O Maidens in your Savage Season

3

Story by **Mari Okada**
Art by **Nao Emoto**

【 *Contents* 】

Meeting 9

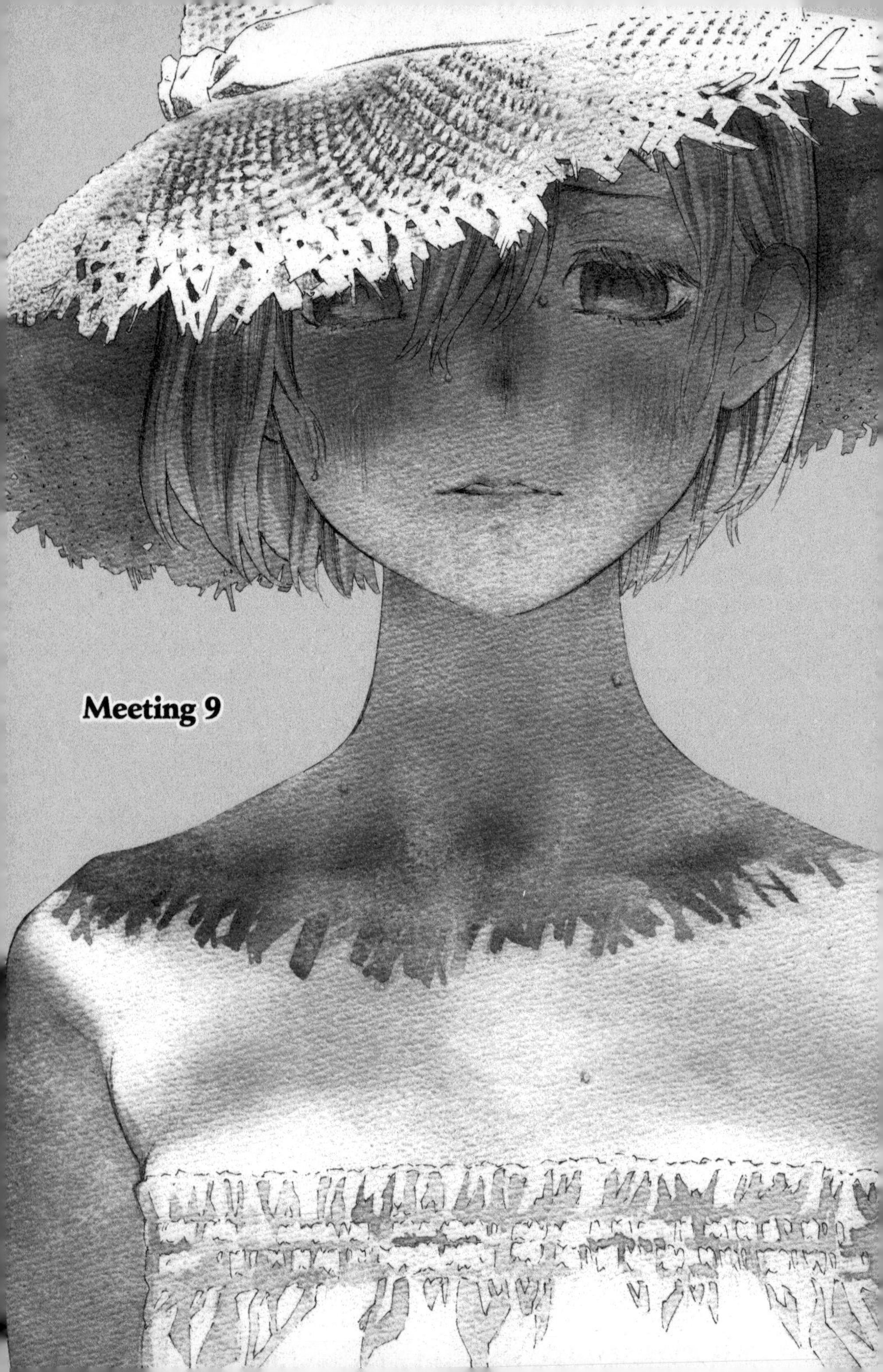

O Maidens in Your Savage Season

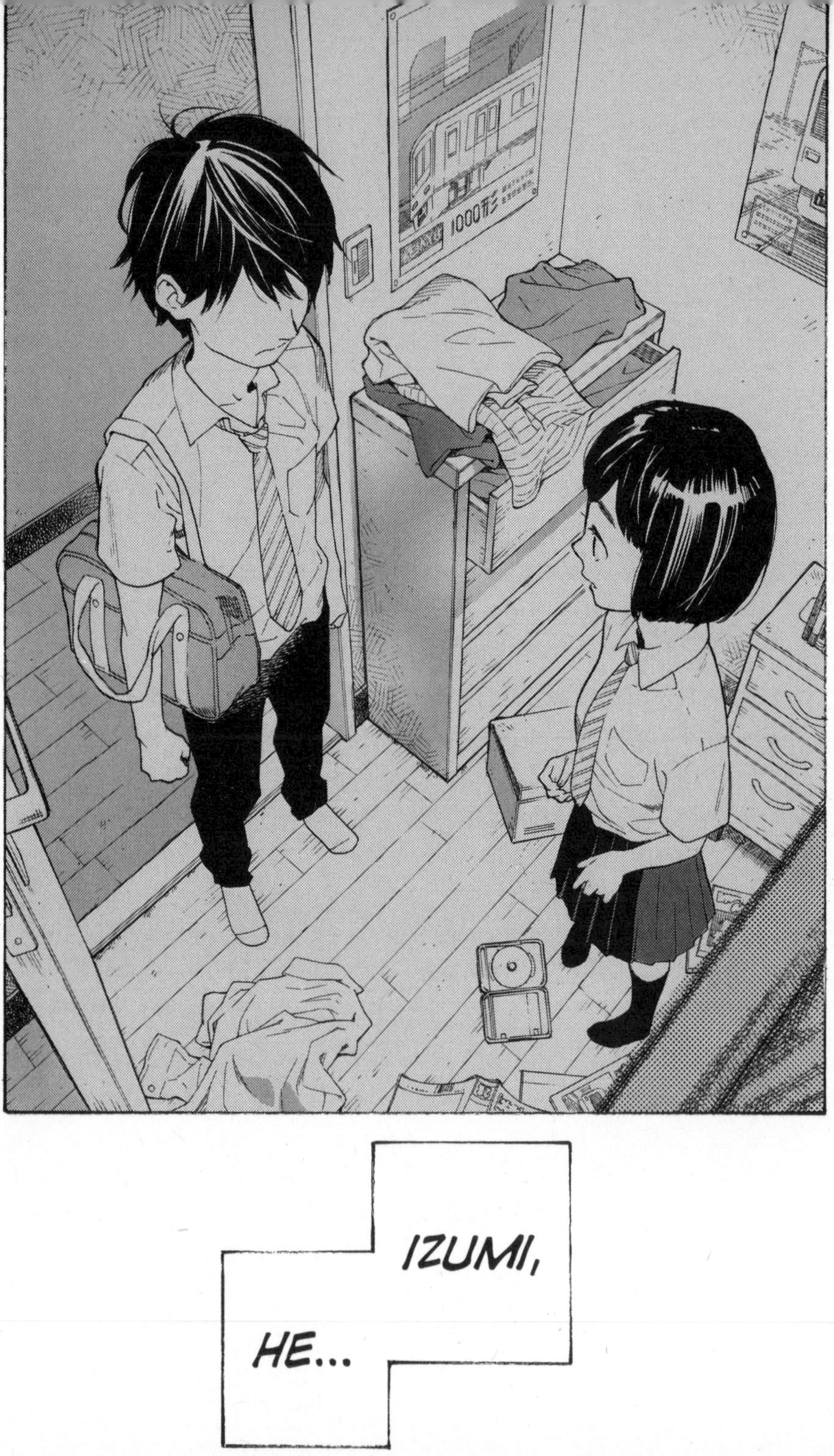

IZUMI,

HE...

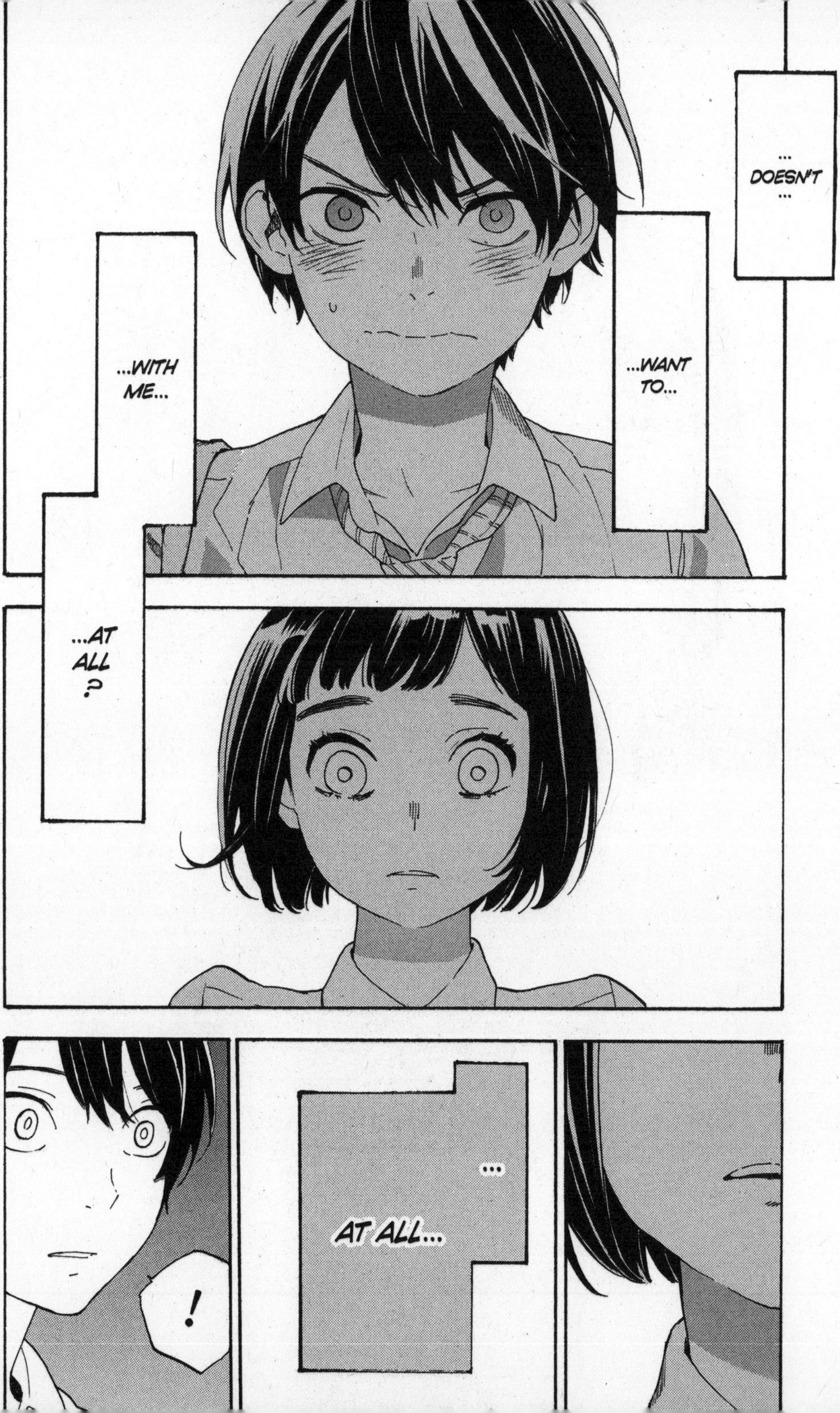
...DOESN'T...
...WANT TO...
...WITH ME...
...AT ALL?
...
AT ALL...
!

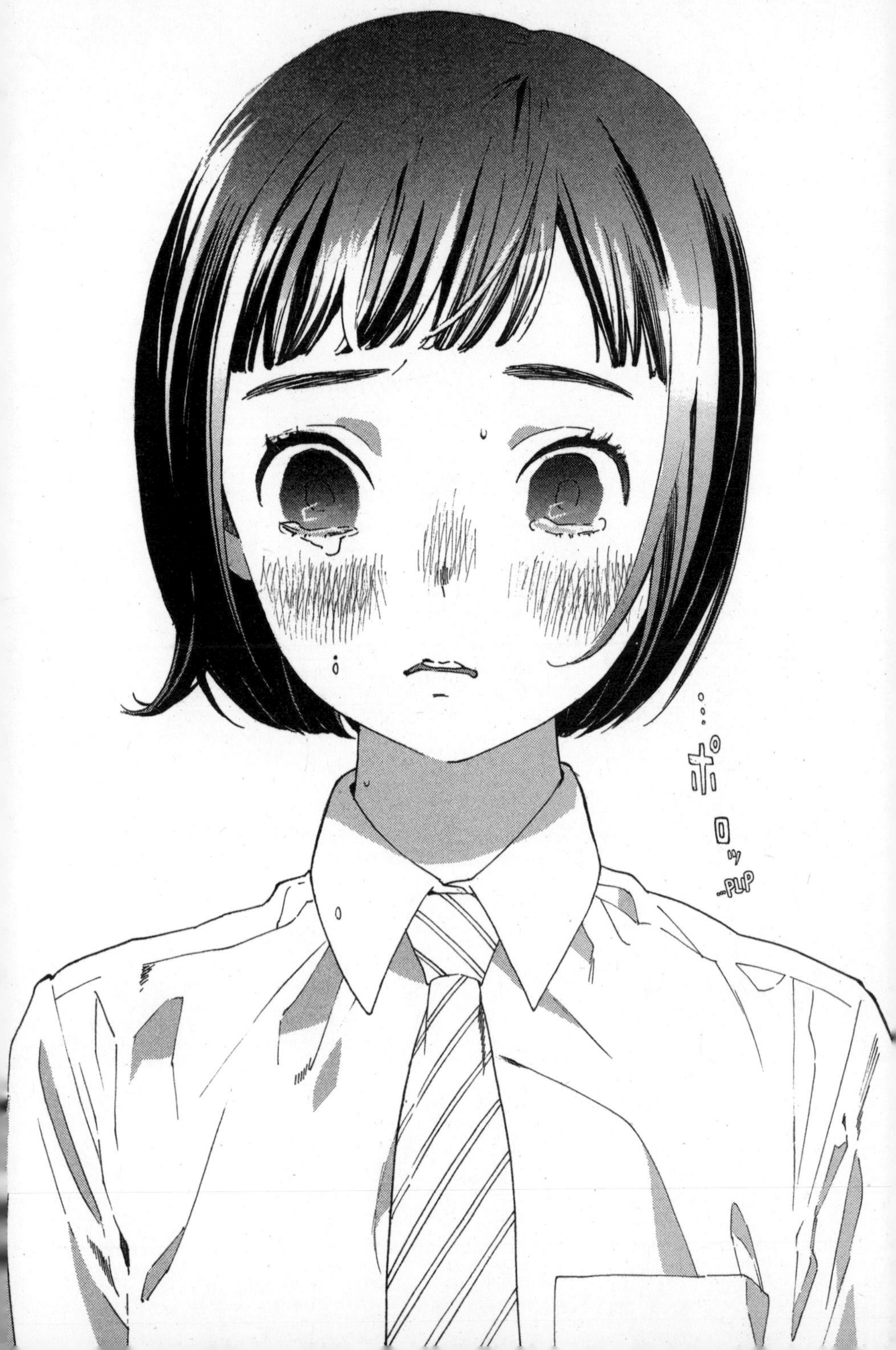
…ポロッ
...PLIP

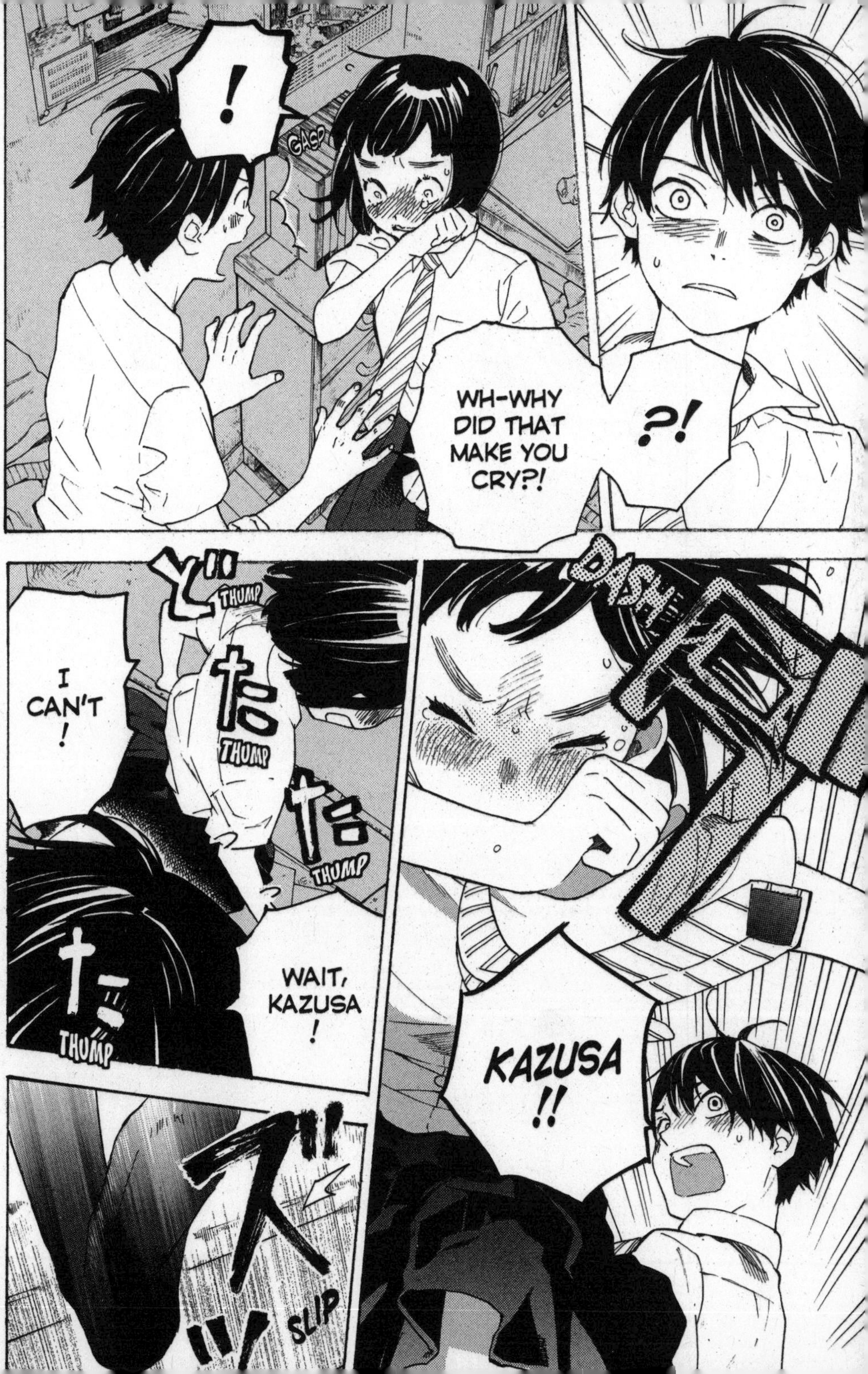
?!
WH-WHY DID THAT MAKE YOU CRY?!
!
GASP
DASH
KAZUSA!!
THUMP
THUMP
THUMP
THUMP
I CAN'T!
WAIT, KAZUSA!
SLIP

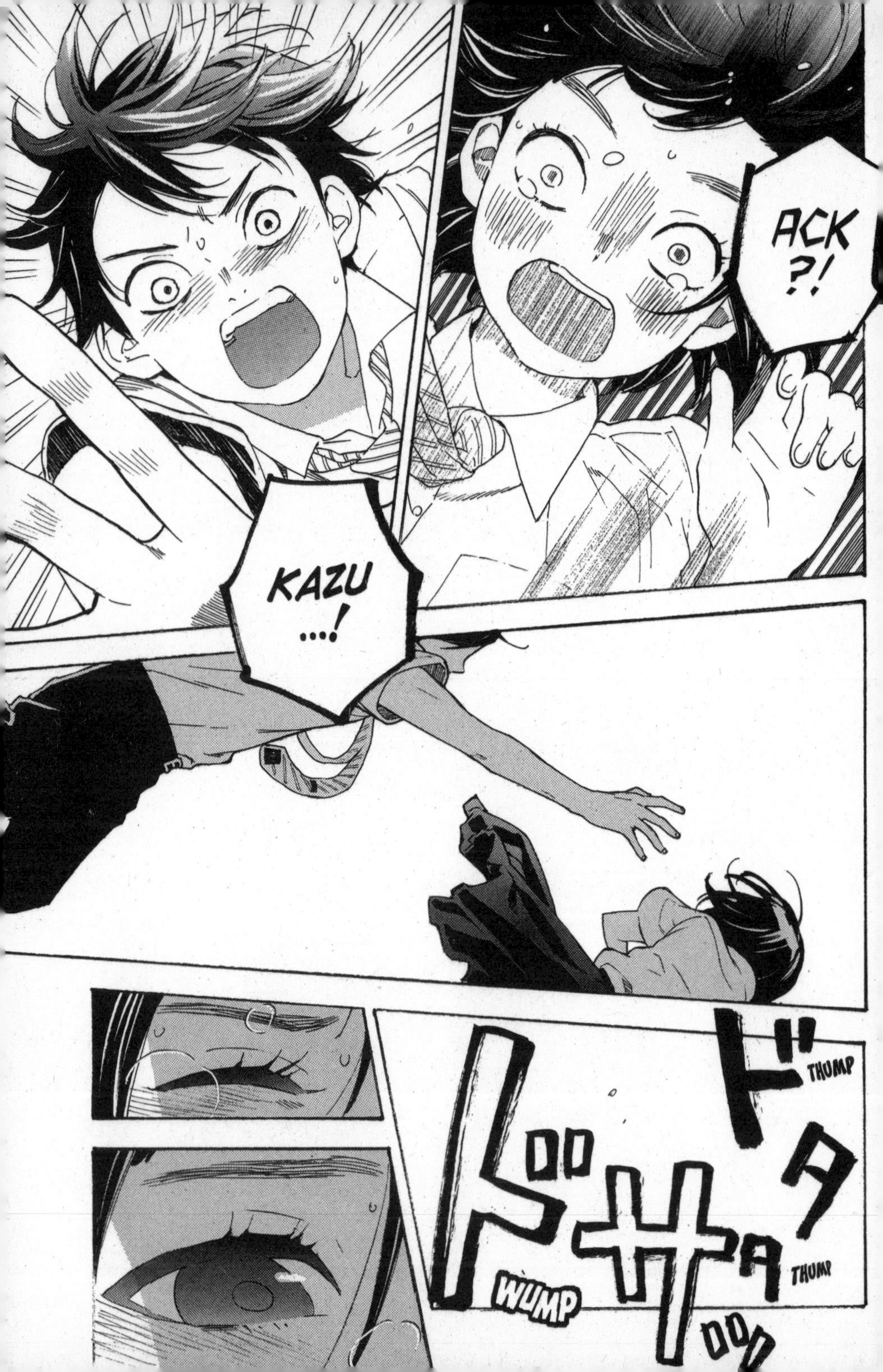
ACK ?!
KAZU ...!
ドタ
THUMP
THUMP
ドサ
WUMP

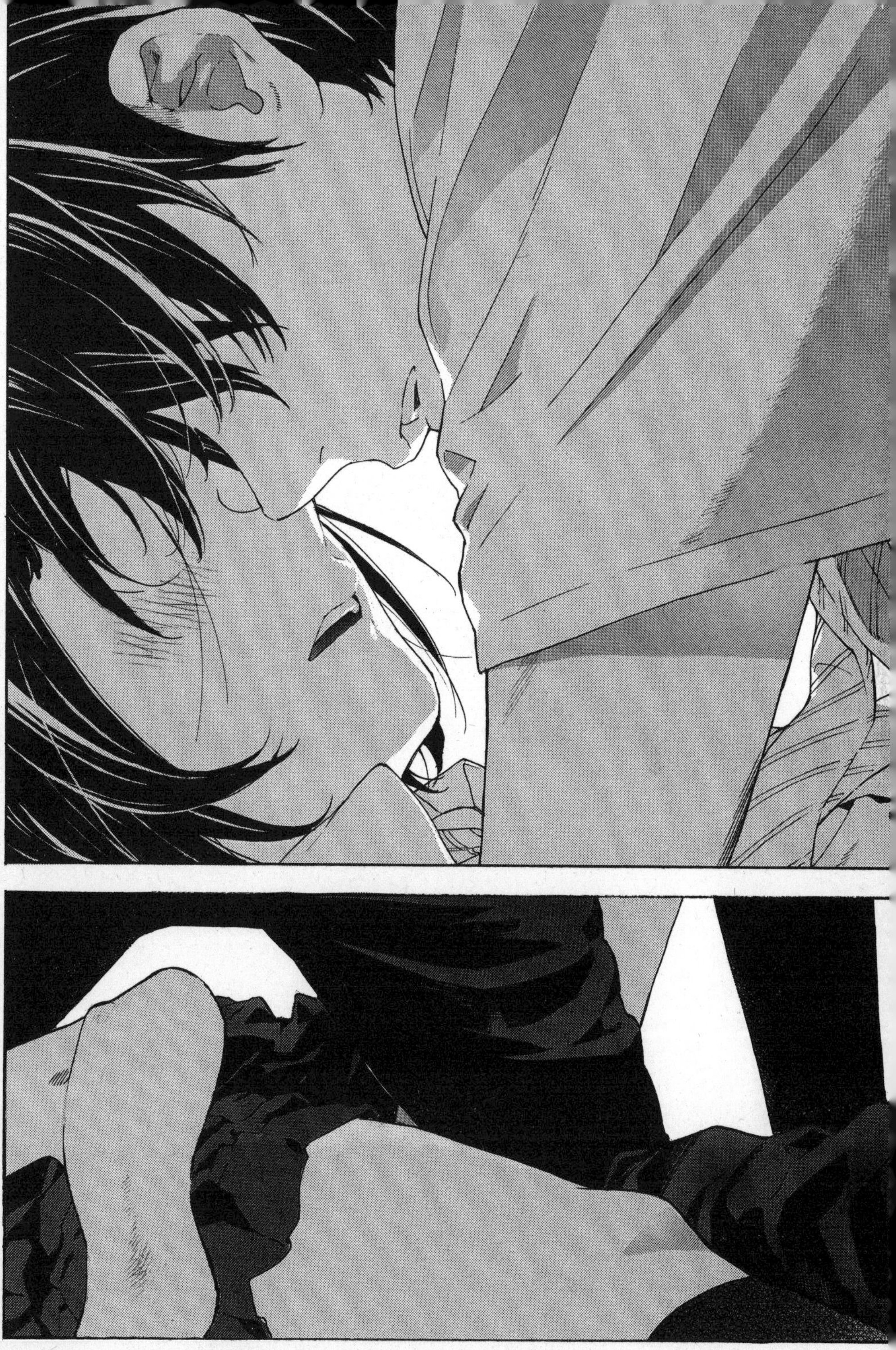

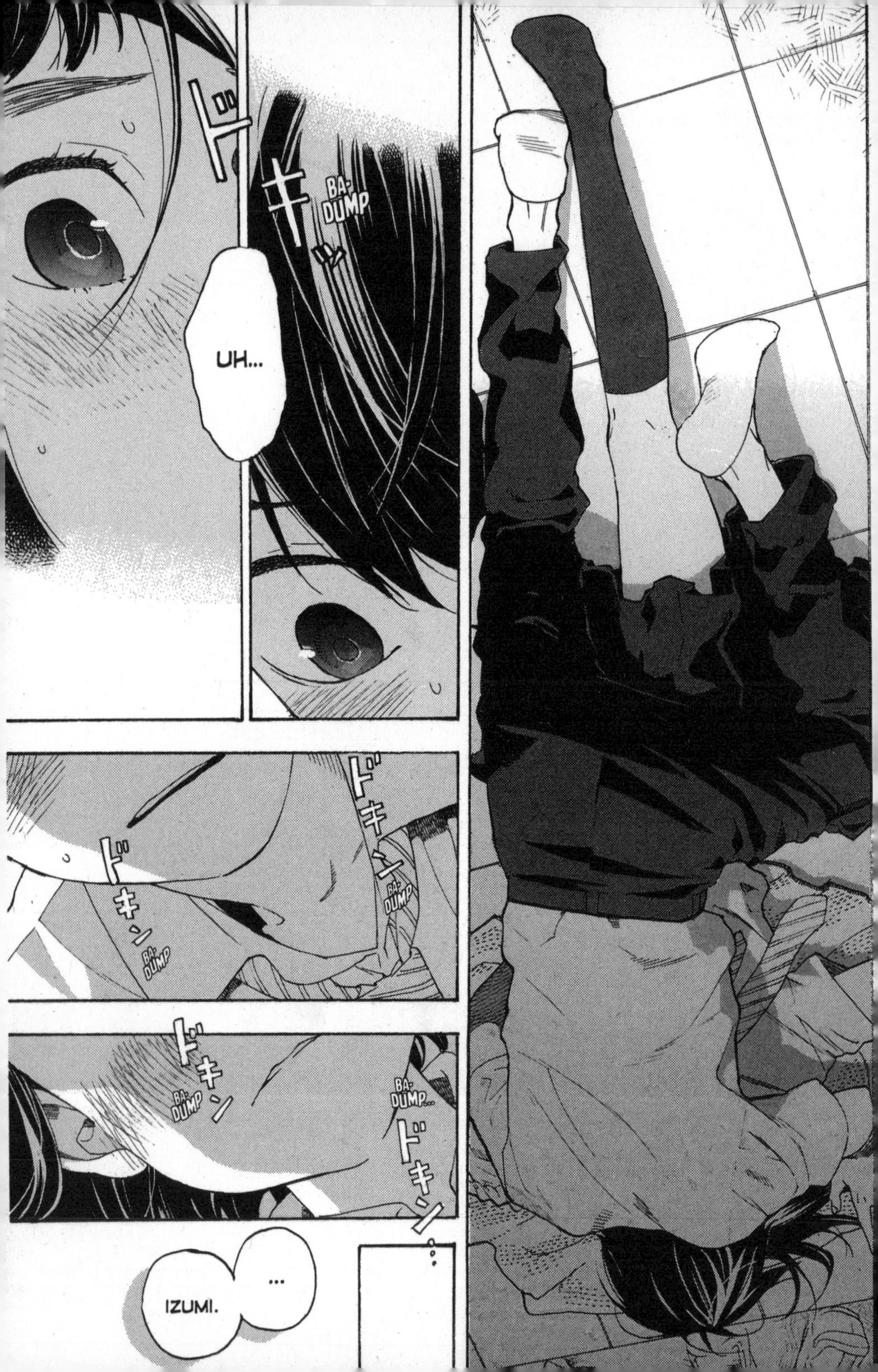
BA-DUMP
UH...
BA-DUMP
BA-DUMP
BA-DUMP...
BA-DUMP
...
IZUMI.

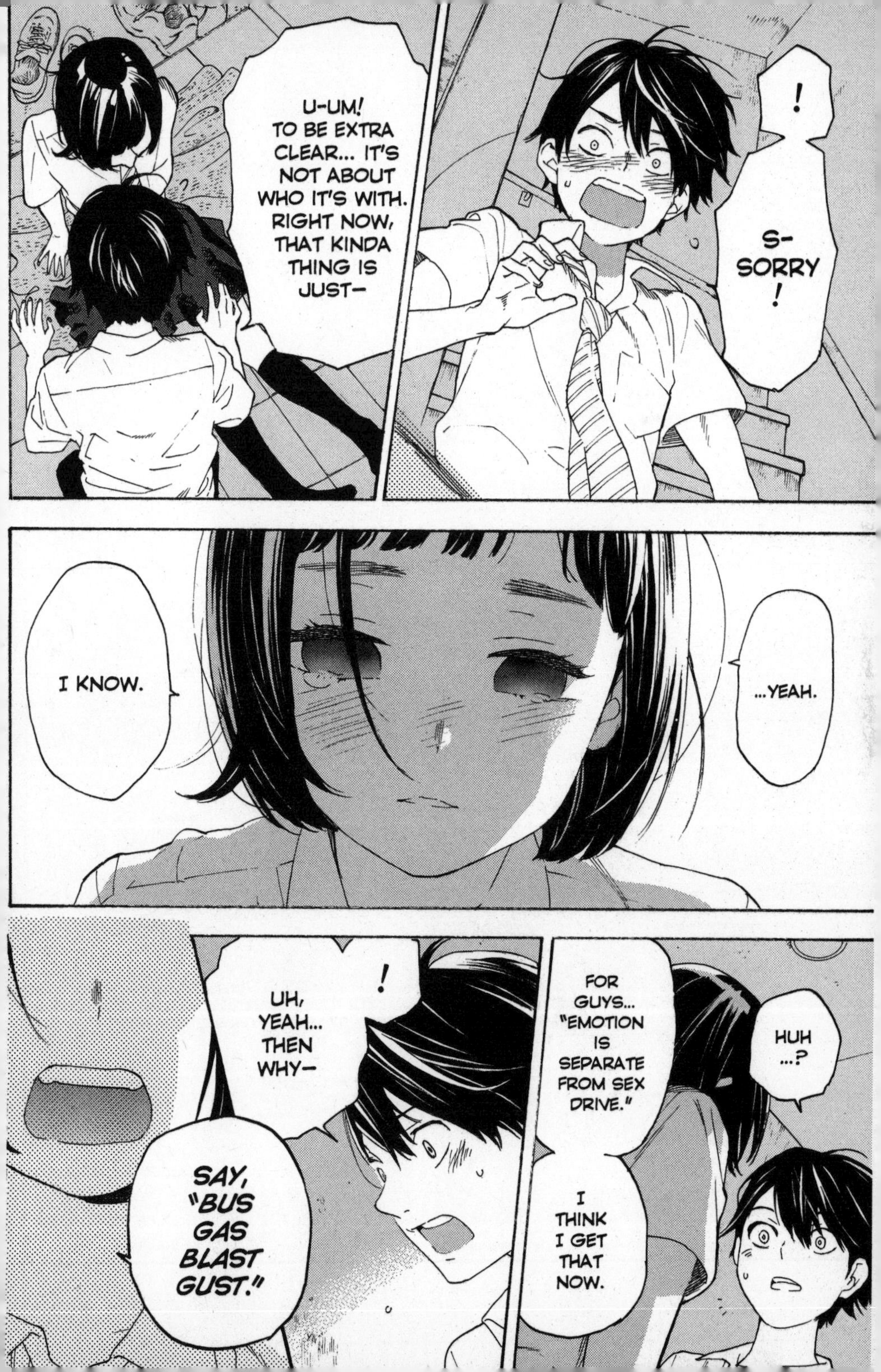
!
S-SORRY!
U-UM! TO BE EXTRA CLEAR... IT'S NOT ABOUT WHO IT'S WITH. RIGHT NOW, THAT KINDA THING IS JUST—
...YEAH.
I KNOW.
HUH...?
FOR GUYS... "EMOTION IS SEPARATE FROM SEX DRIVE."
I THINK I GET THAT NOW.
!
UH, YEAH... THEN WHY—
SAY, "BUS GAS BLAST GUST."

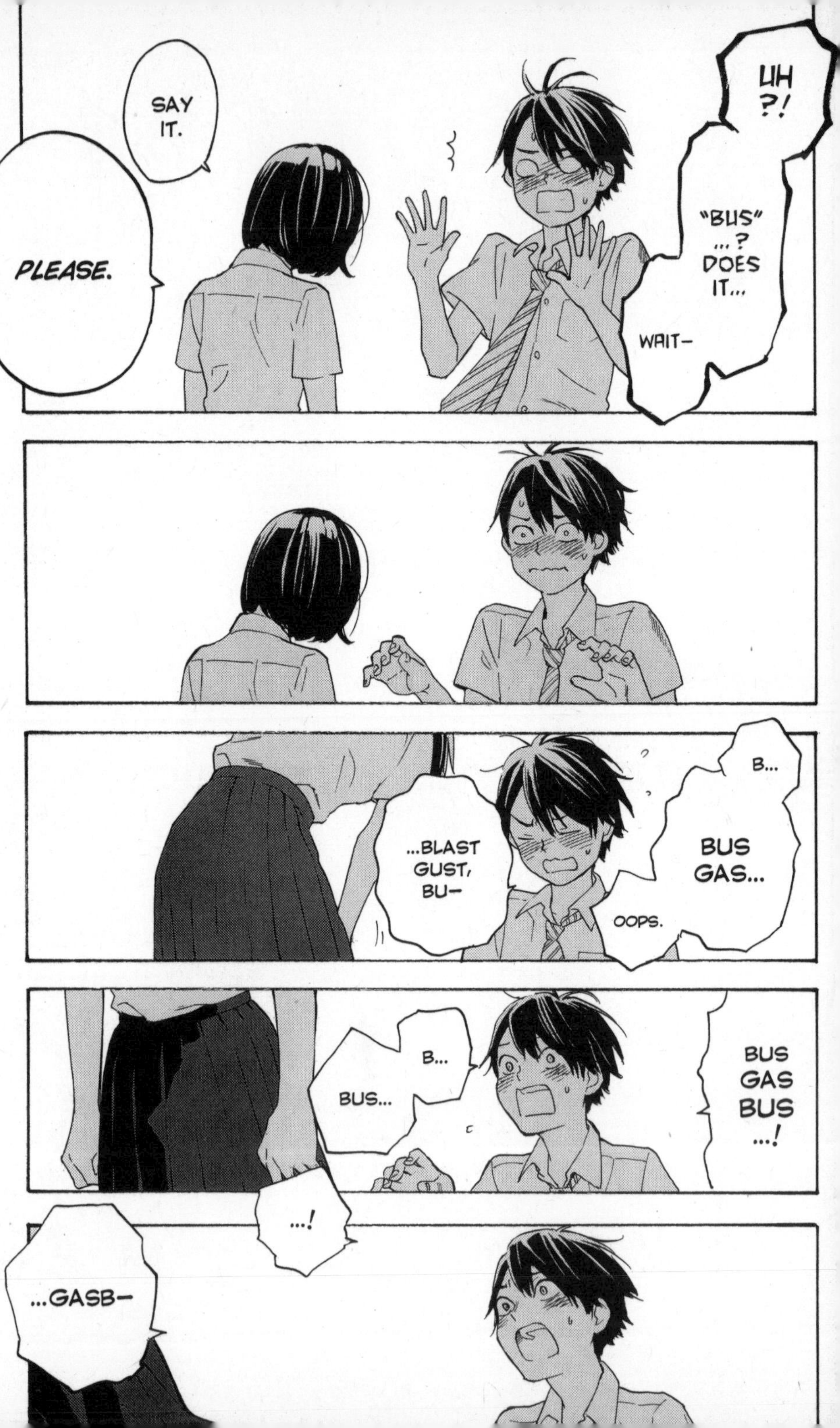
UH ?!
"BUS" ...? DOES IT...
WAIT-
SAY IT.
PLEASE.
B...
BUS GAS...
OOPS.
...BLAST GUST, BU-
BUS GAS BUS ...!
B...
BUS...
...!
...GASB-

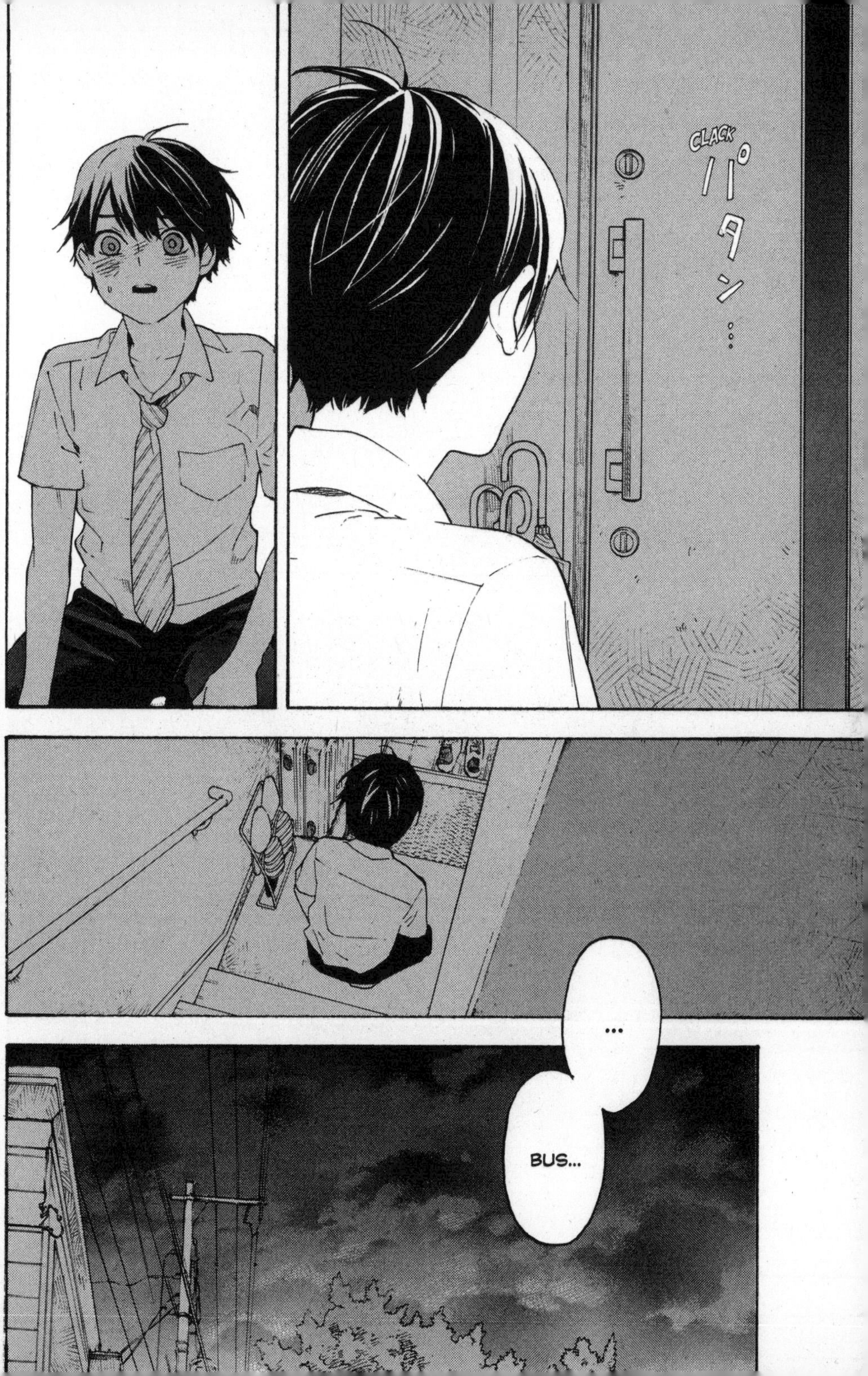
CLACK
パタン…
...
BUS...

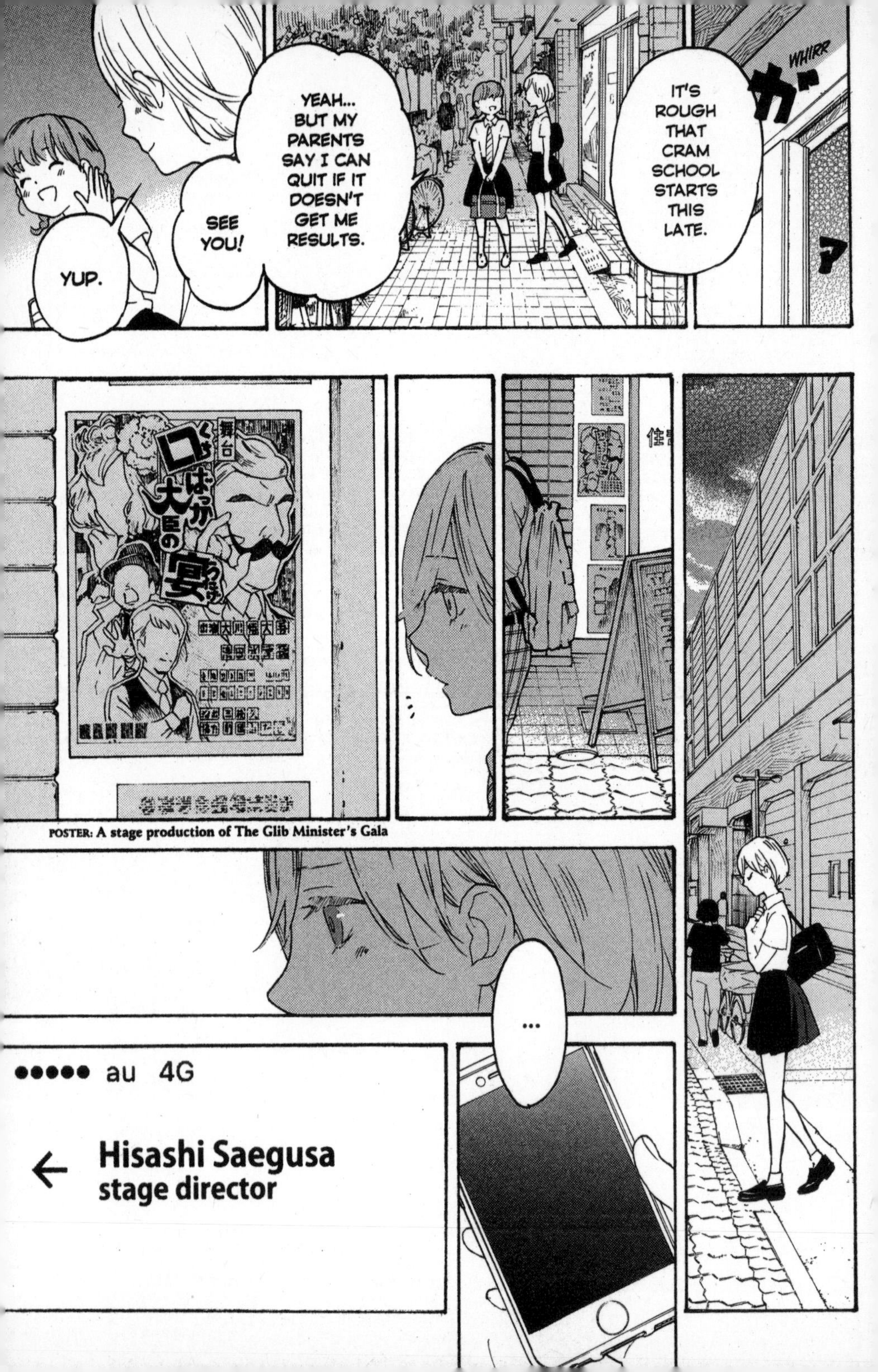
WHIRR
ガァ
IT'S ROUGH THAT CRAM SCHOOL STARTS THIS LATE.
YEAH... BUT MY PARENTS SAY I CAN QUIT IF IT DOESN'T GET ME RESULTS.
SEE YOU!
YUP.
舞台
口ばっか大臣の宴
POSTER: A stage production of The Glib Minister's Gala
...
●●●●● au 4G
← Hisashi Saegusa
stage director

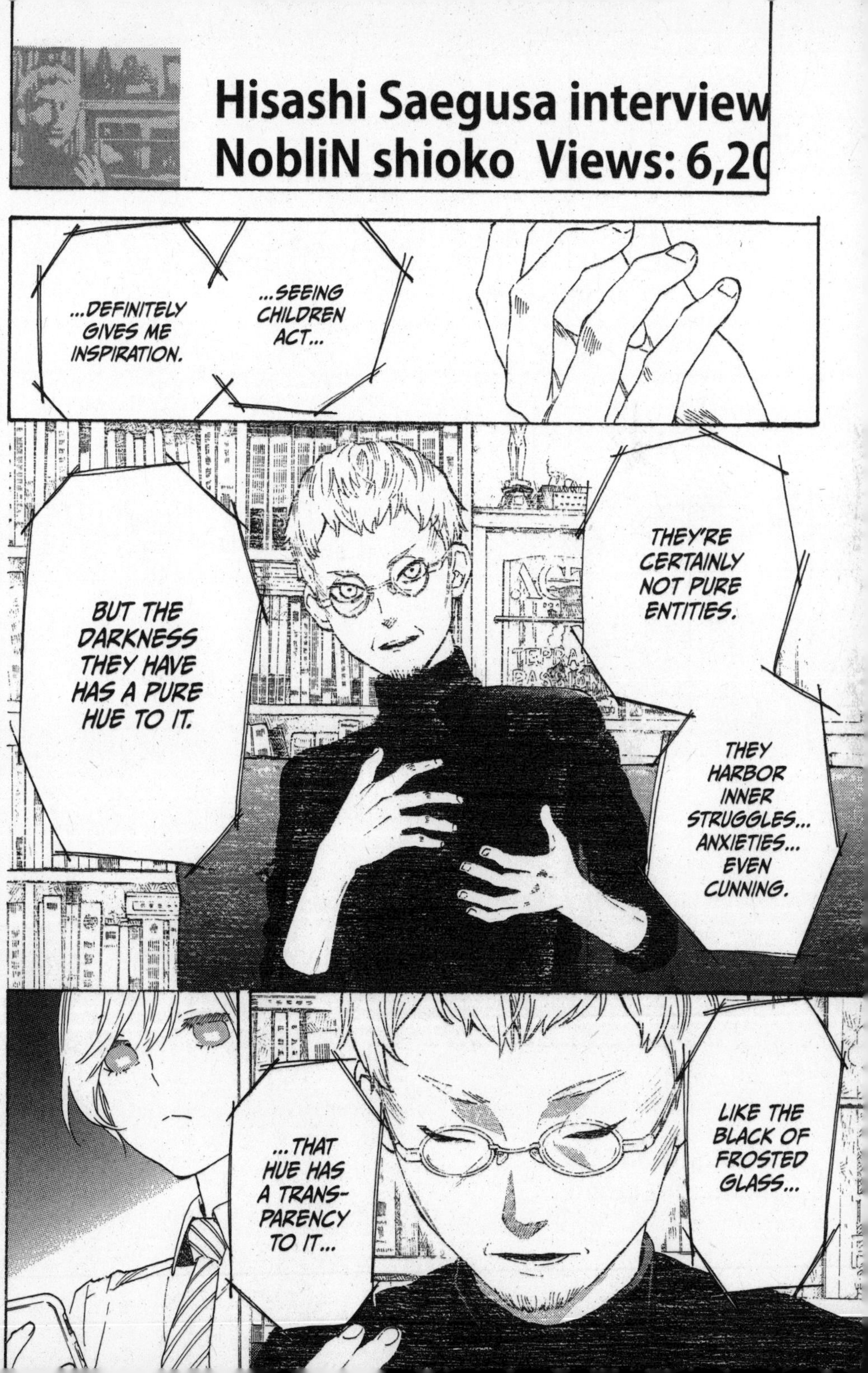
Hisashi Saegusa interview
NobliN shioko Views: 6,20
...SEEING CHILDREN ACT...
...DEFINITELY GIVES ME INSPIRATION.
THEY'RE CERTAINLY NOT PURE ENTITIES.
THEY HARBOR INNER STRUGGLES... ANXIETIES... EVEN CUNNING.
BUT THE DARKNESS THEY HAVE HAS A PURE HUE TO IT.
LIKE THE BLACK OF FROSTED GLASS...
...THAT HUE HAS A TRANS-PARENCY TO IT...

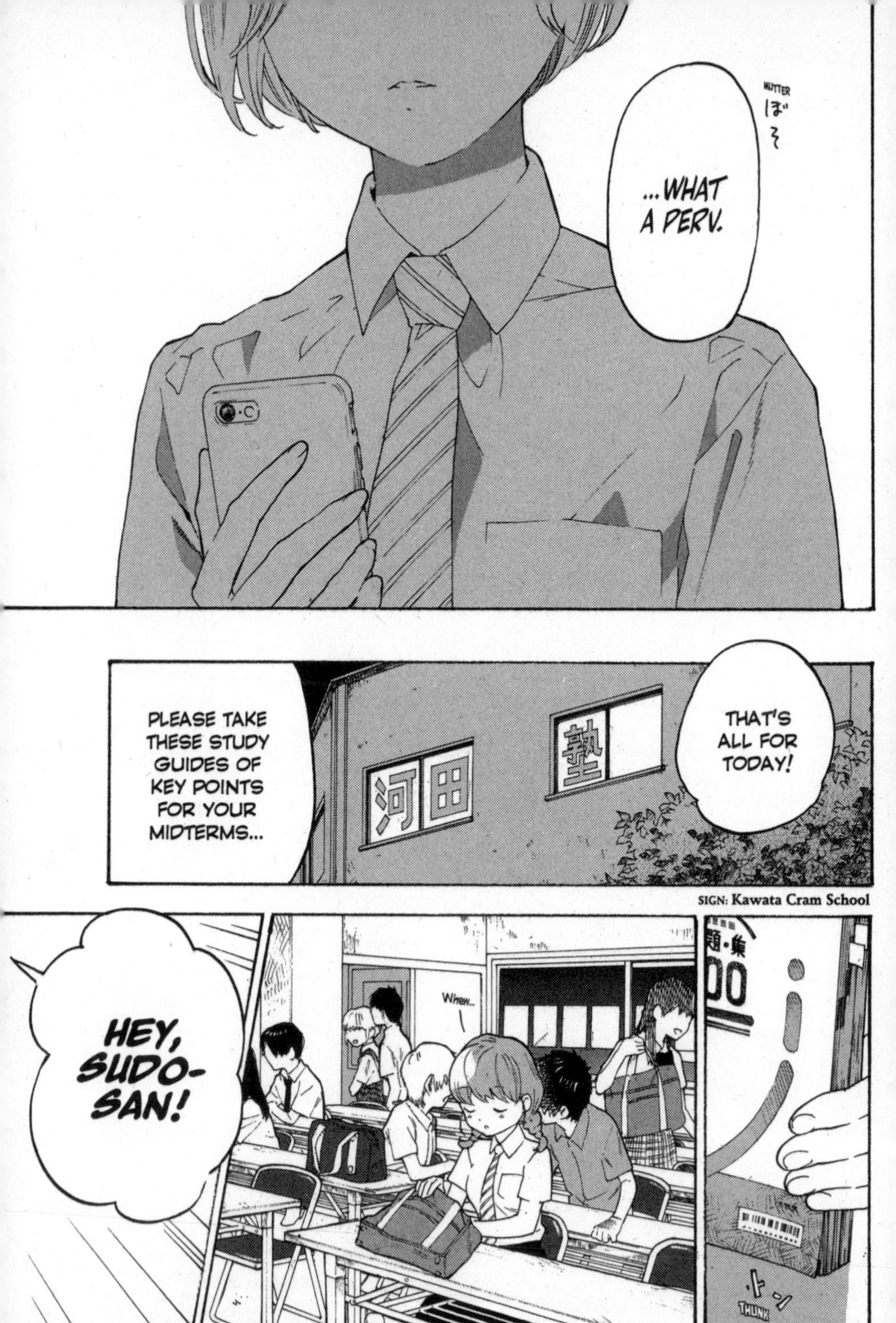
MUTTER
ぼそ
...WHAT A PERV.
THAT'S ALL FOR TODAY!
PLEASE TAKE THESE STUDY GUIDES OF KEY POINTS FOR YOUR MIDTERMS...
SIGN: Kawata Cram School
トン
THUNK
Whew...
HEY, SUDO-SAN!

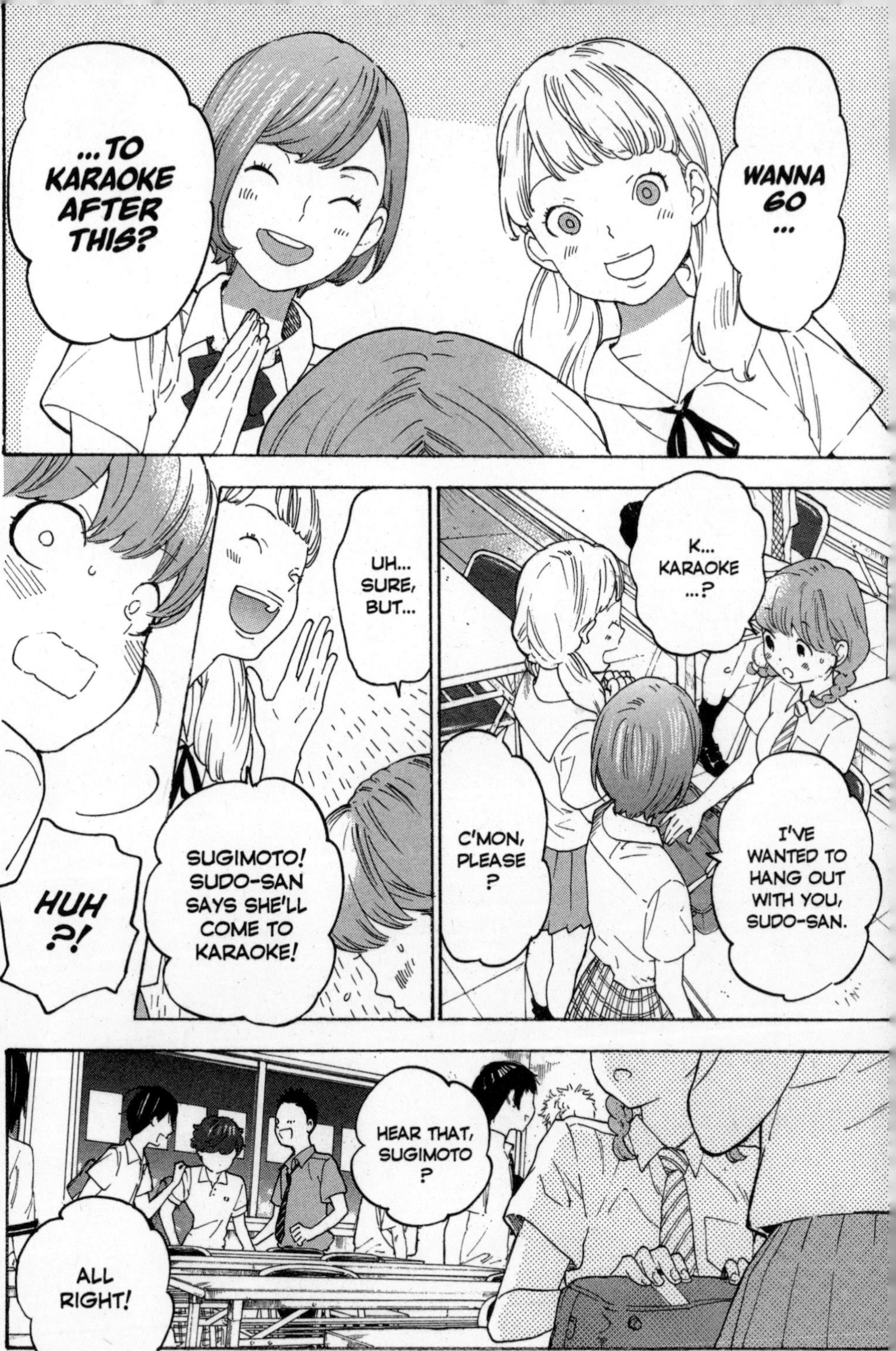
WANNA GO ...
...TO KARAOKE AFTER THIS?
K... KARAOKE ...?
I'VE WANTED TO HANG OUT WITH YOU, SUDO-SAN.
C'MON, PLEASE?
UH... SURE, BUT...
SUGIMOTO! SUDO-SAN SAYS SHE'LL COME TO KARAOKE!
HUH?!
HEAR THAT, SUGIMOTO?
ALL RIGHT!

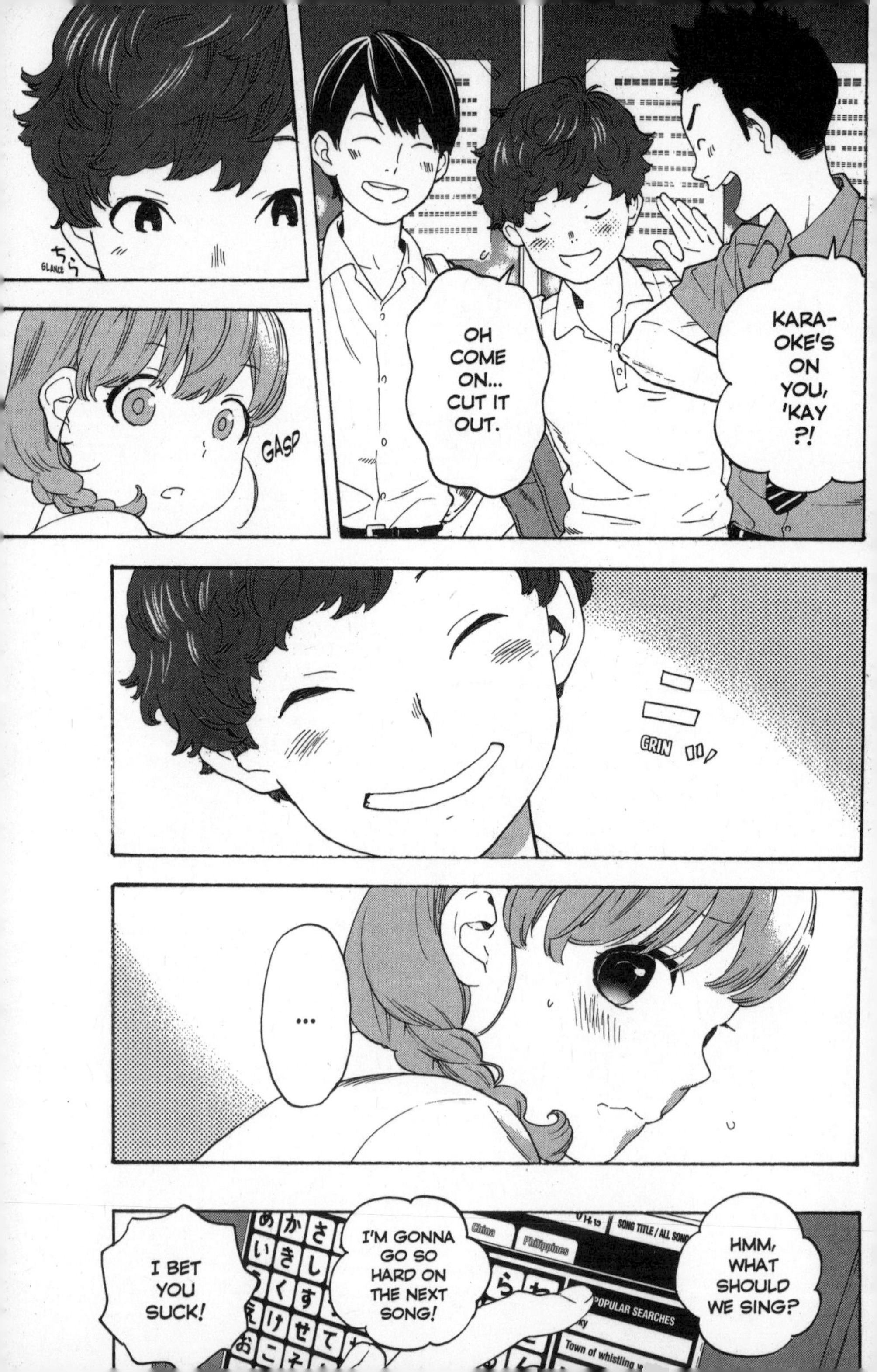
KARA-OKE'S ON YOU, 'KAY?!
OH COME ON... CUT IT OUT.
ちら
GLANCE
GASP
GRIN
...
HMM, WHAT SHOULD WE SING?
I'M GONNA GO SO HARD ON THE NEXT SONG!
I BET YOU SUCK!
China
Philippines
POPULAR SEARCHES

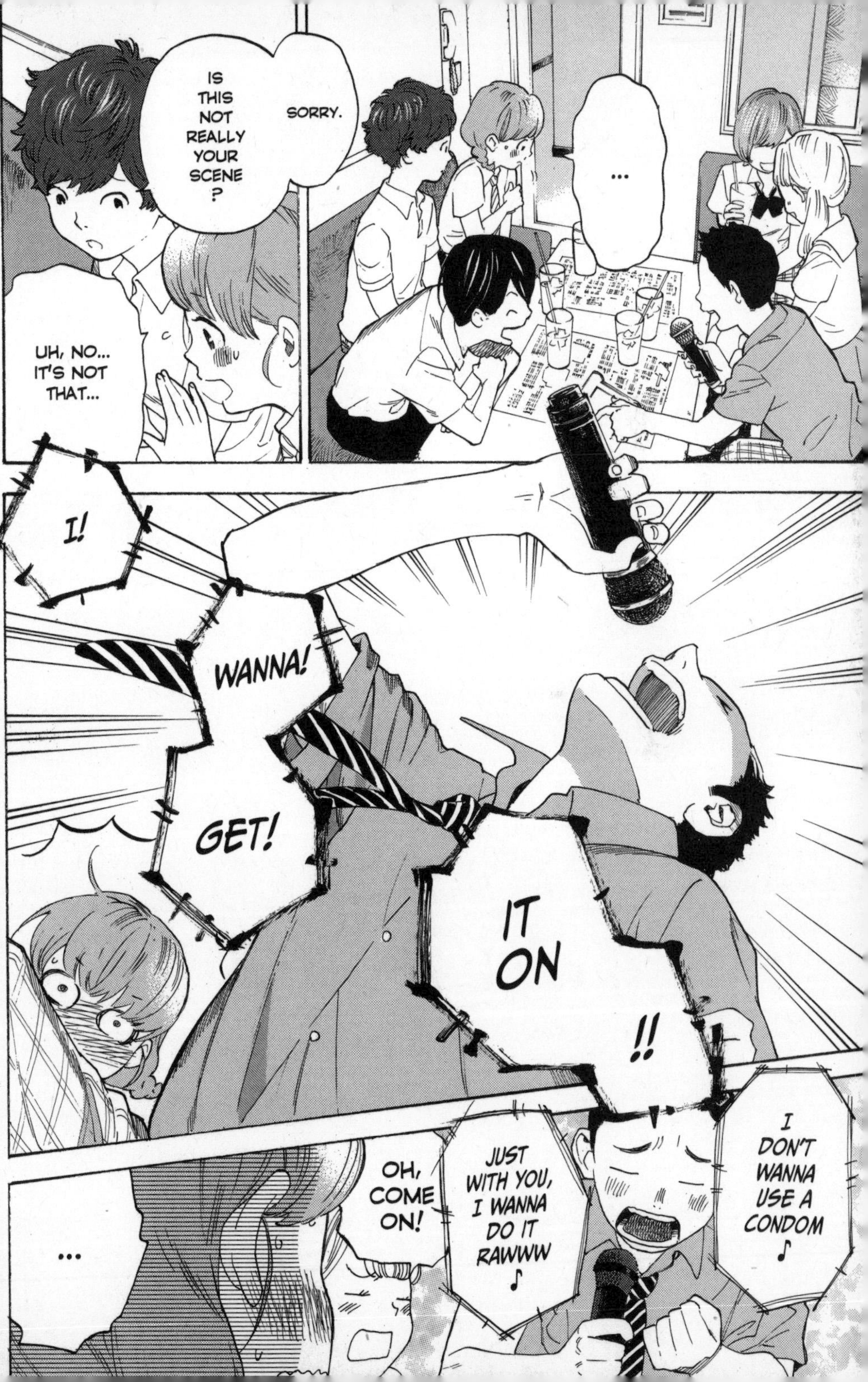
...
SORRY.
IS THIS NOT REALLY YOUR SCENE?
UH, NO... IT'S NOT THAT...
I!
WANNA!
GET!
IT ON!!
I DON'T WANNA USE A CONDOM ♪
JUST WITH YOU, I WANNA DO IT RAWWW ♪
OH, COME ON!
...

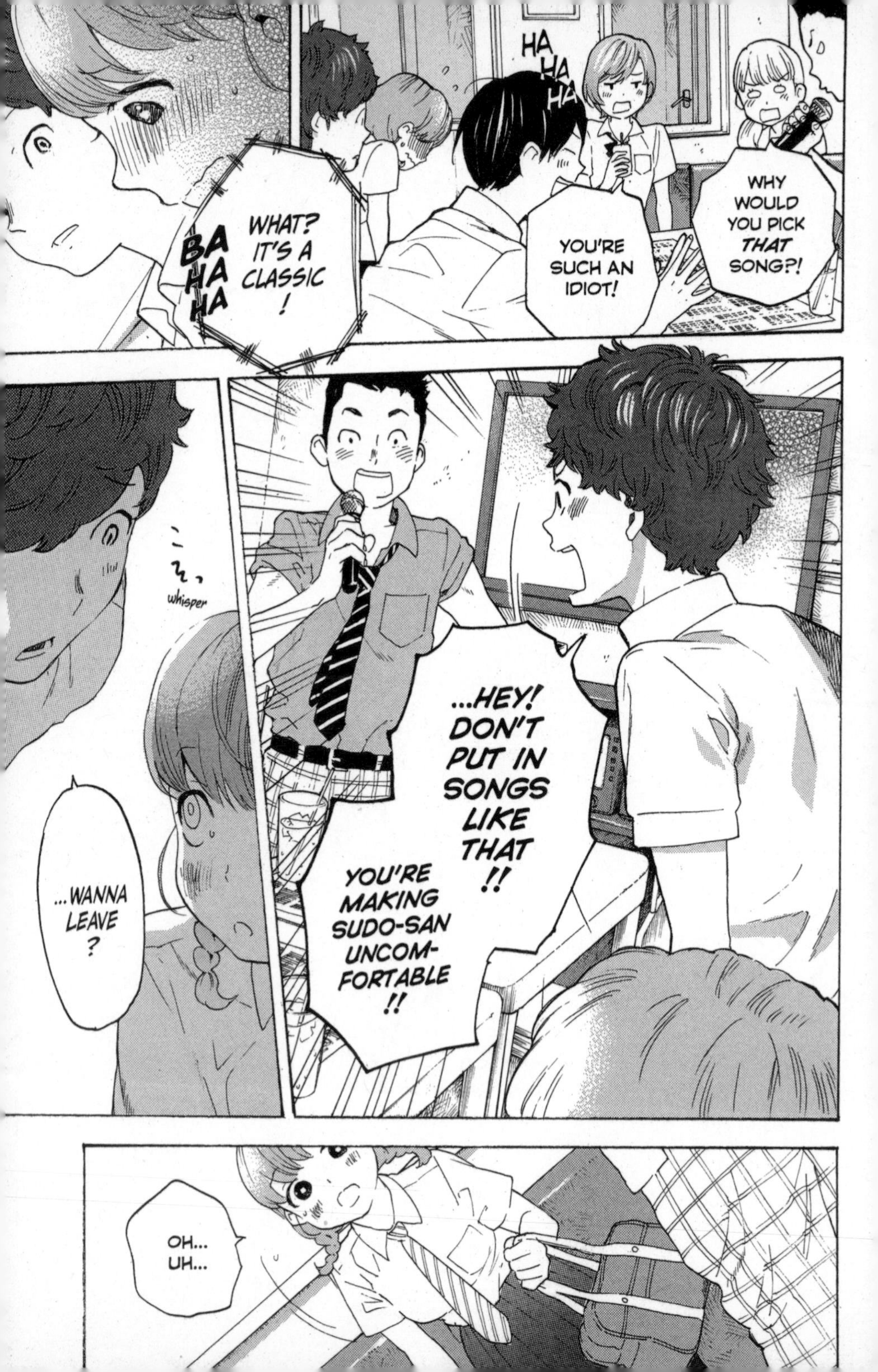
WHY WOULD YOU PICK *THAT* SONG?!
HA HA HA
YOU'RE SUCH AN IDIOT!
WHAT? IT'S A CLASSIC!
BA HA HA
...HEY! DON'T PUT IN SONGS LIKE THAT!!
YOU'RE MAKING SUDO-SAN UNCOMFORTABLE!!
whisper
...WANNA LEAVE?
OH... UH...

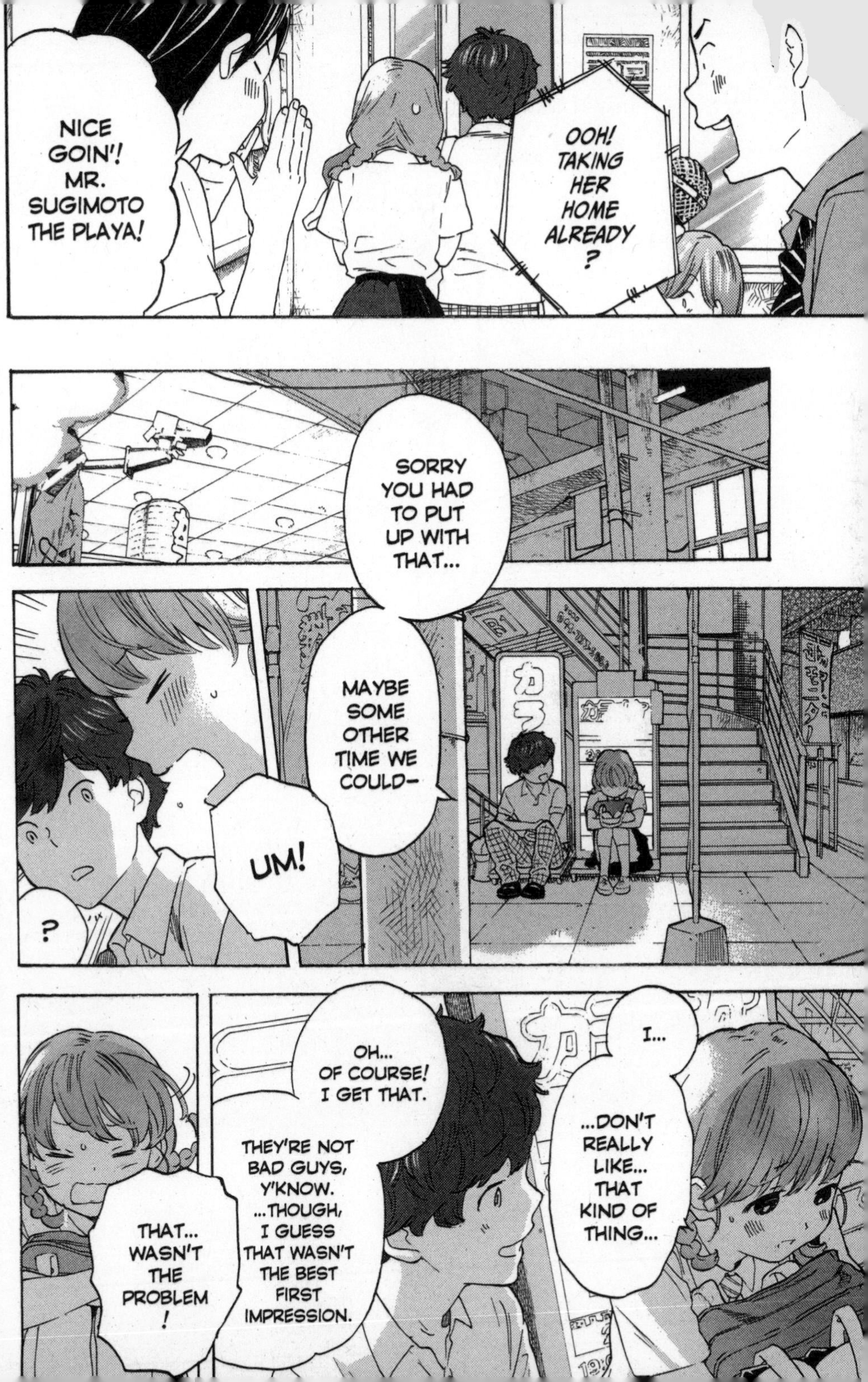
OOH! TAKING HER HOME ALREADY?
NICE GOIN'! MR. SUGIMOTO THE PLAYA!
SORRY YOU HAD TO PUT UP WITH THAT...
MAYBE SOME OTHER TIME WE COULD-
UM!
?
I...
...DON'T REALLY LIKE... THAT KIND OF THING...
OH... OF COURSE! I GET THAT.
THEY'RE NOT BAD GUYS, Y'KNOW. ...THOUGH, I GUESS THAT WASN'T THE BEST FIRST IMPRESSION.
THAT... WASN'T THE PROBLEM!

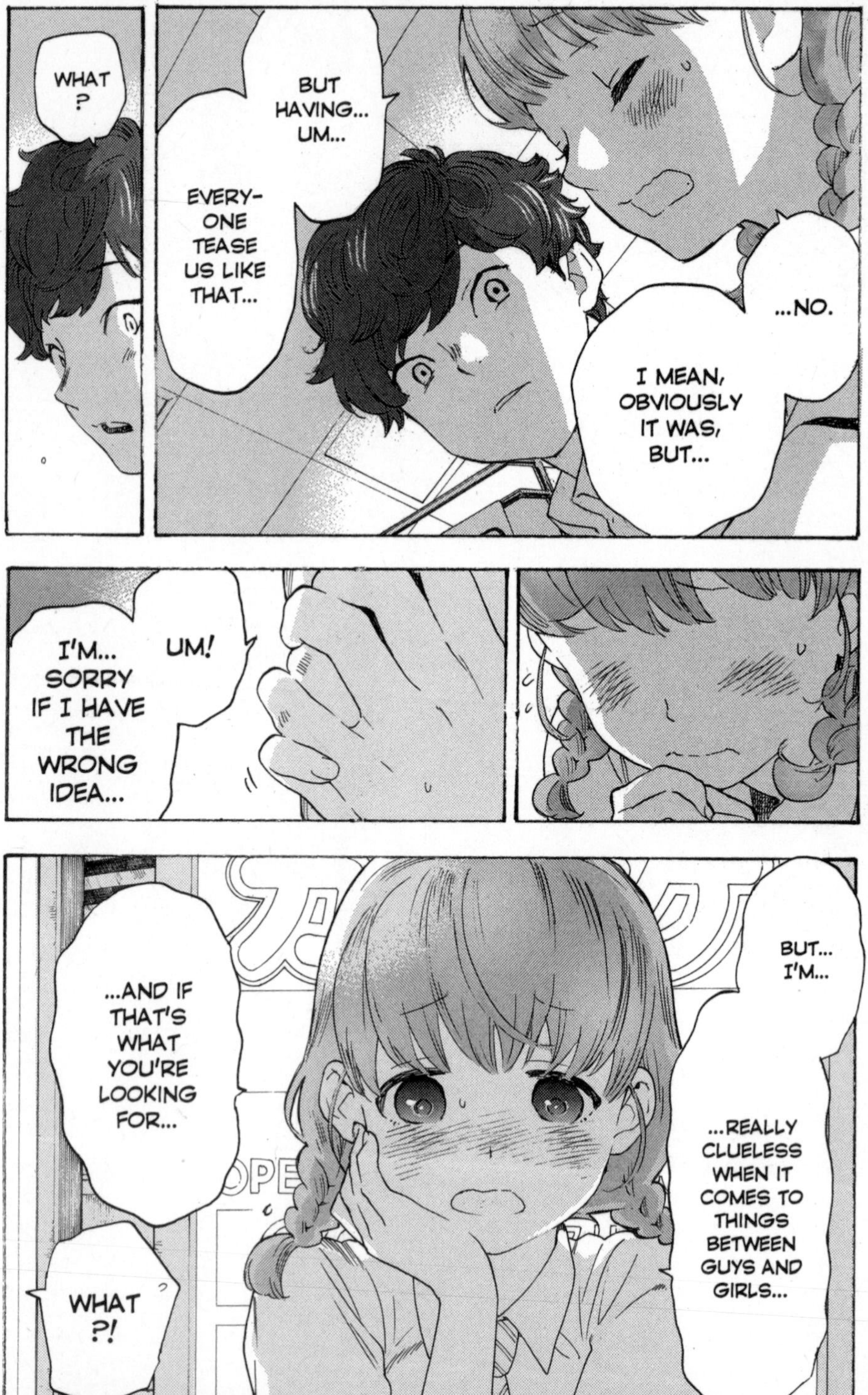
BUT HAVING... UM...
EVERY-ONE TEASE US LIKE THAT...
...NO.
I MEAN, OBVIOUSLY IT WAS, BUT...
WHAT?
UM!
I'M... SORRY IF I HAVE THE WRONG IDEA...
BUT... I'M...
...REALLY CLUELESS WHEN IT COMES TO THINGS BETWEEN GUYS AND GIRLS...
...AND IF THAT'S WHAT YOU'RE LOOKING FOR...
WHAT?!

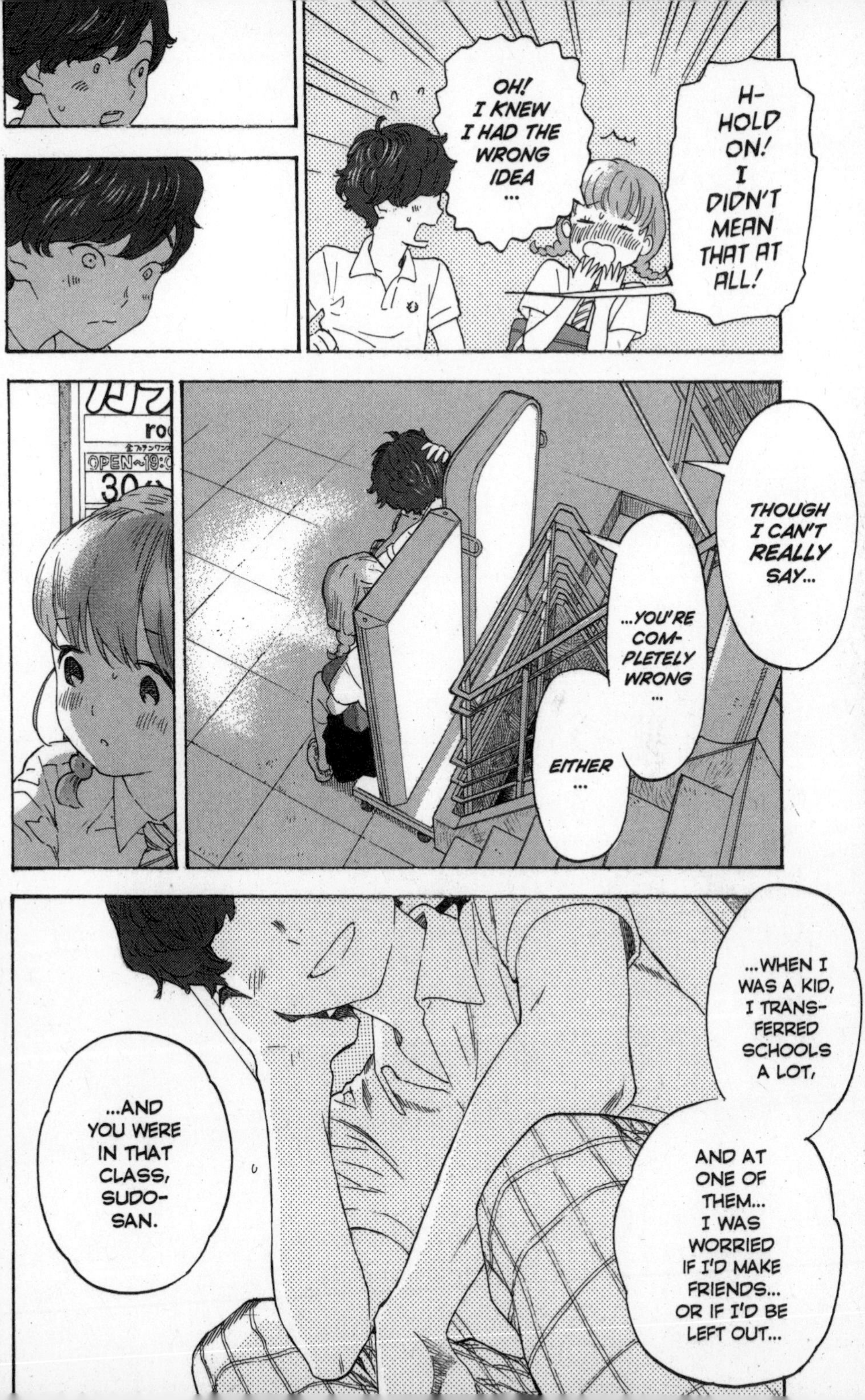
H-HOLD ON! I DIDN'T MEAN THAT AT ALL!
OH! I KNEW I HAD THE WRONG IDEA ...
THOUGH I CAN'T REALLY SAY...
...YOU'RE COMPLETELY WRONG ...
EITHER ...
...WHEN I WAS A KID, I TRANSFERRED SCHOOLS A LOT,
AND AT ONE OF THEM... I WAS WORRIED IF I'D MAKE FRIENDS... OR IF I'D BE LEFT OUT...
...AND YOU WERE IN THAT CLASS, SUDO-SAN.

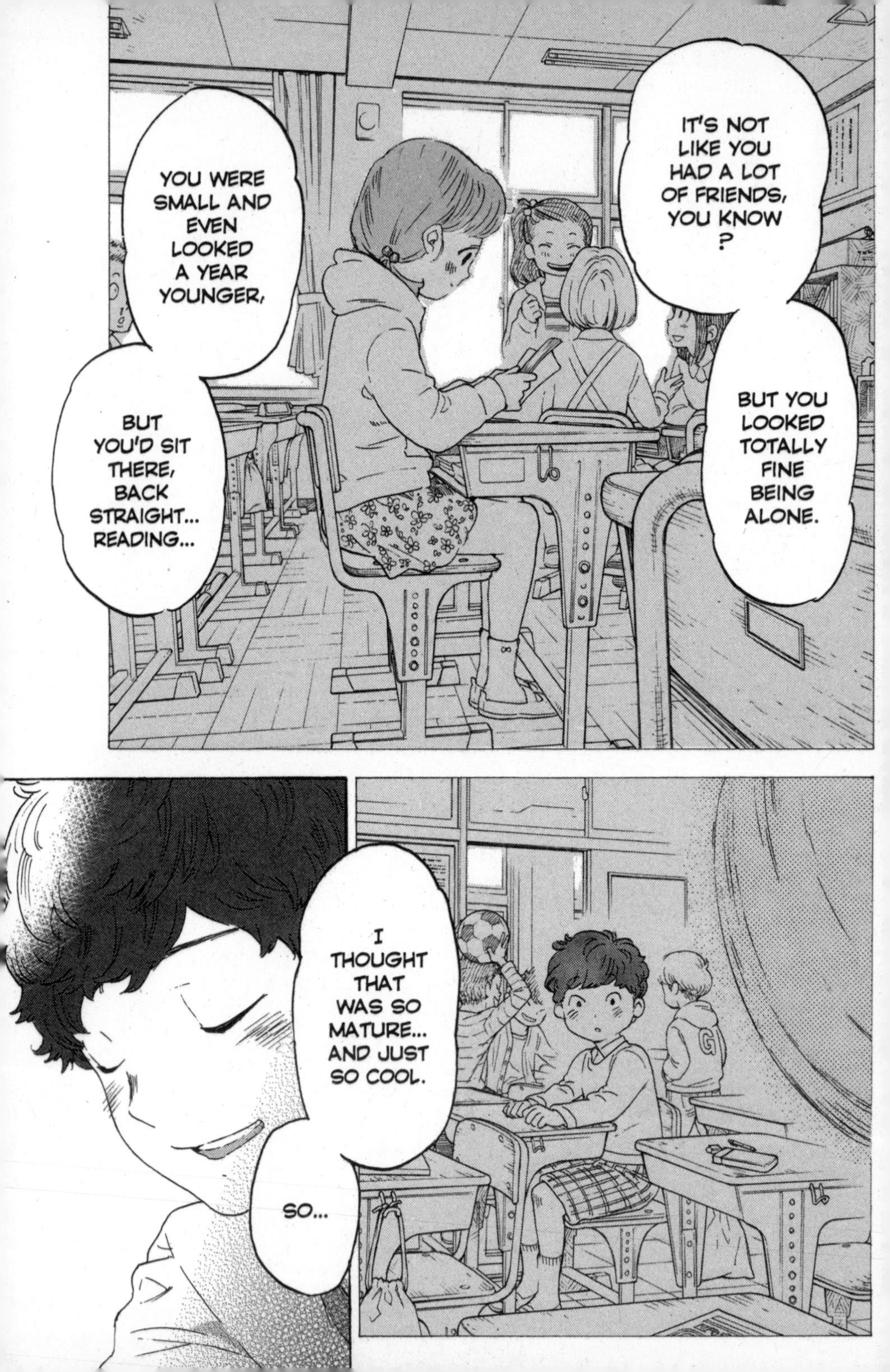
IT'S NOT LIKE YOU HAD A LOT OF FRIENDS, YOU KNOW?
BUT YOU LOOKED TOTALLY FINE BEING ALONE.
YOU WERE SMALL AND EVEN LOOKED A YEAR YOUNGER,
BUT YOU'D SIT THERE, BACK STRAIGHT... READING...
I THOUGHT THAT WAS SO MATURE... AND JUST SO COOL.
SO...

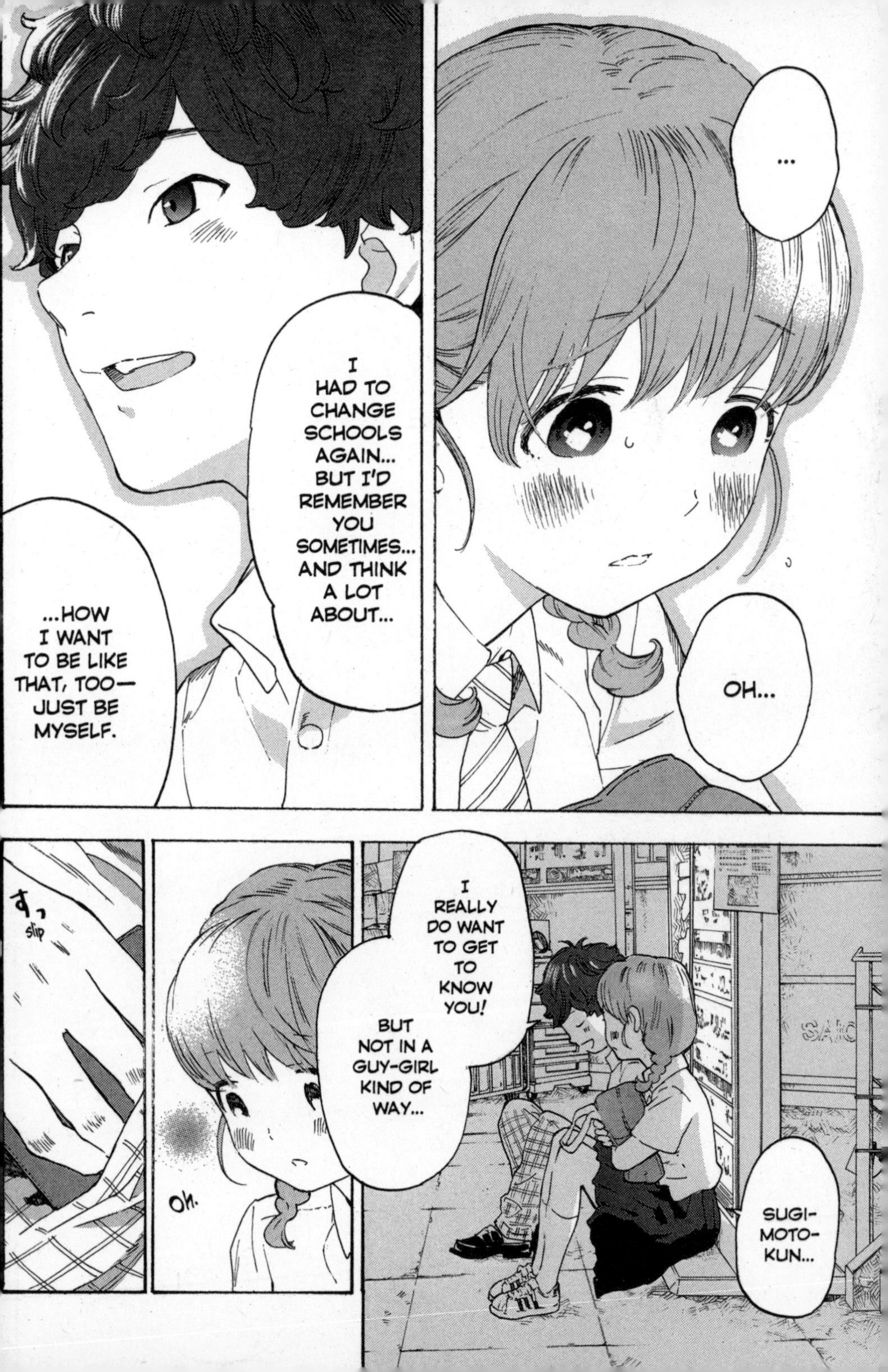
...
OH...
I HAD TO CHANGE SCHOOLS AGAIN... BUT I'D REMEMBER YOU SOMETIMES... AND THINK A LOT ABOUT...
...HOW I WANT TO BE LIKE THAT, TOO— JUST BE MYSELF.
I REALLY DO WANT TO GET TO KNOW YOU!
BUT NOT IN A GUY-GIRL KIND OF WAY...
SUGI-MOTO-KUN...
Oh.
す,
slip

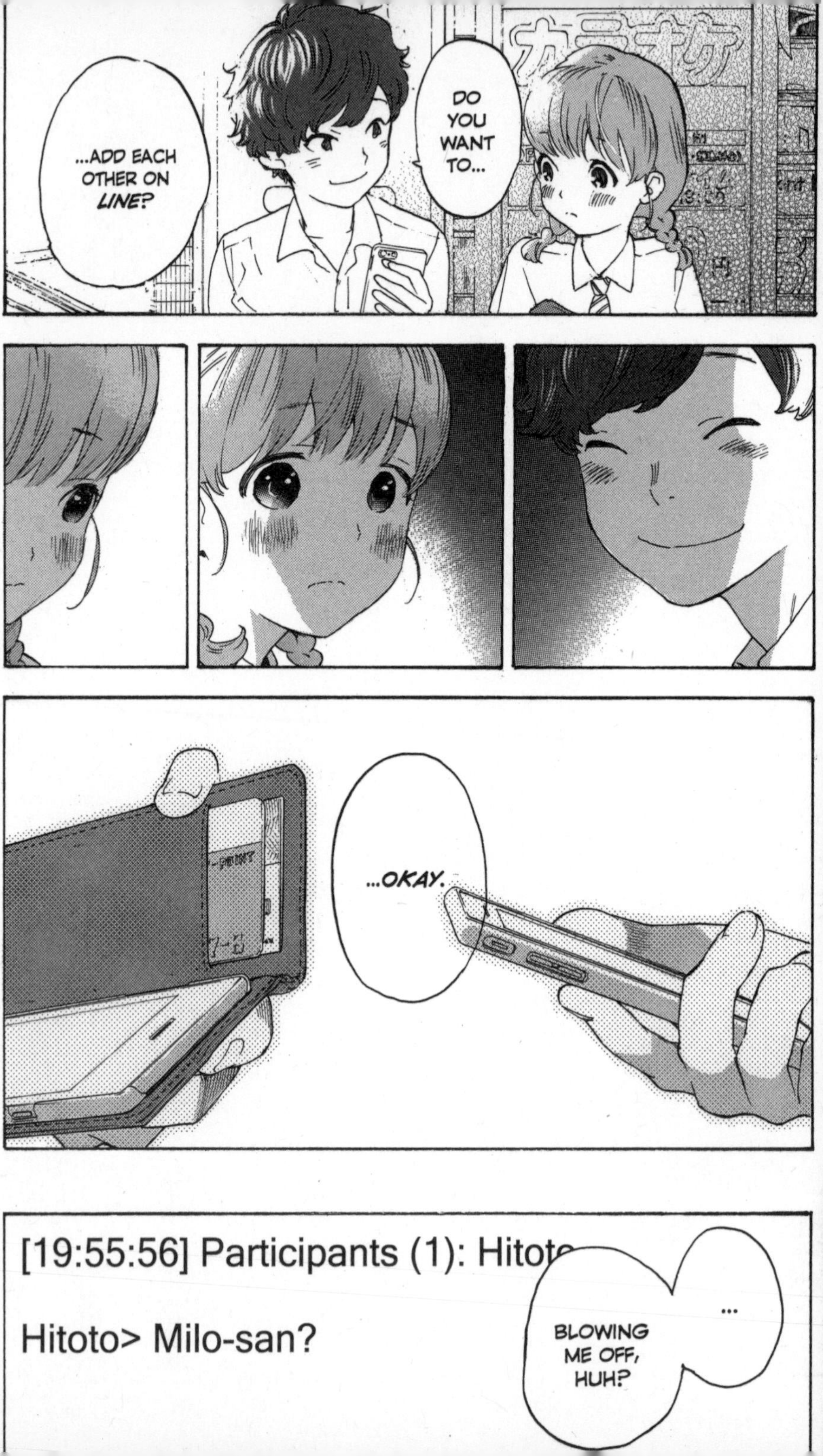
DO YOU WANT TO...
...ADD EACH OTHER ON *LINE*?
...OKAY.
[19:55:56] Participants (1): Hitot
Hitoto> Milo-san?
... BLOWING ME OFF, HUH?

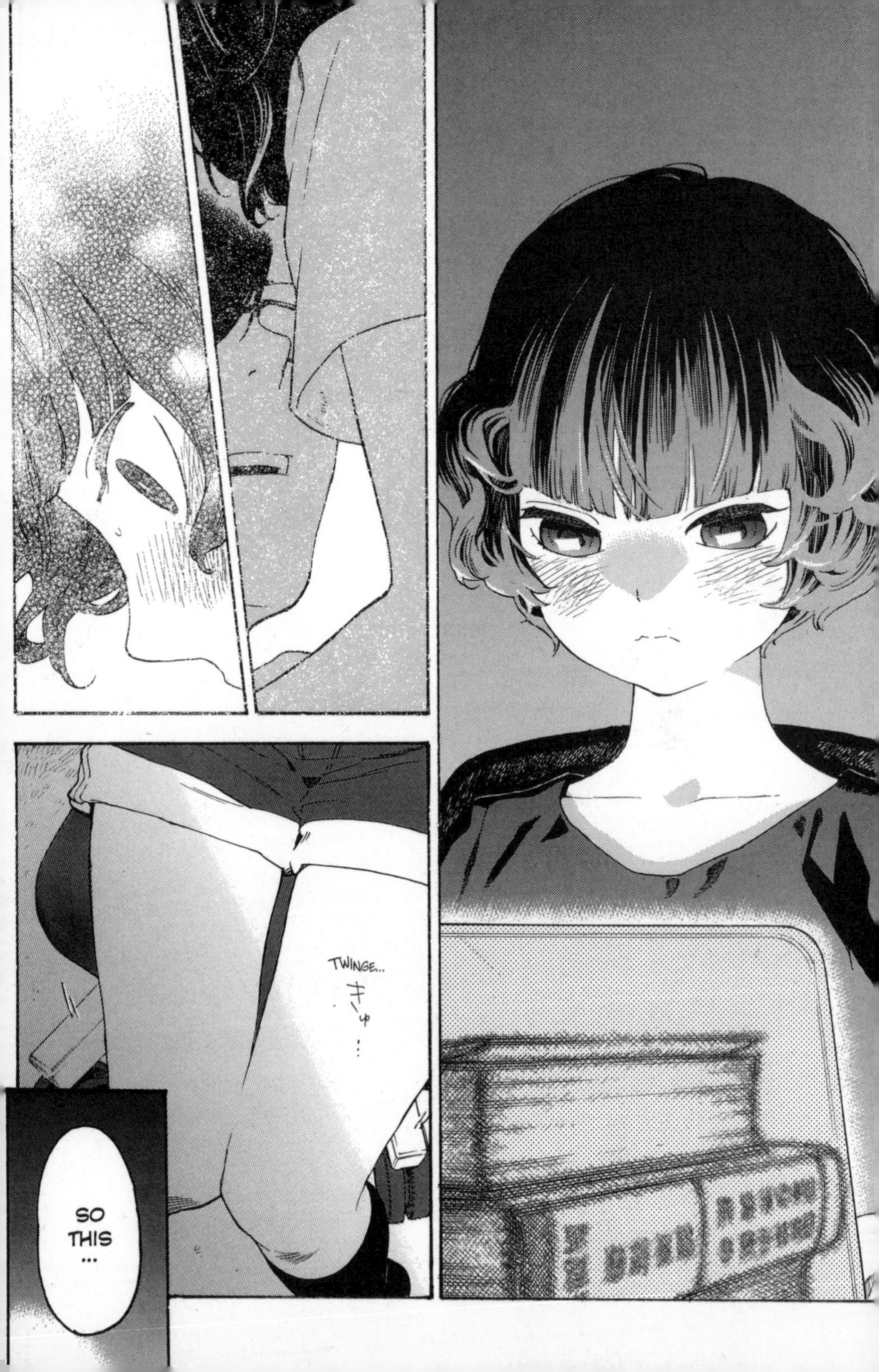
TWINGE...
キゅ…
SO THIS...

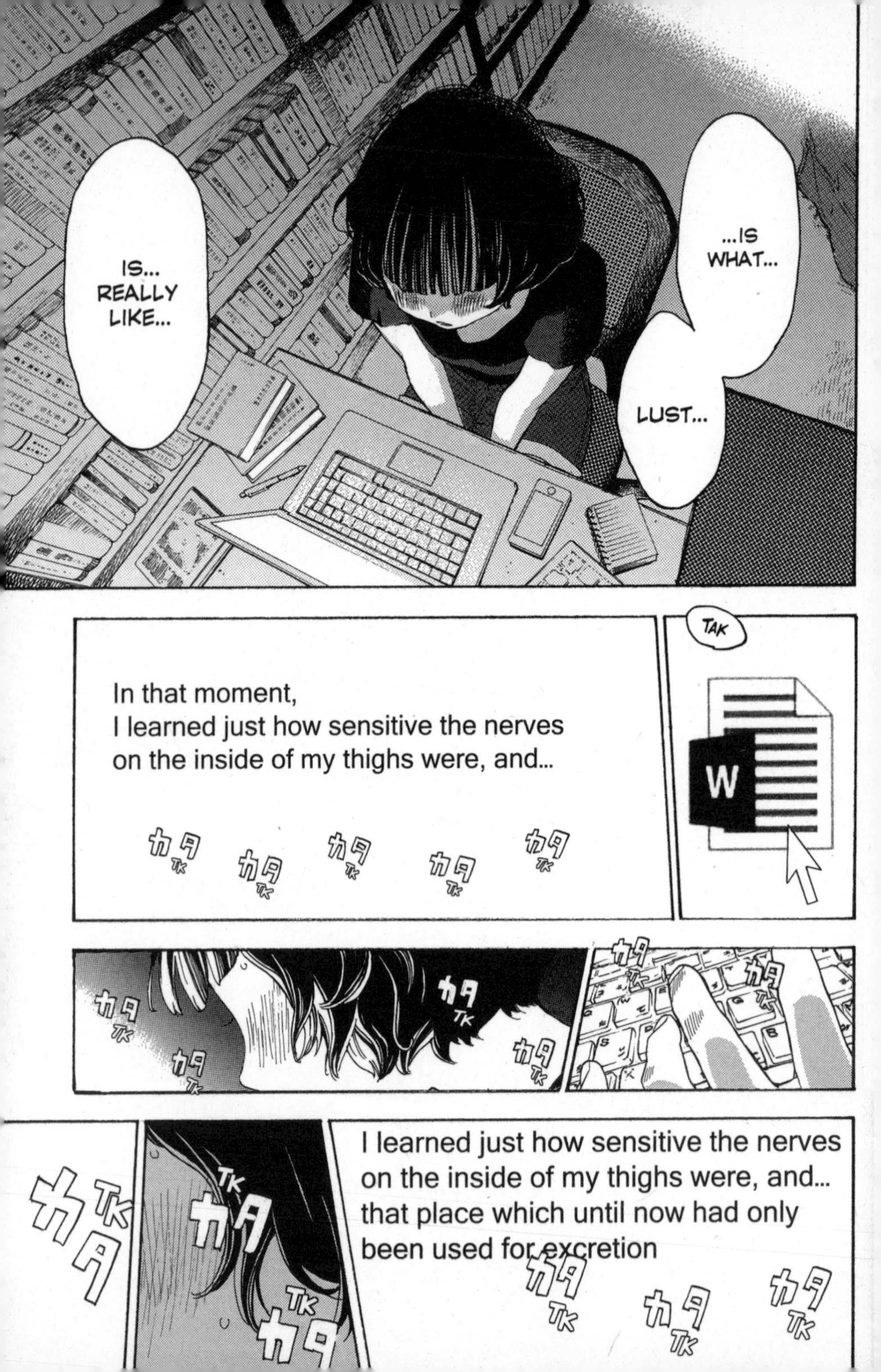
...IS WHAT...
LUST...
IS... REALLY LIKE...
TAK
W
In that moment,
I learned just how sensitive the nerves on the inside of my thighs were, and...
カタ TK
カタ TK
カタ TK
カタ TK
カタ TK
カタ TK
カタ TK
カタ TK
カタ TK
カタ TK
カタ TK
I learned just how sensitive the nerves on the inside of my thighs were, and... that place which until now had only been used for excretion
カタ TK
カタ TK
カタ TK
TK カタ
TK カタ
TK カタ

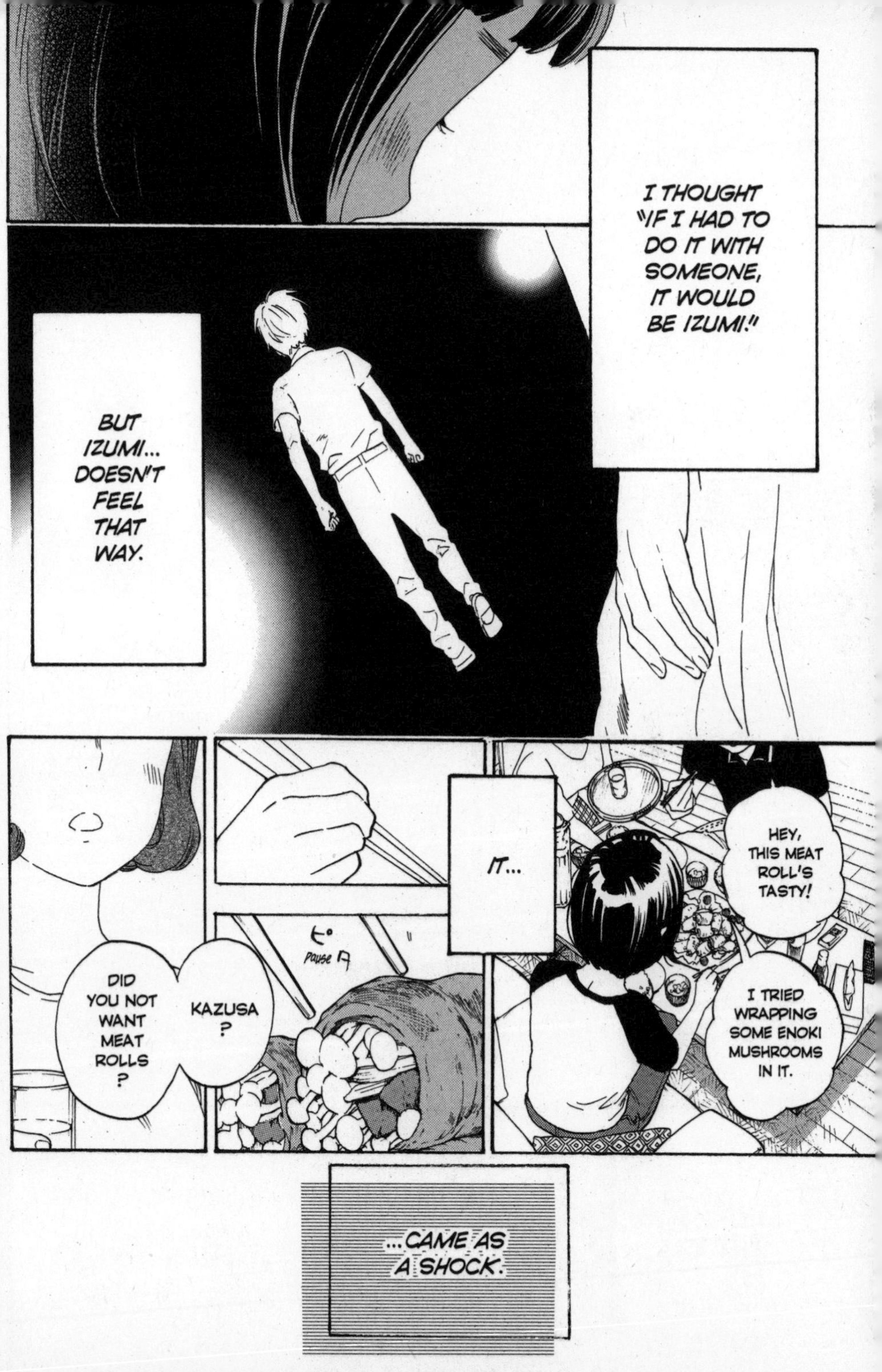
I THOUGHT "IF I HAD TO DO IT WITH SOMEONE, IT WOULD BE IZUMI."
BUT IZUMI... DOESN'T FEEL THAT WAY.
HEY, THIS MEAT ROLL'S TASTY!
IT...
I TRIED WRAPPING SOME ENOKI MUSHROOMS IN IT.
pause
KAZUSA?
DID YOU NOT WANT MEAT ROLLS?
...CAME AS A SHOCK.

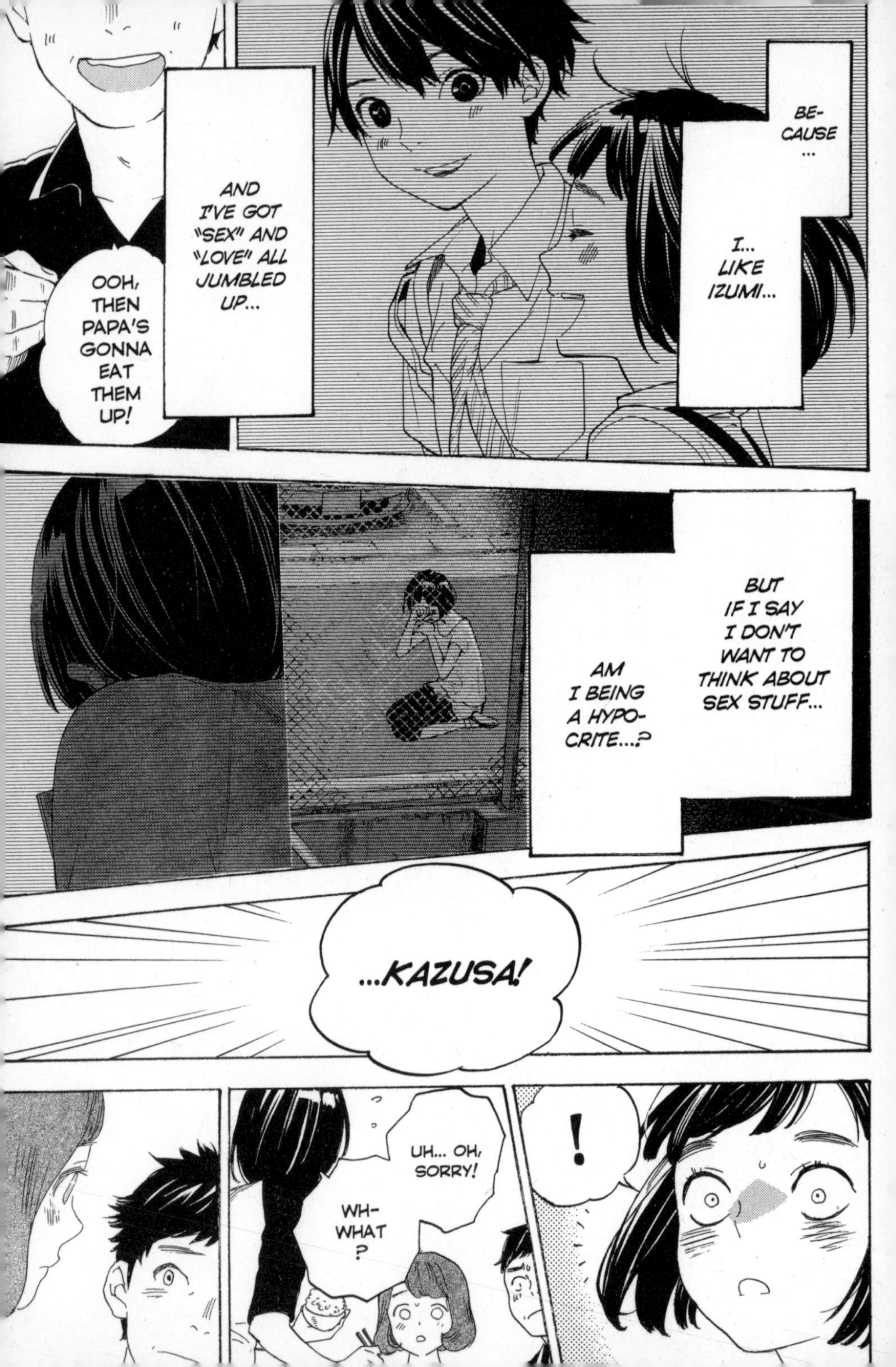
BE-CAUSE ...
I... LIKE IZUMI...
AND I'VE GOT "SEX" AND "LOVE" ALL JUMBLED UP...
OOH, THEN PAPA'S GONNA EAT THEM UP!
BUT IF I SAY I DON'T WANT TO THINK ABOUT SEX STUFF...
AM I BEING A HYPOCRITE...?
...KAZUSA!
!
UH... OH, SORRY!
WH-WHAT?

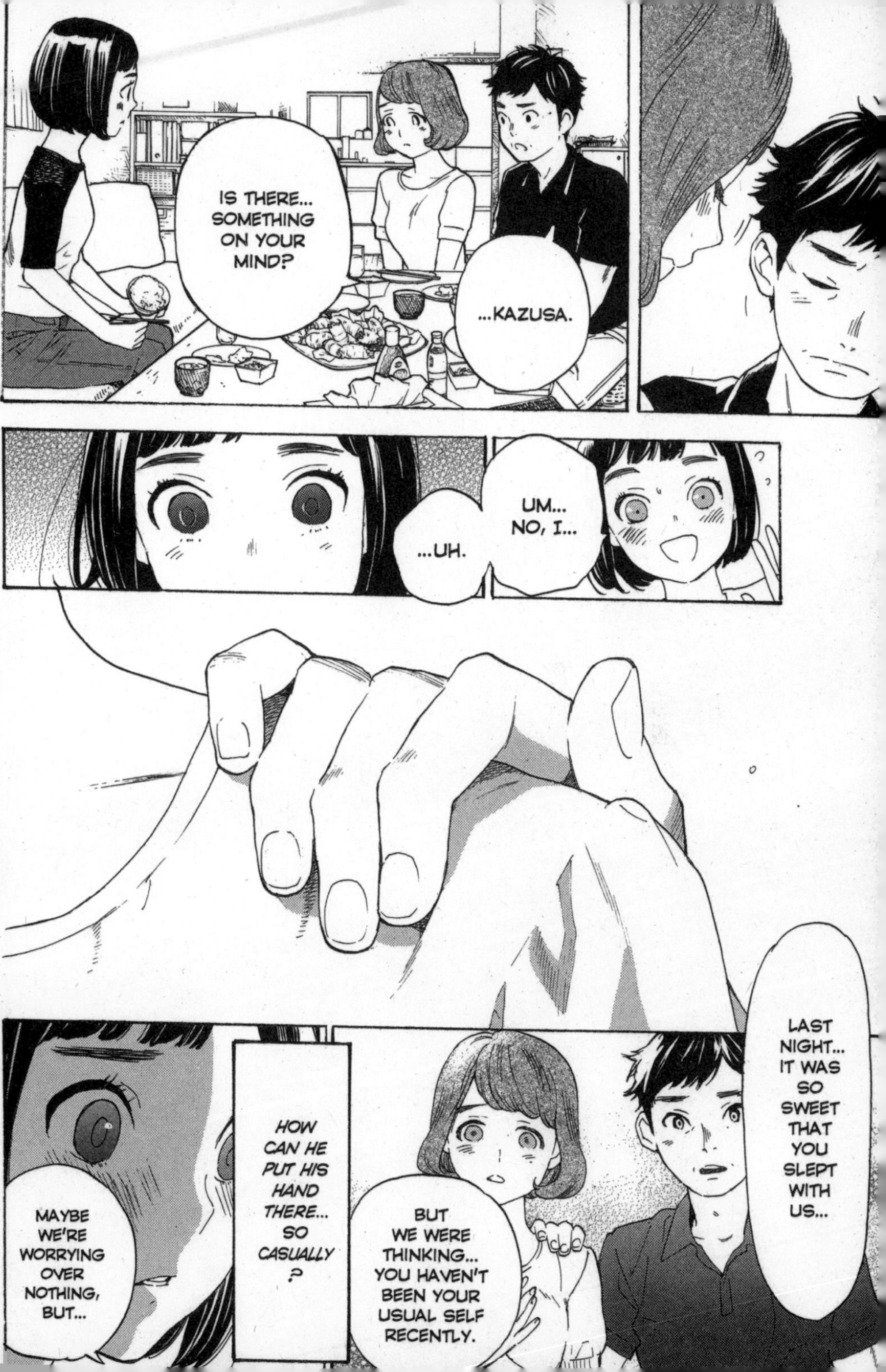
...KAZUSA.
IS THERE... SOMETHING ON YOUR MIND?
UM... NO, I...
...UH.
LAST NIGHT... IT WAS SO SWEET THAT YOU SLEPT WITH US...
BUT WE WERE THINKING... YOU HAVEN'T BEEN YOUR USUAL SELF RECENTLY.
HOW CAN HE PUT HIS HAND THERE... SO CASUALLY?
MAYBE WE'RE WORRYING OVER NOTHING, BUT...

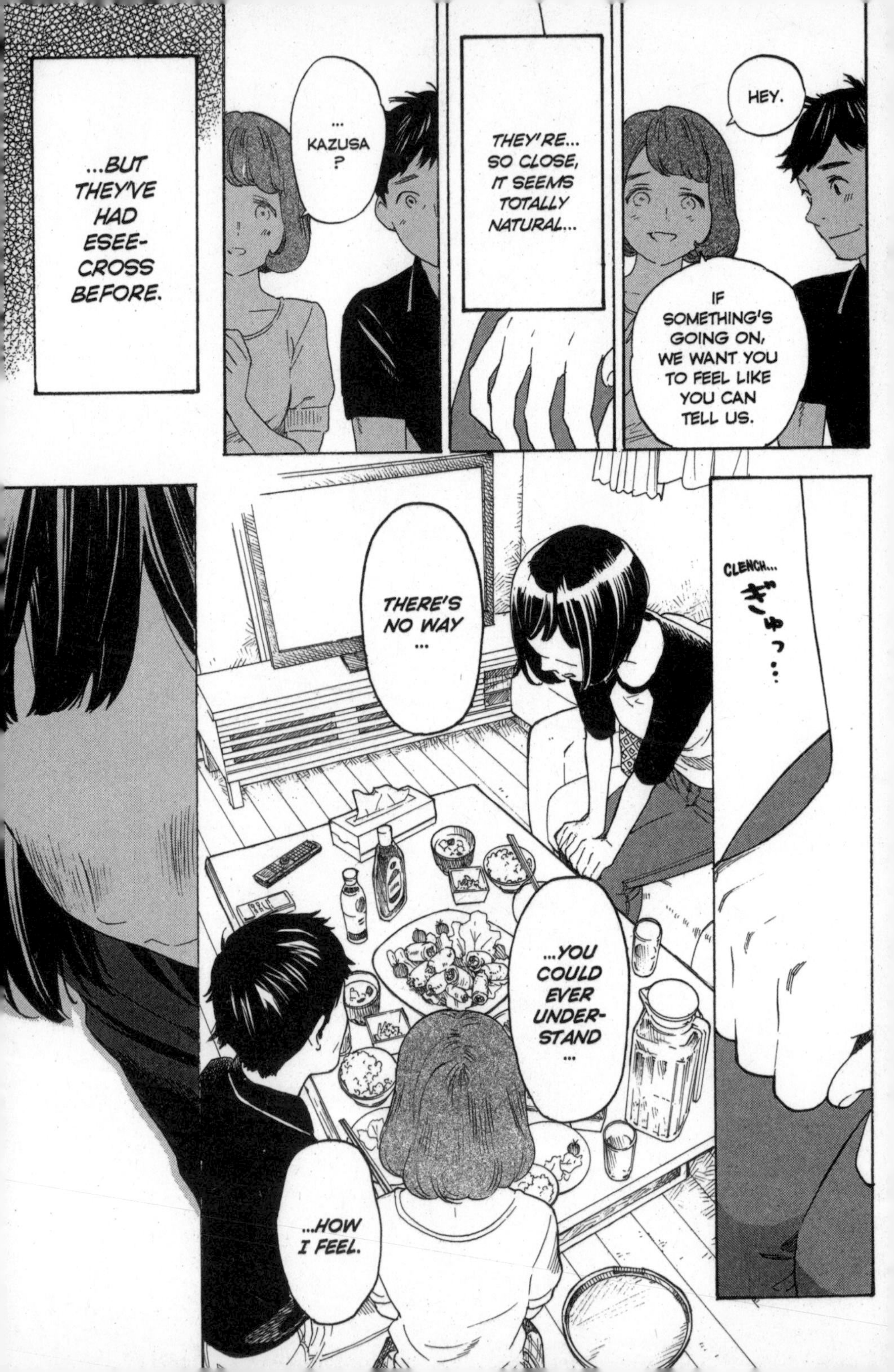
HEY.
IF SOMETHING'S GOING ON, WE WANT YOU TO FEEL LIKE YOU CAN TELL US.
THEY'RE... SO CLOSE, IT SEEMS TOTALLY NATURAL...
... KAZUSA ?
...BUT THEY'VE HAD ESEE-CROSS BEFORE.
CLENCH...
ぎゅっ…
THERE'S NO WAY ...
...YOU COULD EVER UNDER-STAND ...
...HOW I FEEL.

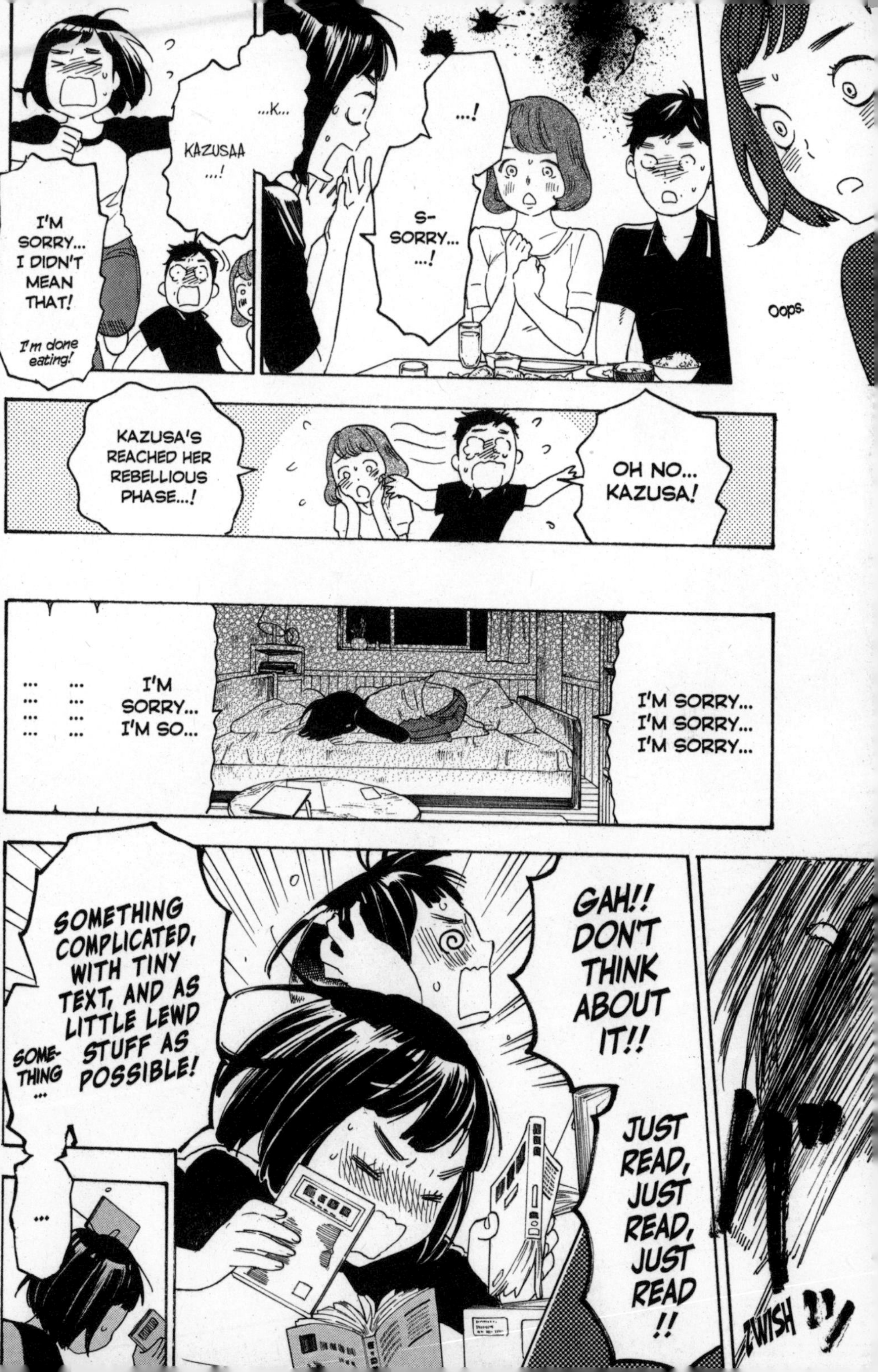
Oops.
...!
...K...
KAZUSAA ...!
S-SORRY... ...!
I'M SORRY... I DIDN'T MEAN THAT!
I'm done eating!
OH NO... KAZUSA!
KAZUSA'S REACHED HER REBELLIOUS PHASE...!
I'M SORRY... I'M SORRY... I'M SORRY...
I'M SORRY... I'M SO...
... ...
... ...
ZWISH
GAH!! DON'T THINK ABOUT IT!!
JUST READ, JUST READ, JUST READ!!
SOMETHING COMPLICATED, WITH TINY TEXT, AND AS LITTLE LEWD STUFF AS POSSIBLE!
SOME-THING ...
...

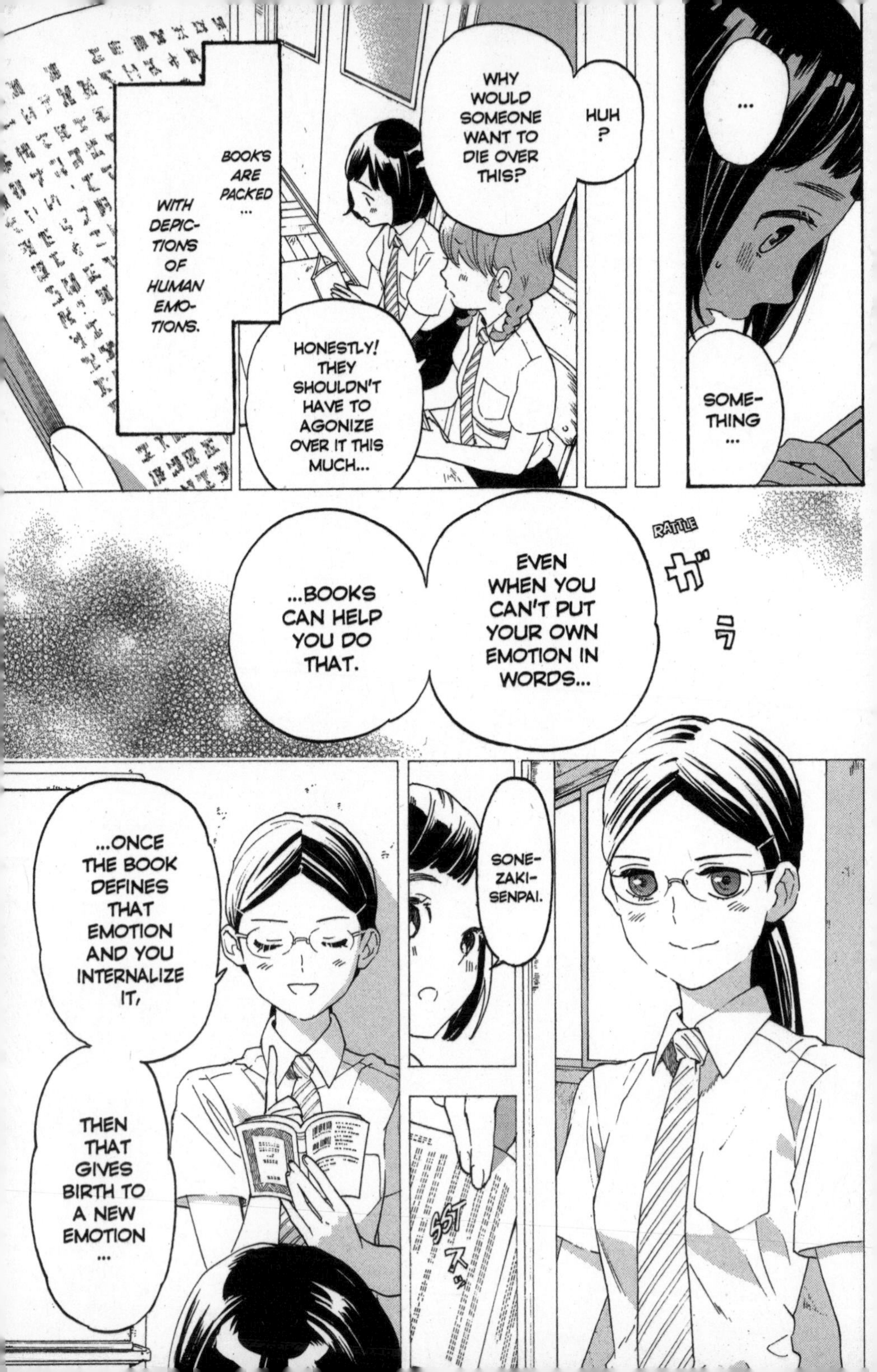
...
SOME-THING ...
HUH ?
WHY WOULD SOMEONE WANT TO DIE OVER THIS?
HONESTLY! THEY SHOULDN'T HAVE TO AGONIZE OVER IT THIS MUCH...
BOOKS ARE PACKED ...
WITH DEPIC-TIONS OF HUMAN EMO-TIONS.
RATTLE
ガラ
EVEN WHEN YOU CAN'T PUT YOUR OWN EMOTION IN WORDS...
...BOOKS CAN HELP YOU DO THAT.
SONE-ZAKI-SENPAI.
SST
ス
...ONCE THE BOOK DEFINES THAT EMOTION AND YOU INTERNALIZE IT,
THEN THAT GIVES BIRTH TO A NEW EMOTION ...

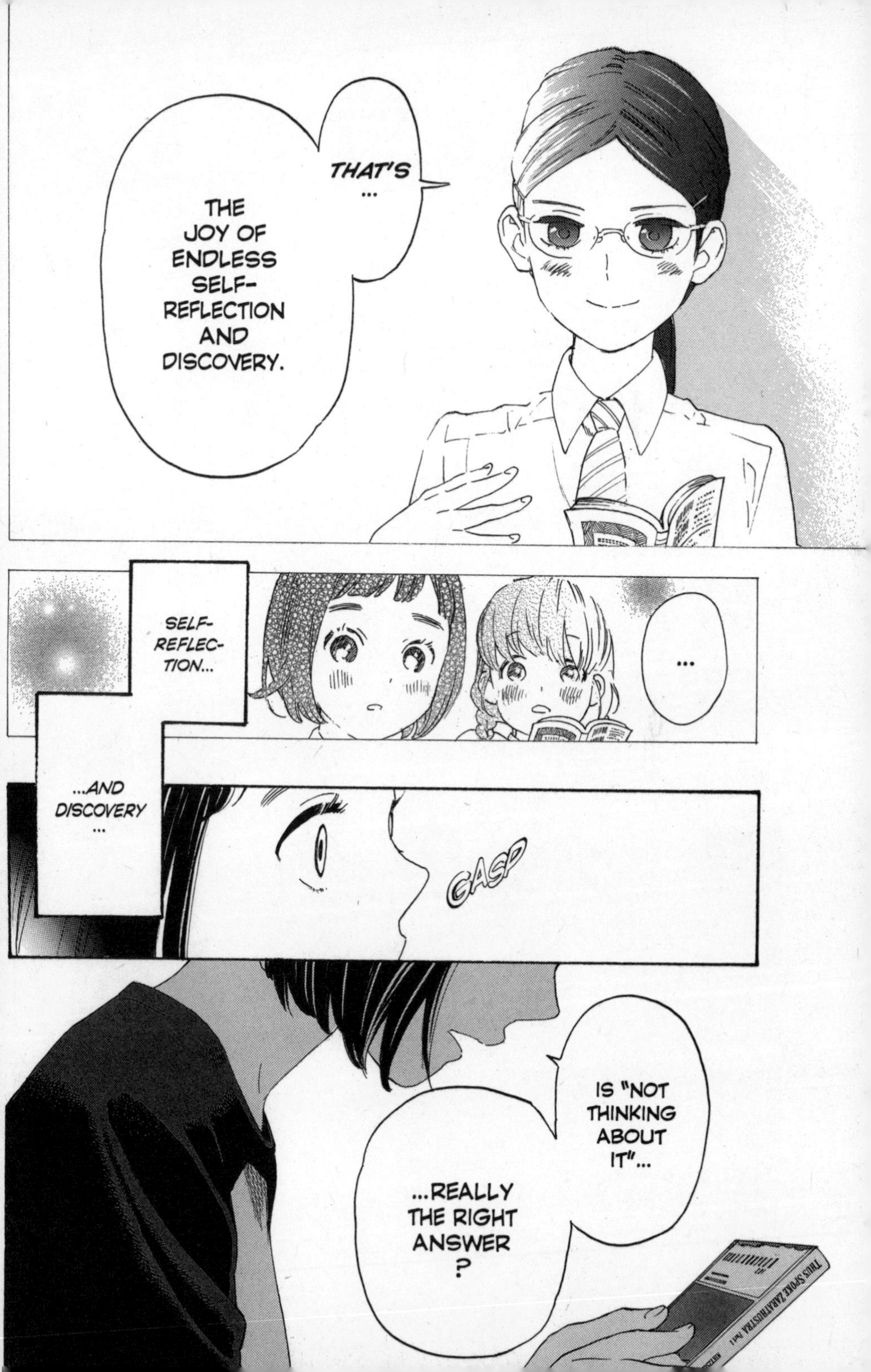
THAT'S ...
THE JOY OF ENDLESS SELF-REFLECTION AND DISCOVERY.
...
SELF-REFLECTION...
...AND DISCOVERY ...
GASP
IS "NOT THINKING ABOUT IT"...
...REALLY THE RIGHT ANSWER ?
THUS SPOKE ZARATHUSTRA

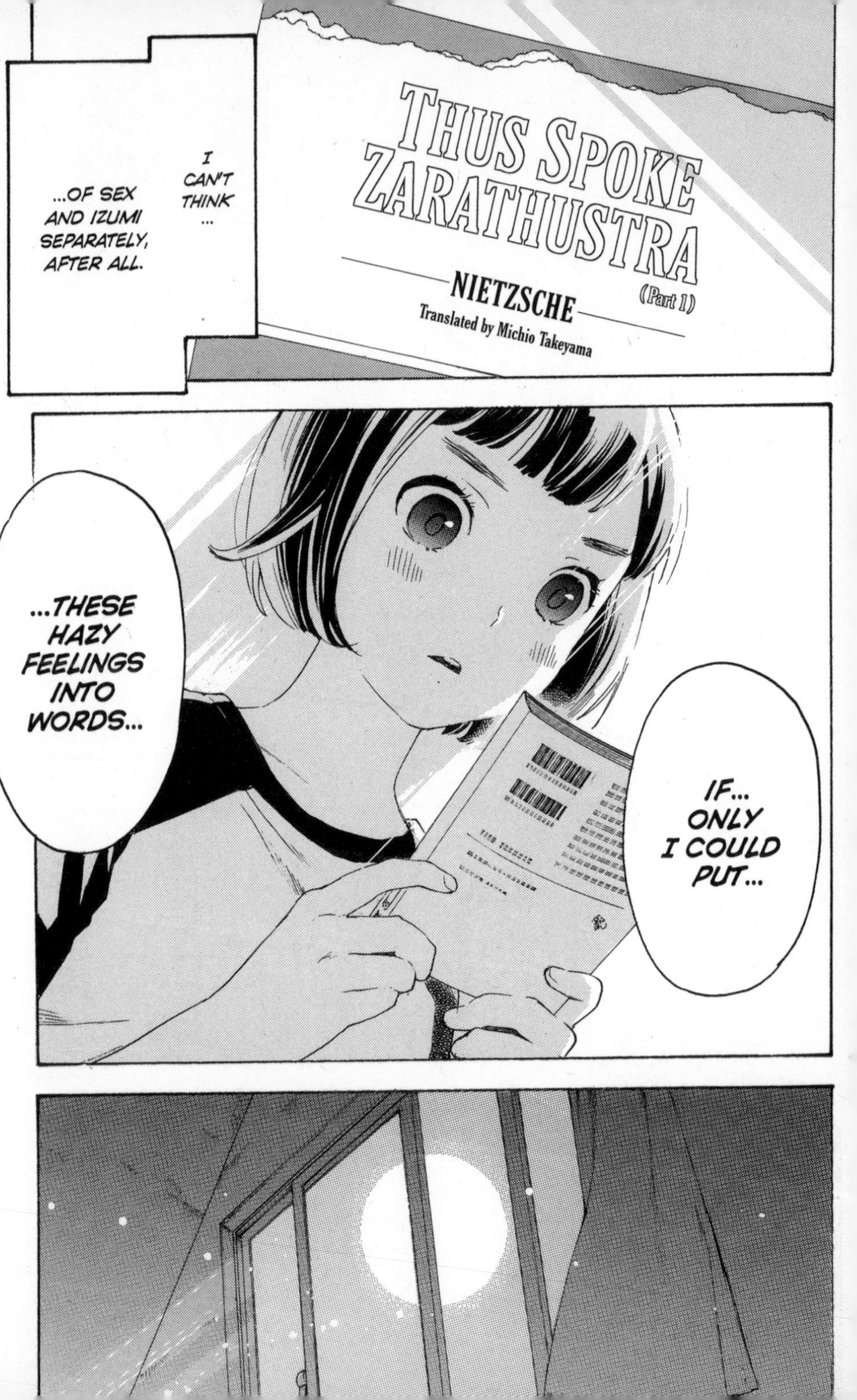
THUS SPOKE ZARATHUSTRA
(Part 1)
NIETZSCHE
Translated by Michio Takeyama
I CAN'T THINK ...
...OF SEX AND IZUMI SEPARATELY, AFTER ALL.
IF... ONLY I COULD PUT...
...THESE HAZY FEELINGS INTO WORDS...

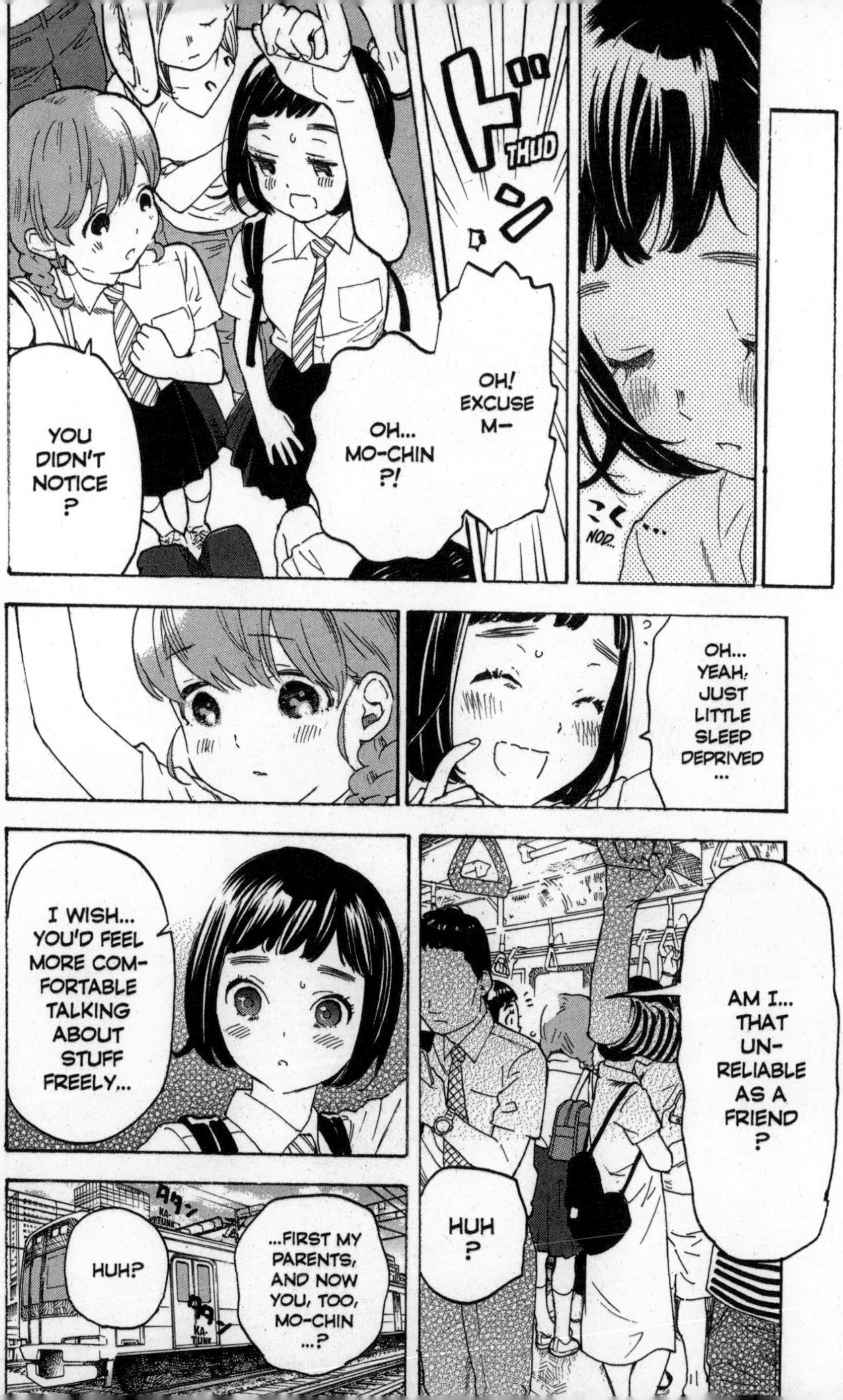
NOD...
THUD
OH! EXCUSE M—
OH... MO-CHIN ?!
YOU DIDN'T NOTICE ?
OH... YEAH, JUST LITTLE SLEEP DEPRIVED ...
AM I... THAT UN-RELIABLE AS A FRIEND ?
HUH ?
I WISH... YOU'D FEEL MORE COM-FORTABLE TALKING ABOUT STUFF FREELY...
KA-TUNK
...FIRST MY PARENTS, AND NOW YOU, TOO, MO-CHIN ...?
HUH?
KA-TUNK

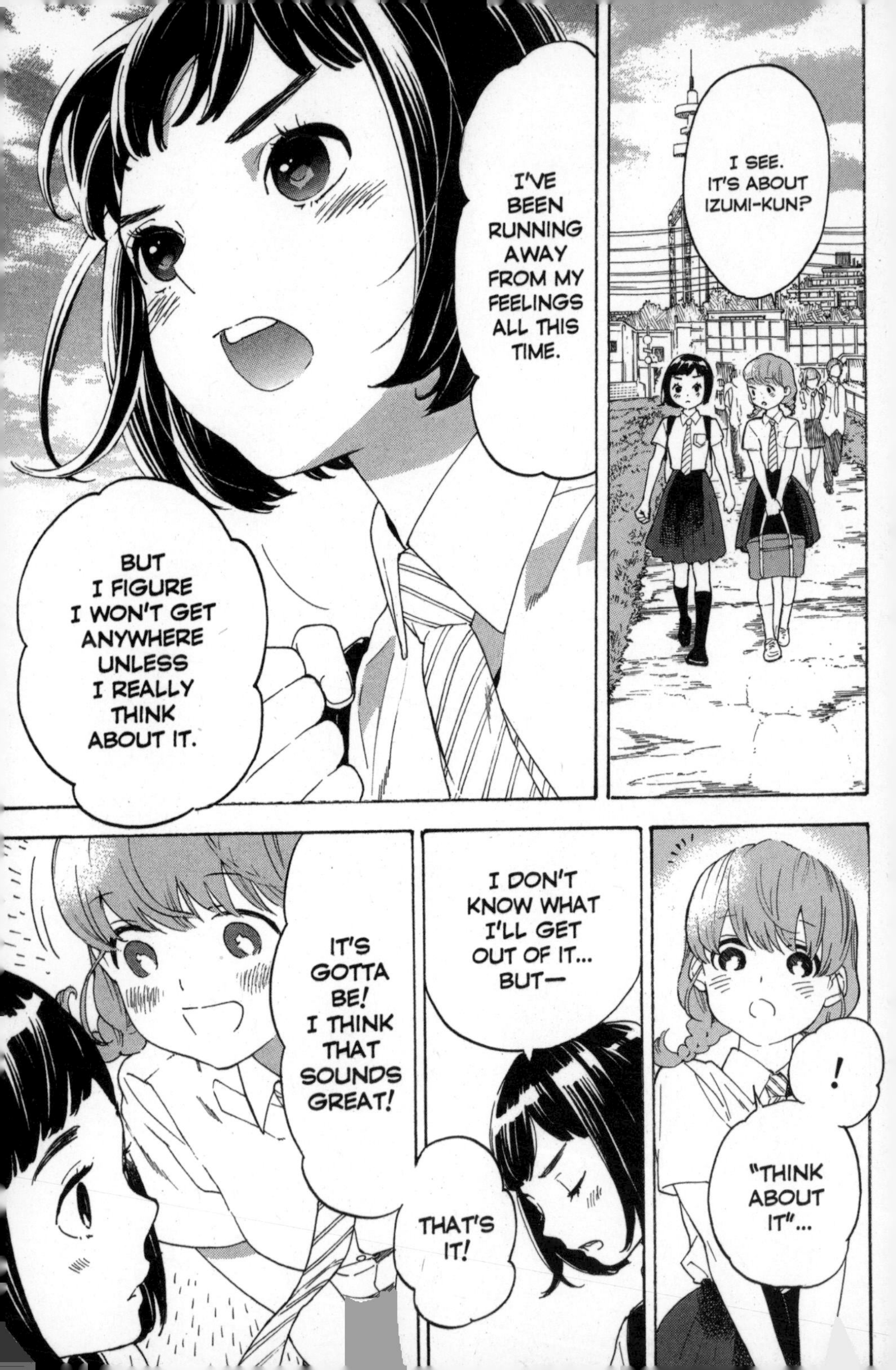
I SEE. IT'S ABOUT IZUMI-KUN?
I'VE BEEN RUNNING AWAY FROM MY FEELINGS ALL THIS TIME.
BUT I FIGURE I WON'T GET ANYWHERE UNLESS I REALLY THINK ABOUT IT.
!
"THINK ABOUT IT"...
I DON'T KNOW WHAT I'LL GET OUT OF IT... BUT—
THAT'S IT!
IT'S GOTTA BE! I THINK THAT SOUNDS GREAT!

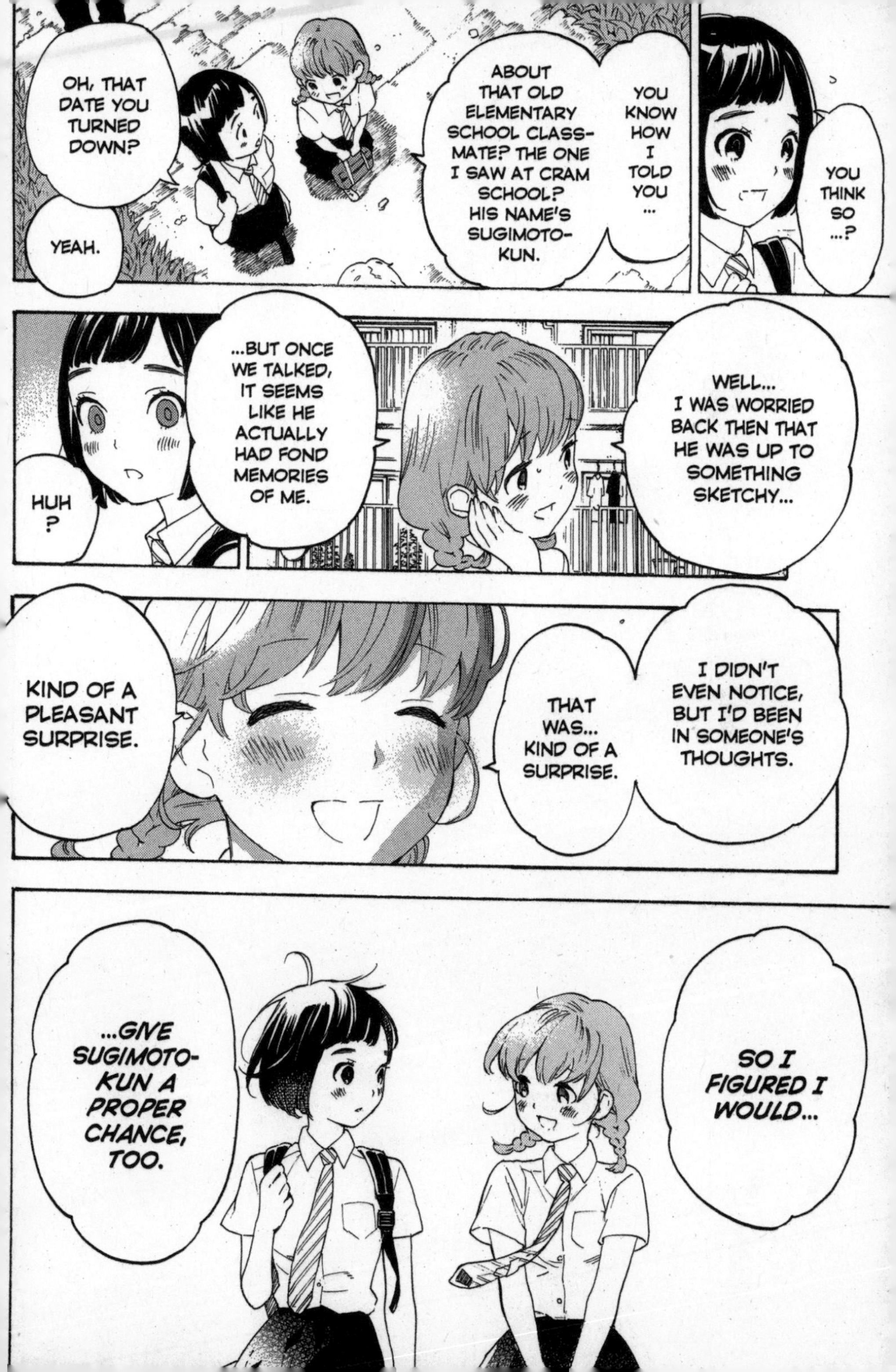
YOU THINK SO ...?
YOU KNOW HOW I TOLD YOU ...
ABOUT THAT OLD ELEMENTARY SCHOOL CLASS-MATE? THE ONE I SAW AT CRAM SCHOOL? HIS NAME'S SUGIMOTO-KUN.
OH, THAT DATE YOU TURNED DOWN?
YEAH.
WELL... I WAS WORRIED BACK THEN THAT HE WAS UP TO SOMETHING SKETCHY...
...BUT ONCE WE TALKED, IT SEEMS LIKE HE ACTUALLY HAD FOND MEMORIES OF ME.
HUH?
I DIDN'T EVEN NOTICE, BUT I'D BEEN IN SOMEONE'S THOUGHTS.
THAT WAS... KIND OF A SURPRISE.
KIND OF A PLEASANT SURPRISE.
SO I FIGURED I WOULD...
...GIVE SUGIMOTO-KUN A PROPER CHANCE, TOO.

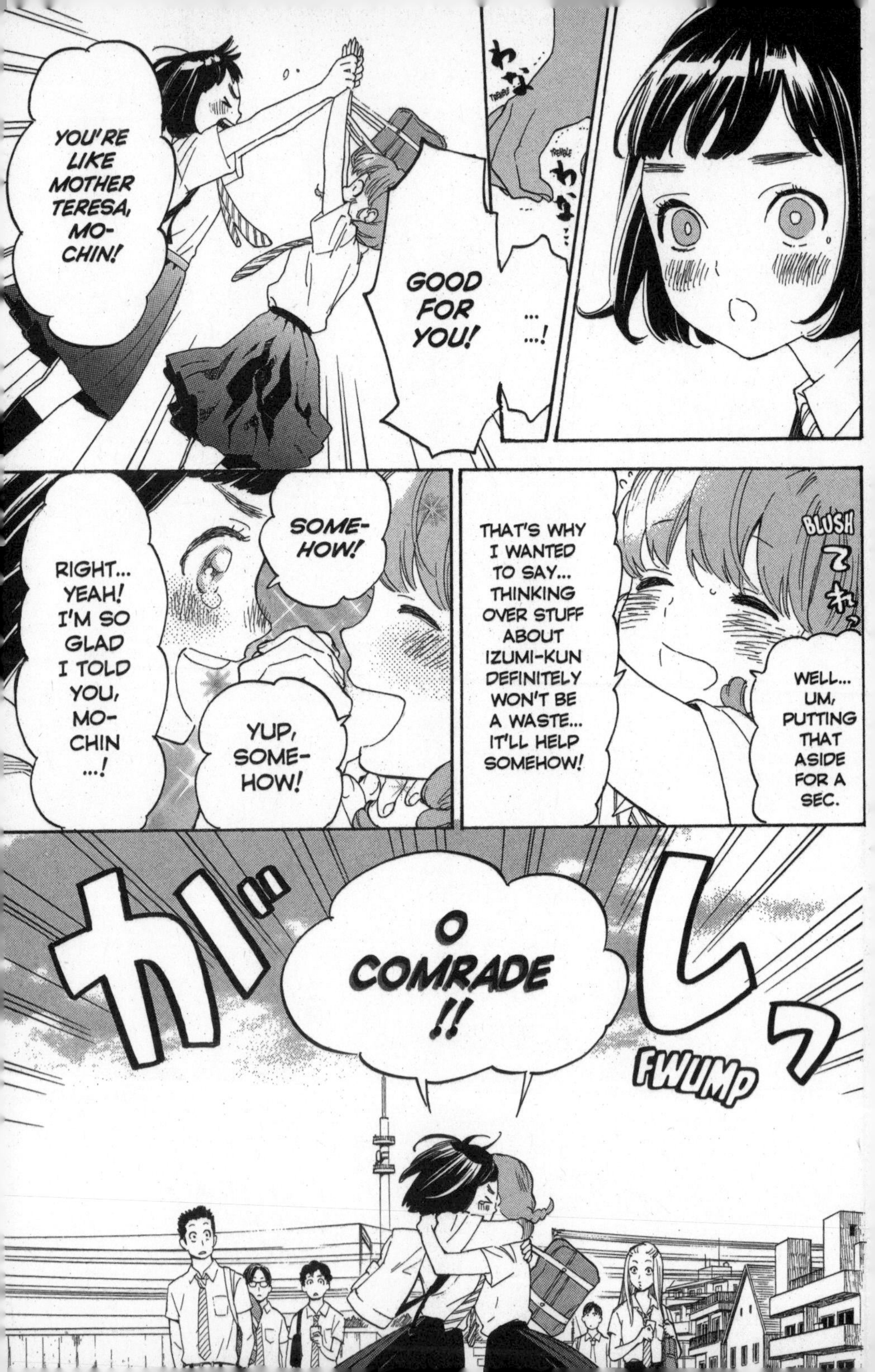
TREMBLE
TREMBLE
... ...!
GOOD FOR YOU!
YOU'RE LIKE MOTHER TERESA, MO-CHIN!
BLUSH
WELL... UM, PUTTING THAT ASIDE FOR A SEC.
THAT'S WHY I WANTED TO SAY... THINKING OVER STUFF ABOUT IZUMI-KUN DEFINITELY WON'T BE A WASTE... IT'LL HELP SOMEHOW!
SOME-HOW!
YUP, SOME-HOW!
RIGHT... YEAH! I'M SO GLAD I TOLD YOU, MO-CHIN ...!
O COMRADE !!
FWUMP

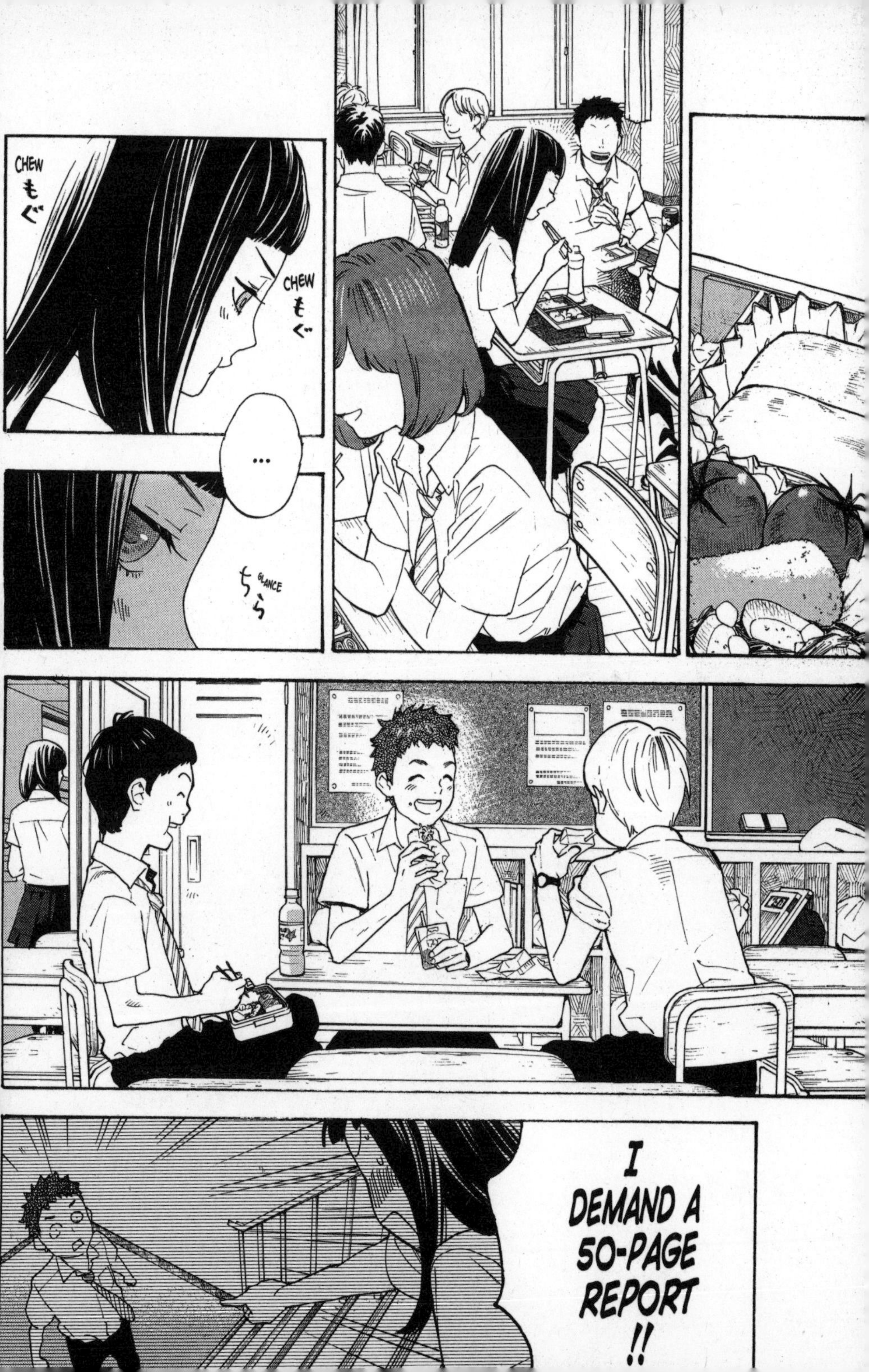
CHEW
もぐ
CHEW
もぐ
...
ちら
GLANCE
I DEMAND A 50-PAGE REPORT!!

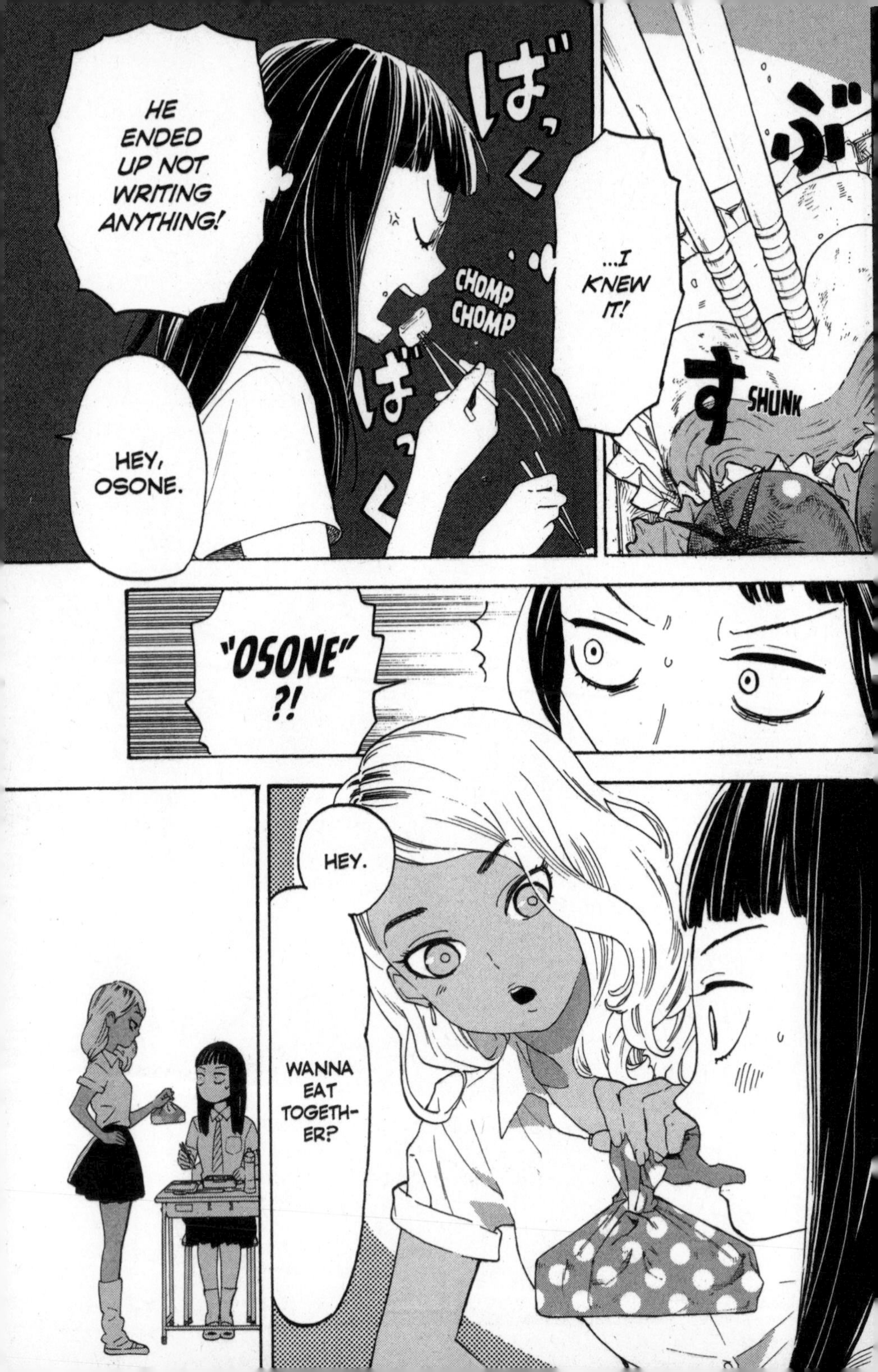
ぶ
す
SHUNK
...I KNEW IT!
HE ENDED UP NOT WRITING ANYTHING!
ばっく
ばっく
CHOMP CHOMP
HEY, OSONE.
"OSONE" ?!
HEY.
WANNA EAT TOGETH-ER?

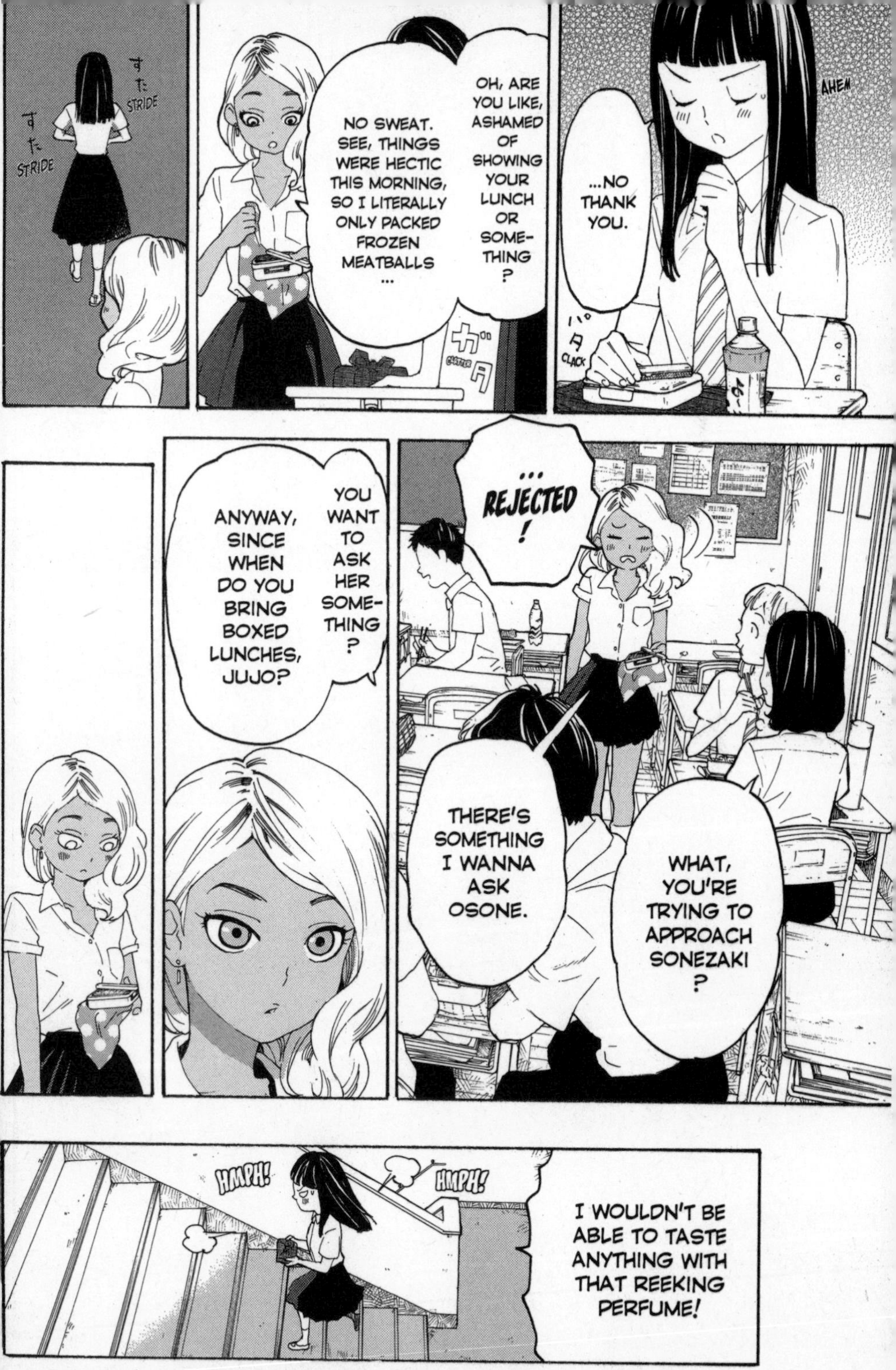
AHEM
...NO THANK YOU.
パタ CLACK
OH, ARE YOU LIKE, ASHAMED OF SHOWING YOUR LUNCH OR SOMETHING?
NO SWEAT. SEE, THINGS WERE HECTIC THIS MORNING, SO I LITERALLY ONLY PACKED FROZEN MEATBALLS...
ガタ CLATTER
すた STRIDE
すた STRIDE
...REJECTED!
WHAT, YOU'RE TRYING TO APPROACH SONEZAKI?
THERE'S SOMETHING I WANNA ASK OSONE.
YOU WANT TO ASK HER SOMETHING?
ANYWAY, SINCE WHEN DO YOU BRING BOXED LUNCHES, JUJO?
HMPH!
HMPH!
I WOULDN'T BE ABLE TO TASTE ANYTHING WITH THAT REEKING PERFUME!

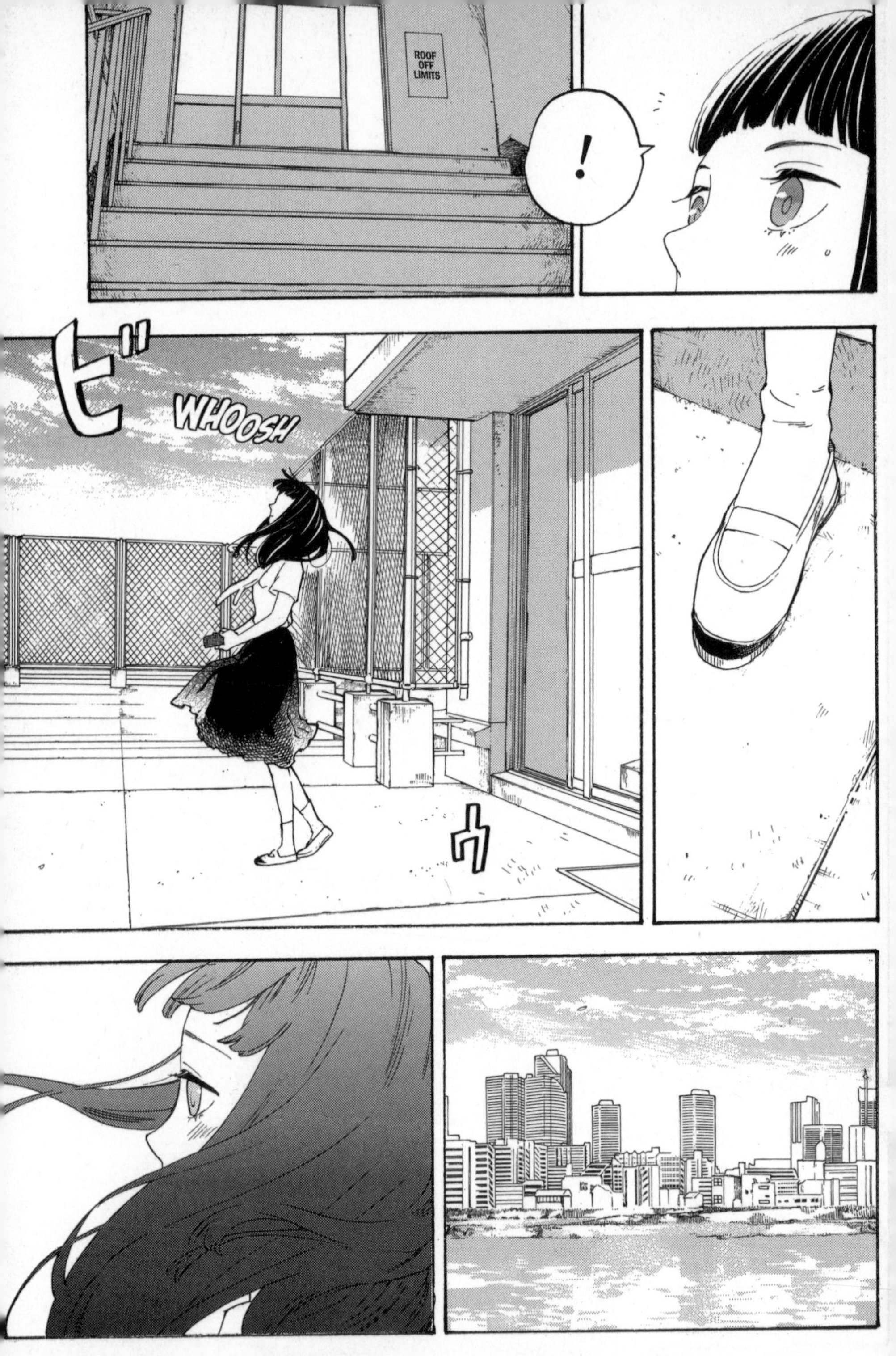
!
ROOF OFF LIMITS
ビ
WHOOSH

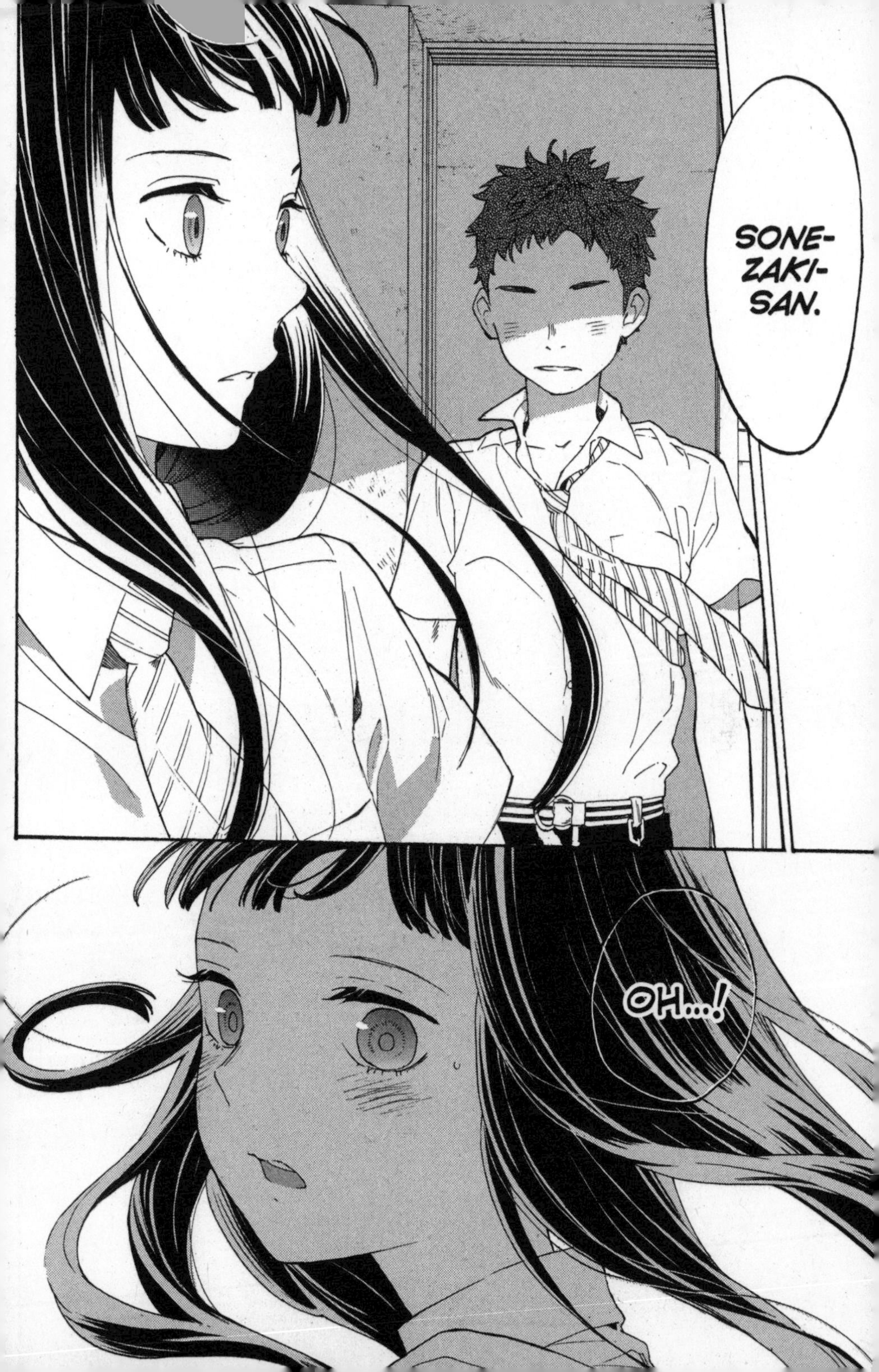
SONE-
ZAKI-
SAN.
OH...!

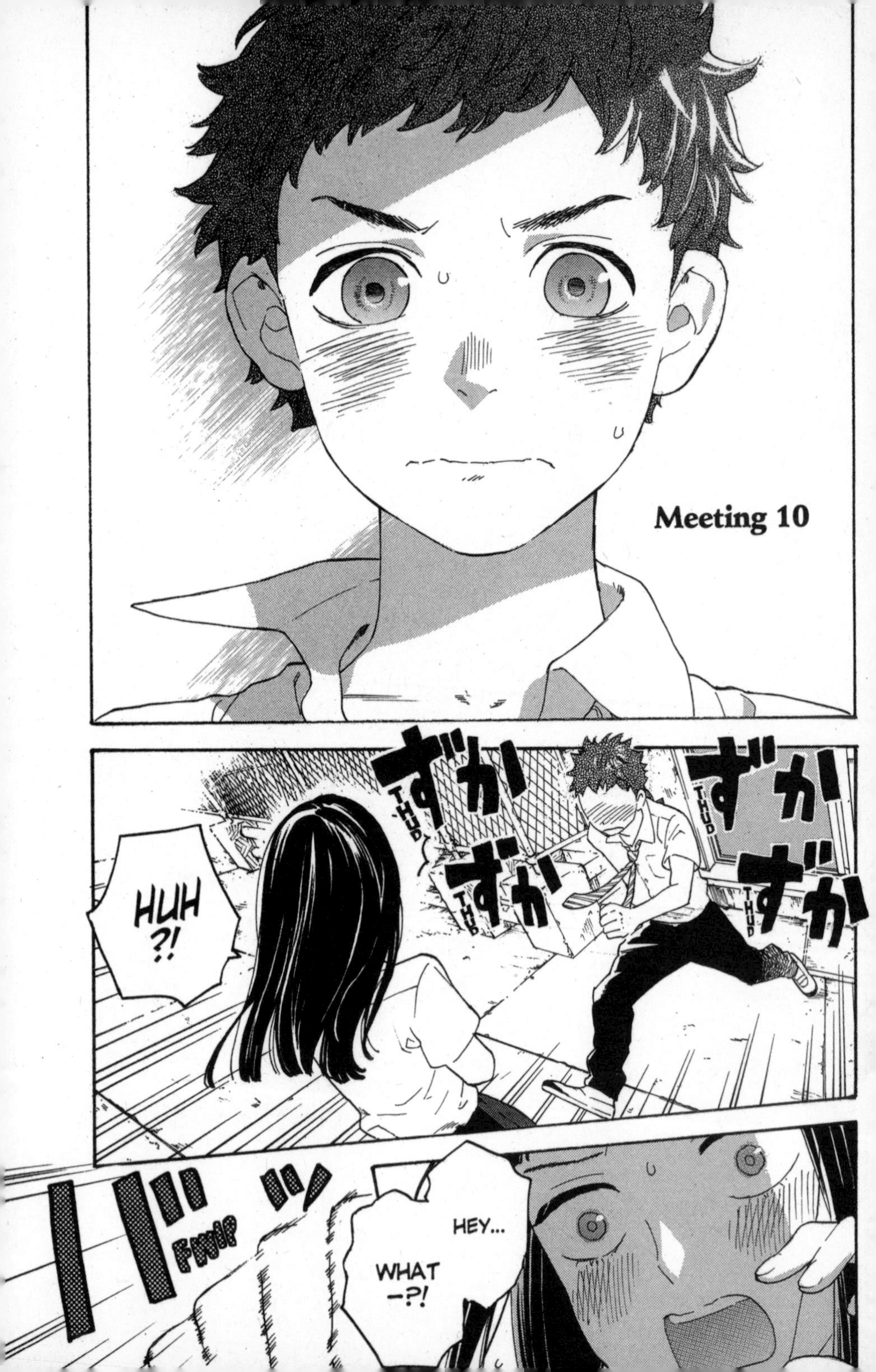
Meeting 10
ずか THUD
ずか THUD
ずか THUD
ずか THUD
HUH ?!
HEY...
WHAT —?!
FWIP

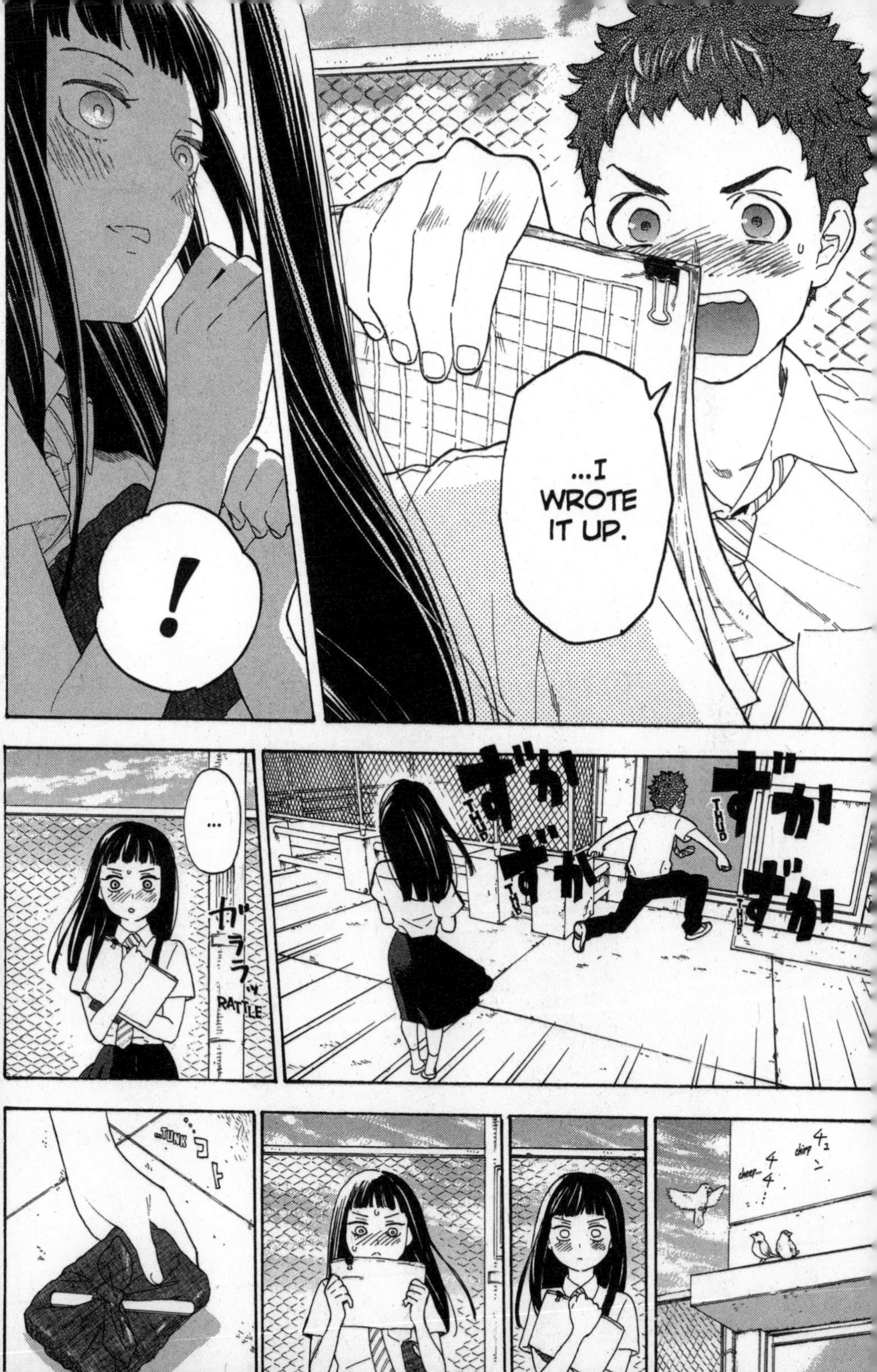
...I WROTE IT UP.
!
ずかずか
THUD
THUD
ずかずか
THUD
THUD
...
ガララ
RATTLE
chirp
cheep...
...TUNK
コト

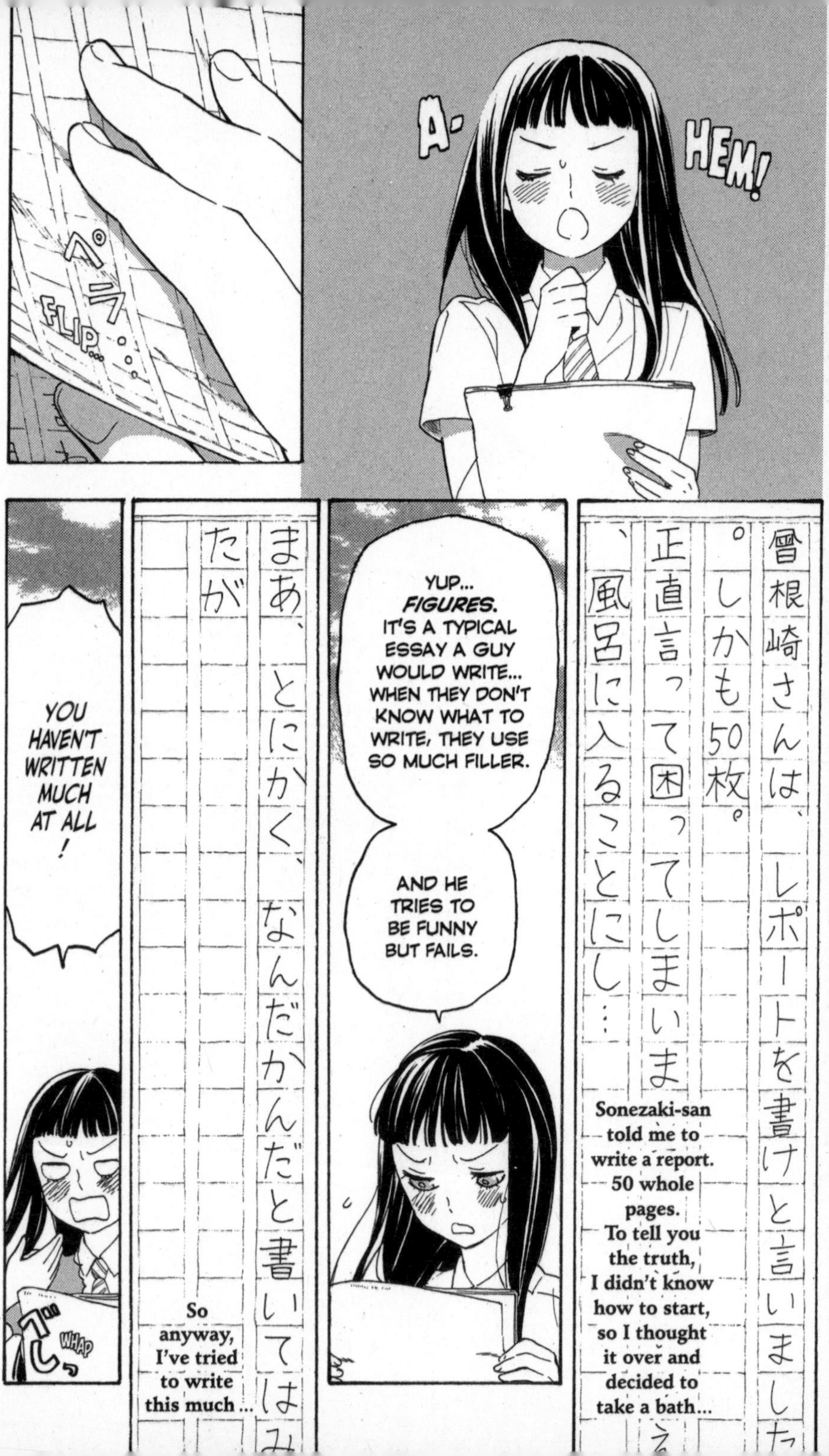
A-
HEM!
ペラ
FLIP...
曽根崎さんは、レポートを書けと言いました
。しかも50枚。
正直言って困ってしまいま
、風呂に入ることにし…
Sonezaki-san told me to write a report. 50 whole pages. To tell you the truth, I didn't know how to start, so I thought it over and decided to take a bath...
YUP... FIGURES. IT'S A TYPICAL ESSAY A GUY WOULD WRITE... WHEN THEY DON'T KNOW WHAT TO WRITE, THEY USE SO MUCH FILLER.
AND HE TRIES TO BE FUNNY BUT FAILS.
まあ、とにかく、なんだかんだと書いてはみ
たが
So anyway, I've tried to write this much ...
YOU HAVEN'T WRITTEN MUCH AT ALL!
WHAP

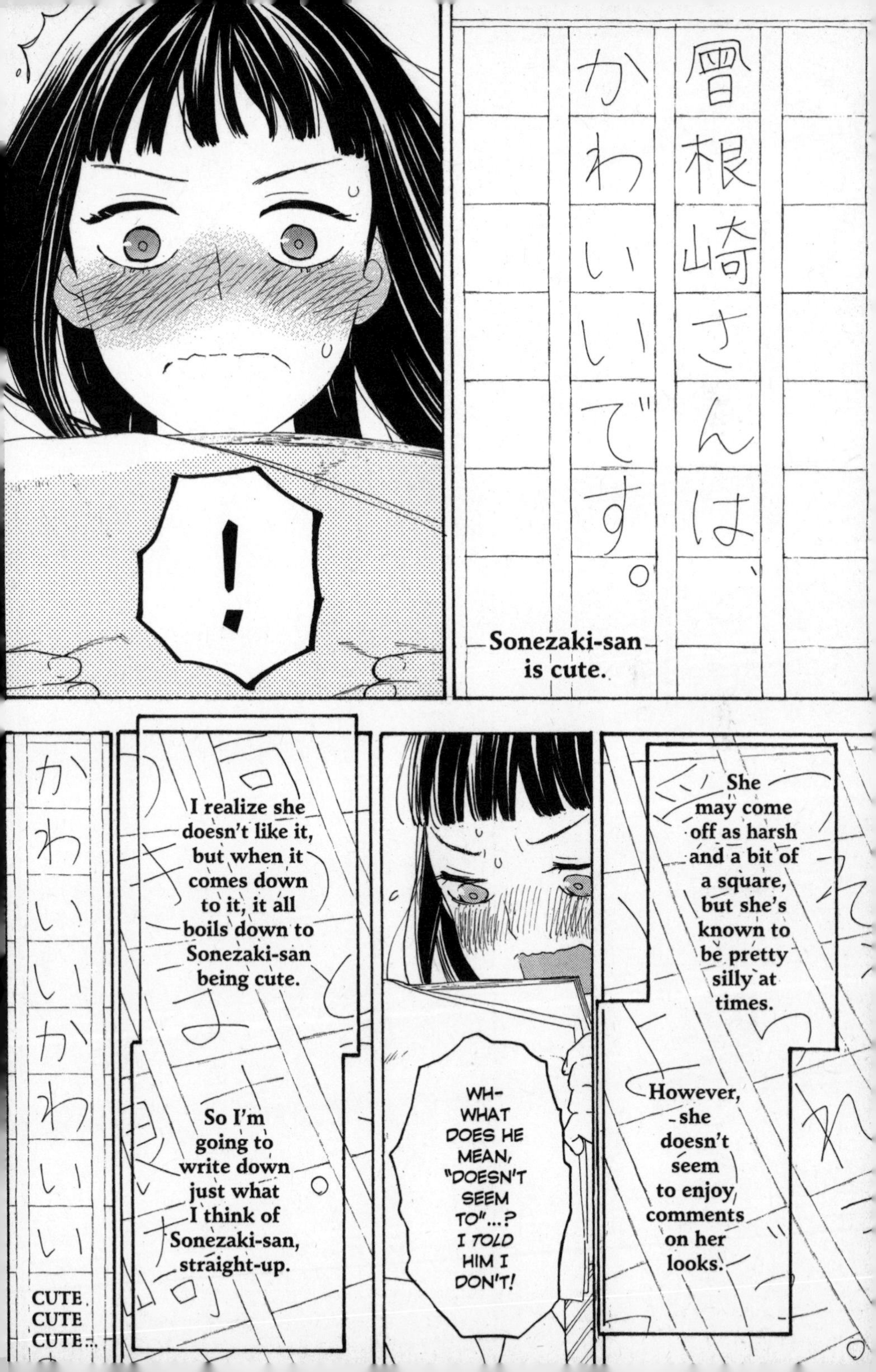
曽根崎さんは、かわいいです。
Sonezaki-san is cute.
!
She may come off as harsh and a bit of a square, but she's known to be pretty silly at times.
However, she doesn't seem to enjoy comments on her looks.
WH-WHAT DOES HE MEAN, "DOESN'T SEEM TO"...? I TOLD HIM I DON'T!
I realize she doesn't like it, but when it comes down to it, it all boils down to Sonezaki-san being cute.
So I'm going to write down just what I think of Sonezaki-san, straight-up.
かわいいかわいい
CUTE CUTE CUTE...

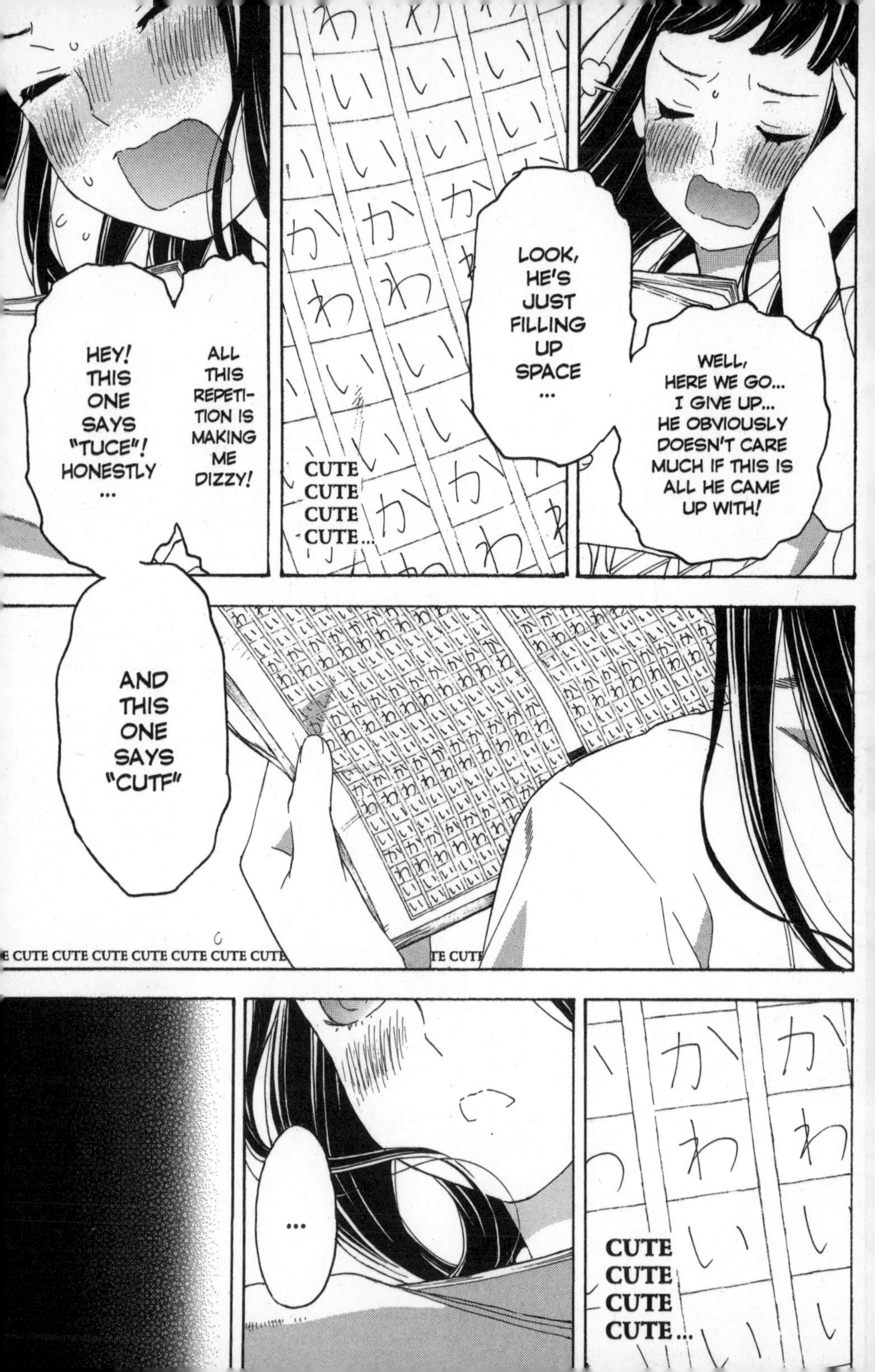
WELL, HERE WE GO... I GIVE UP... HE OBVIOUSLY DOESN'T CARE MUCH IF THIS IS ALL HE CAME UP WITH!
LOOK, HE'S JUST FILLING UP SPACE...
CUTE CUTE CUTE CUTE...
ALL THIS REPETITION IS MAKING ME DIZZY!
HEY! THIS ONE SAYS "TUCE"! HONESTLY...
AND THIS ONE SAYS "CUTF"
CUTE CUTE CUTE CUTE CUTE CUTE CUTE
CUTE CUTE CUTE CUTE...
...

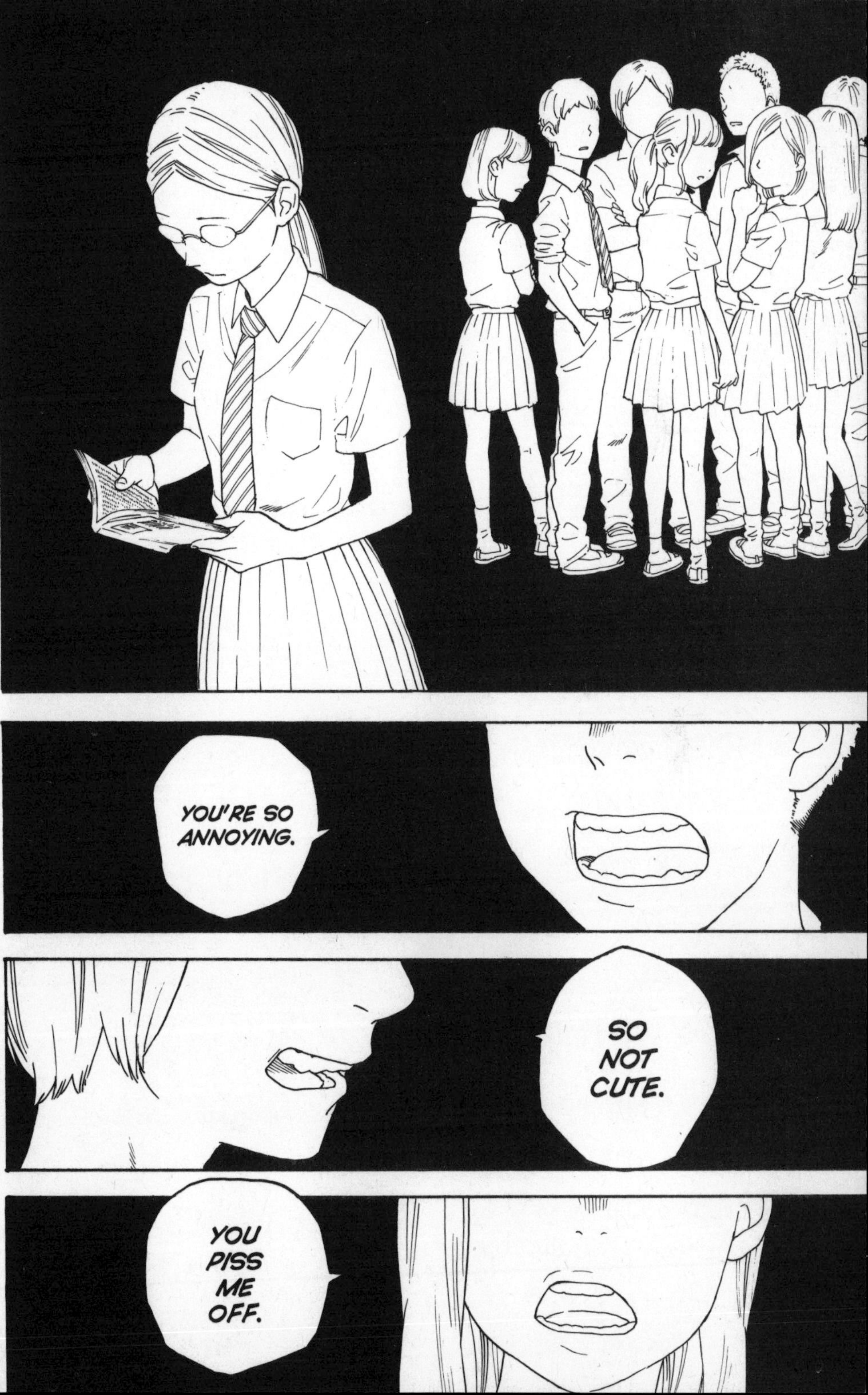
YOU'RE SO ANNOYING.
SO NOT CUTE.
YOU PISS ME OFF.

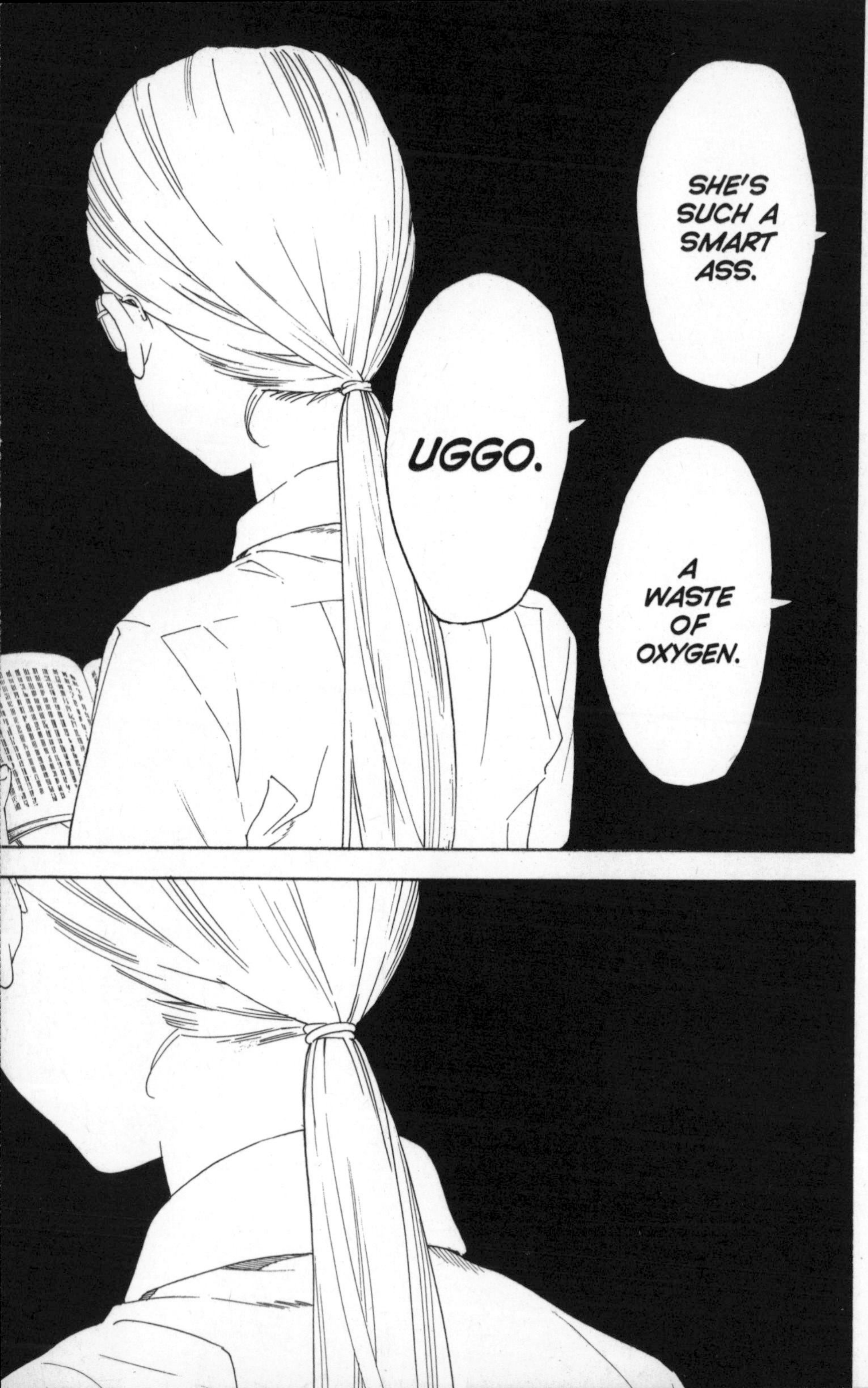
SHE'S SUCH A SMART ASS.
UGGO.
A WASTE OF OXYGEN.

かわいい
CUTE

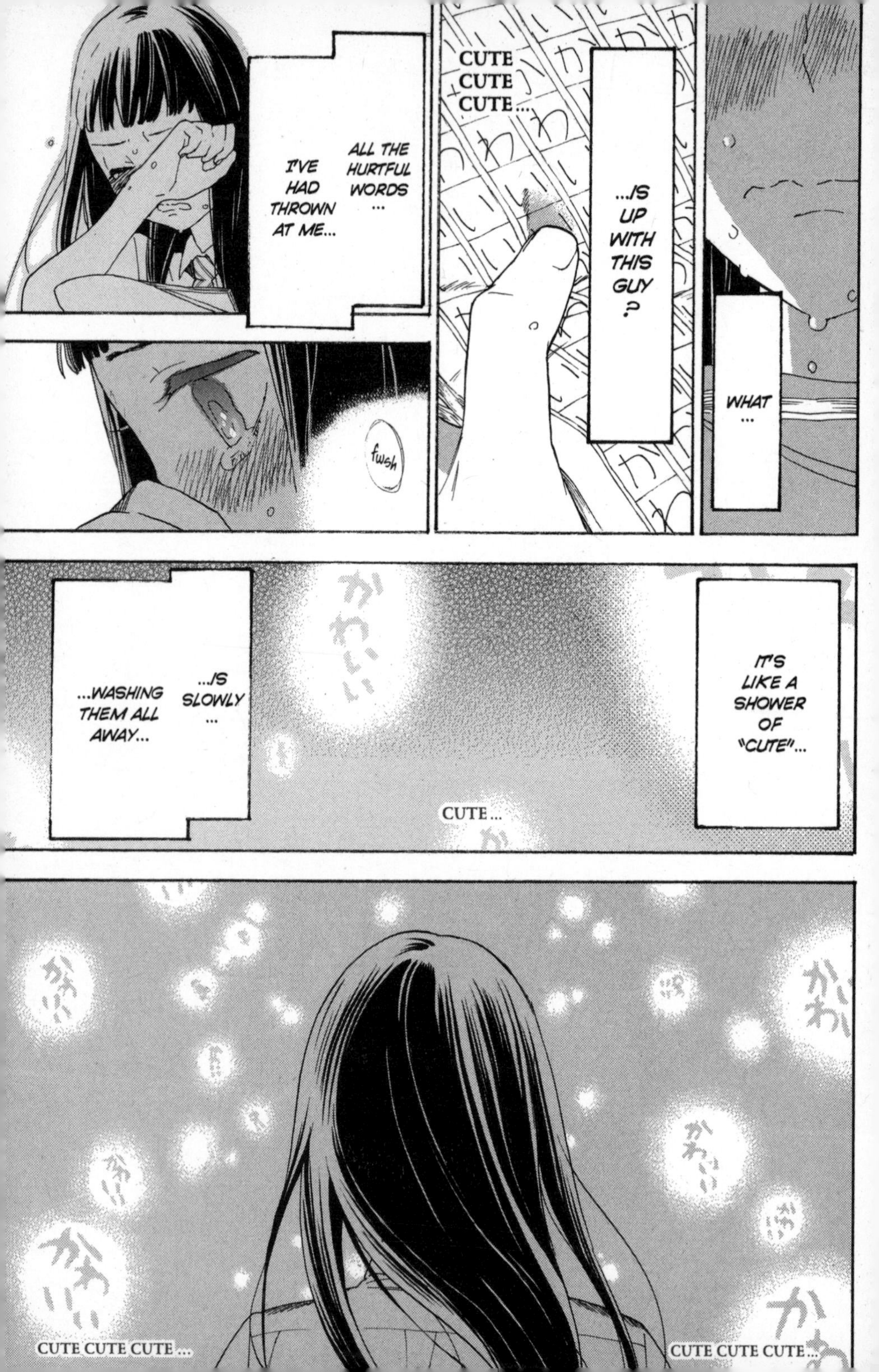
WHAT ...
...IS UP WITH THIS GUY?
CUTE
CUTE
CUTE...
ALL THE HURTFUL WORDS ...
I'VE HAD THROWN AT ME...
fwsh
IT'S LIKE A SHOWER OF "CUTE"...
CUTE...
...IS SLOWLY ...
...WASHING THEM ALL AWAY...
CUTE CUTE CUTE...
CUTE CUTE CUTE...

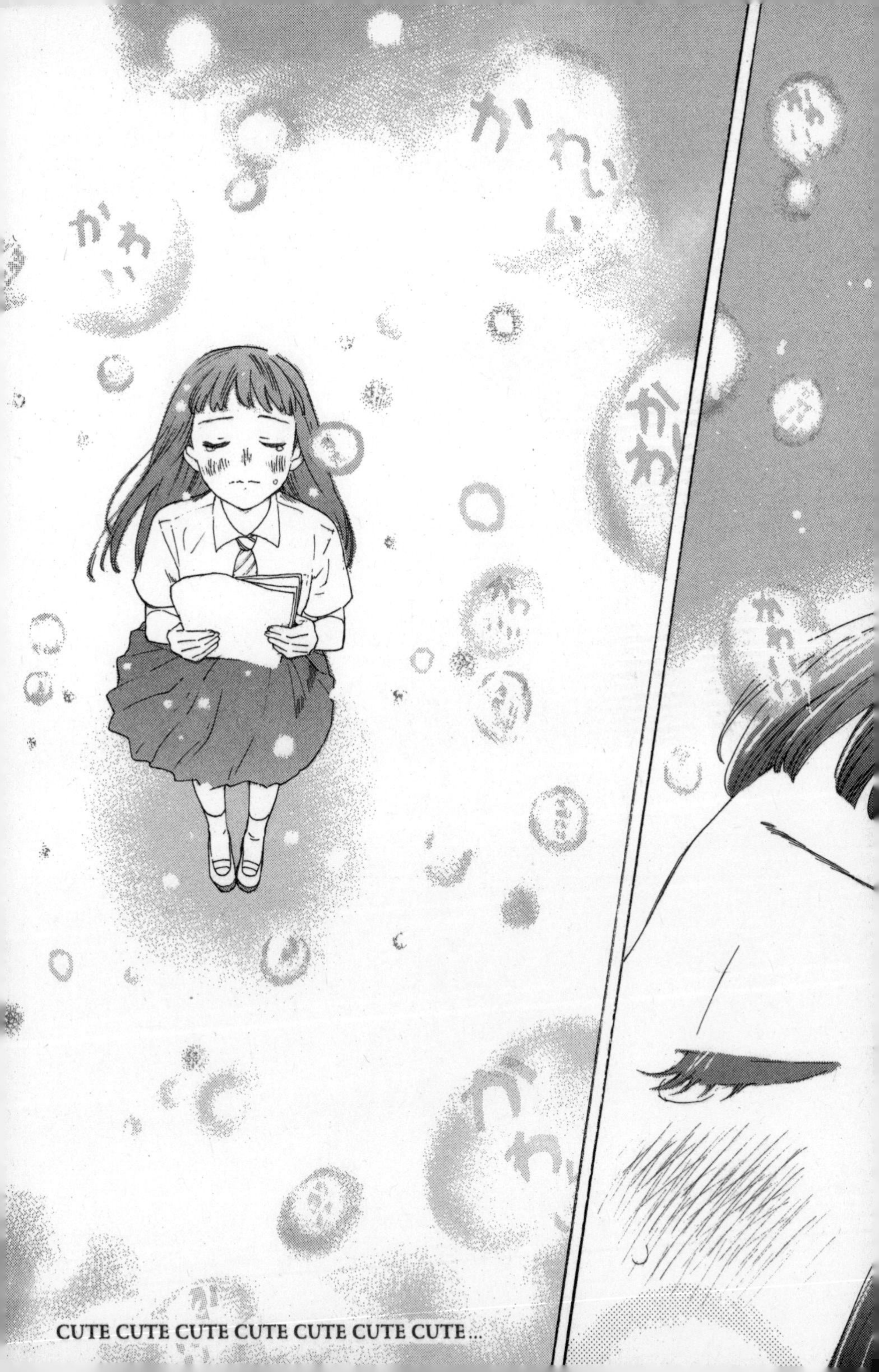
CUTE CUTE CUTE CUTE CUTE CUTE CUTE...

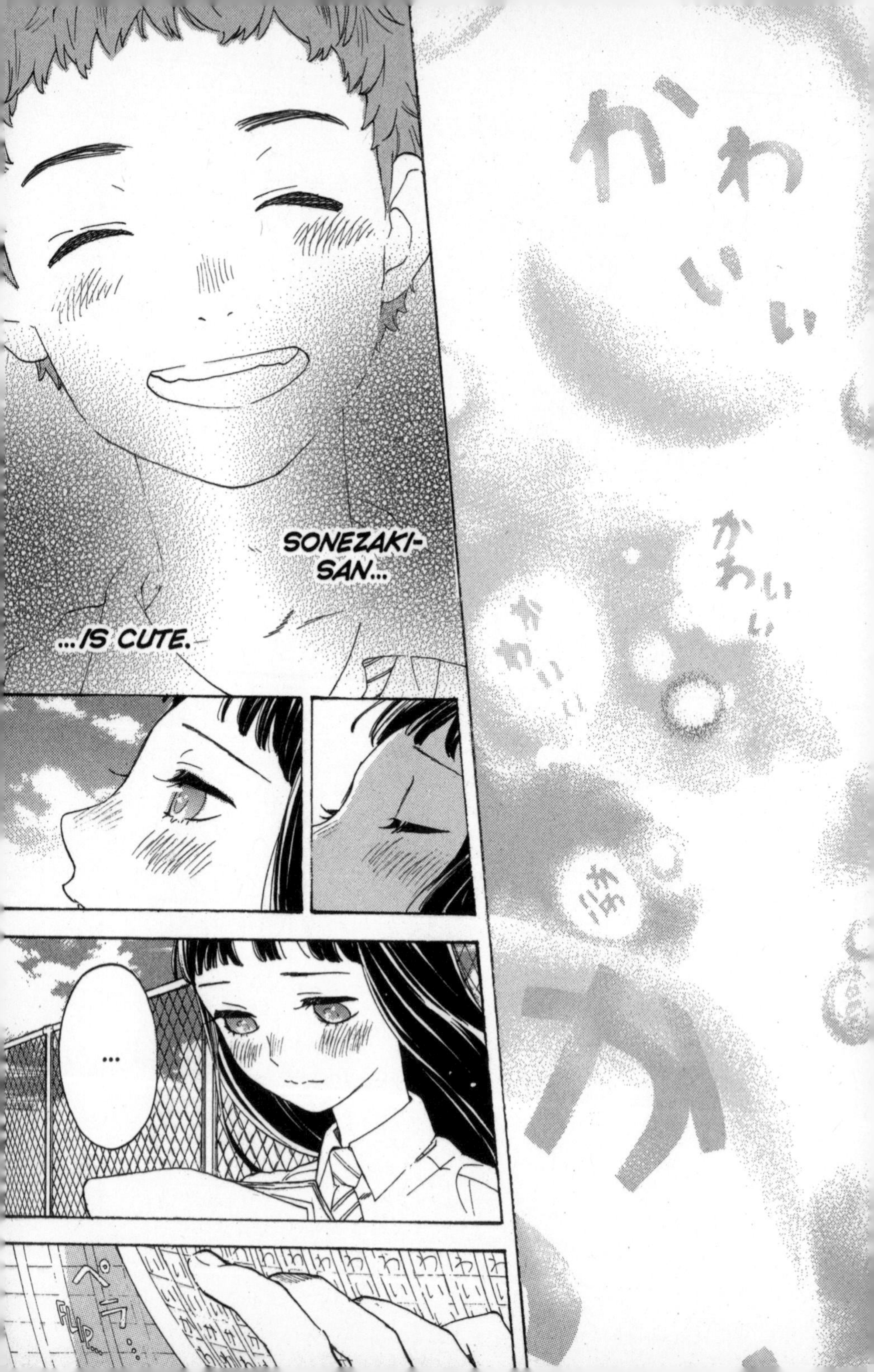

かわいい
かわいい
SONEZAKI-SAN...
...IS CUTE.
...
ペラ
FLIP...

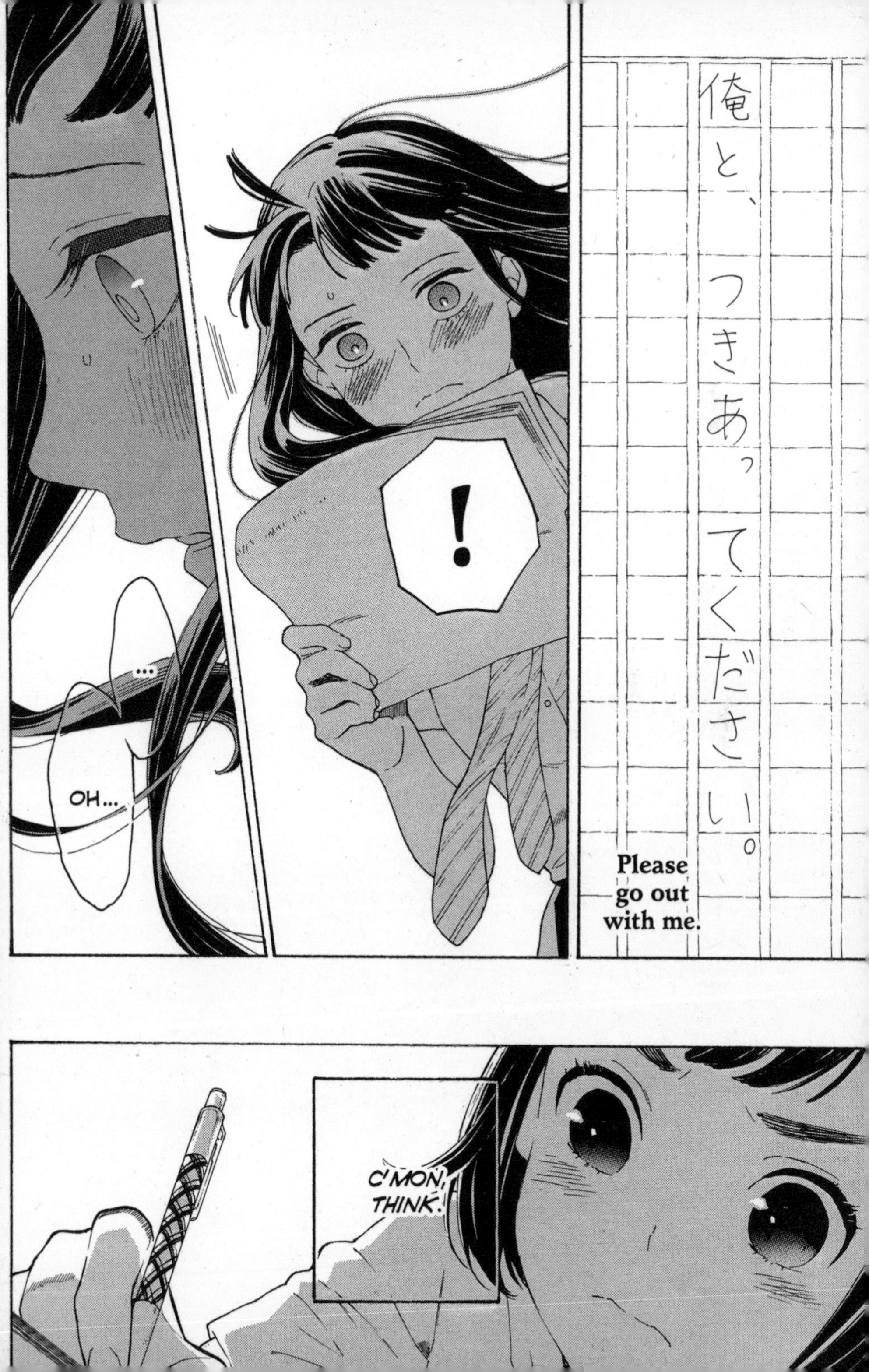
俺と、つきあってください。
Please go out with me.
!
...
OH...
C'MON, THINK.

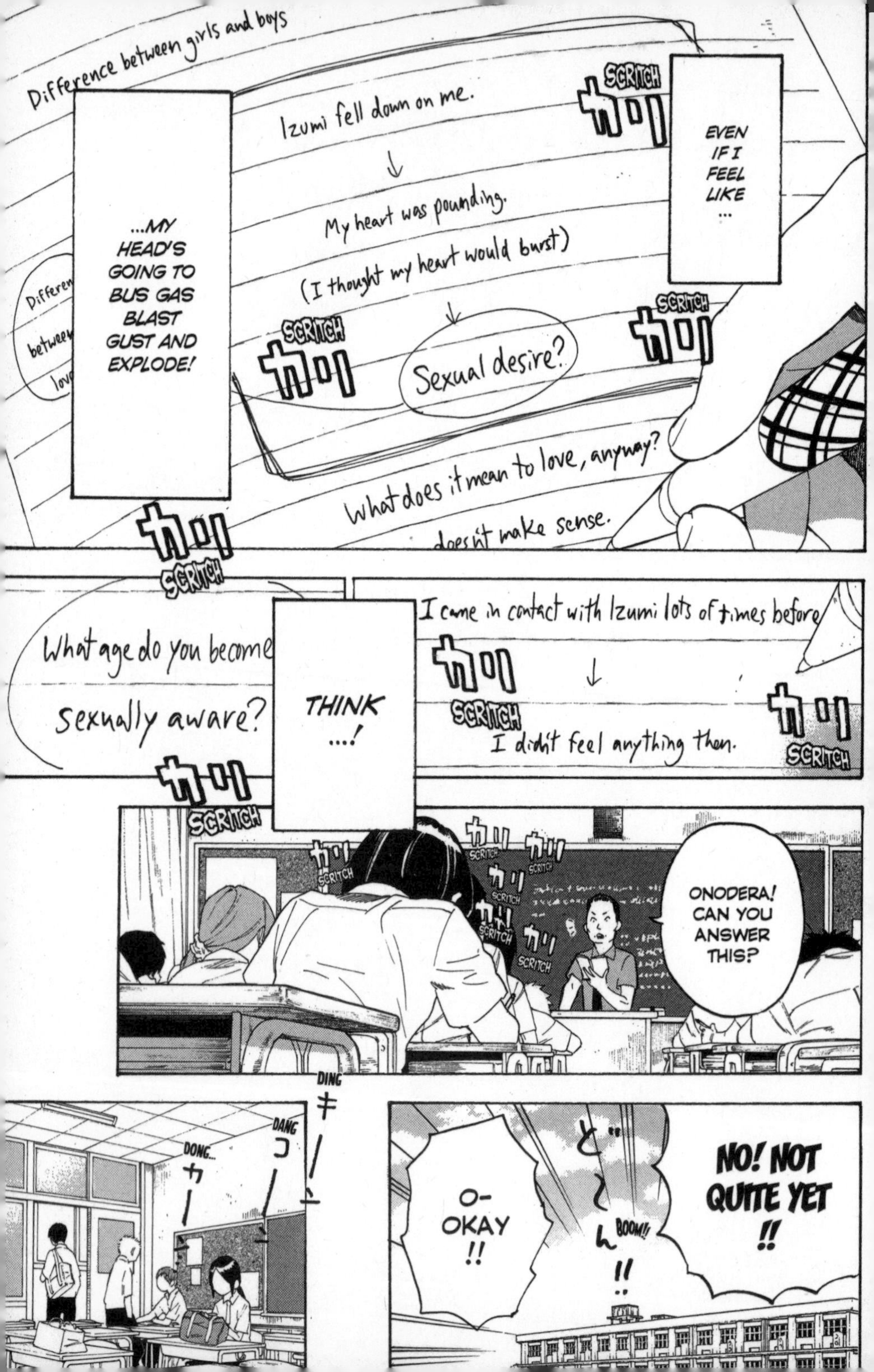
EVEN IF I FEEL LIKE …
SCRITCH
Difference between girls and boys
Izumi fell down on me.
My heart was pounding.
(I thought my heart would burst)
SCRITCH
Sexual desire?
SCRITCH
What does it mean to love, anyway?
doesn't make sense.
…MY HEAD'S GOING TO BUS GAS BLAST GUST AND EXPLODE!
SCRITCH
I came in contact with Izumi lots of times before
SCRITCH
SCRITCH
I didn't feel anything then.
THINK …!
What age do you become sexually aware?
SCRITCH
ONODERA! CAN YOU ANSWER THIS?
SCRITCH
SCRITCH
SCRITCH
SCRITCH
SCRITCH
SCRITCH
NO! NOT QUITE YET!!
BOOM!!
O-OKAY!!
DING
DANG
DONG…

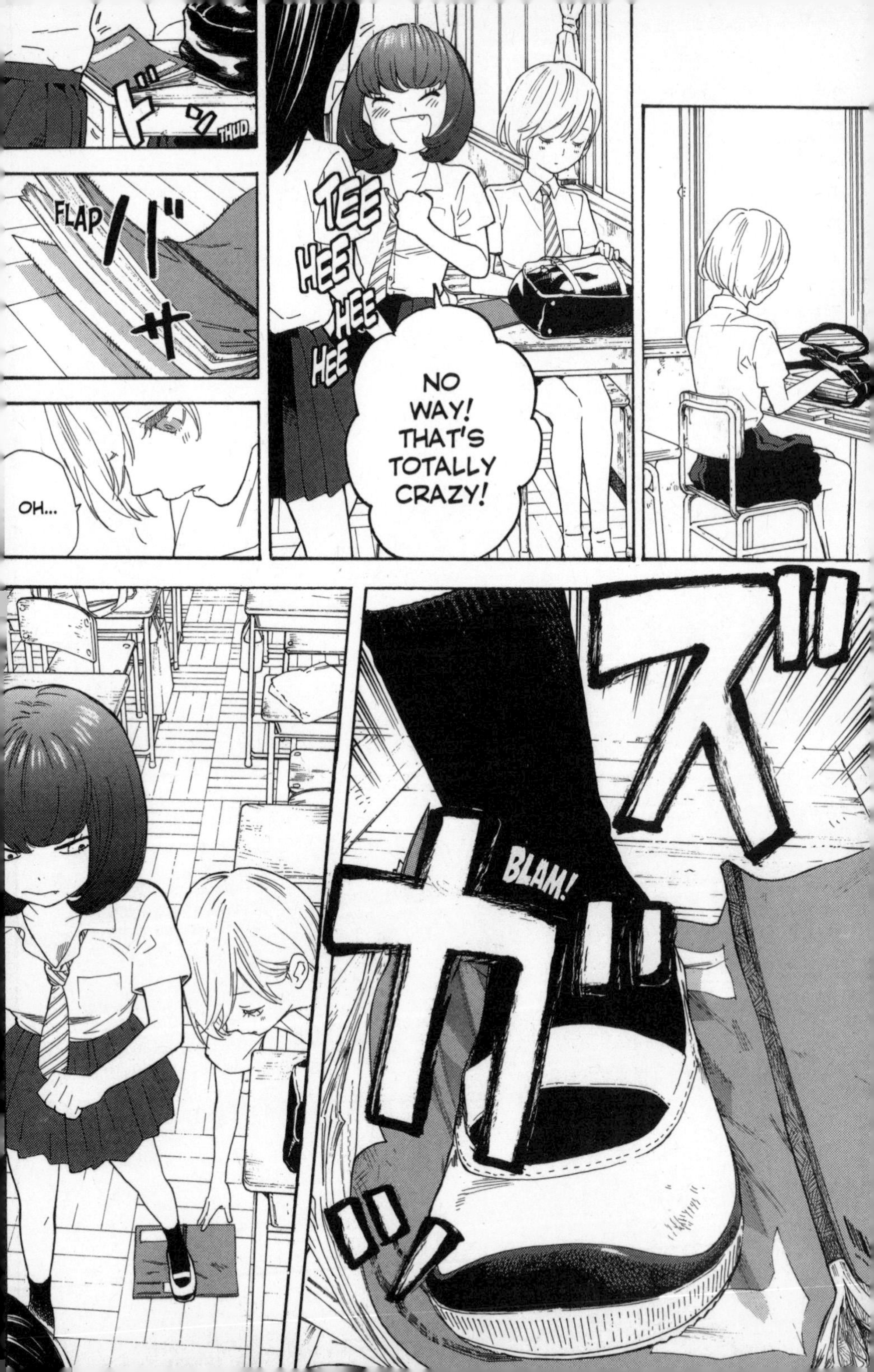
TEE HEE HEE HEE
NO WAY! THAT'S TOTALLY CRAZY!
THUD
FLAP
OH...
BLAM!

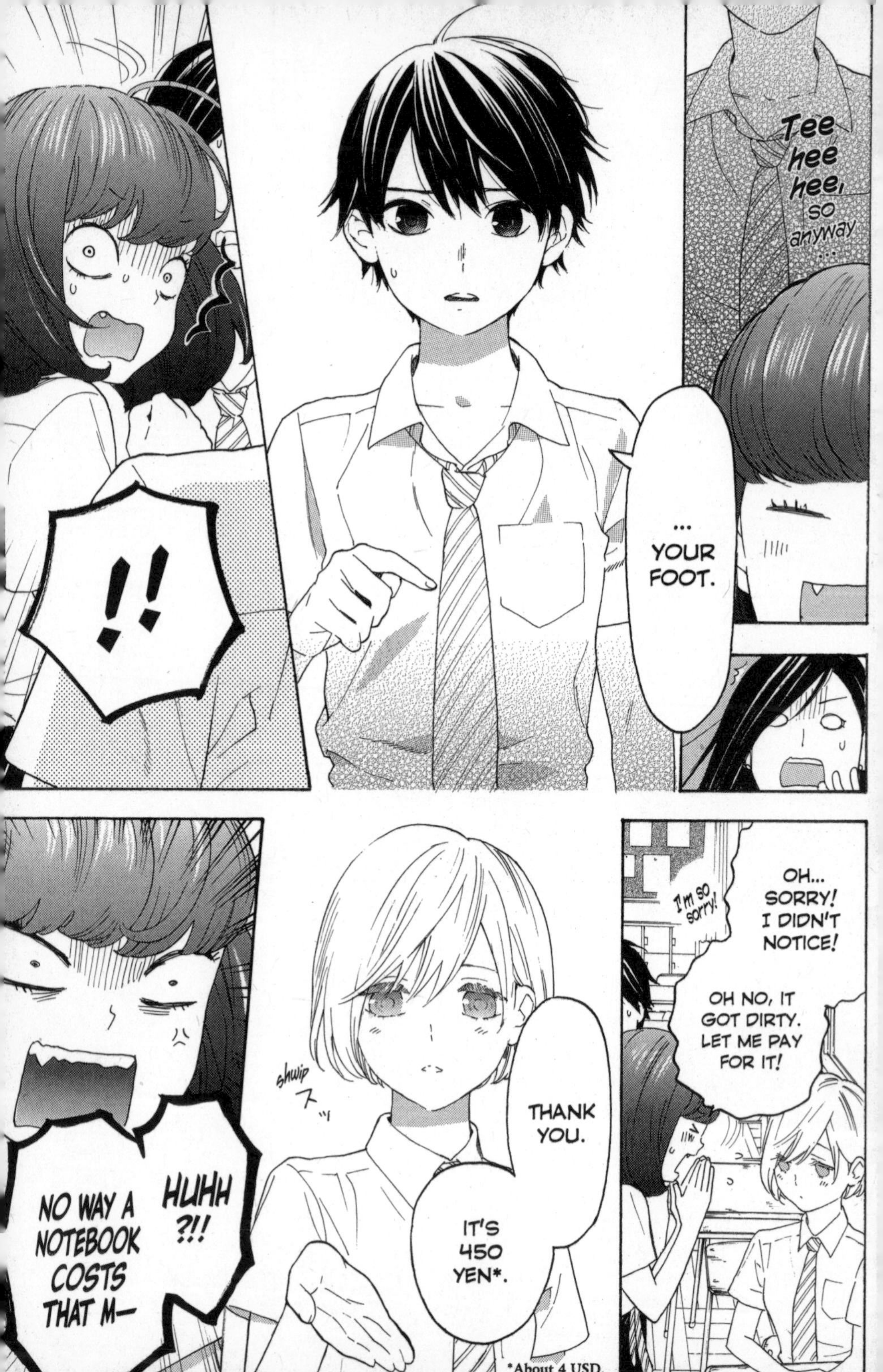
Tee hee hee, so anyway ...
... YOUR FOOT.
!!
OH... SORRY! I DIDN'T NOTICE!
I'm so sorry!
OH NO, IT GOT DIRTY. LET ME PAY FOR IT!
shwip
THANK YOU.
IT'S 450 YEN*.
HUHH ?!!
NO WAY A NOTEBOOK COSTS THAT M—

*About 4 USD.

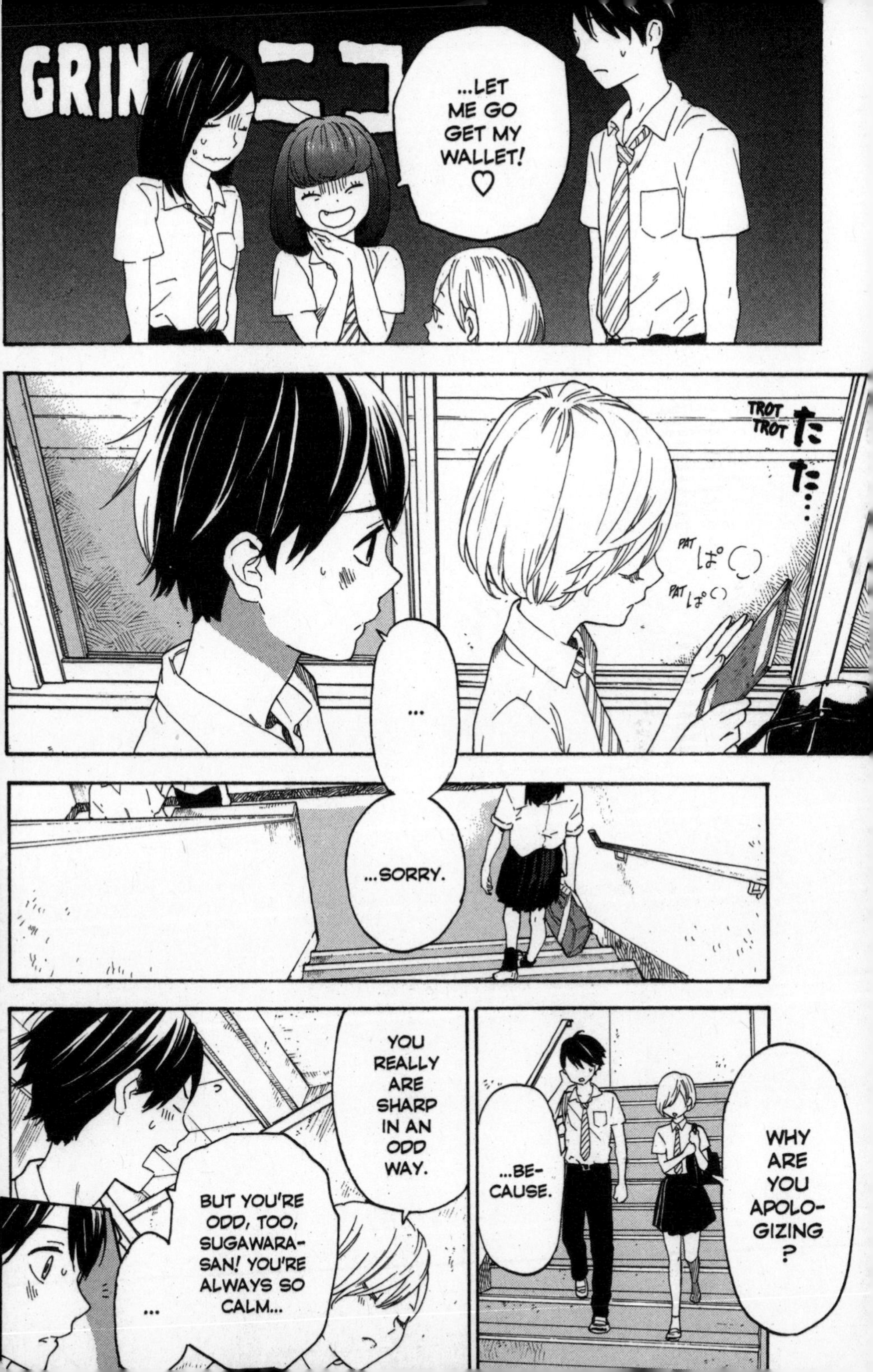
GRIN
...LET ME GO GET MY WALLET! ♡
TROT TROT たた…
PAT ぱ
PAT ぱ
...
...SORRY.
WHY ARE YOU APOLOGIZING?
...BECAUSE.
YOU REALLY ARE SHARP IN AN ODD WAY.
BUT YOU'RE ODD, TOO, SUGAWARA-SAN! YOU'RE ALWAYS SO CALM...
...

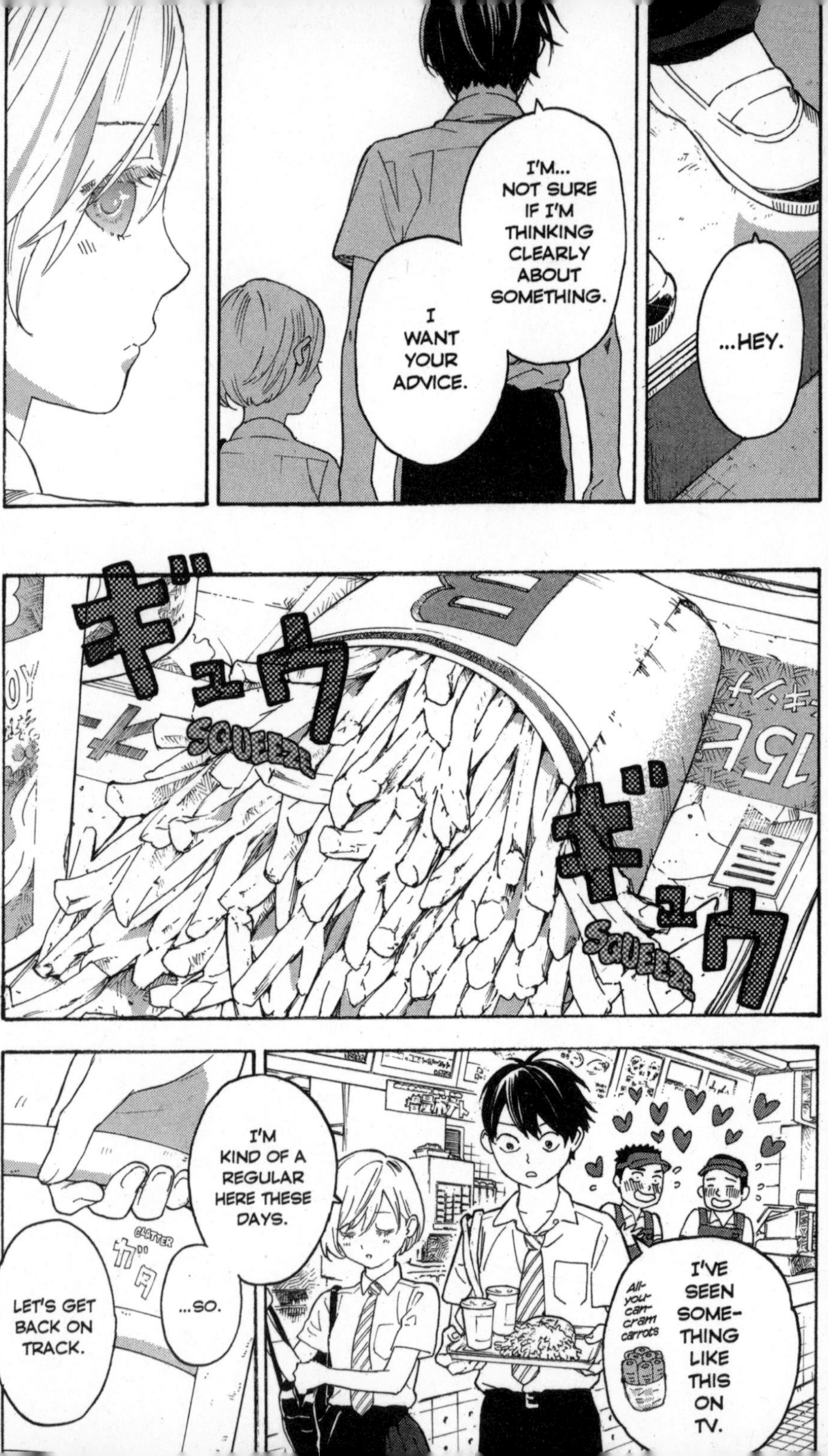
...HEY.
I'M... NOT SURE IF I'M THINKING CLEARLY ABOUT SOMETHING.
I WANT YOUR ADVICE.
ギュウ
SQUEEZ
ギュウ
SQUEEZ
I'VE SEEN SOMETHING LIKE THIS ON TV.
All-you-can-cram carrots
I'M KIND OF A REGULAR HERE THESE DAYS.
カタ
CLATTER
...SO.
LET'S GET BACK ON TRACK.

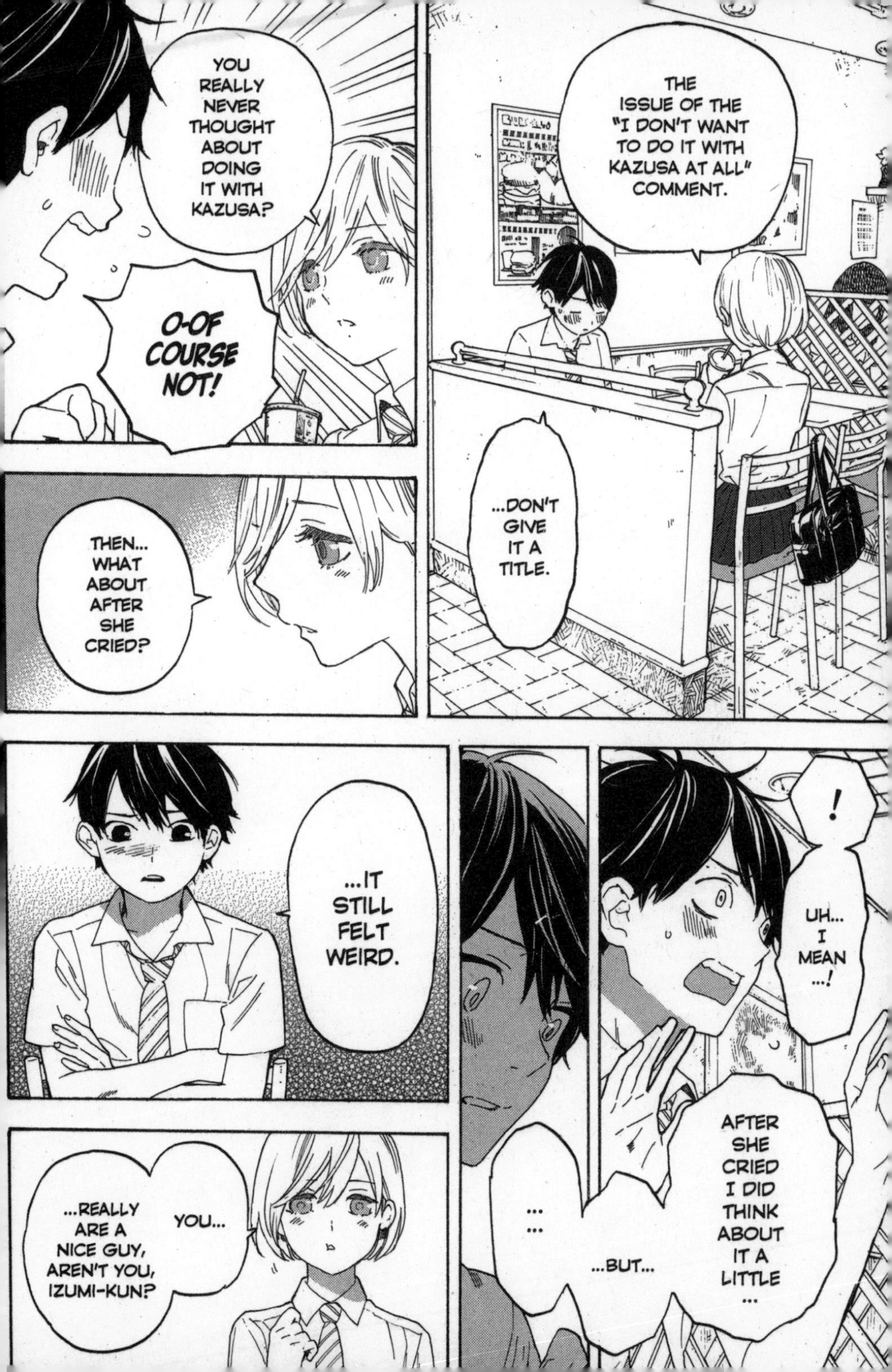
THE ISSUE OF THE "I DON'T WANT TO DO IT WITH KAZUSA AT ALL" COMMENT.
...DON'T GIVE IT A TITLE.
YOU REALLY NEVER THOUGHT ABOUT DOING IT WITH KAZUSA?
O-OF COURSE NOT!
THEN... WHAT ABOUT AFTER SHE CRIED?
!
UH... I MEAN...!
AFTER SHE CRIED I DID THINK ABOUT IT A LITTLE...
...BUT...
......
...IT STILL FELT WEIRD.
YOU...
...REALLY ARE A NICE GUY, AREN'T YOU, IZUMI-KUN?

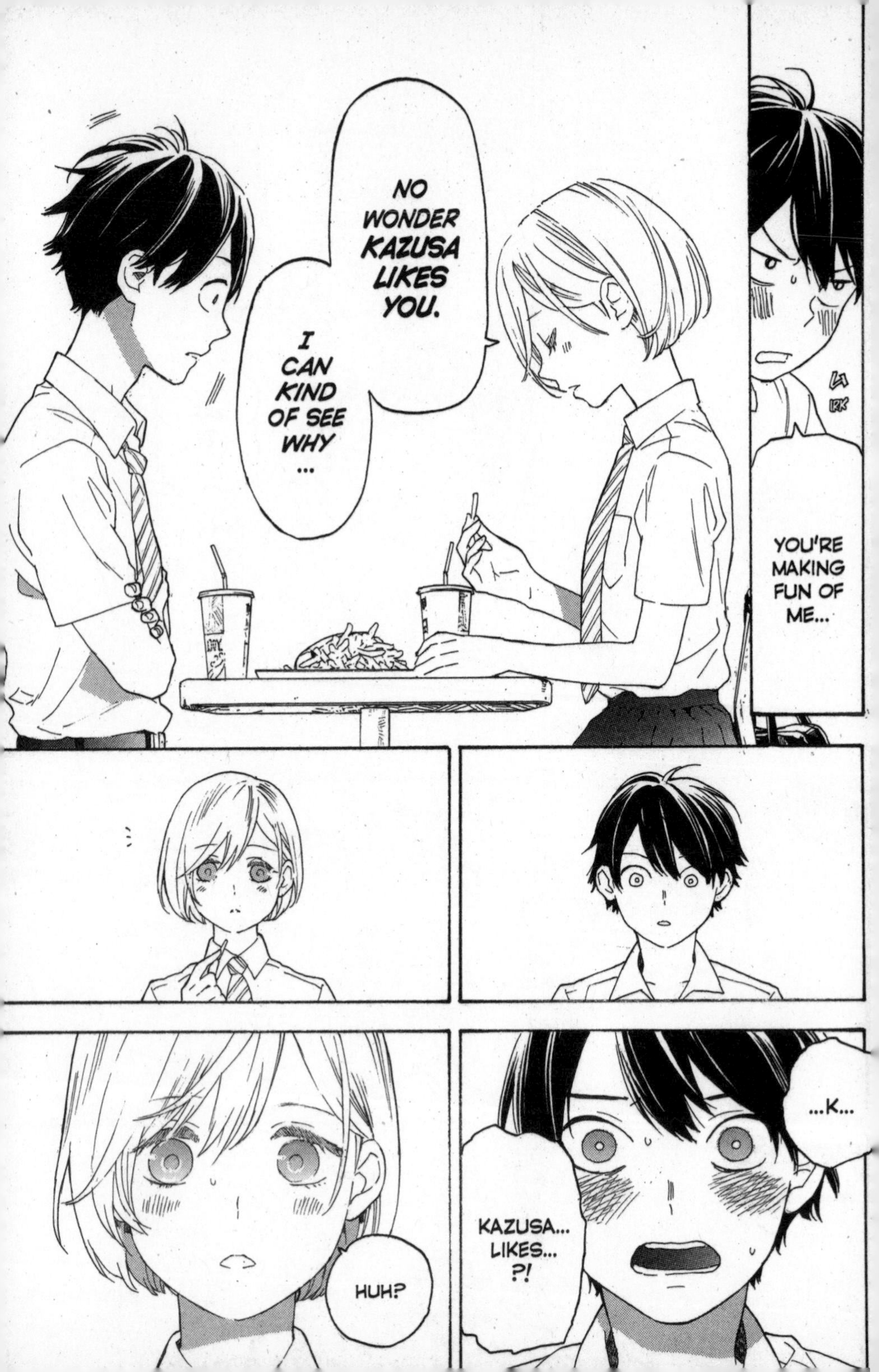
IRK
YOU'RE MAKING FUN OF ME...
NO WONDER KAZUSA LIKES YOU.
I CAN KIND OF SEE WHY ...
...K...
KAZUSA... LIKES... ?!
HUH?

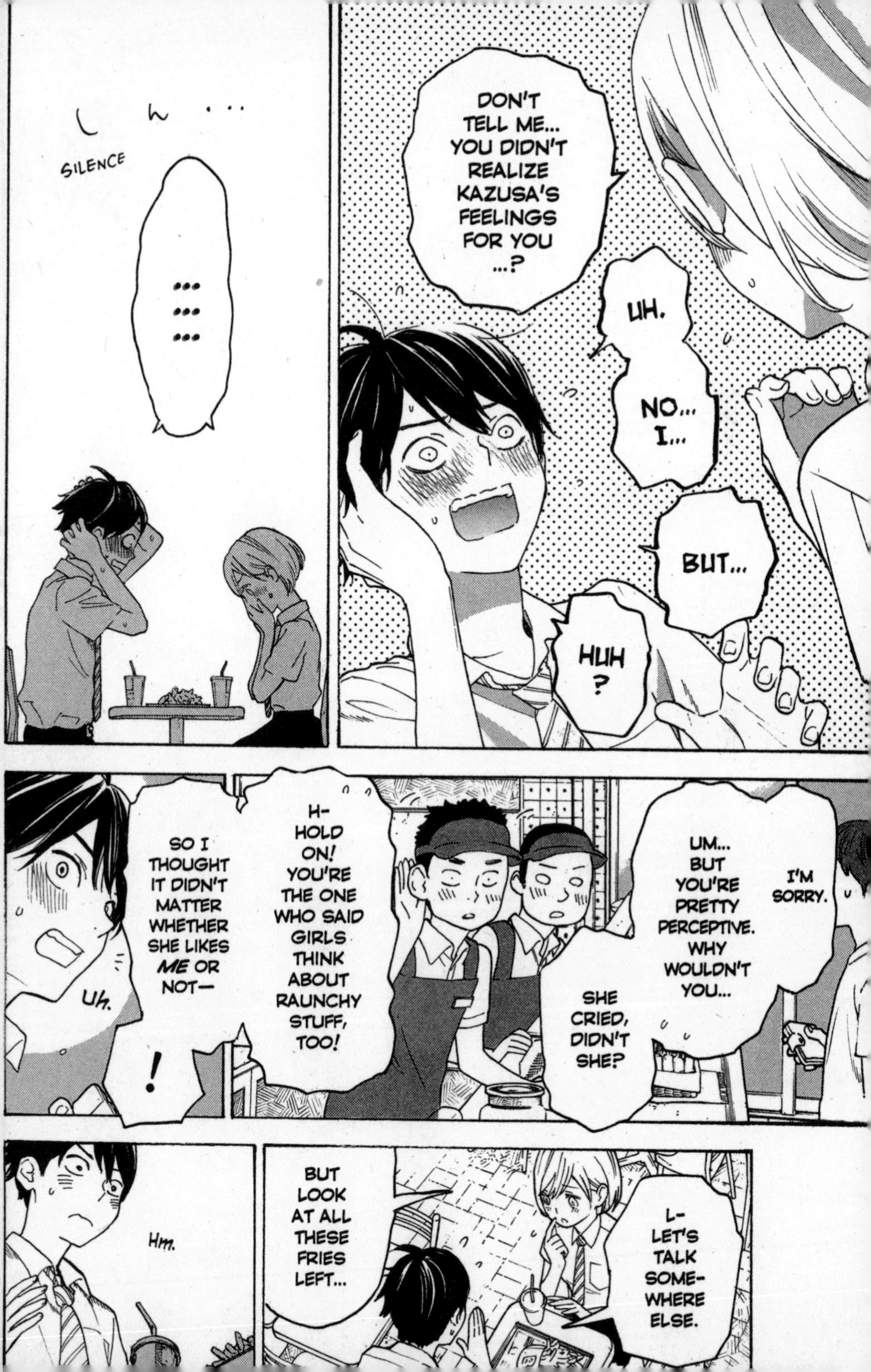
DON'T TELL ME... YOU DIDN'T REALIZE KAZUSA'S FEELINGS FOR YOU ...?
UH.
NO... I...
BUT...
HUH ?
しん...
SILENCE
... ...
I'M SORRY.
UM... BUT YOU'RE PRETTY PERCEPTIVE. WHY WOULDN'T YOU...
SHE CRIED, DIDN'T SHE?
H- HOLD ON! YOU'RE THE ONE WHO SAID GIRLS THINK ABOUT RAUNCHY STUFF, TOO!
SO I THOUGHT IT DIDN'T MATTER WHETHER SHE LIKES *ME* OR NOT—
!
Uh.
L- LET'S TALK SOME- WHERE ELSE.
BUT LOOK AT ALL THESE FRIES LEFT...
Hm.

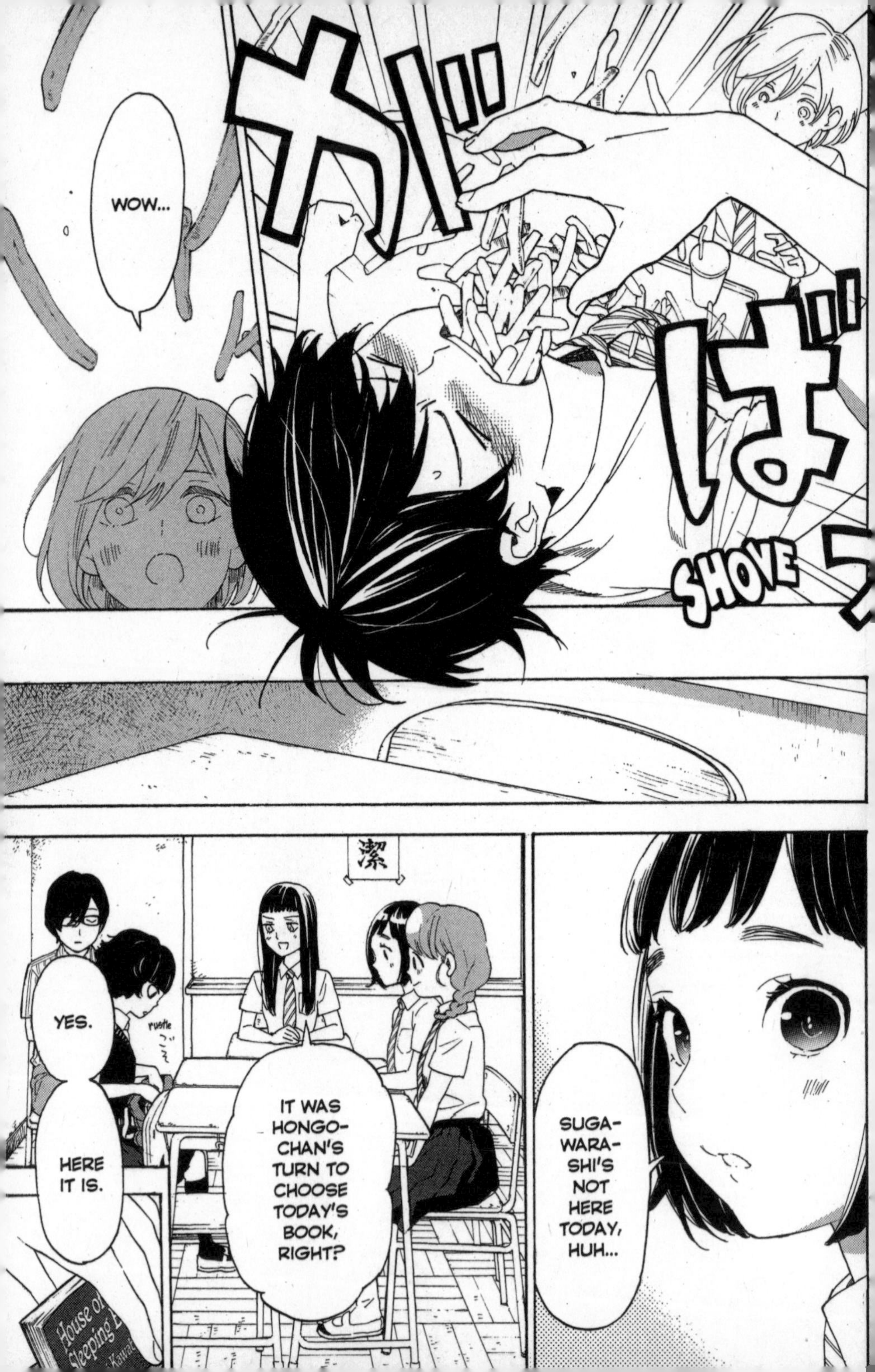
ば
SHOVE
カバ
WOW...
SUGA-WARA-SHI'S NOT HERE TODAY, HUH...
潔
IT WAS HONGO-CHAN'S TURN TO CHOOSE TODAY'S BOOK, RIGHT?
YES.
rustle
HERE IT IS.

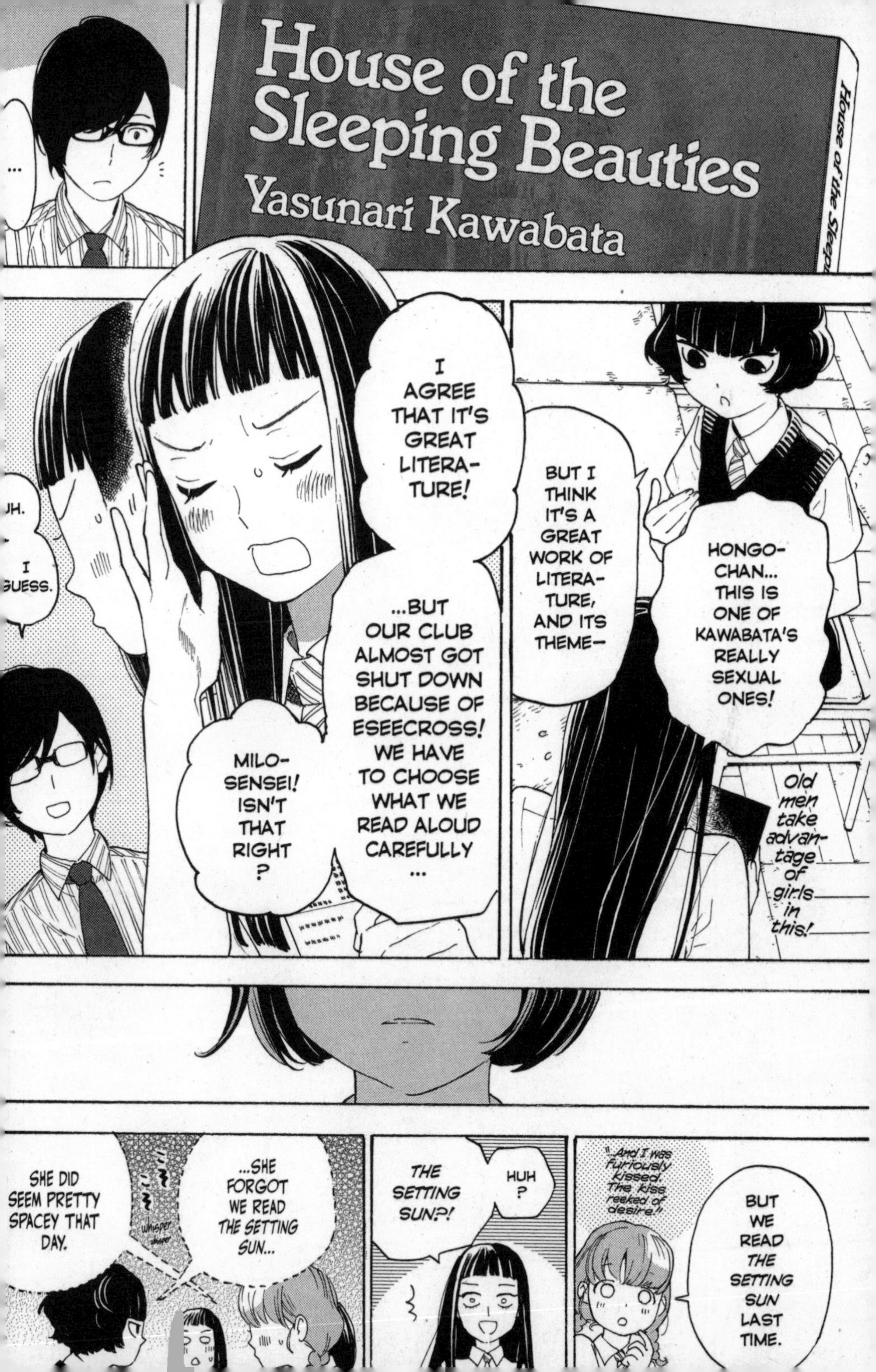
House of the Sleeping Beauties
Yasunari Kawabata
House of the Sleep
...
HONGO-CHAN... THIS IS ONE OF KAWABATA'S REALLY SEXUAL ONES!
Old men take advantage of girls in this!
BUT I THINK IT'S A GREAT WORK OF LITERATURE, AND ITS THEME—
I AGREE THAT IT'S GREAT LITERATURE!
...BUT OUR CLUB ALMOST GOT SHUT DOWN BECAUSE OF ESEECROSS! WE HAVE TO CHOOSE WHAT WE READ ALOUD CAREFULLY...
MILO-SENSEI! ISN'T THAT RIGHT?
UH. I GUESS.
"...And I was furiously kissed. The kiss reeked of desire."
BUT WE READ THE SETTING SUN LAST TIME.
HUH?
THE SETTING SUN?!
...SHE FORGOT WE READ THE SETTING SUN...
whisper whisper
SHE DID SEEM PRETTY SPACEY THAT DAY.

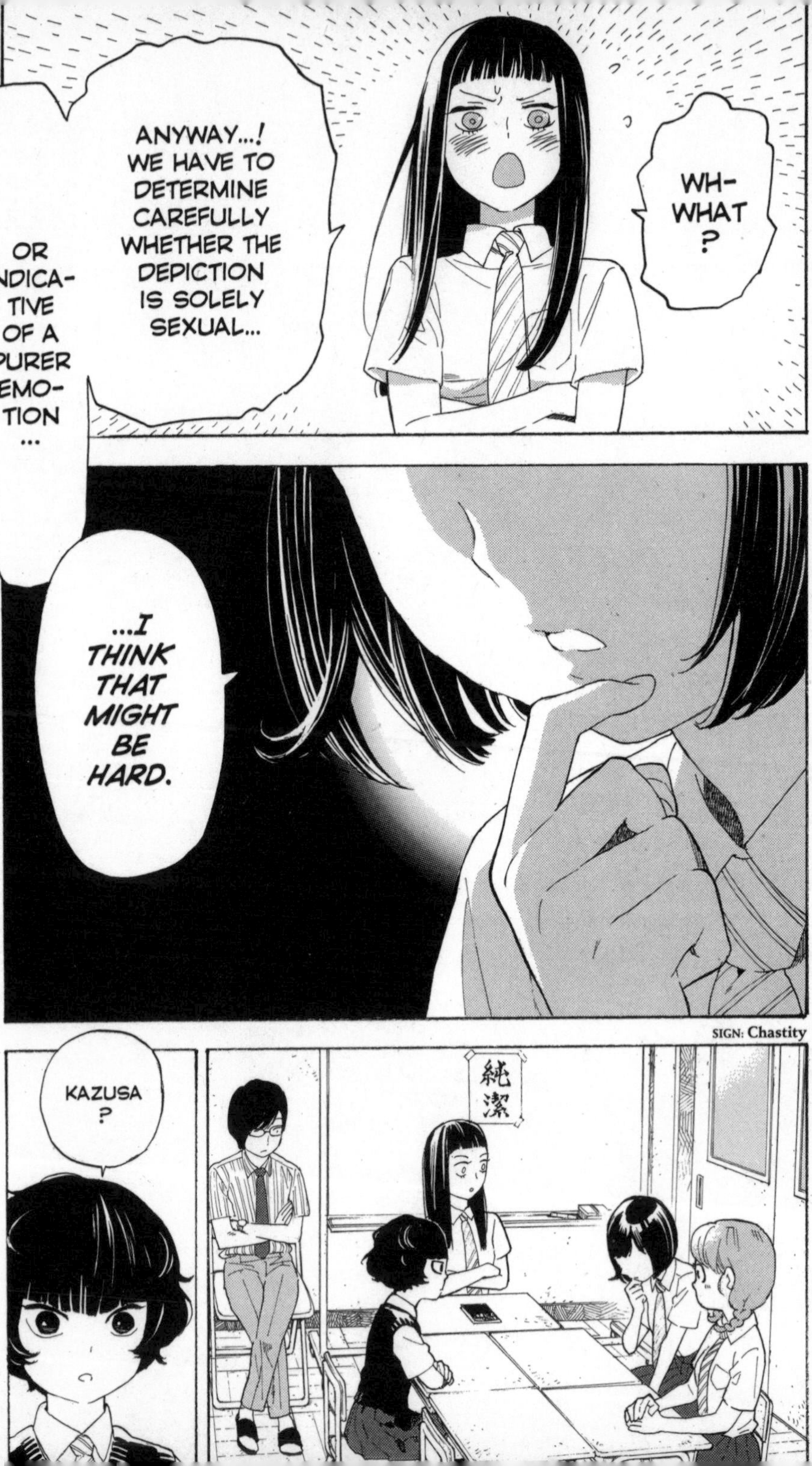
WH-WHAT?
ANYWAY...! WE HAVE TO DETERMINE CAREFULLY WHETHER THE DEPICTION IS SOLELY SEXUAL...
OR INDICATIVE OF A PURER EMOTION...
...I THINK THAT MIGHT BE HARD.
純潔
KAZUSA?
SIGN: Chastity

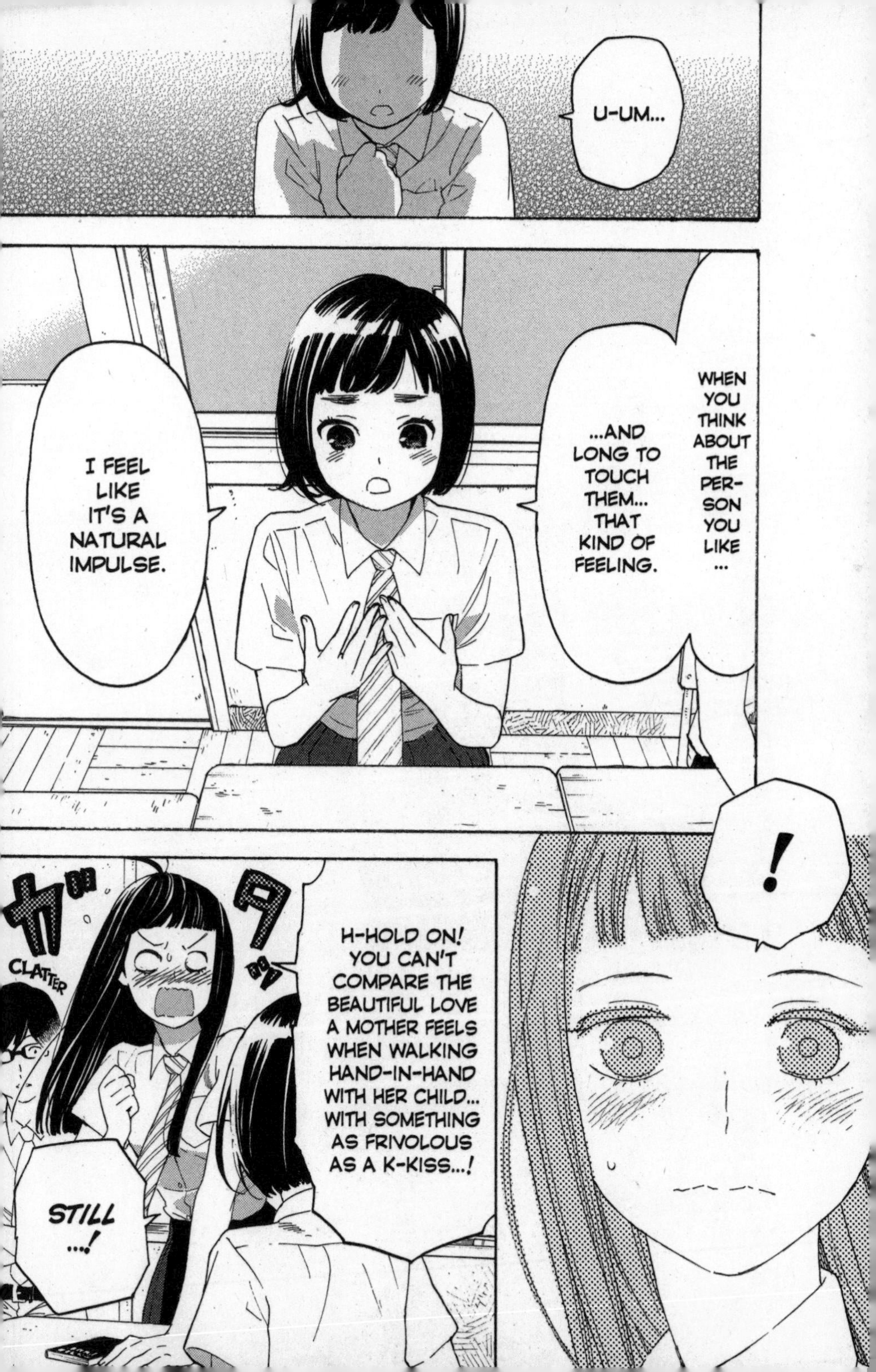
U-UM...
WHEN YOU THINK ABOUT THE PER-SON YOU LIKE...
...AND LONG TO TOUCH THEM... THAT KIND OF FEELING.
I FEEL LIKE IT'S A NATURAL IMPULSE.
!
ガタ
CLATTER
H-HOLD ON! YOU CAN'T COMPARE THE BEAUTIFUL LOVE A MOTHER FEELS WHEN WALKING HAND-IN-HAND WITH HER CHILD... WITH SOMETHING AS FRIVOLOUS AS A K-KISS...!
STILL ...!

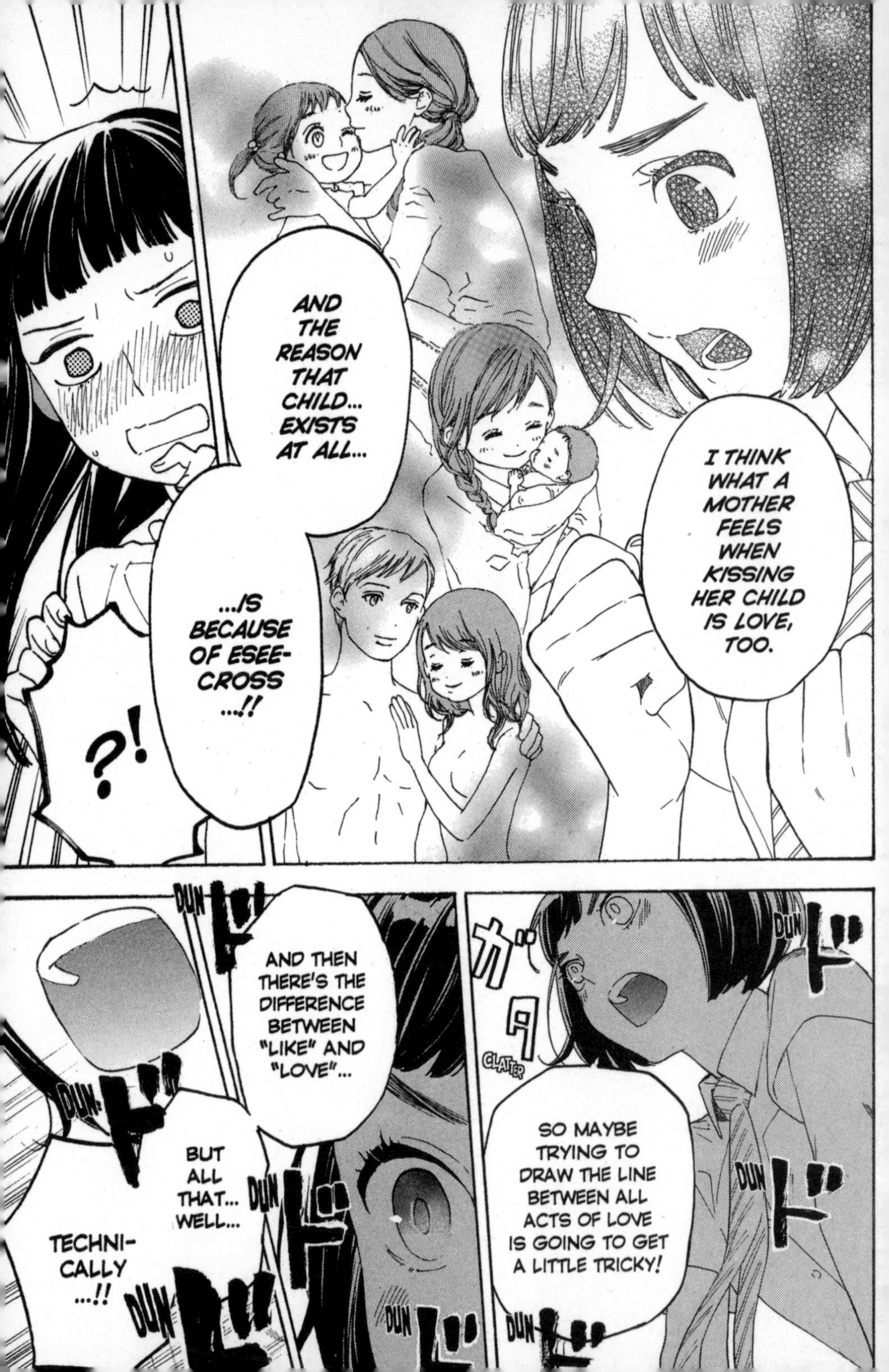

I THINK WHAT A MOTHER FEELS WHEN KISSING HER CHILD IS LOVE, TOO.
AND THE REASON THAT CHILD... EXISTS AT ALL...
...IS BECAUSE OF ESEE-CROSS ...!!
?!
DUN
CLATTER
SO MAYBE TRYING TO DRAW THE LINE BETWEEN ALL ACTS OF LOVE IS GOING TO GET A LITTLE TRICKY!
DUN
DUN
DUN
AND THEN THERE'S THE DIFFERENCE BETWEEN "LIKE" AND "LOVE"...
DUN
BUT ALL THAT... WELL...
DUN
TECHNI-CALLY ...!!
DUN
DUN

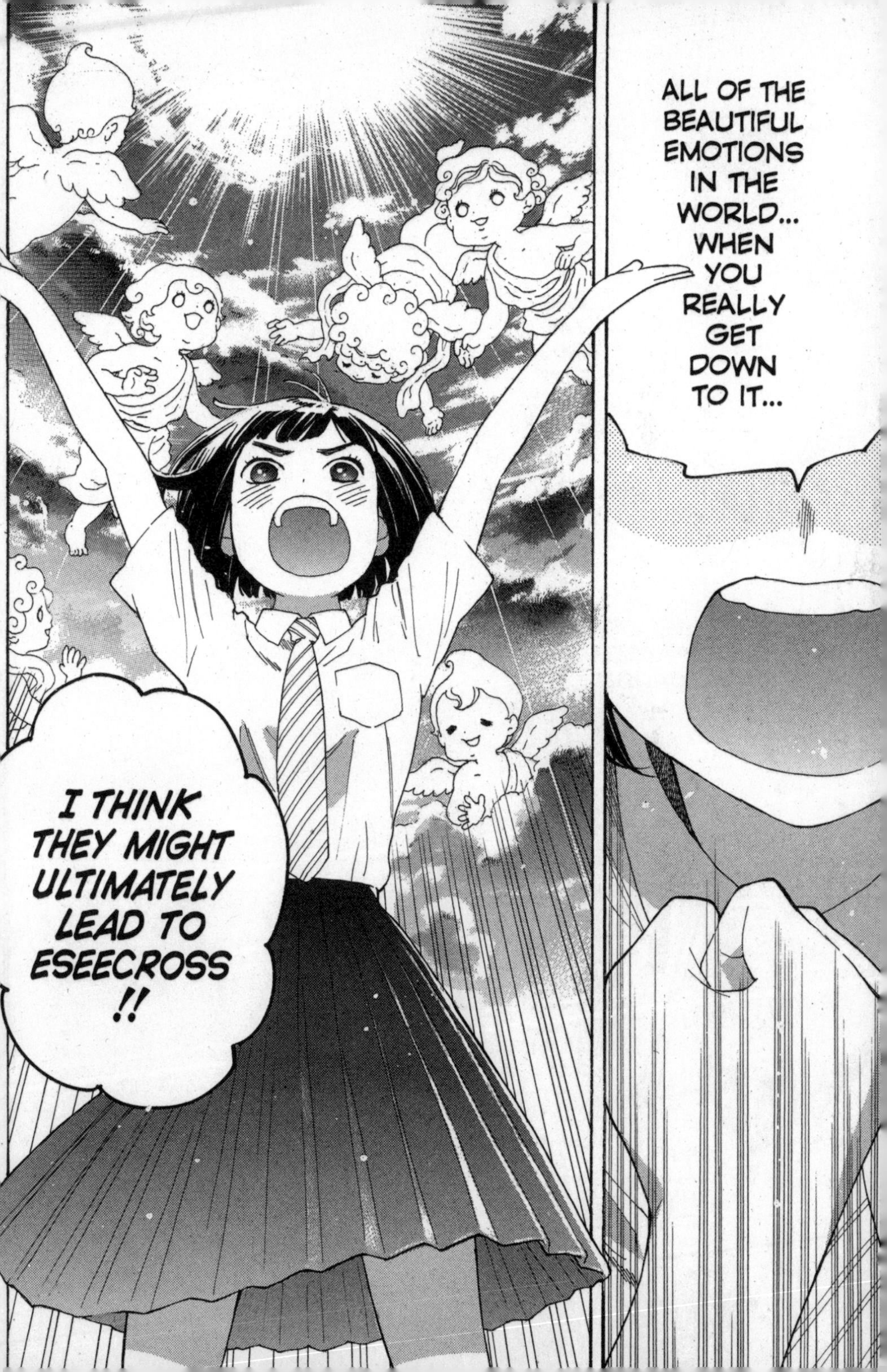
ALL OF THE BEAUTIFUL EMOTIONS IN THE WORLD... WHEN YOU REALLY GET DOWN TO IT...
I THINK THEY MIGHT ULTIMATELY LEAD TO ESEECROSS!!

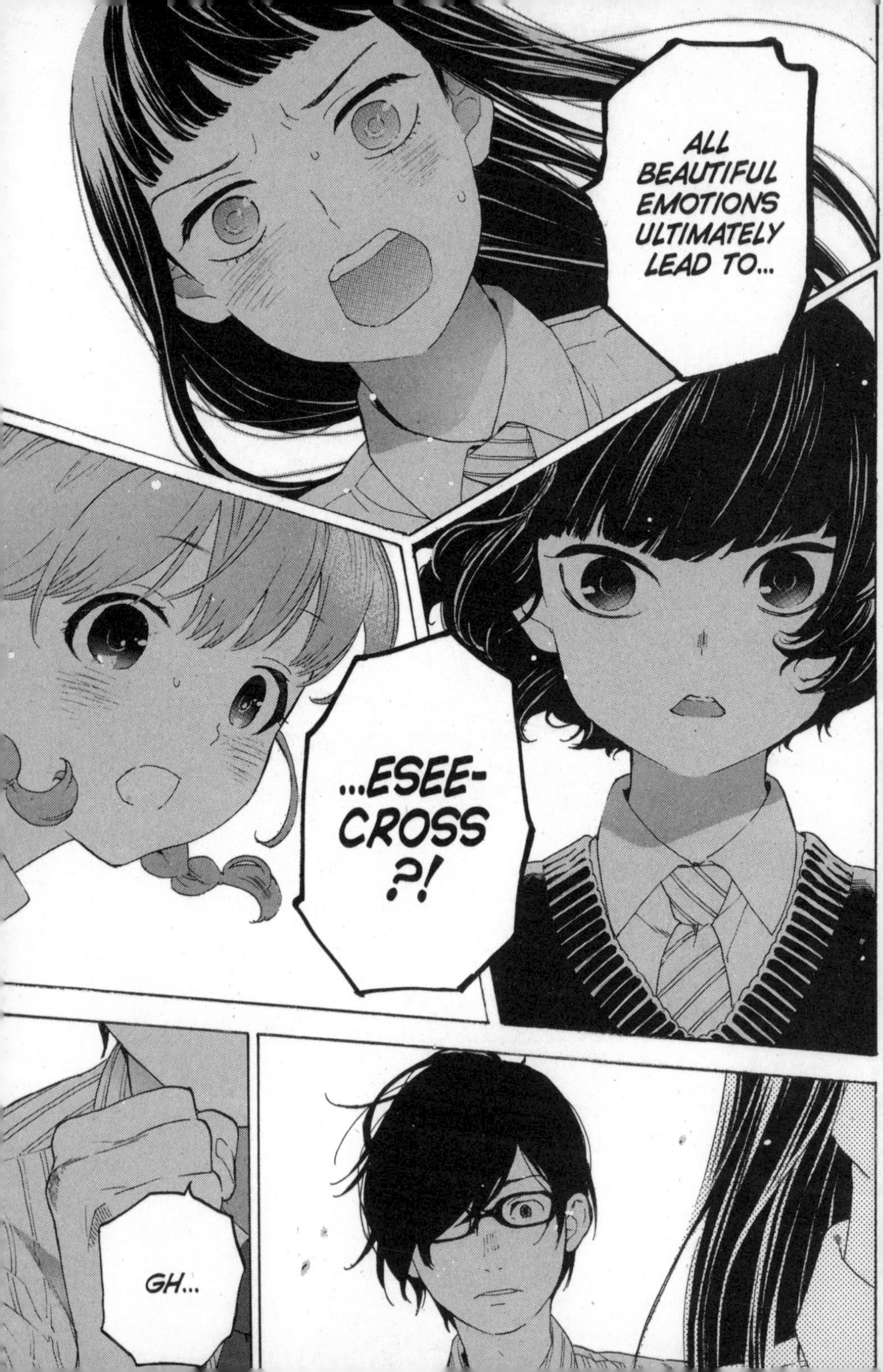
ALL BEAUTIFUL EMOTIONS ULTIMATELY LEAD TO...
...ESEE-CROSS?!
GH...

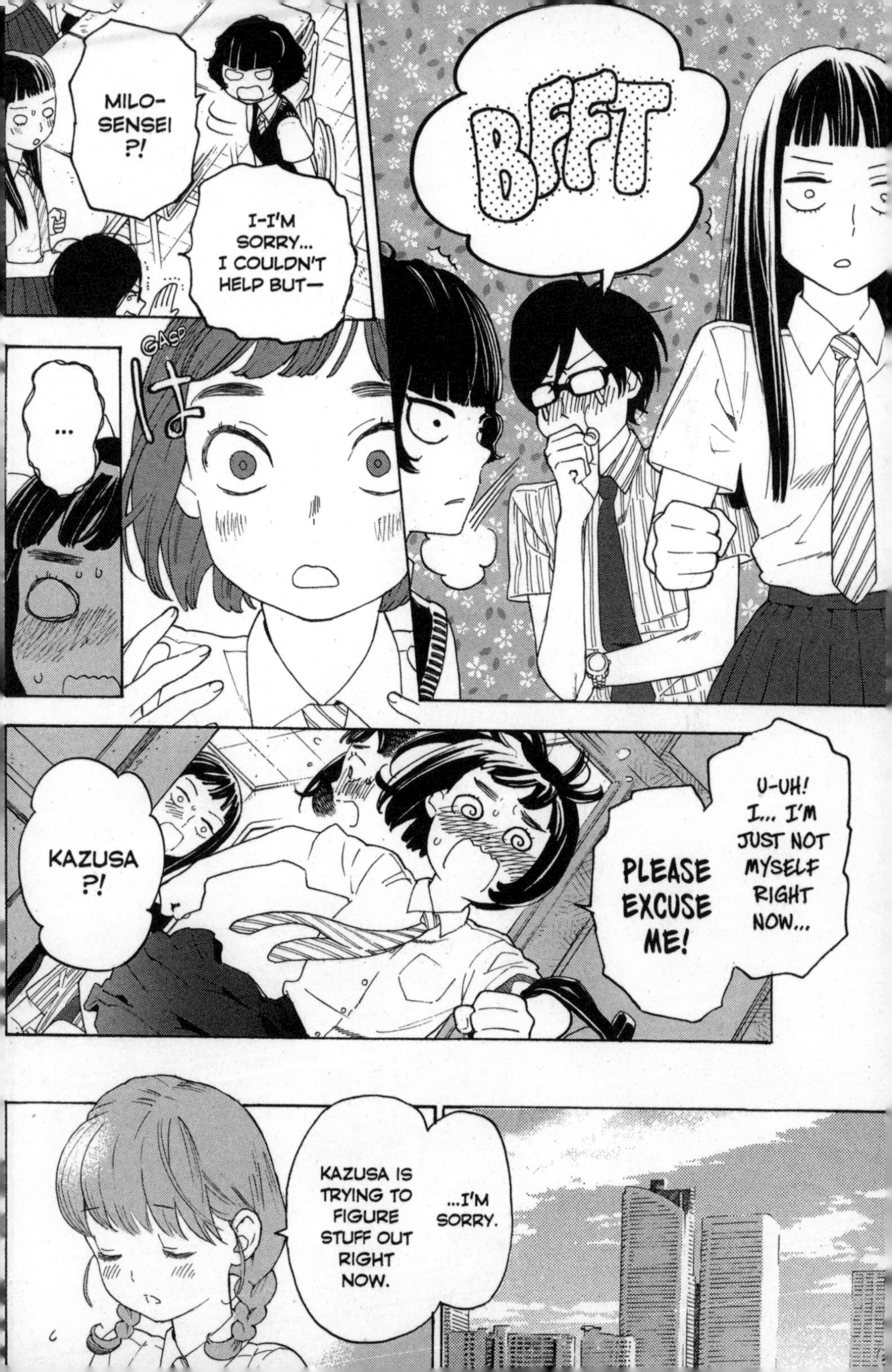
BFFT
MILO-SENSEI ?!
I-I'M SORRY... I COULDN'T HELP BUT—
GASP
...
U-UH! I... I'M JUST NOT MYSELF RIGHT NOW...
PLEASE EXCUSE ME!
KAZUSA ?!
...I'M SORRY.
KAZUSA IS TRYING TO FIGURE STUFF OUT RIGHT NOW.

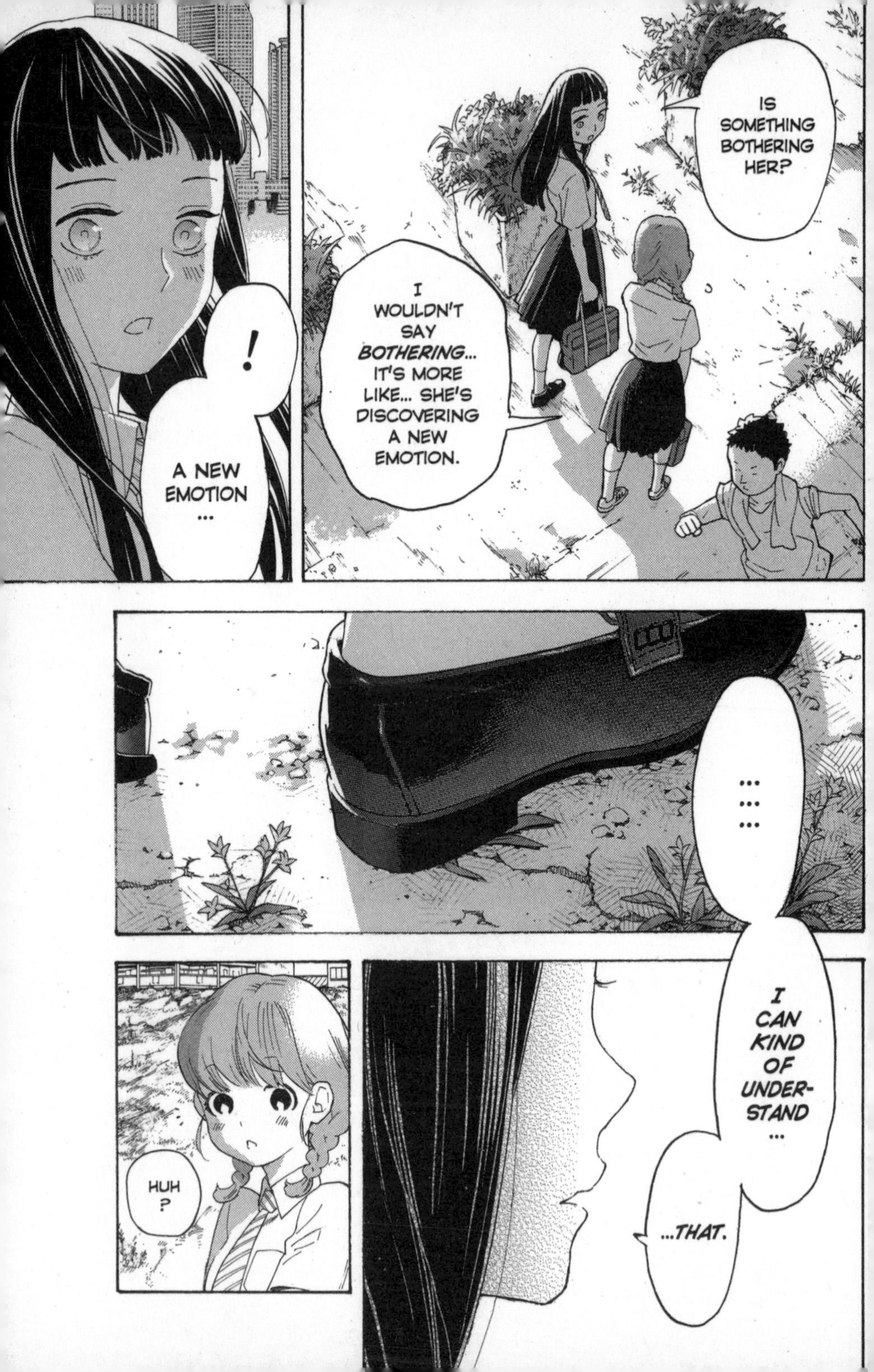
IS SOMETHING BOTHERING HER?
I WOULDN'T SAY *BOTHERING*... IT'S MORE LIKE... SHE'S DISCOVERING A NEW EMOTION.
!
A NEW EMOTION ...
... ...
I CAN KIND OF UNDER-STAND ...
...THAT.
HUH?

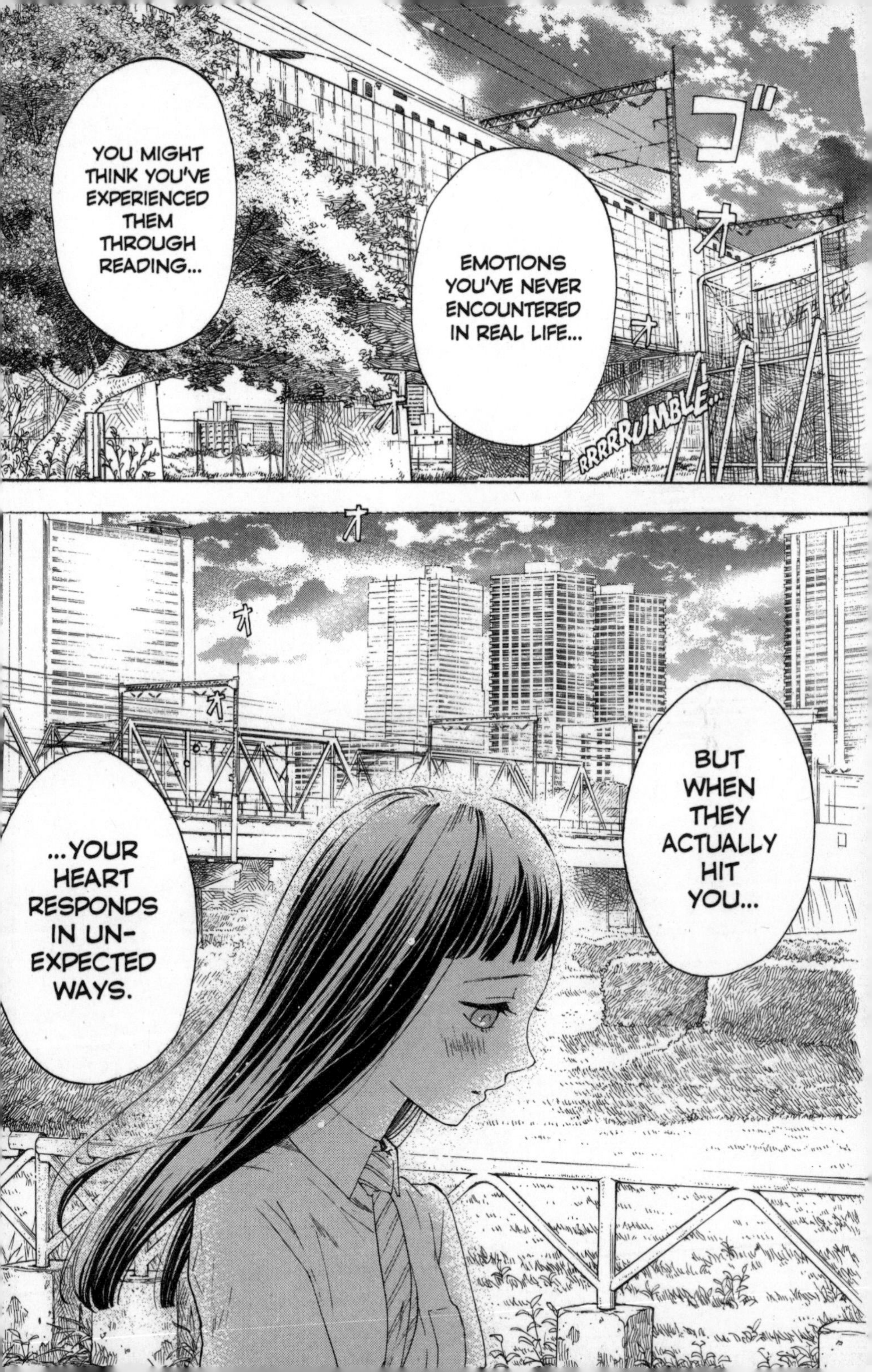
ゴオオオ
EMOTIONS YOU'VE NEVER ENCOUNTERED IN REAL LIFE...
YOU MIGHT THINK YOU'VE EXPERIENCED THEM THROUGH READING...
RRRRRUMBLE...
オオオ
BUT WHEN THEY ACTUALLY HIT YOU...
...YOUR HEART RESPONDS IN UN-EXPECTED WAYS.

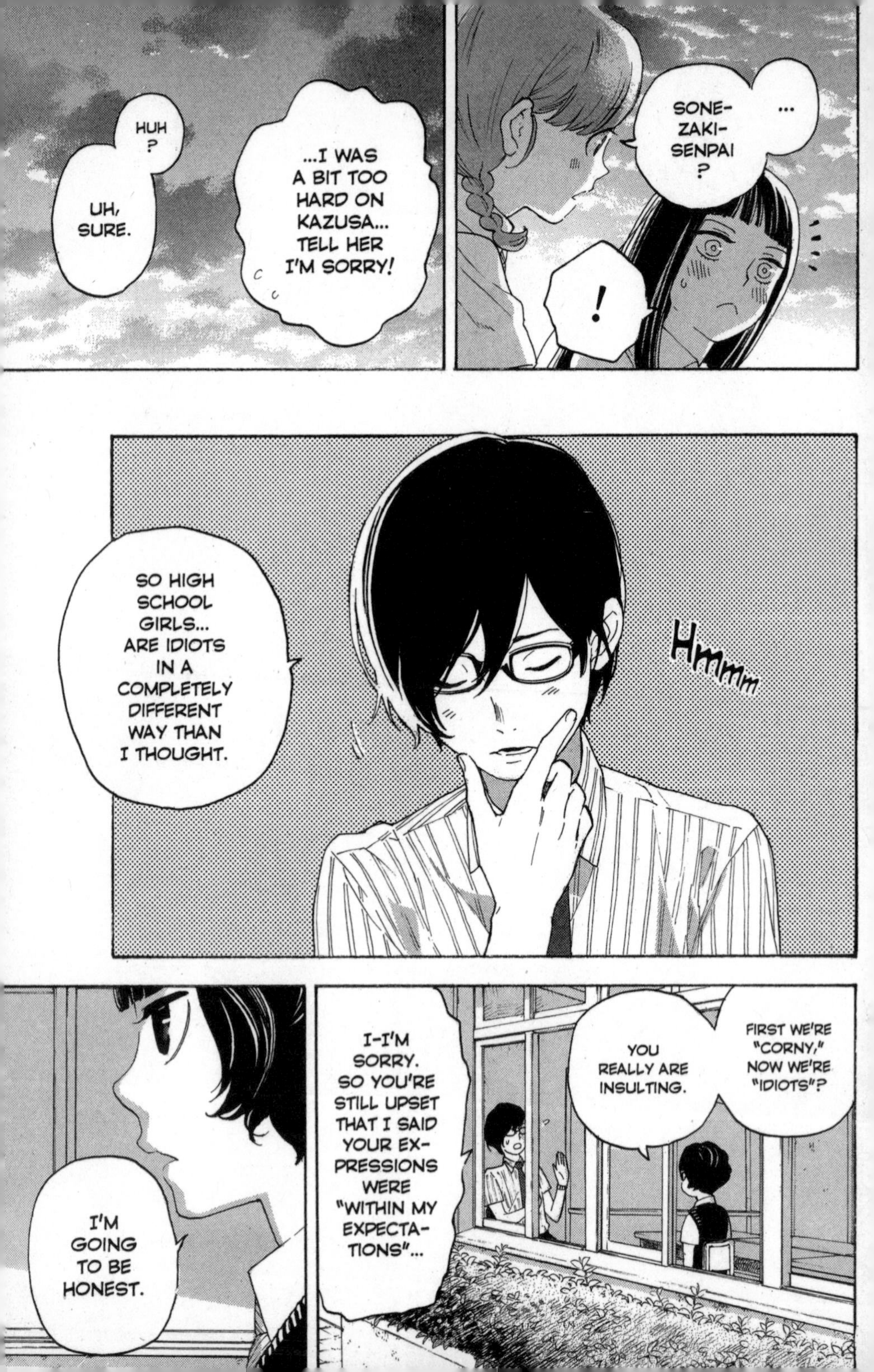
...
SONE-ZAKI-SENPAI?
!
...I WAS A BIT TOO HARD ON KAZUSA... TELL HER I'M SORRY!
HUH?
UH, SURE.
Hmmm
SO HIGH SCHOOL GIRLS... ARE IDIOTS IN A COMPLETELY DIFFERENT WAY THAN I THOUGHT.
FIRST WE'RE "CORNY," NOW WE'RE "IDIOTS"?
YOU REALLY ARE INSULTING.
I-I'M SORRY. SO YOU'RE STILL UPSET THAT I SAID YOUR EX-PRESSIONS WERE "WITHIN MY EXPECTA-TIONS"...
I'M GOING TO BE HONEST.

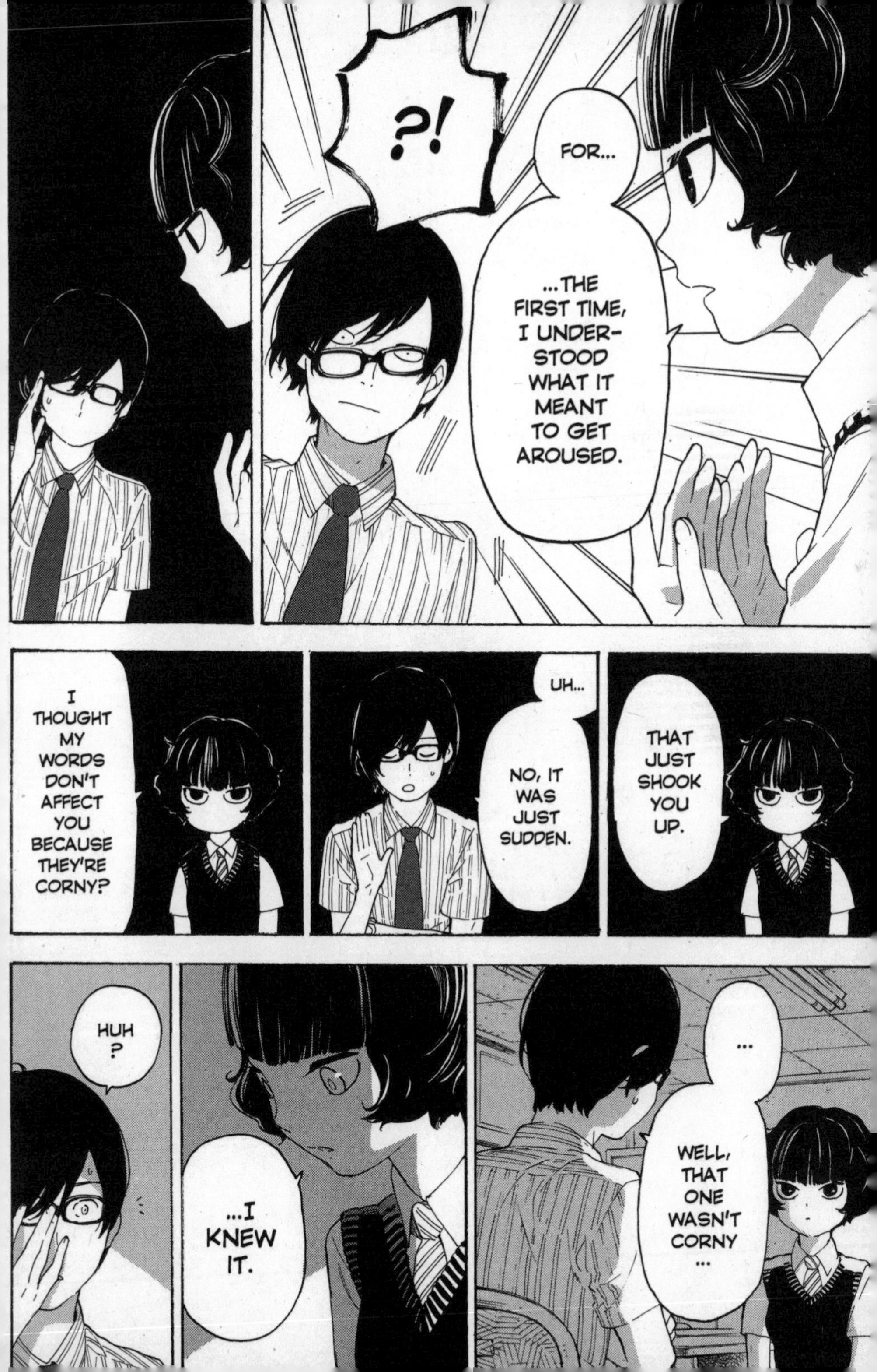
FOR...
...THE FIRST TIME, I UNDERSTOOD WHAT IT MEANT TO GET AROUSED.
?!
THAT JUST SHOOK YOU UP.
UH...
NO, IT WAS JUST SUDDEN.
I THOUGHT MY WORDS DON'T AFFECT YOU BECAUSE THEY'RE CORNY?
...
WELL, THAT ONE WASN'T CORNY ...
...I KNEW IT.
HUH ?

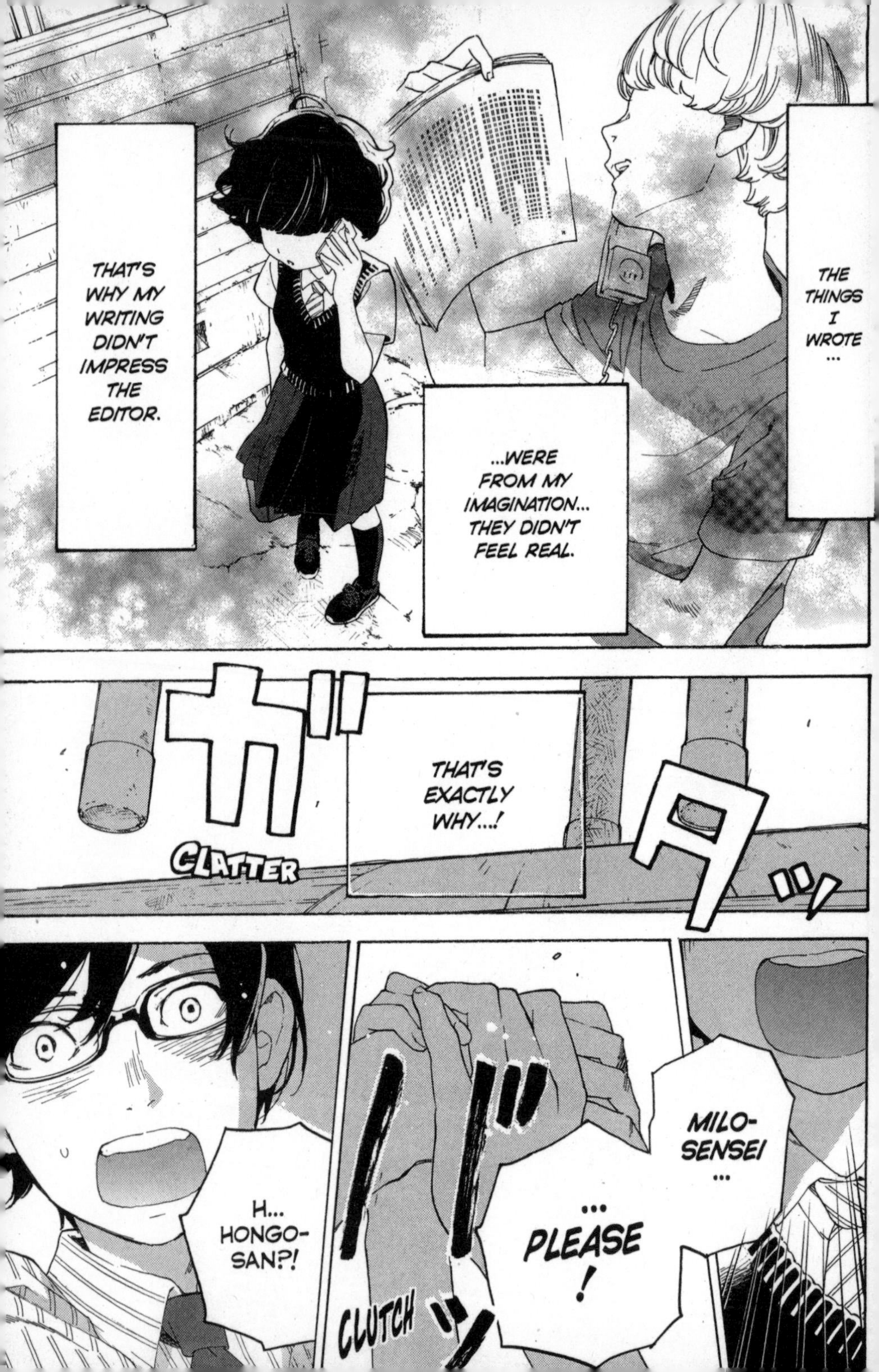
THE THINGS I WROTE...
...WERE FROM MY IMAGINATION... THEY DIDN'T FEEL REAL.
THAT'S WHY MY WRITING DIDN'T IMPRESS THE EDITOR.
ガタッ!
THAT'S EXACTLY WHY...!
CLATTER
MILO-SENSEI...
...PLEASE!
CLUTCH
H... HONGO-SAN?!

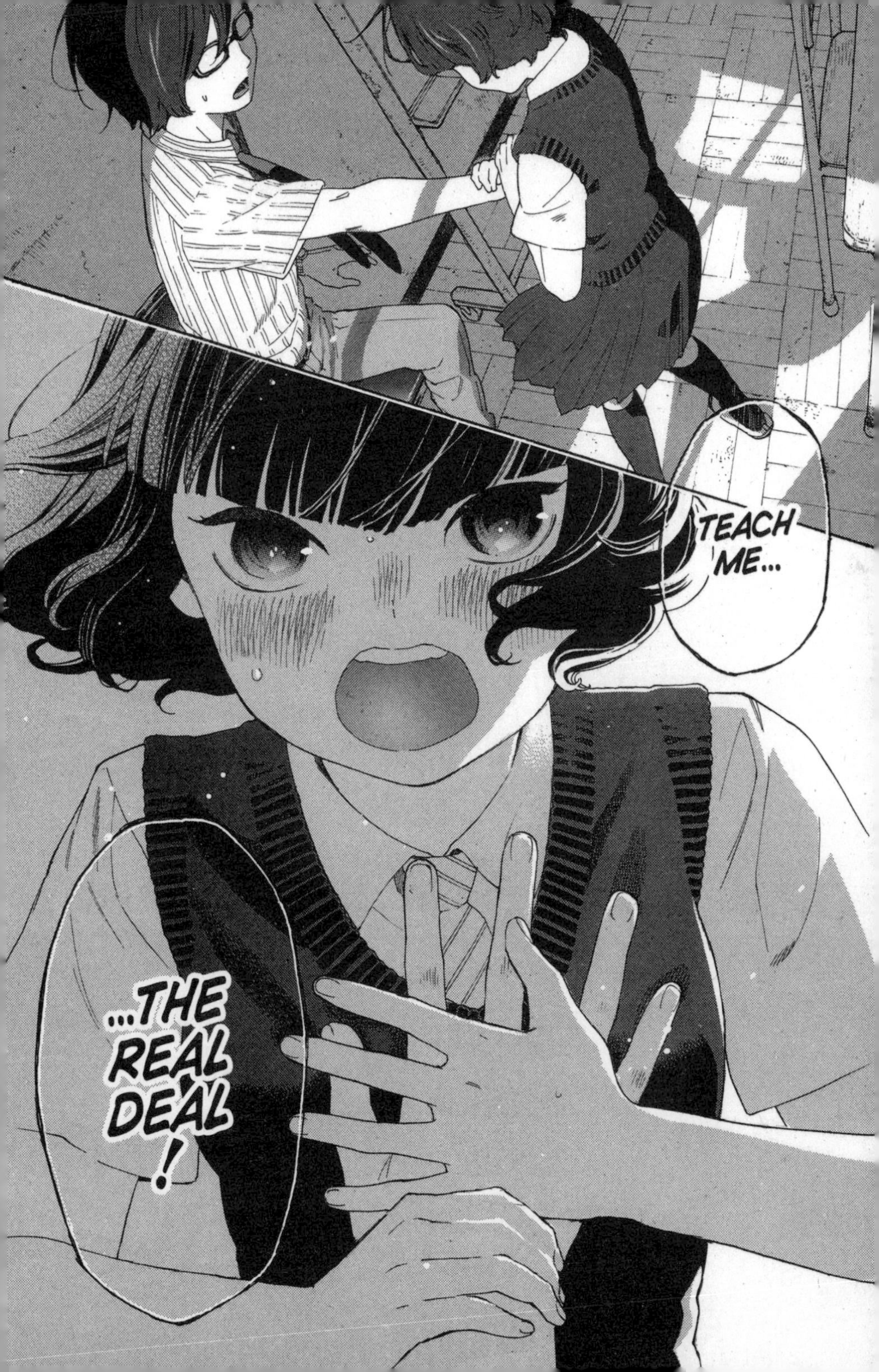
TEACH ME...
...THE REAL DEAL!

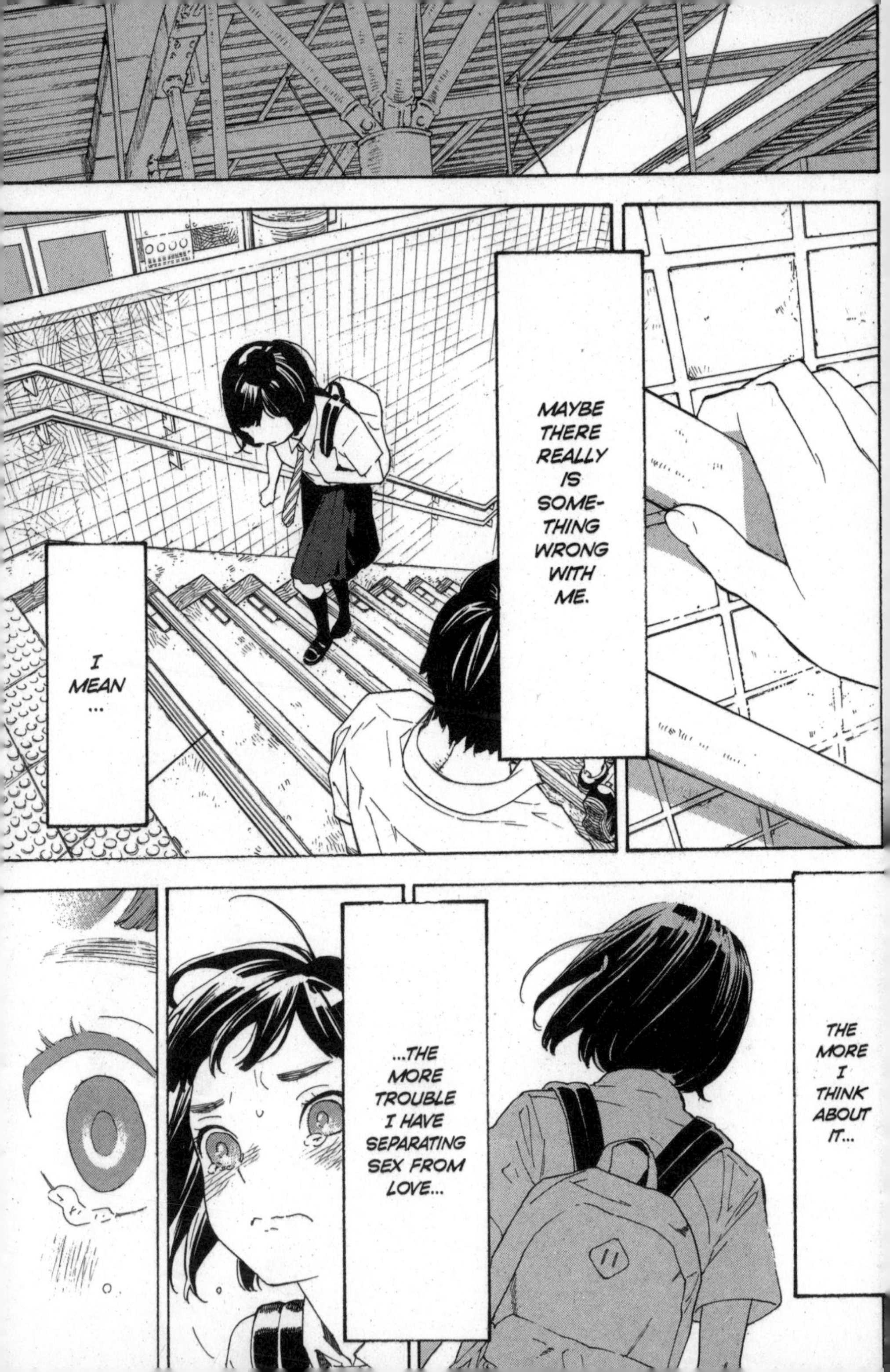
MAYBE THERE REALLY IS SOME-THING WRONG WITH ME.
I MEAN ...
THE MORE I THINK ABOUT IT...
...THE MORE TROUBLE I HAVE SEPARATING SEX FROM LOVE...

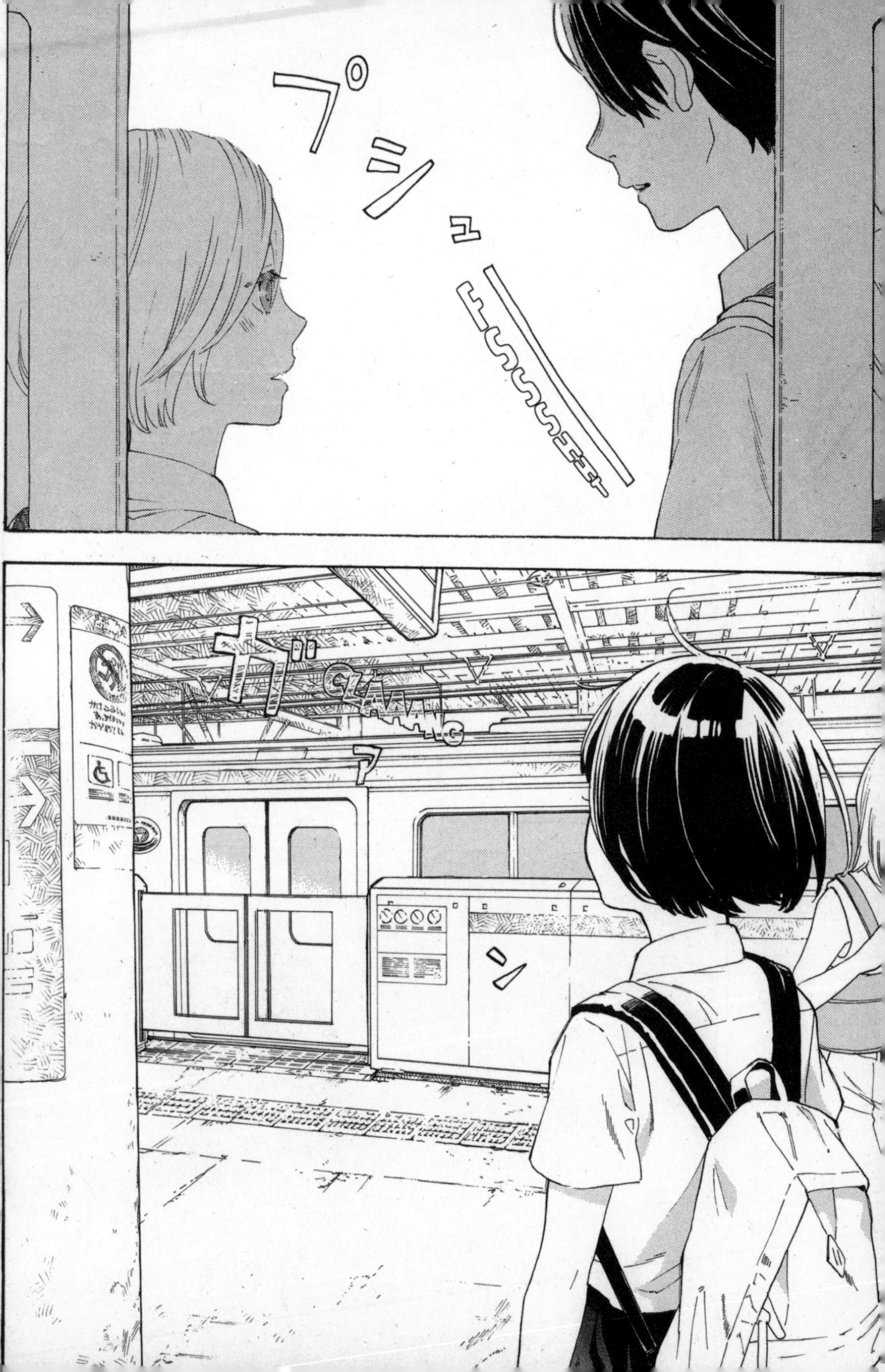
プシュ
FSSSSHHT
ガアン
CLAAANG

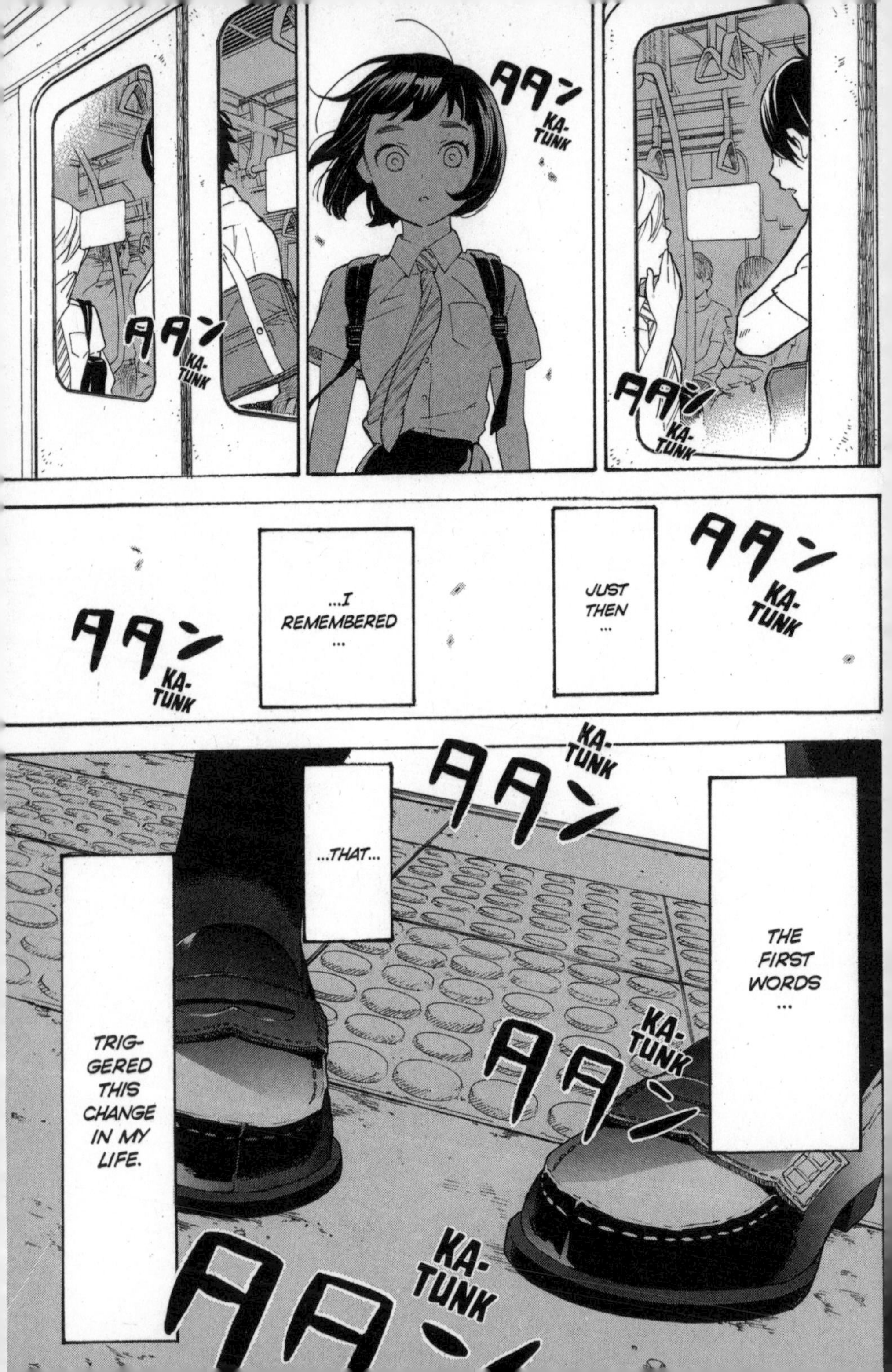

タタン
KA-TUNK
タタン
KA-TUNK
タタン
KA-TUNK
タタン
KA-TUNK
JUST THEN ...
...I REMEMBERED ...
タタン
KA-TUNK
THE FIRST WORDS ...
タタン
KA-TUNK
...THAT...
タタン
KA-TUNK
TRIG-GERED THIS CHANGE IN MY LIFE.
タタン
KA-TUNK

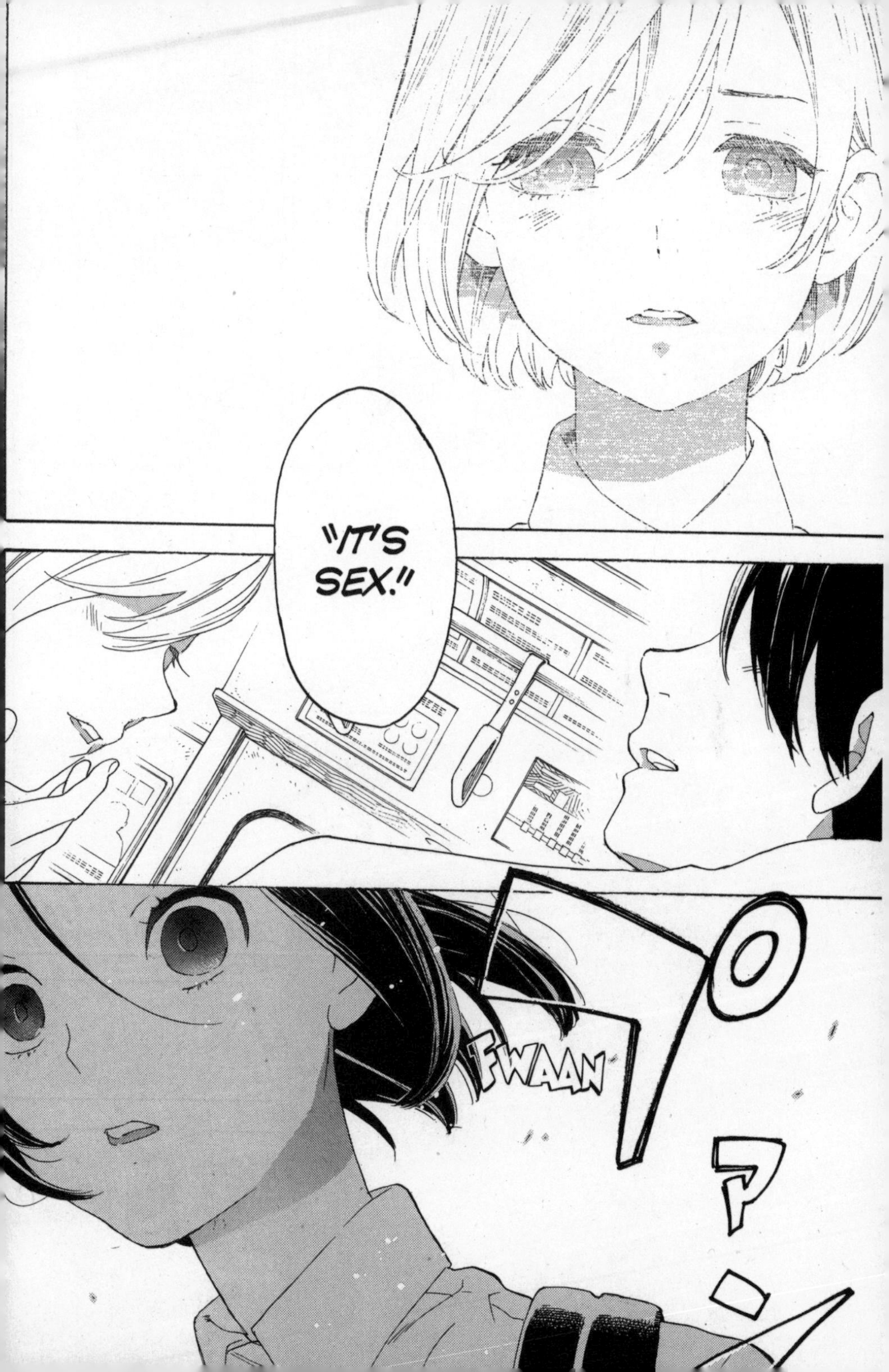
"IT'S SEX."
FWAAN

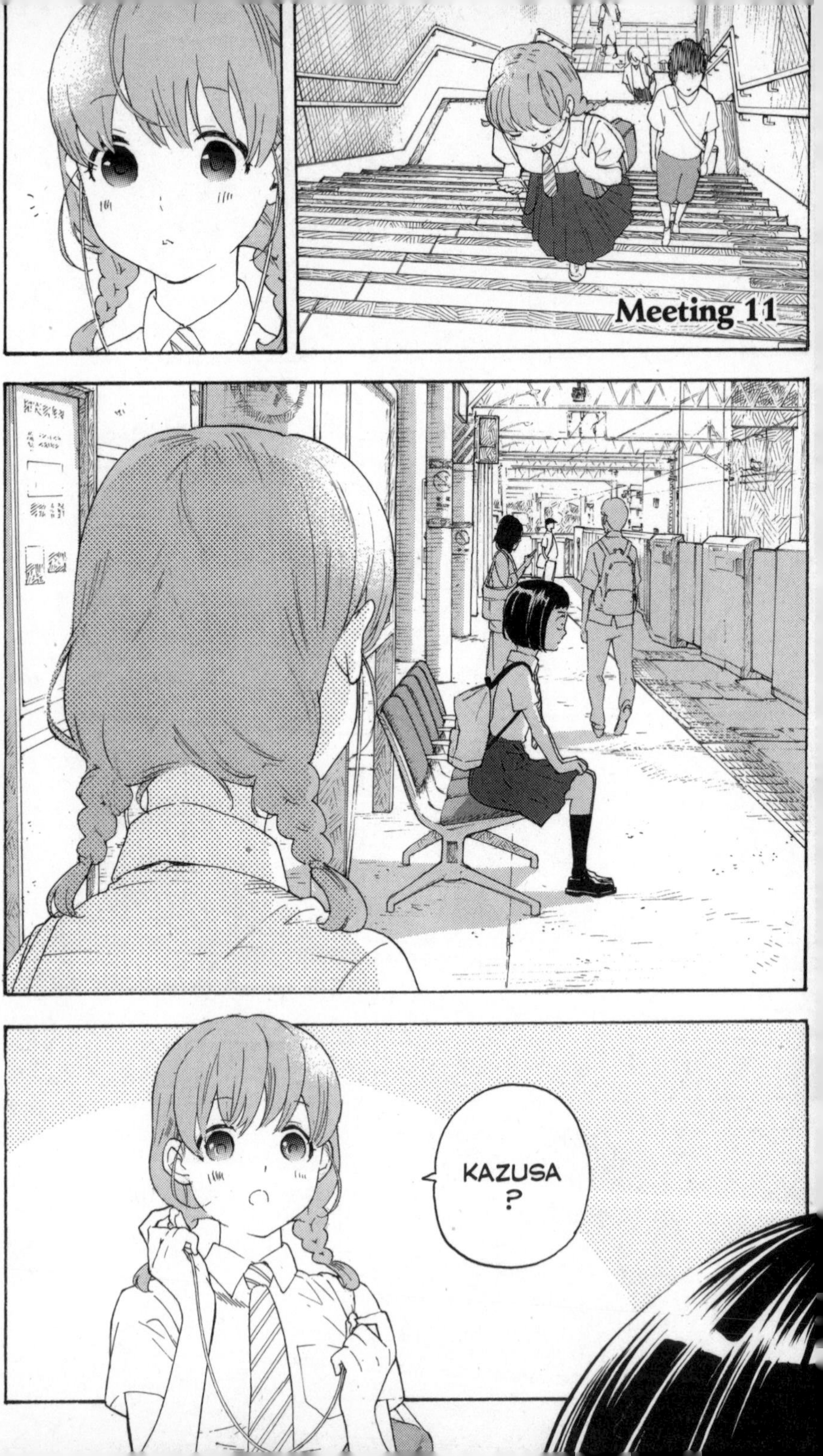
Meeting 11
KAZUSA?

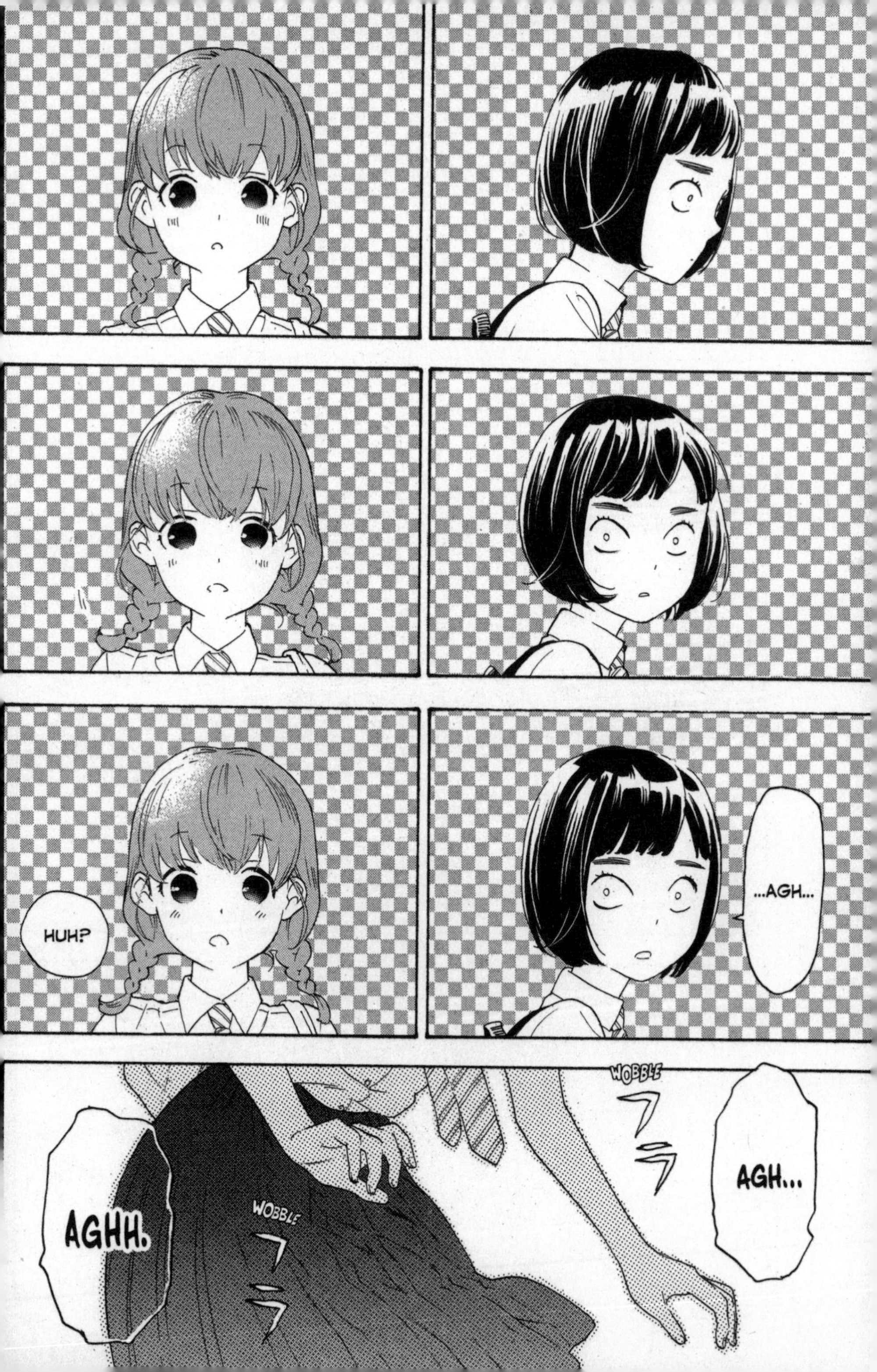
...AGH...
HUH?
WOBBLE
AGH...
WOBBLE
AGHH.

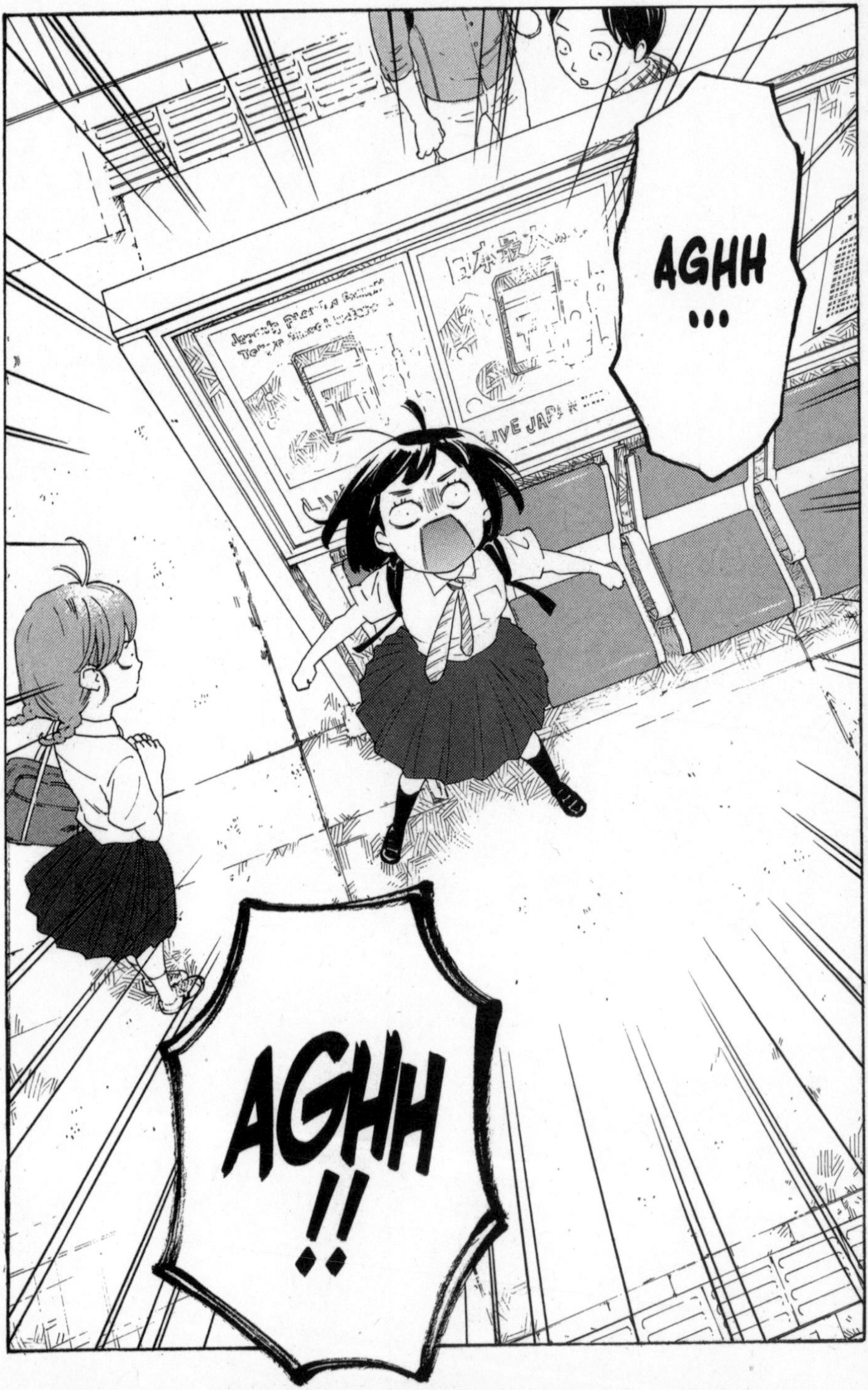
AGHH ...
AGHH !!

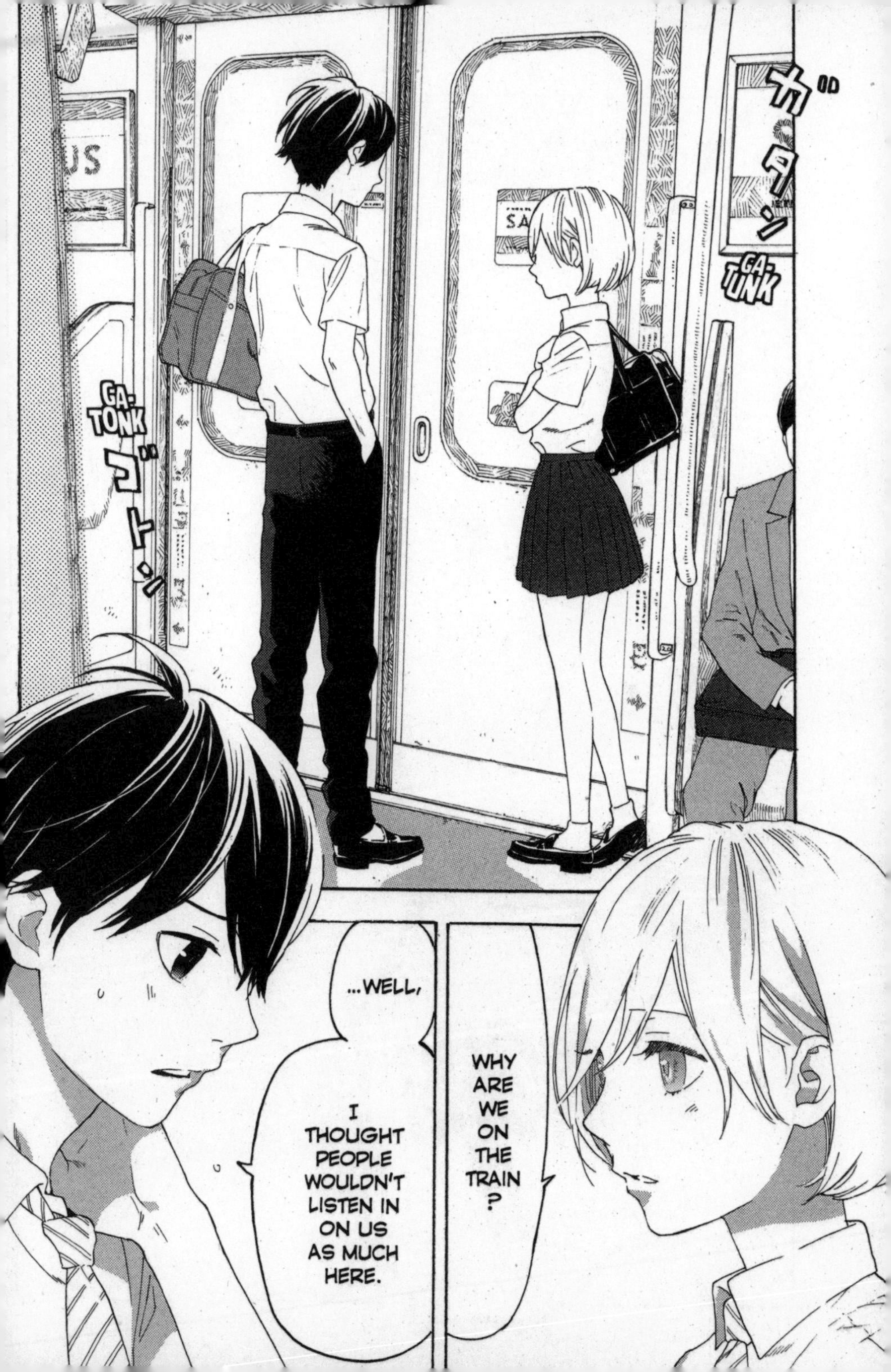
カタン
GA-TUNK
GA-TONK
ゴトッ
WHY ARE WE ON THE TRAIN?
...WELL,
I THOUGHT PEOPLE WOULDN'T LISTEN IN ON US AS MUCH HERE.

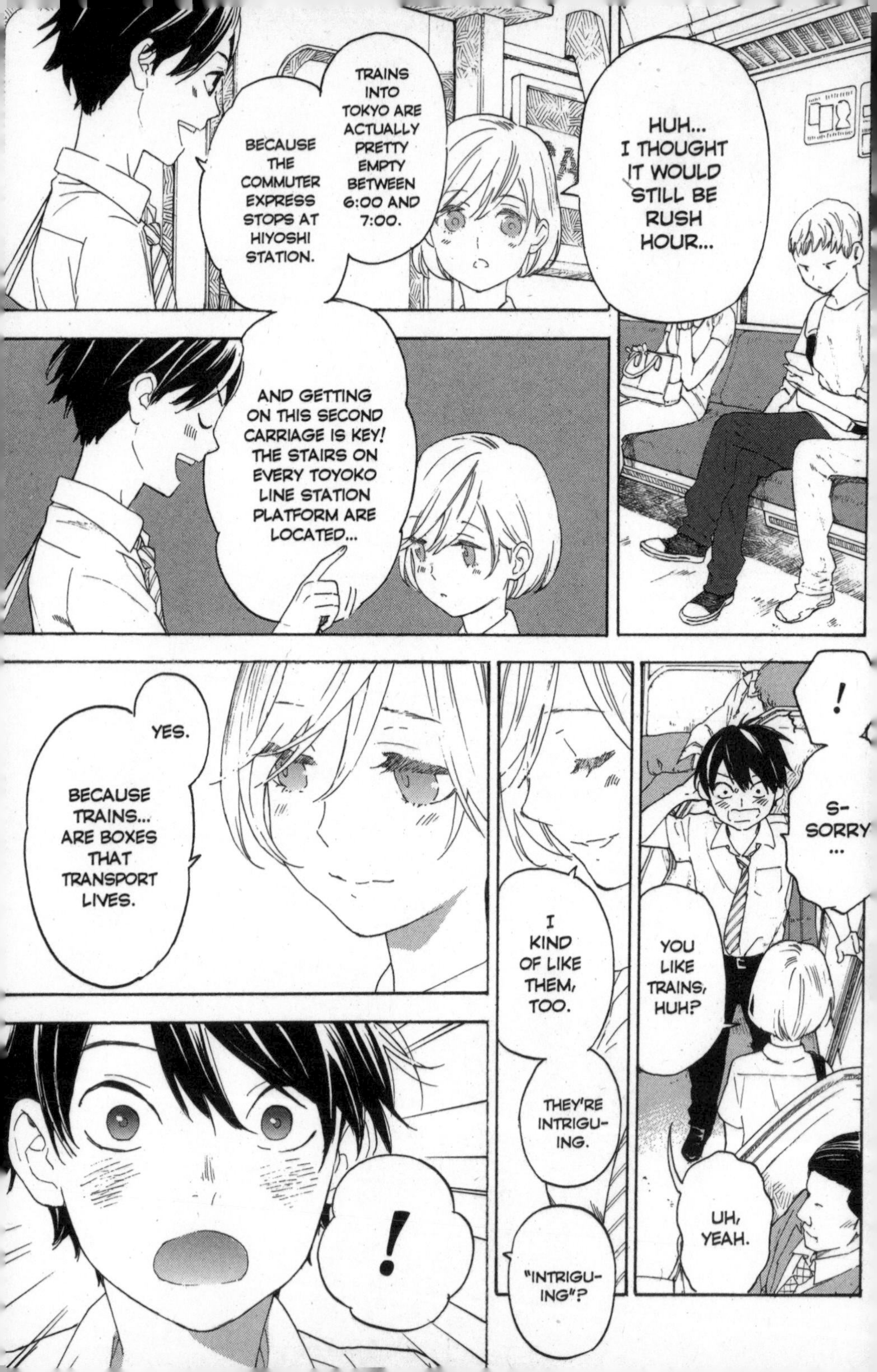
HUH... I THOUGHT IT WOULD STILL BE RUSH HOUR...
TRAINS INTO TOKYO ARE ACTUALLY PRETTY EMPTY BETWEEN 6:00 AND 7:00.
BECAUSE THE COMMUTER EXPRESS STOPS AT HIYOSHI STATION.
AND GETTING ON THIS SECOND CARRIAGE IS KEY! THE STAIRS ON EVERY TOYOKO LINE STATION PLATFORM ARE LOCATED...
!
S-SORRY...
YOU LIKE TRAINS, HUH?
UH, YEAH.
I KIND OF LIKE THEM, TOO.
THEY'RE INTRIGU-ING.
"INTRIGU-ING"?
YES.
BECAUSE TRAINS... ARE BOXES THAT TRANSPORT LIVES.
!

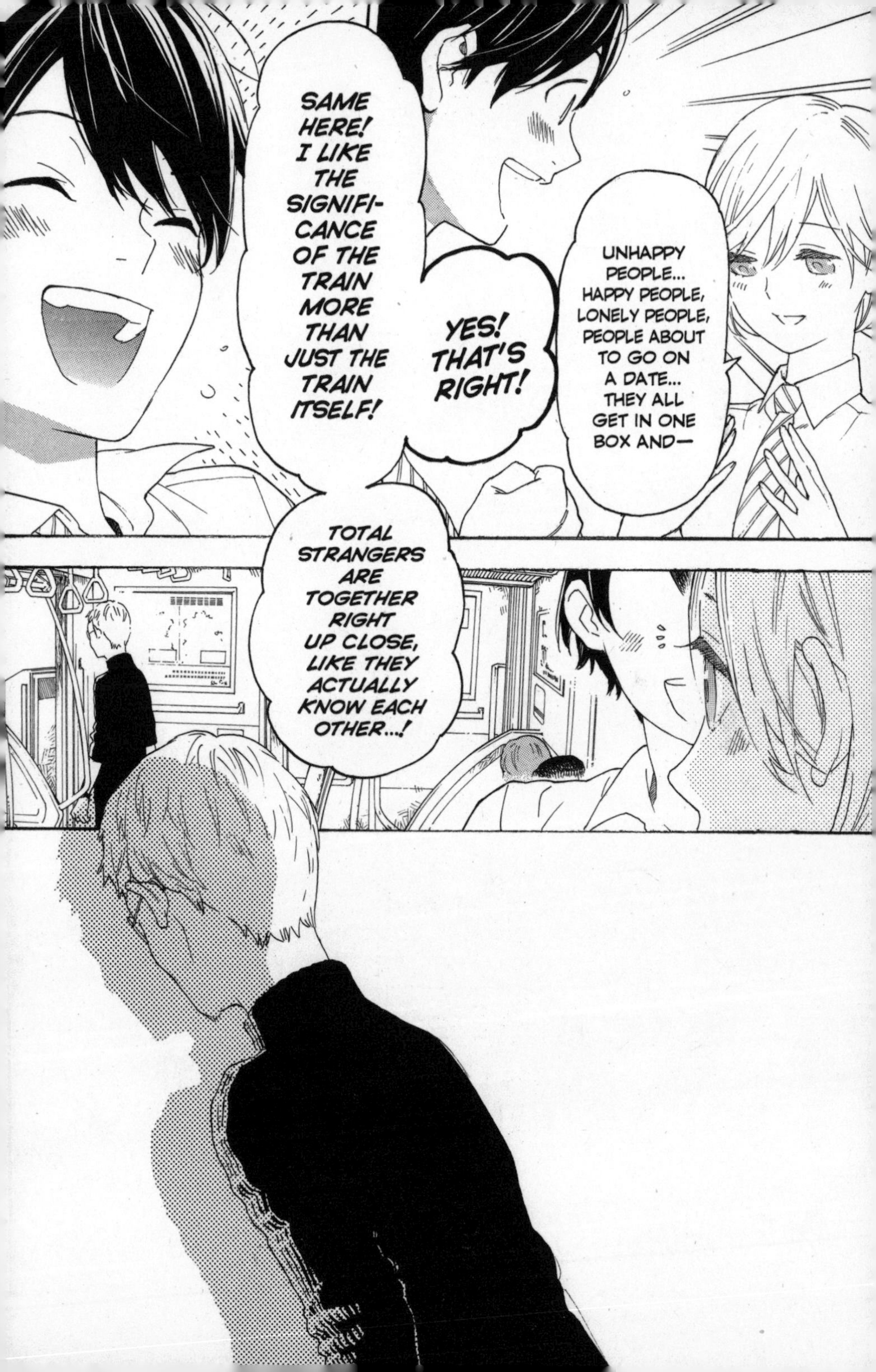
UNHAPPY PEOPLE... HAPPY PEOPLE, LONELY PEOPLE, PEOPLE ABOUT TO GO ON A DATE... THEY ALL GET IN ONE BOX AND—
YES! THAT'S RIGHT!
SAME HERE! I LIKE THE SIGNIFI-CANCE OF THE TRAIN MORE THAN JUST THE TRAIN ITSELF!
TOTAL STRANGERS ARE TOGETHER RIGHT UP CLOSE, LIKE THEY ACTUALLY KNOW EACH OTHER...!

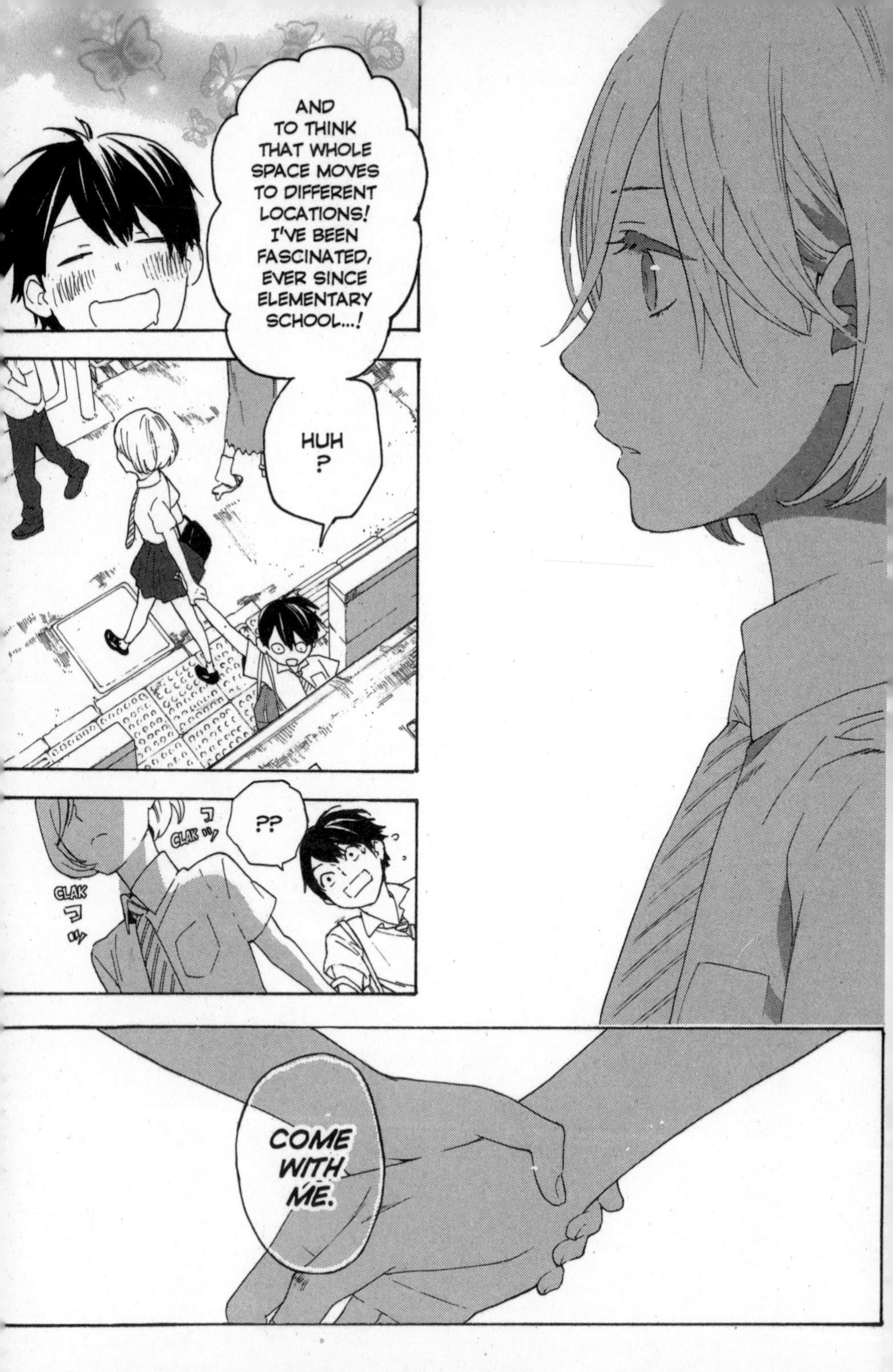
AND TO THINK THAT WHOLE SPACE MOVES TO DIFFERENT LOCATIONS! I'VE BEEN FASCINATED, EVER SINCE ELEMENTARY SCHOOL...!
HUH?
??
CLAK
CLAK
COME WITH ME.

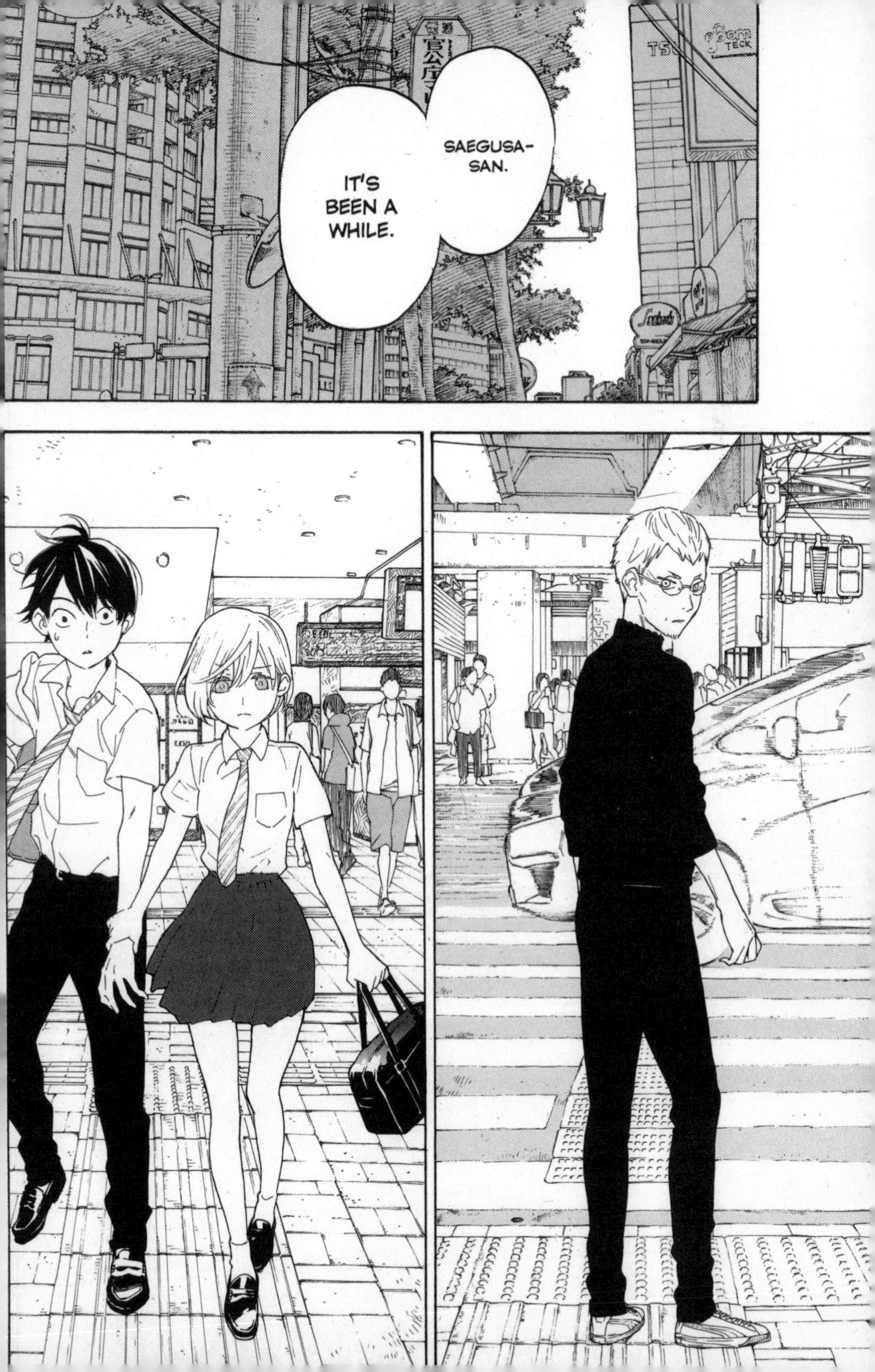
SAEGUSA-SAN.
IT'S BEEN A WHILE.

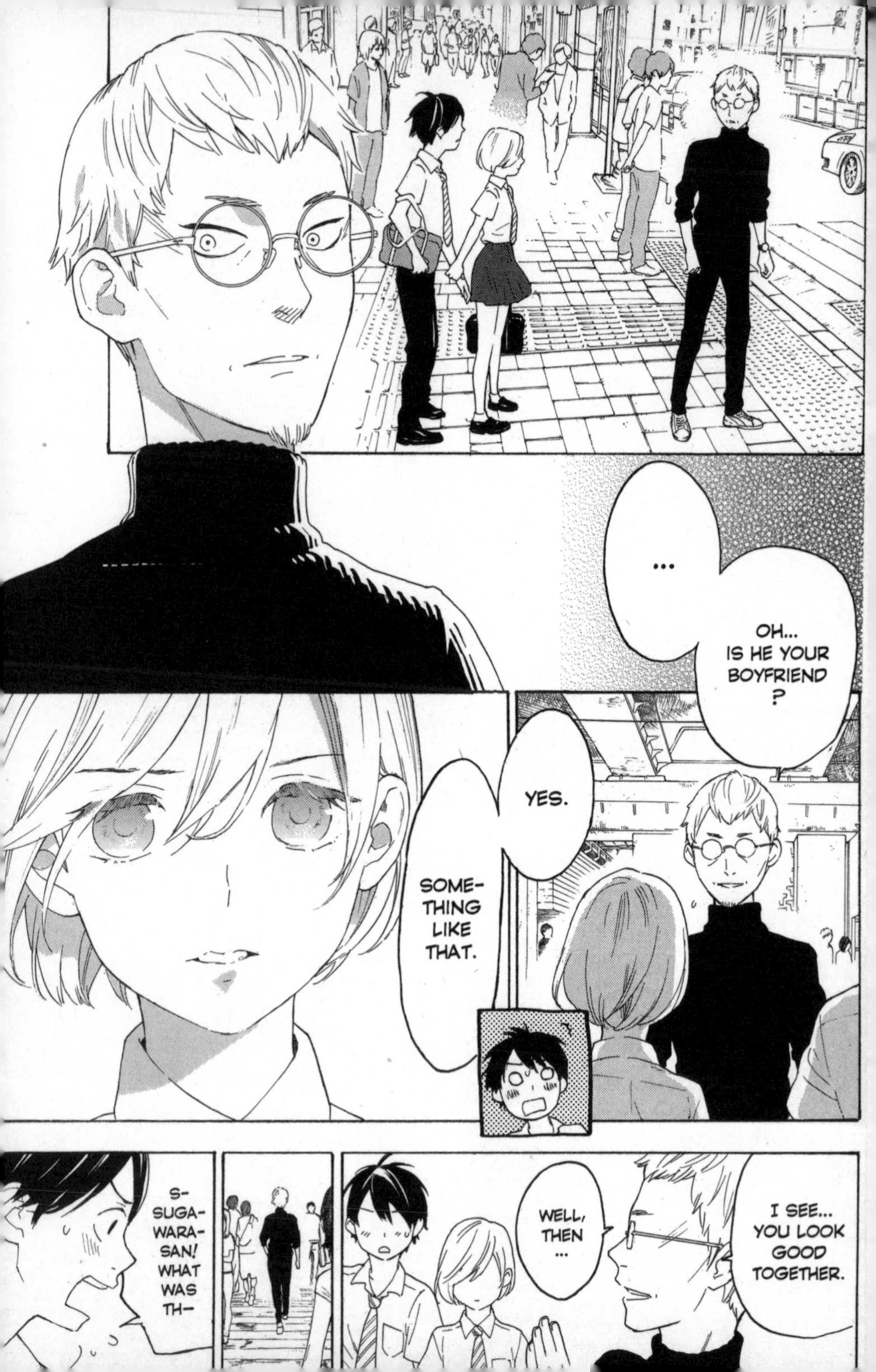
...
OH... IS HE YOUR BOYFRIEND ?
YES.
SOMETHING LIKE THAT.
I SEE... YOU LOOK GOOD TOGETHER.
WELL, THEN ...
S-SUGAWARA-SAN! WHAT WAS TH-

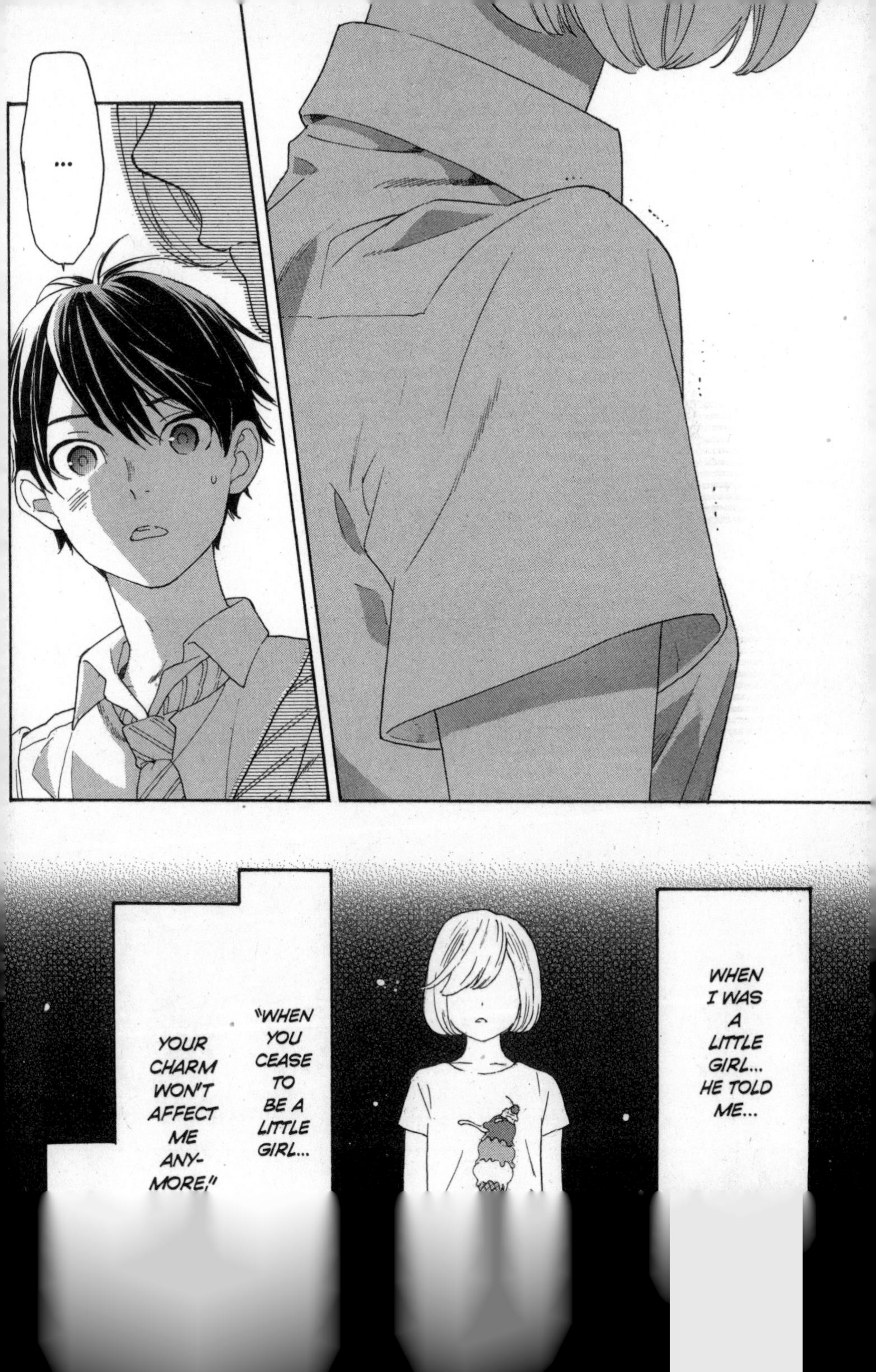
...
WHEN I WAS A LITTLE GIRL... HE TOLD ME...
"WHEN YOU CEASE TO BE A LITTLE GIRL...
YOUR CHARM WON'T AFFECT ME ANY-MORE."

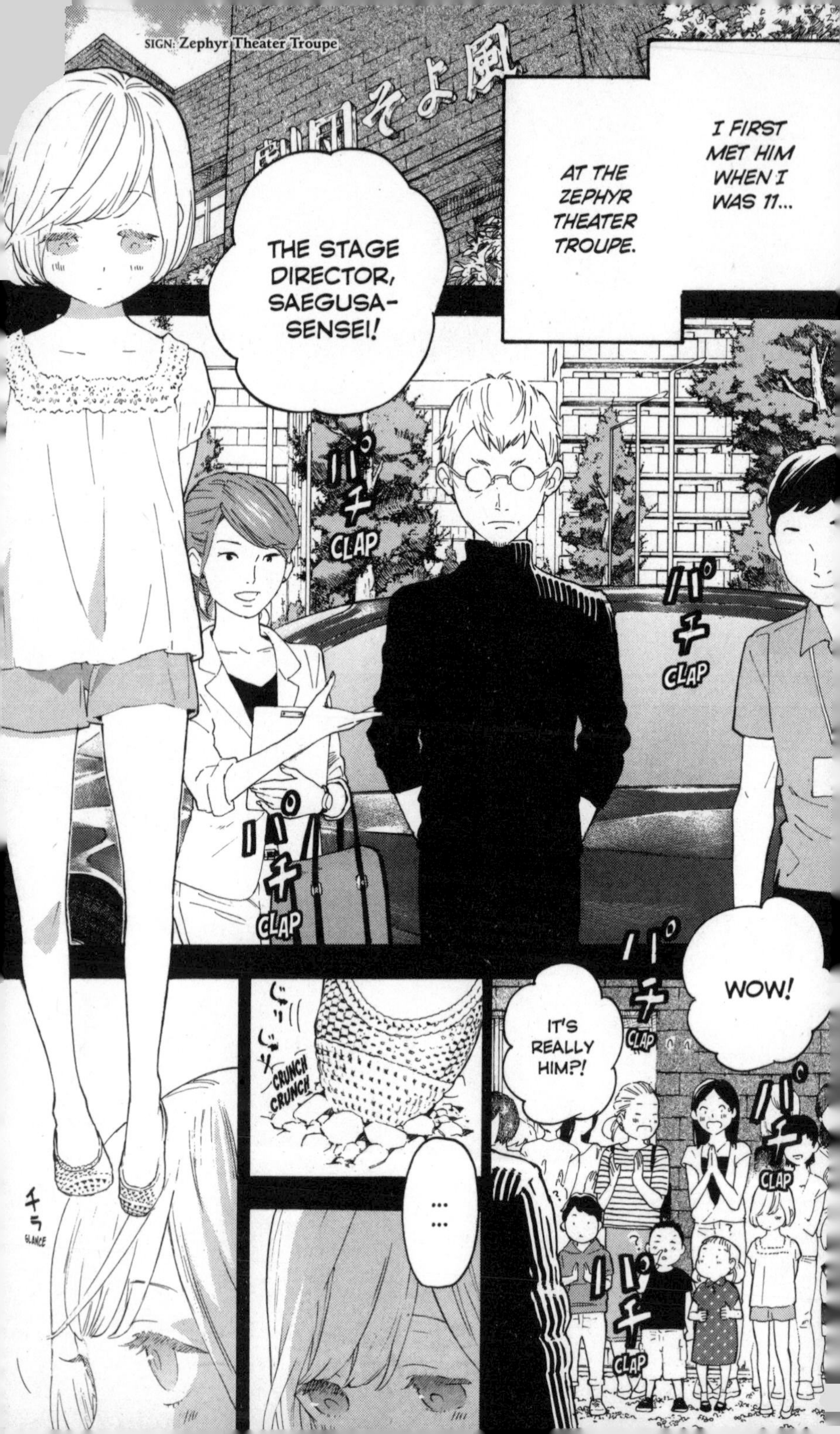
I FIRST MET HIM WHEN I WAS 11...
AT THE ZEPHYR THEATER TROUPE.
SIGN: Zephyr Theater Troupe
THE STAGE DIRECTOR, SAEGUSA-SENSEI!
CLAP
CLAP
CLAP
WOW!
CLAP
IT'S REALLY HIM?!
CLAP
CLAP
CLAP
CRUNCH CRUNCH
... ...
GLANCE

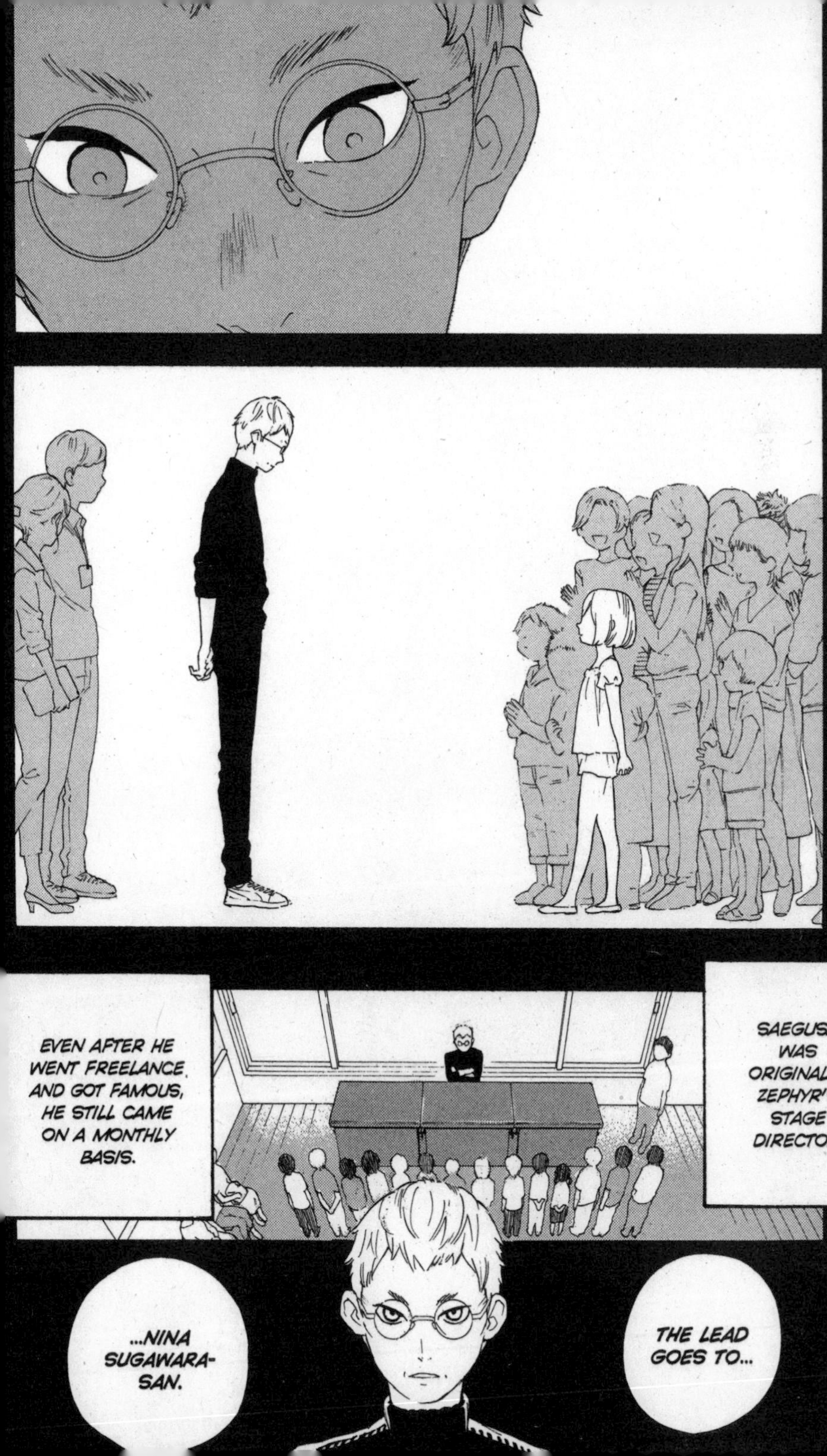
SAEGUSA WAS ORIGINALLY ZEPHYR'S STAGE DIRECTOR.
EVEN AFTER HE WENT FREELANCE AND GOT FAMOUS, HE STILL CAME ON A MONTHLY BASIS.
THE LEAD GOES TO...
...NINA SUGAWARA-SAN.

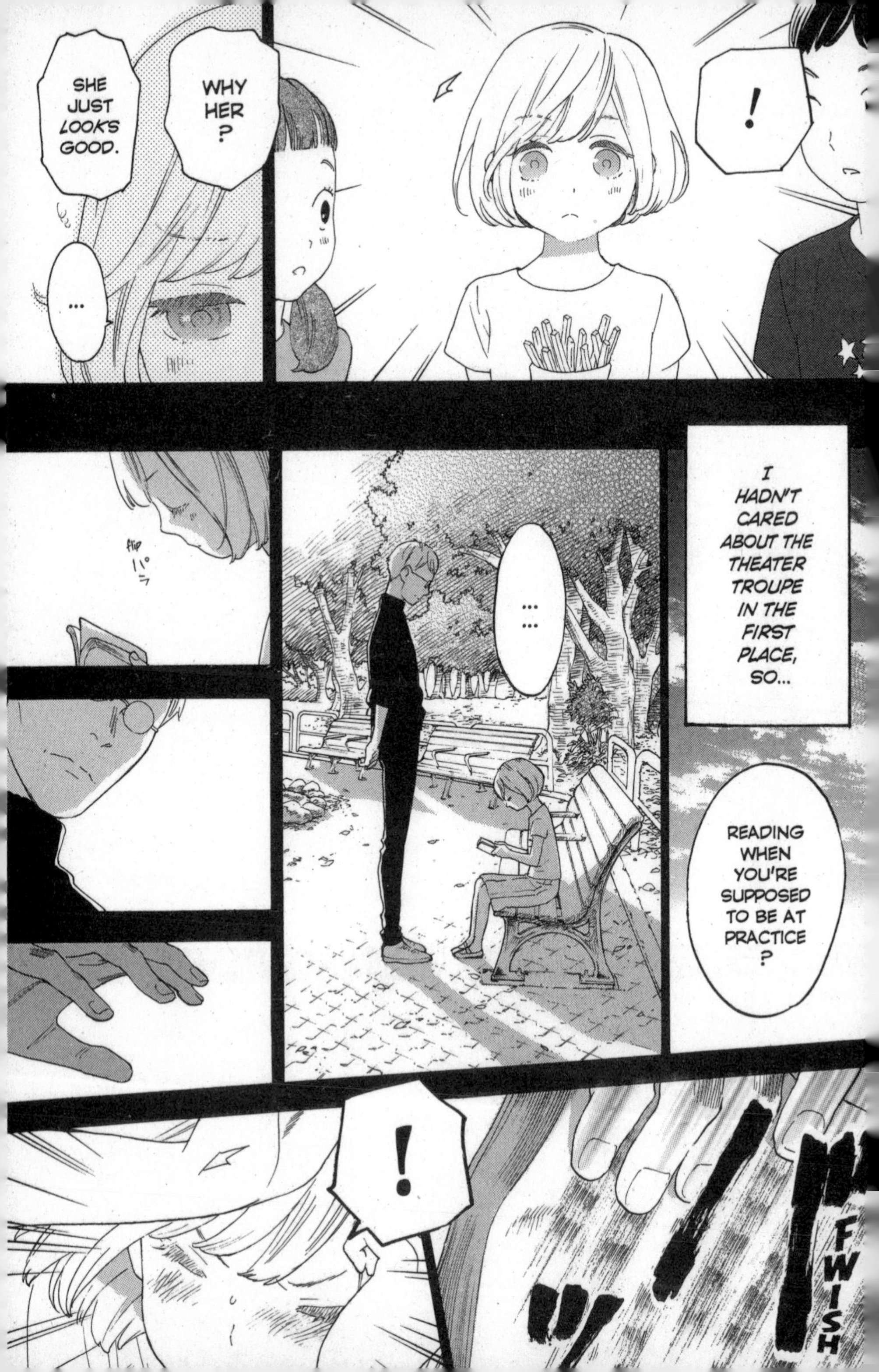
!
WHY HER?
SHE JUST LOOKS GOOD.
...
I HADN'T CARED ABOUT THE THEATER TROUPE IN THE FIRST PLACE, SO...
READING WHEN YOU'RE SUPPOSED TO BE AT PRACTICE?
... ...
flip
パラ
FWISH
!

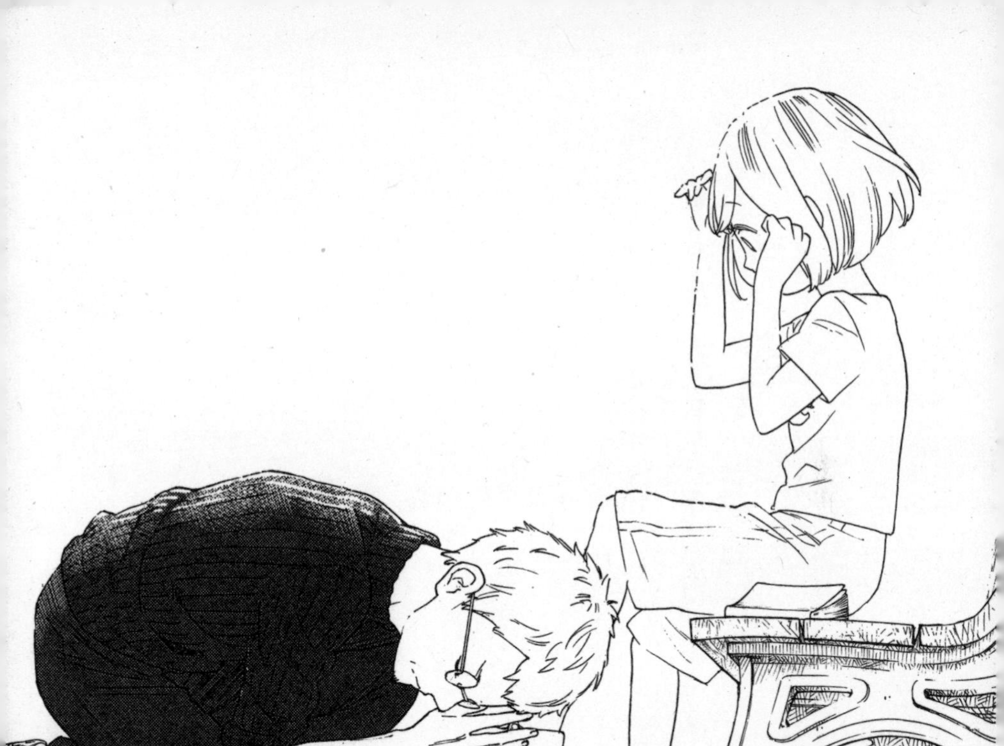

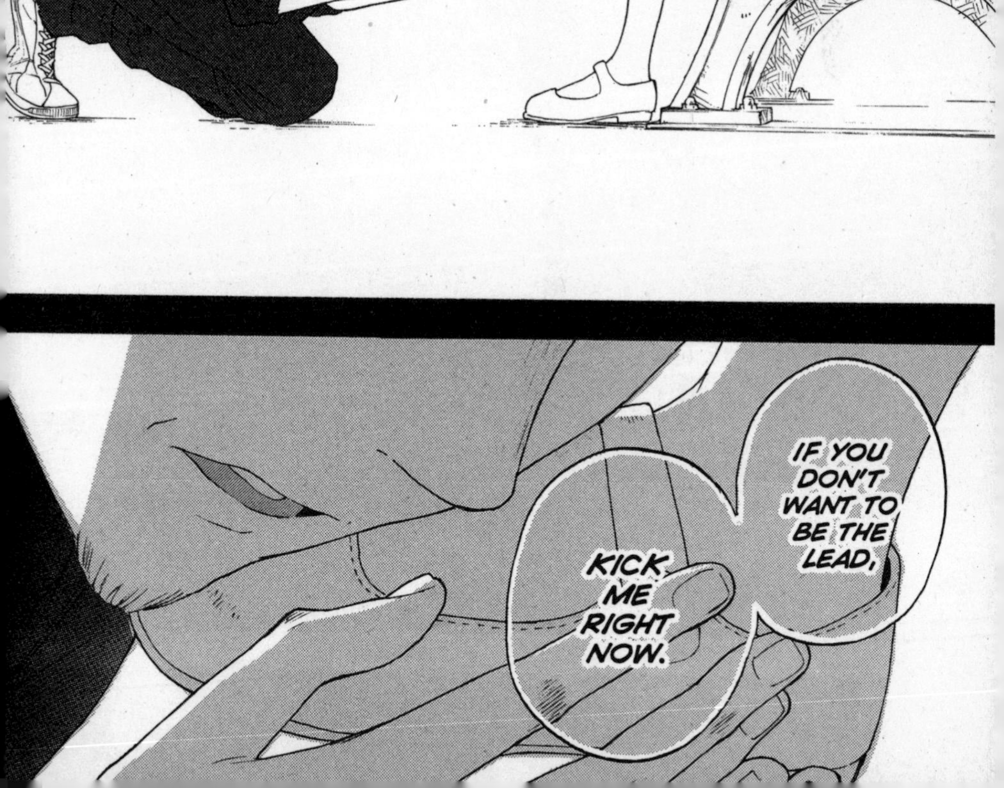
IF YOU DON'T WANT TO BE THE LEAD,
KICK ME RIGHT NOW.

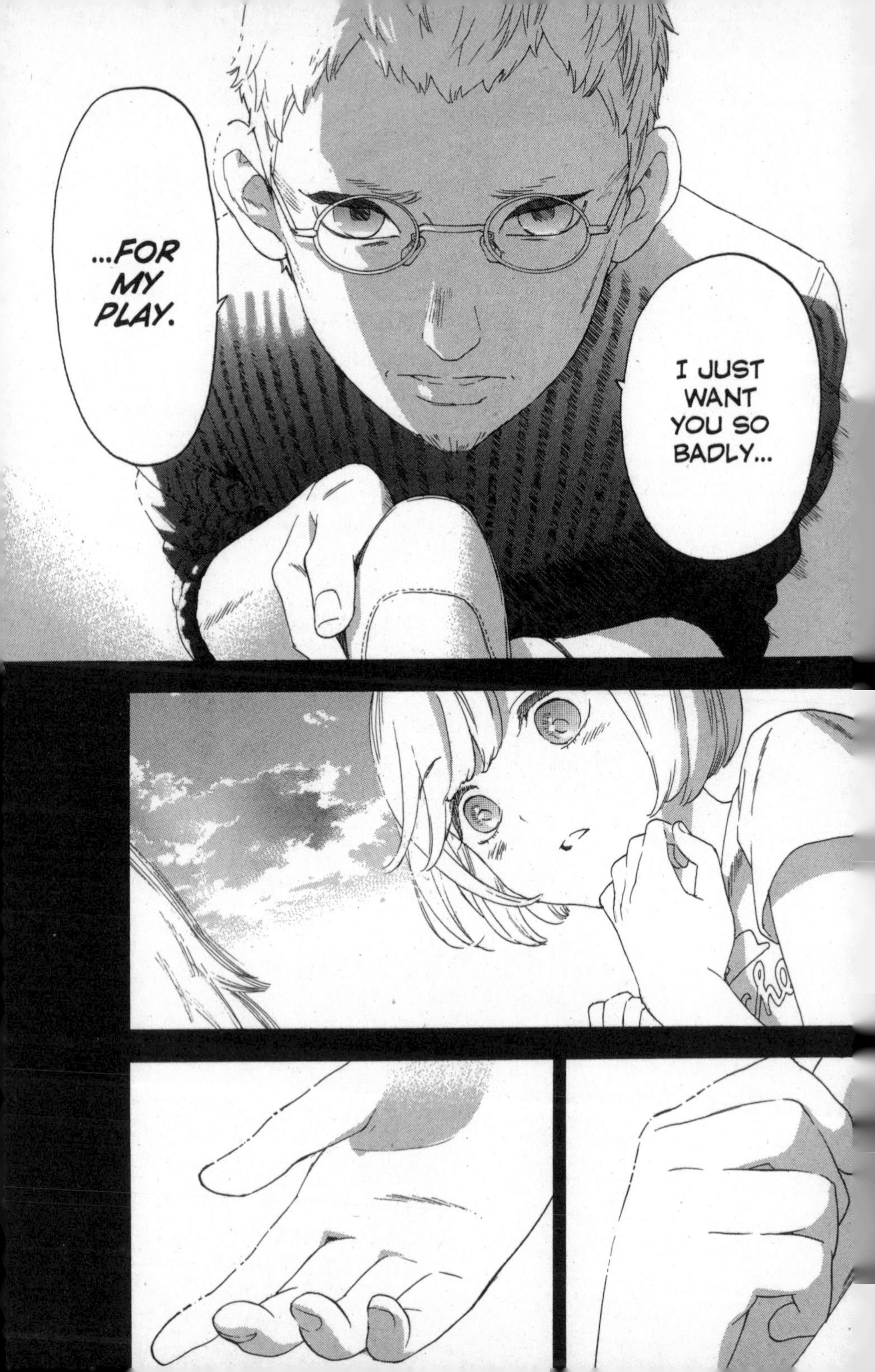
I JUST WANT YOU SO BADLY...
...FOR MY PLAY.

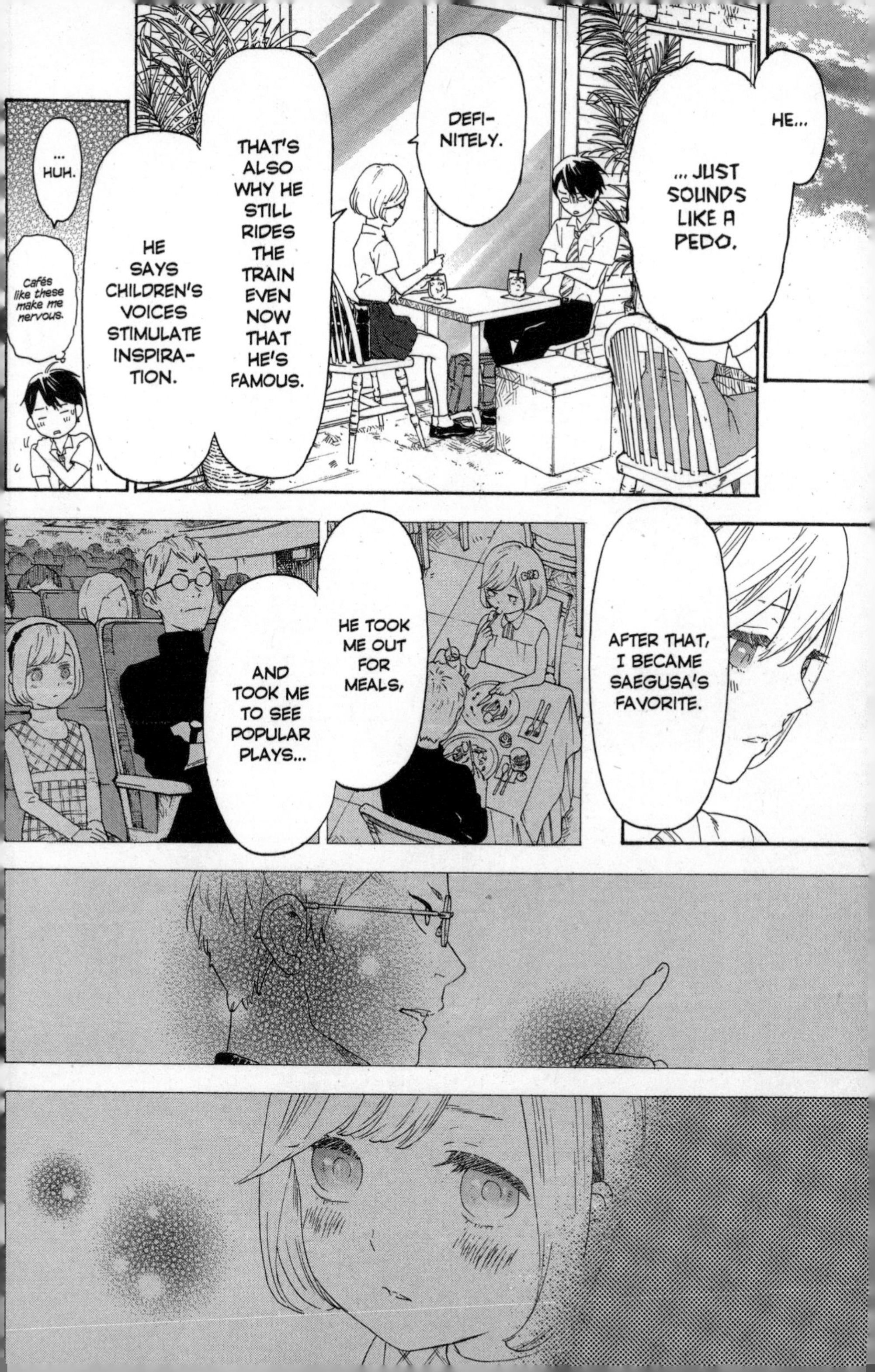
HE...
... JUST SOUNDS LIKE A PEDO.
DEFI-NITELY.
THAT'S ALSO WHY HE STILL RIDES THE TRAIN EVEN NOW THAT HE'S FAMOUS.
HE SAYS CHILDREN'S VOICES STIMULATE INSPIRA-TION.
... HUH.
Cafés like these make me nervous.
AFTER THAT, I BECAME SAEGUSA'S FAVORITE.
HE TOOK ME OUT FOR MEALS,
AND TOOK ME TO SEE POPULAR PLAYS...

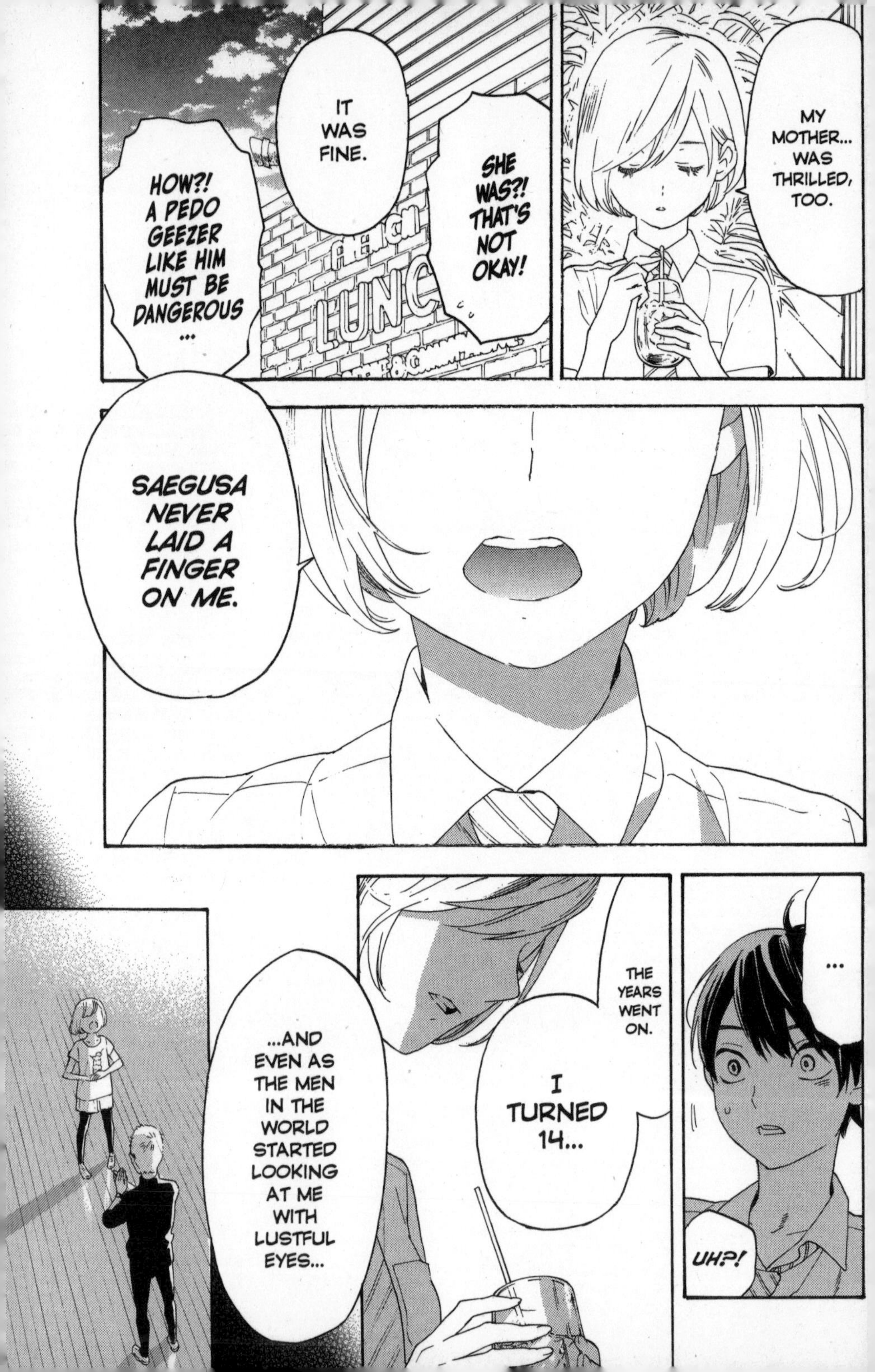
MY MOTHER... WAS THRILLED, TOO.
SHE WAS?! THAT'S NOT OKAY!
HOW?! A PEDO GEEZER LIKE HIM MUST BE DANGEROUS ...
IT WAS FINE.
SAEGUSA NEVER LAID A FINGER ON ME.
...
UH?!
THE YEARS WENT ON.
I TURNED 14...
...AND EVEN AS THE MEN IN THE WORLD STARTED LOOKING AT ME WITH LUSTFUL EYES...

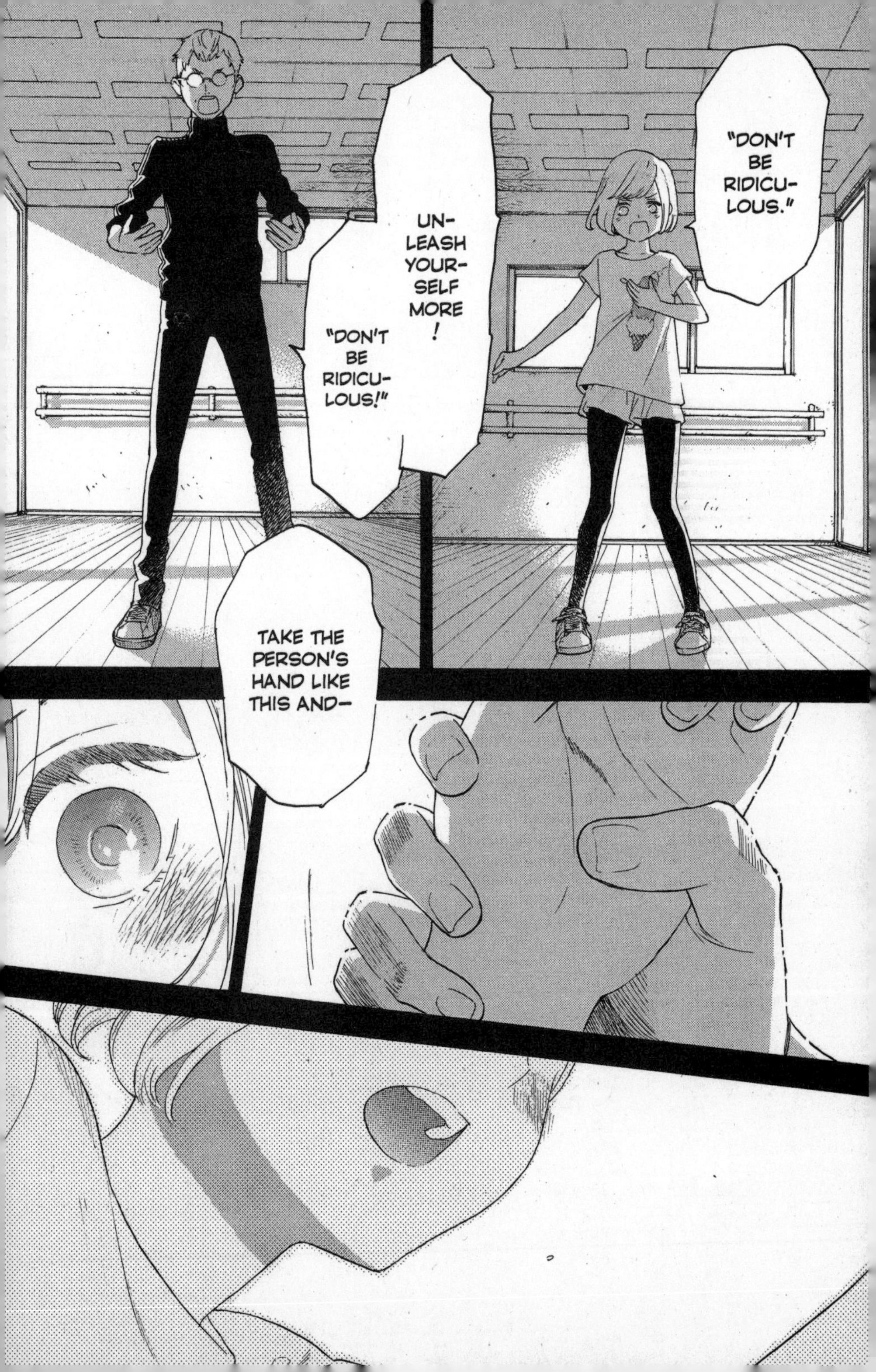
"DON'T BE RIDICU-LOUS."
UN-LEASH YOUR-SELF MORE!
"DON'T BE RIDICU-LOUS!"
TAKE THE PERSON'S HAND LIKE THIS AND–

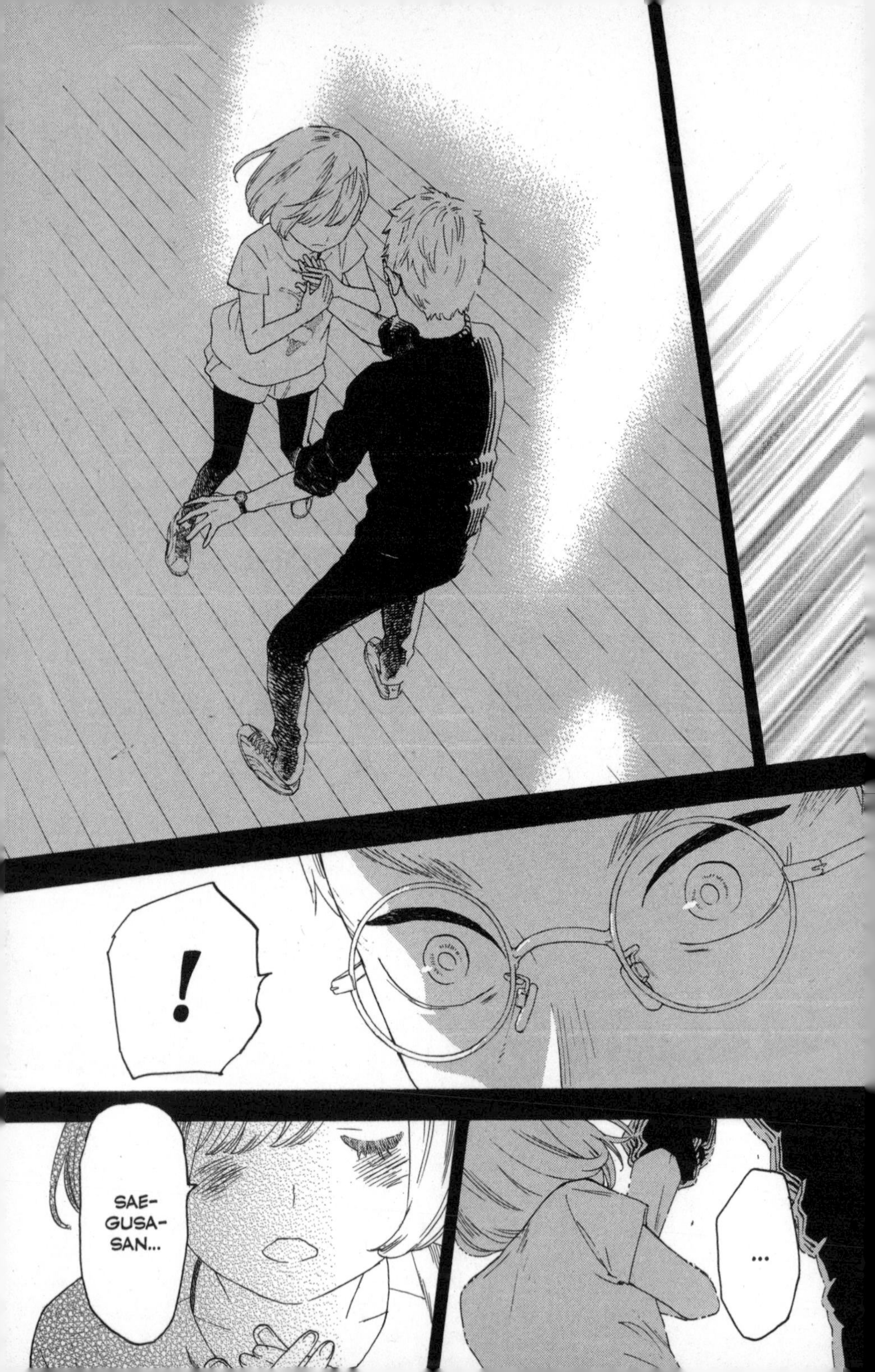
!
...
SAE-GUSA-SAN...

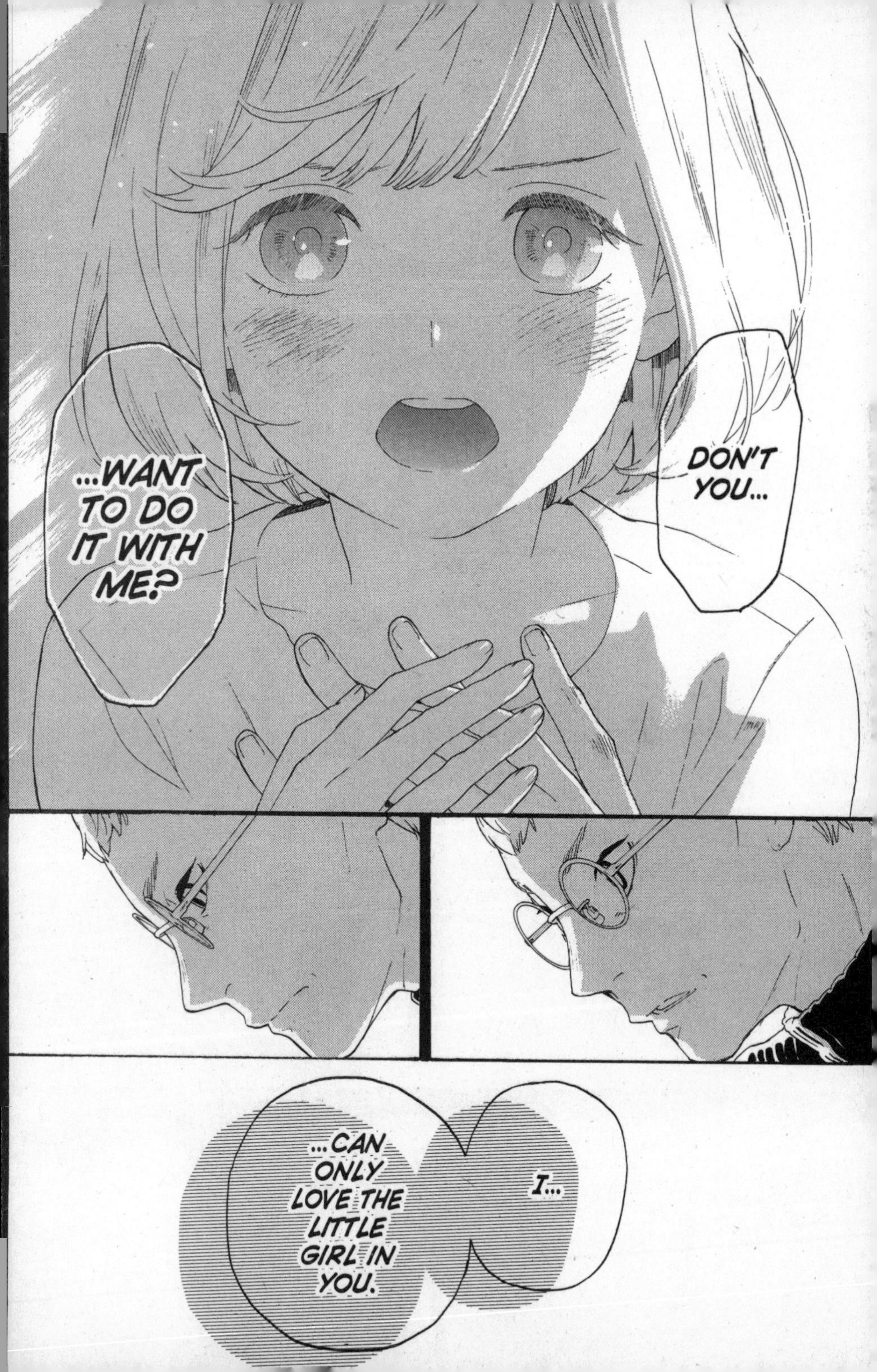
DON'T YOU...
...WANT TO DO IT WITH ME?
I...
...CAN ONLY LOVE THE LITTLE GIRL IN YOU.

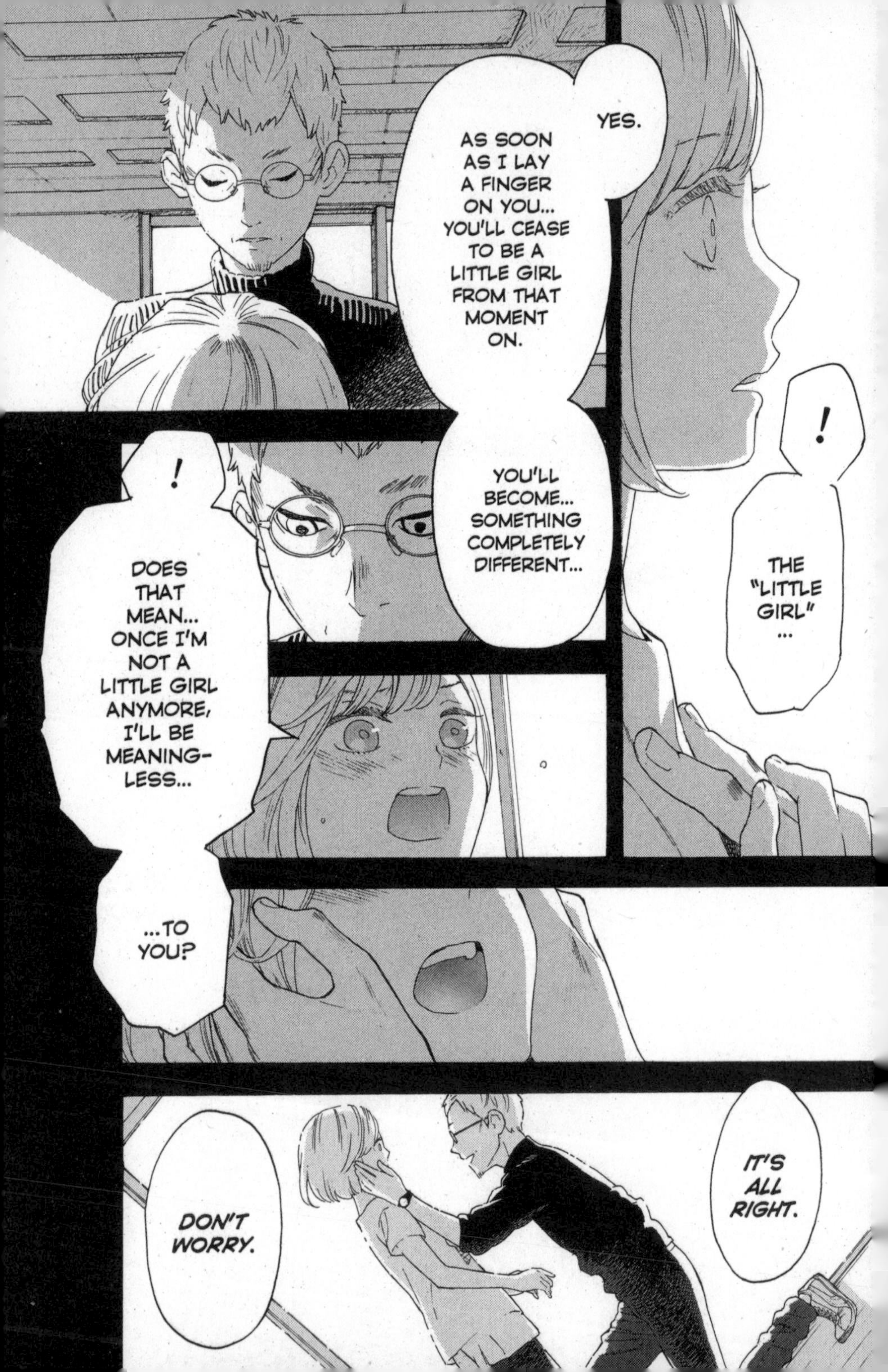
YES.
AS SOON AS I LAY A FINGER ON YOU... YOU'LL CEASE TO BE A LITTLE GIRL FROM THAT MOMENT ON.
YOU'LL BECOME... SOMETHING COMPLETELY DIFFERENT...
!
THE "LITTLE GIRL" ...
!
DOES THAT MEAN... ONCE I'M NOT A LITTLE GIRL ANYMORE, I'LL BE MEANINGLESS...
...TO YOU?
IT'S ALL RIGHT.
DON'T WORRY.

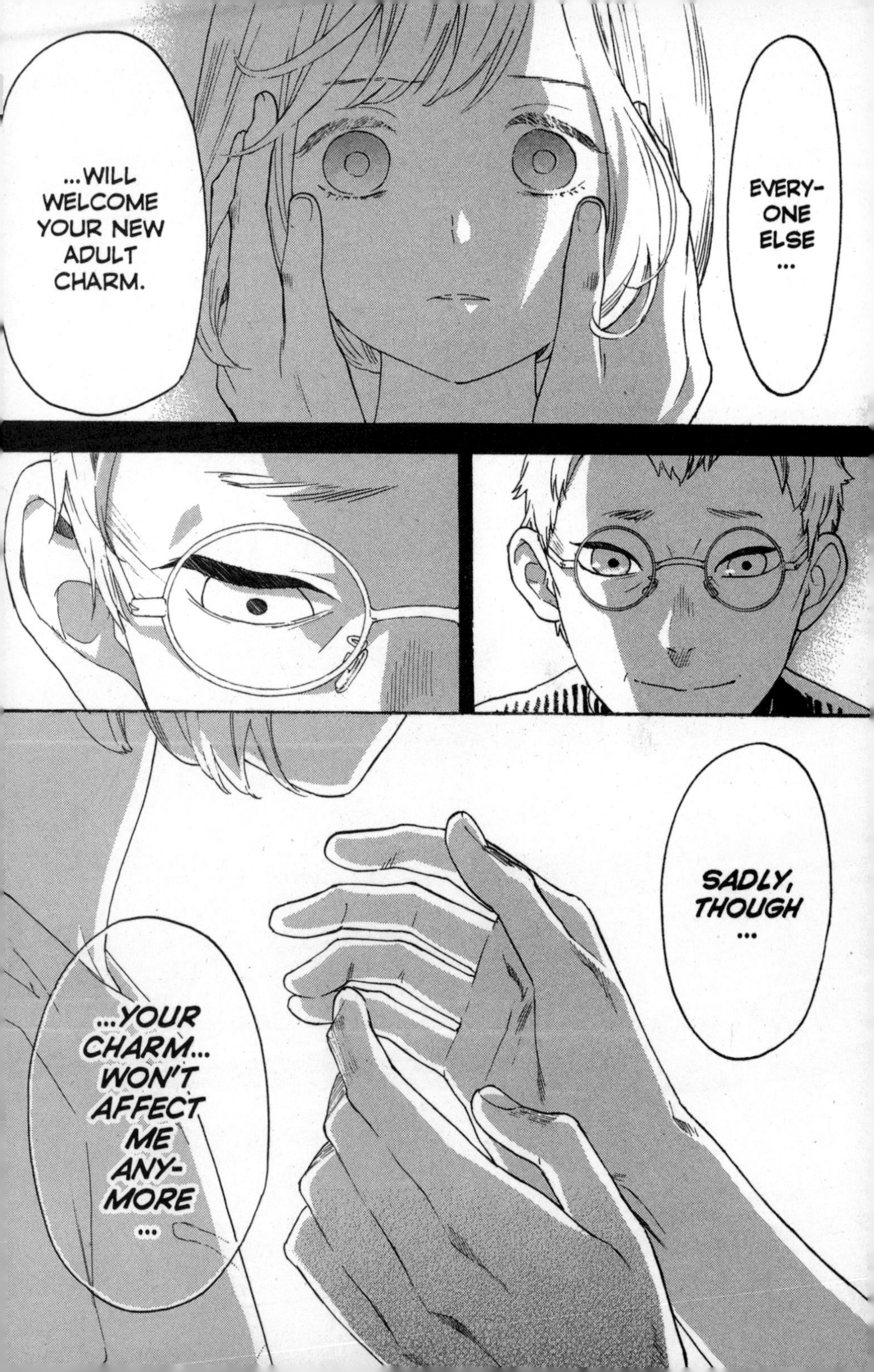
EVERY-ONE ELSE...
...WILL WELCOME YOUR NEW ADULT CHARM.
SADLY, THOUGH...
...YOUR CHARM... WON'T AFFECT ME ANYMORE...

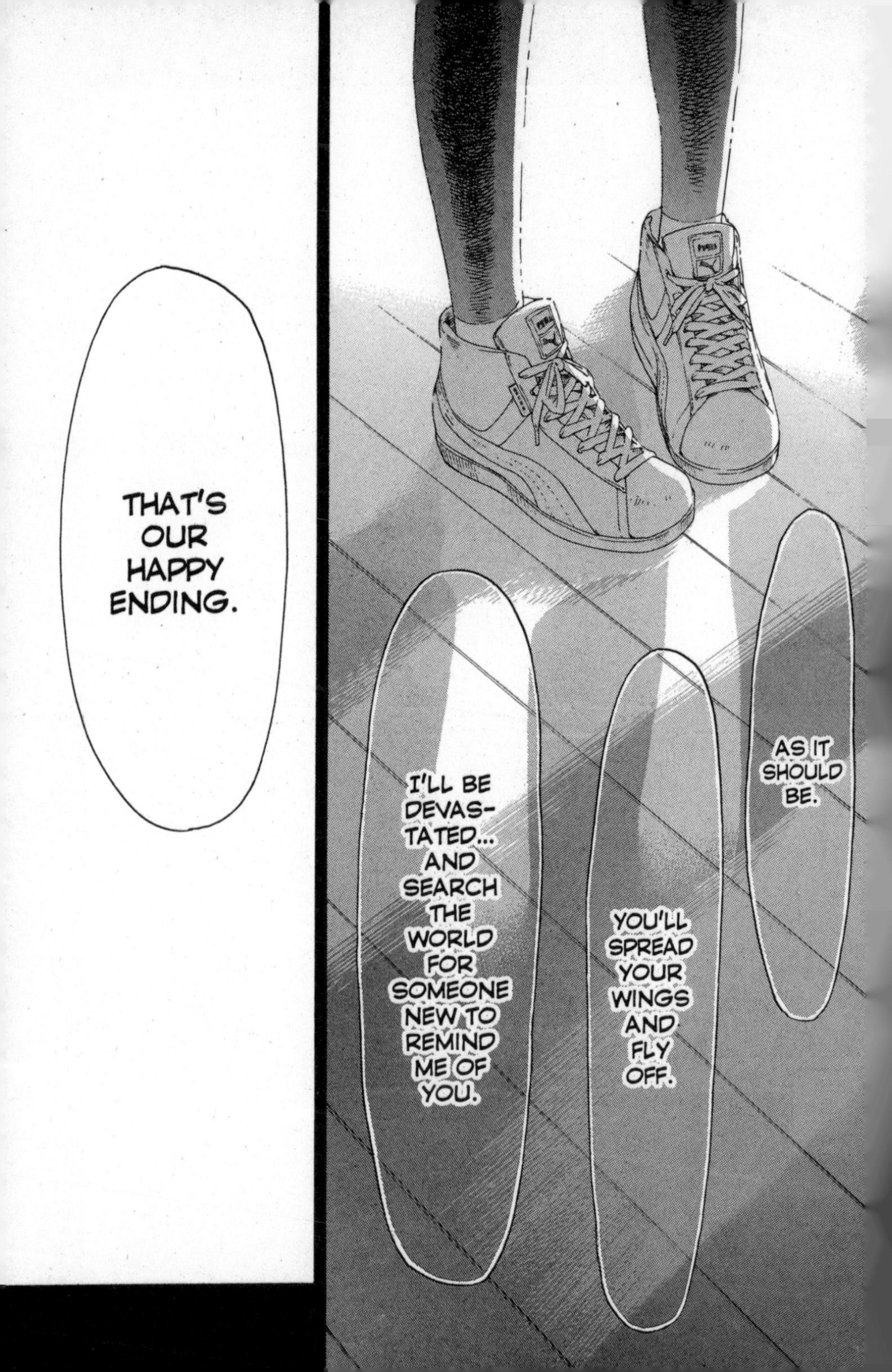
AS IT SHOULD BE.
YOU'LL SPREAD YOUR WINGS AND FLY OFF.
I'LL BE DEVASTATED... AND SEARCH THE WORLD FOR SOMEONE NEW TO REMIND ME OF YOU.
THAT'S OUR HAPPY ENDING.

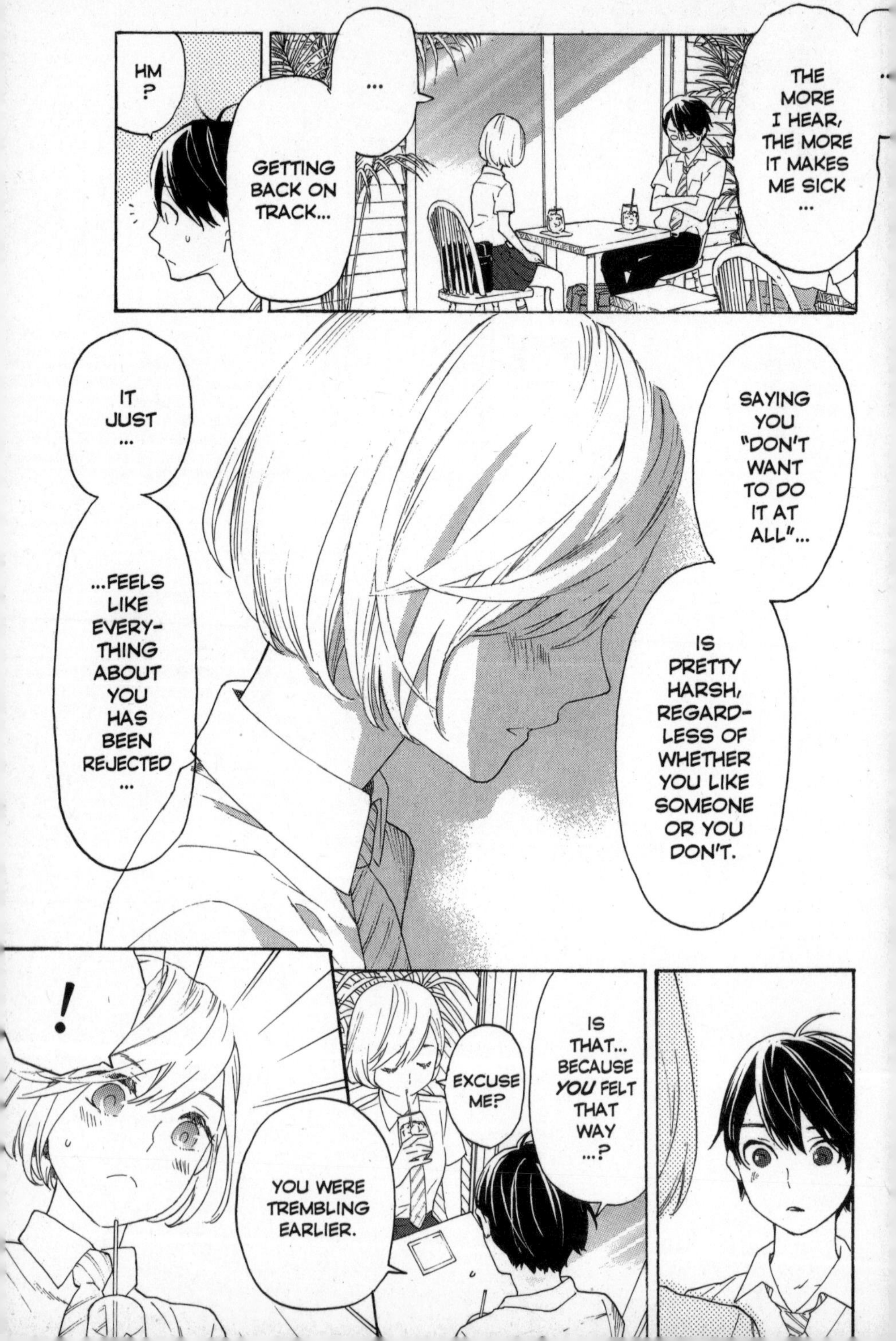
THE MORE I HEAR, THE MORE IT MAKES ME SICK ...
...
GETTING BACK ON TRACK...
HM?
SAYING YOU "DON'T WANT TO DO IT AT ALL"...
IS PRETTY HARSH, REGARDLESS OF WHETHER YOU LIKE SOMEONE OR YOU DON'T.
IT JUST ...
...FEELS LIKE EVERY-THING ABOUT YOU HAS BEEN REJECTED ...
IS THAT... BECAUSE *YOU* FELT THAT WAY ...?
EXCUSE ME?
YOU WERE TREMBLING EARLIER.
!

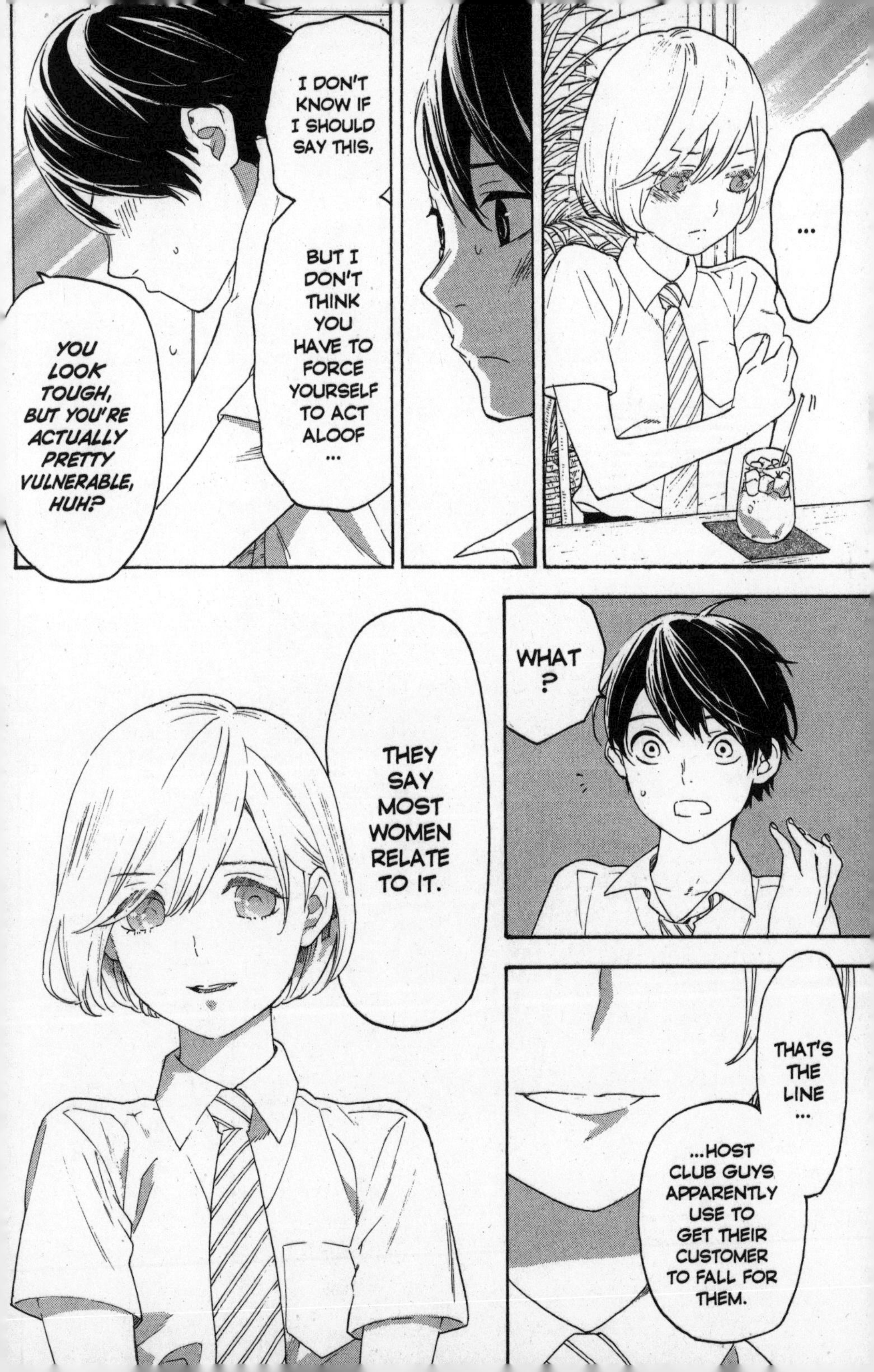
...
I DON'T KNOW IF I SHOULD SAY THIS,
BUT I DON'T THINK YOU HAVE TO FORCE YOURSELF TO ACT ALOOF...
YOU LOOK TOUGH, BUT YOU'RE ACTUALLY PRETTY VULNERABLE, HUH?
WHAT?
THAT'S THE LINE...
...HOST CLUB GUYS APPARENTLY USE TO GET THEIR CUSTOMER TO FALL FOR THEM.
THEY SAY MOST WOMEN RELATE TO IT.

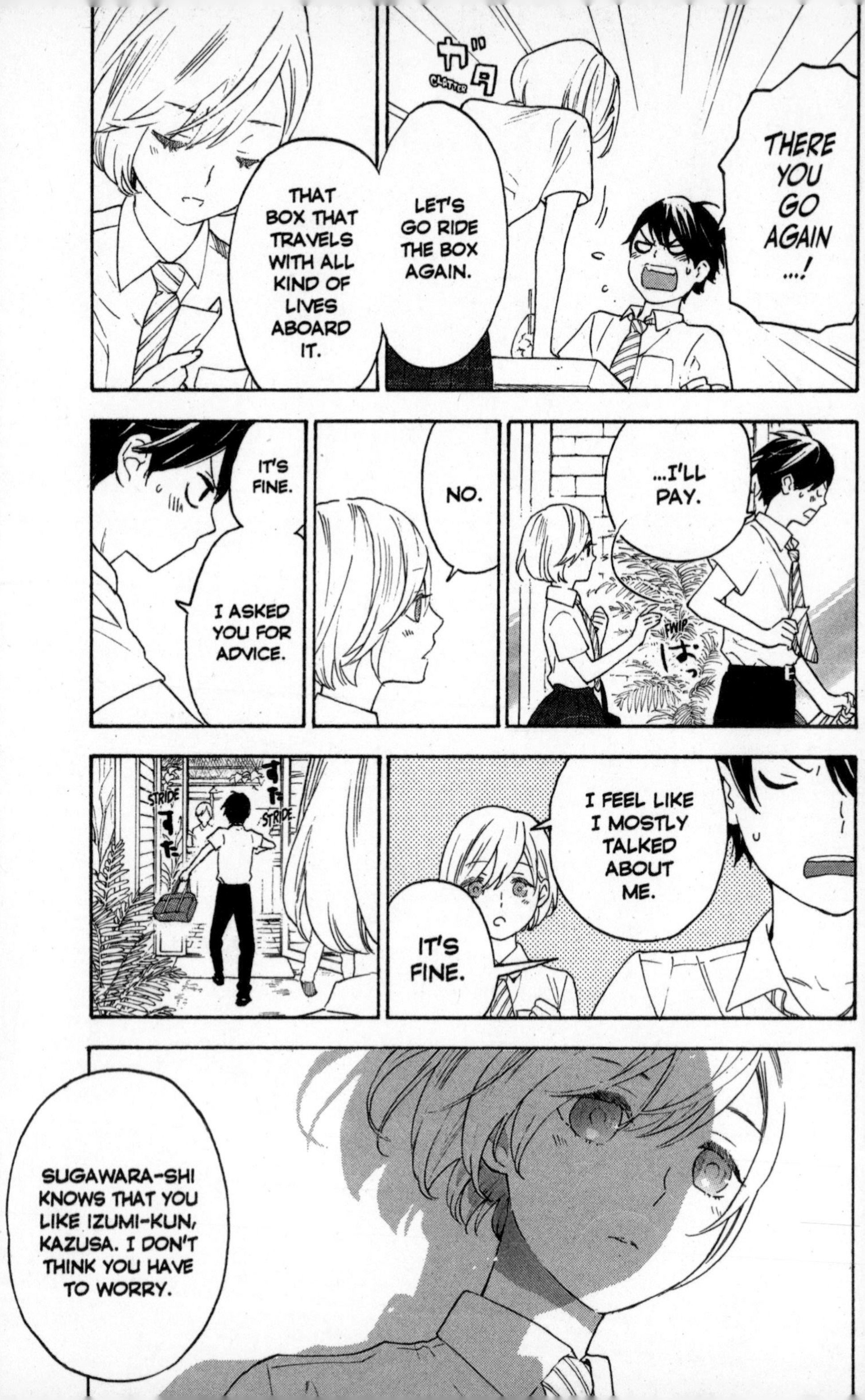
THERE YOU GO AGAIN ...!
CLATTER
LET'S GO RIDE THE BOX AGAIN.
THAT BOX THAT TRAVELS WITH ALL KIND OF LIVES ABOARD IT.
...I'LL PAY.
FWIP
NO.
IT'S FINE.
I ASKED YOU FOR ADVICE.
I FEEL LIKE I MOSTLY TALKED ABOUT ME.
IT'S FINE.
STRIDE
STRIDE
SUGAWARA-SHI KNOWS THAT YOU LIKE IZUMI-KUN, KAZUSA. I DON'T THINK YOU HAVE TO WORRY.

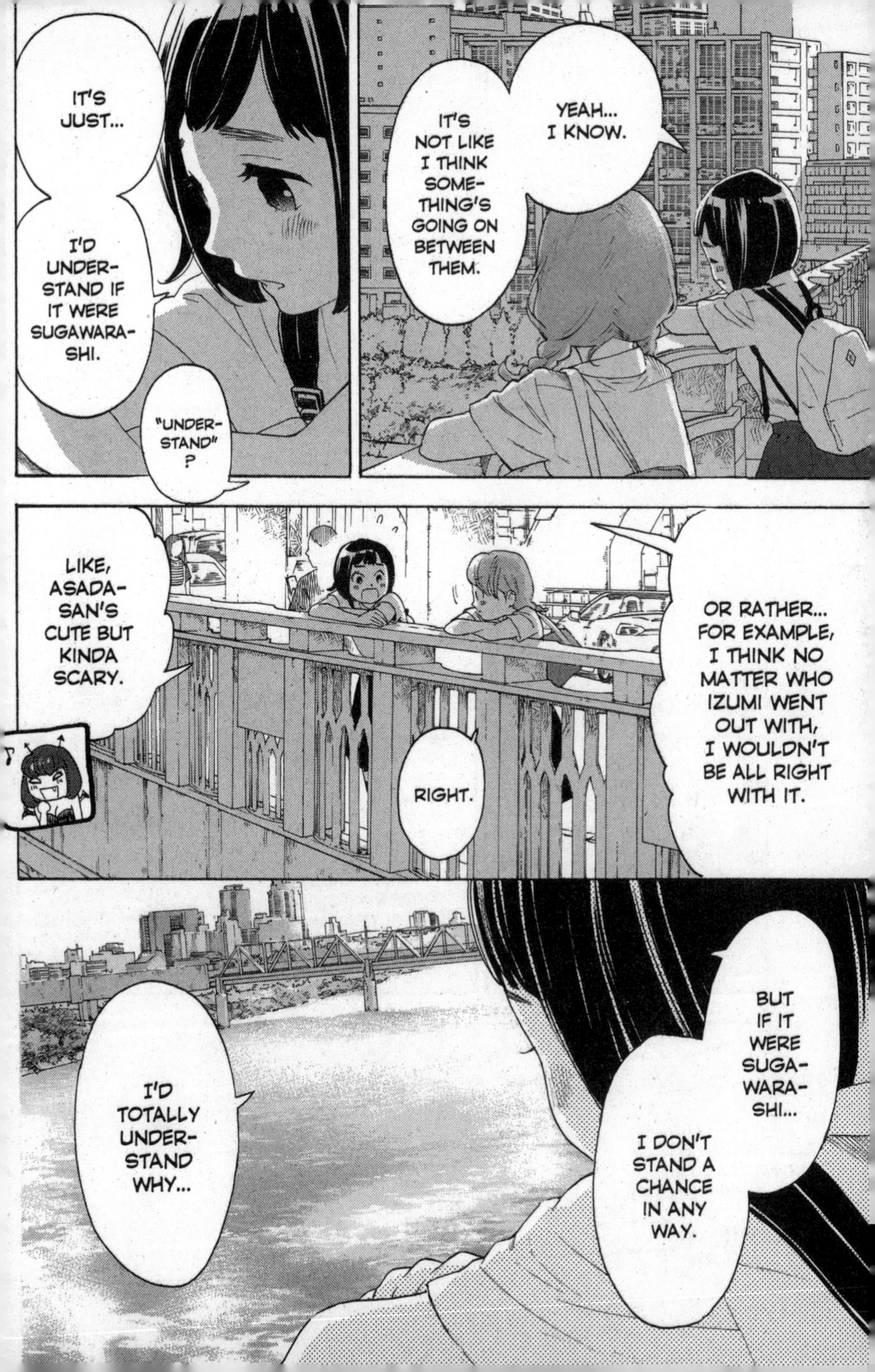
YEAH... I KNOW.
IT'S NOT LIKE I THINK SOMETHING'S GOING ON BETWEEN THEM.
IT'S JUST...
I'D UNDERSTAND IF IT WERE SUGAWARA-SHI.
"UNDERSTAND"?
OR RATHER... FOR EXAMPLE, I THINK NO MATTER WHO IZUMI WENT OUT WITH, I WOULDN'T BE ALL RIGHT WITH IT.
RIGHT.
LIKE, ASADA-SAN'S CUTE BUT KINDA SCARY.
BUT IF IT WERE SUGAWARA-SHI...
I DON'T STAND A CHANCE IN ANY WAY.
I'D TOTALLY UNDERSTAND WHY...

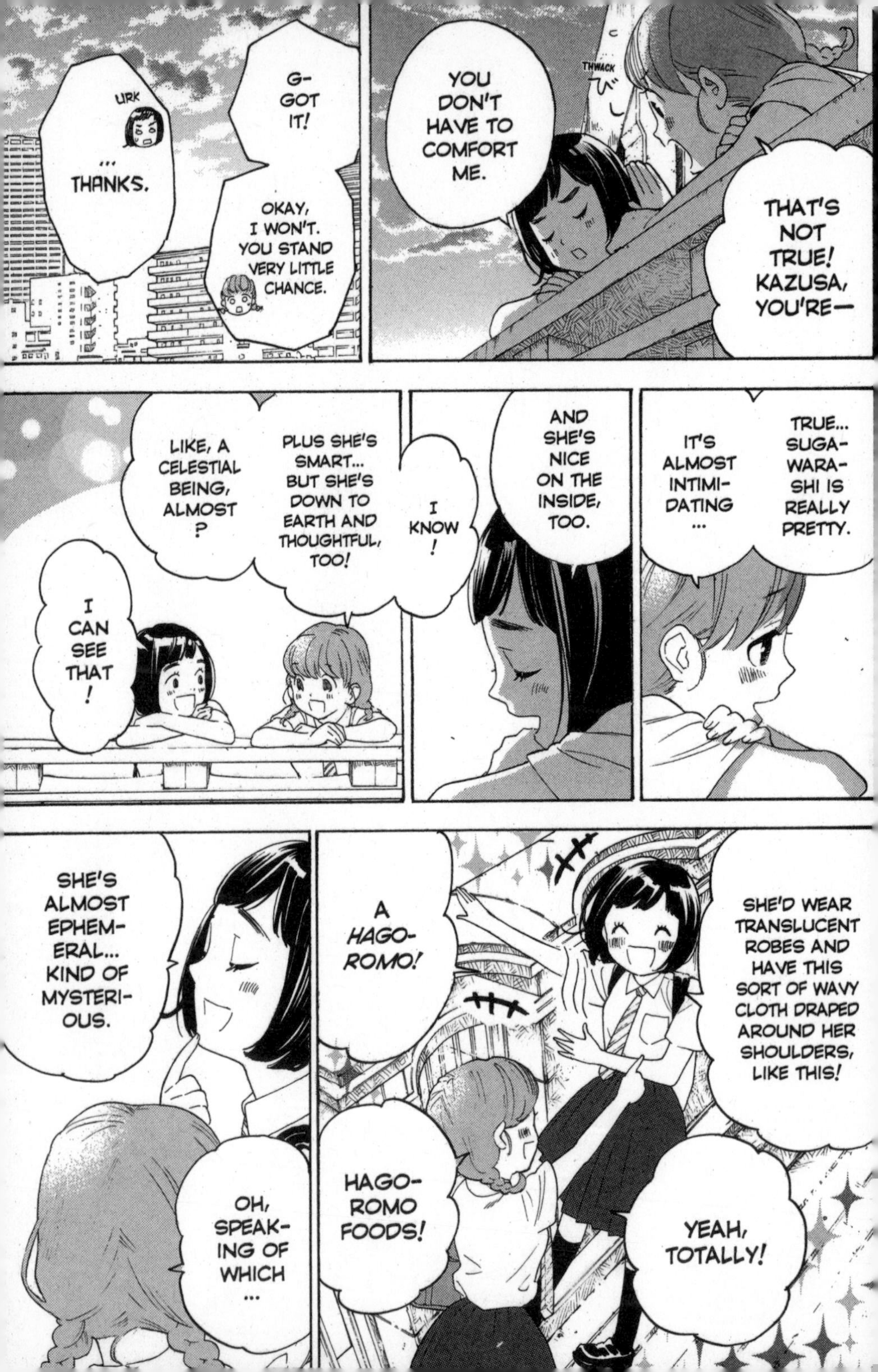
THAT'S NOT TRUE! KAZUSA, YOU'RE—
THWACK
YOU DON'T HAVE TO COMFORT ME.
G-GOT IT!
OKAY, I WON'T. YOU STAND VERY LITTLE CHANCE.
URK
... THANKS.
TRUE... SUGAWARASHI IS REALLY PRETTY.
IT'S ALMOST INTIMIDATING...
AND SHE'S NICE ON THE INSIDE, TOO.
I KNOW!
PLUS SHE'S SMART... BUT SHE'S DOWN TO EARTH AND THOUGHTFUL, TOO!
LIKE, A CELESTIAL BEING, ALMOST?
I CAN SEE THAT!
SHE'D WEAR TRANSLUCENT ROBES AND HAVE THIS SORT OF WAVY CLOTH DRAPED AROUND HER SHOULDERS, LIKE THIS!
A *HAGOROMO*!
YEAH, TOTALLY!
HAGOROMO FOODS!
SHE'S ALMOST EPHEMERAL... KIND OF MYSTERIOUS.
OH, SPEAKING OF WHICH...

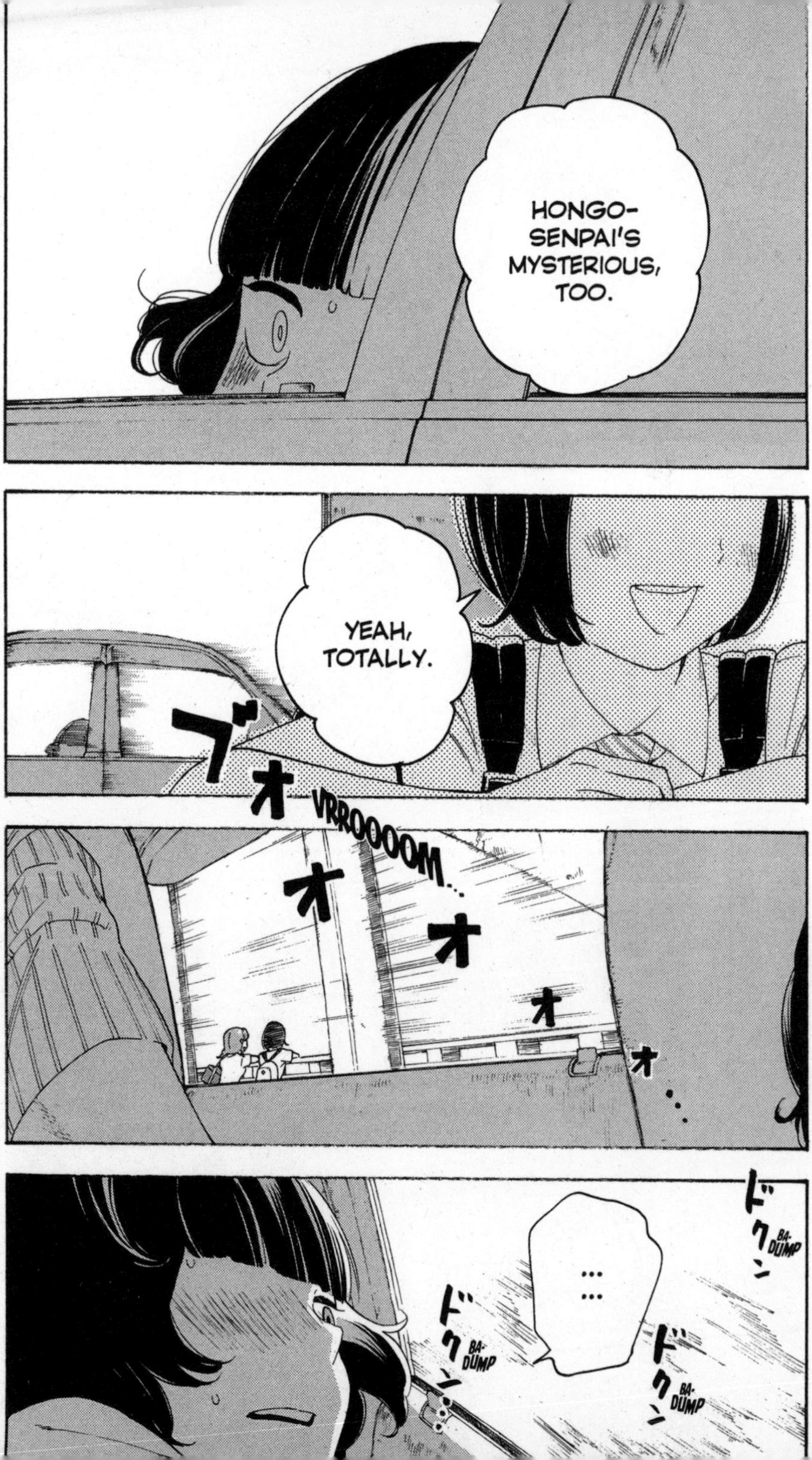
HONGO-SENPAI'S MYSTERIOUS, TOO.
YEAH, TOTALLY.
ブオ
VRROOOOM...
オオオオ...
ドクン
BA-DUMP
......
ドクン
BA-DUMP
ドクン
BA-DUMP

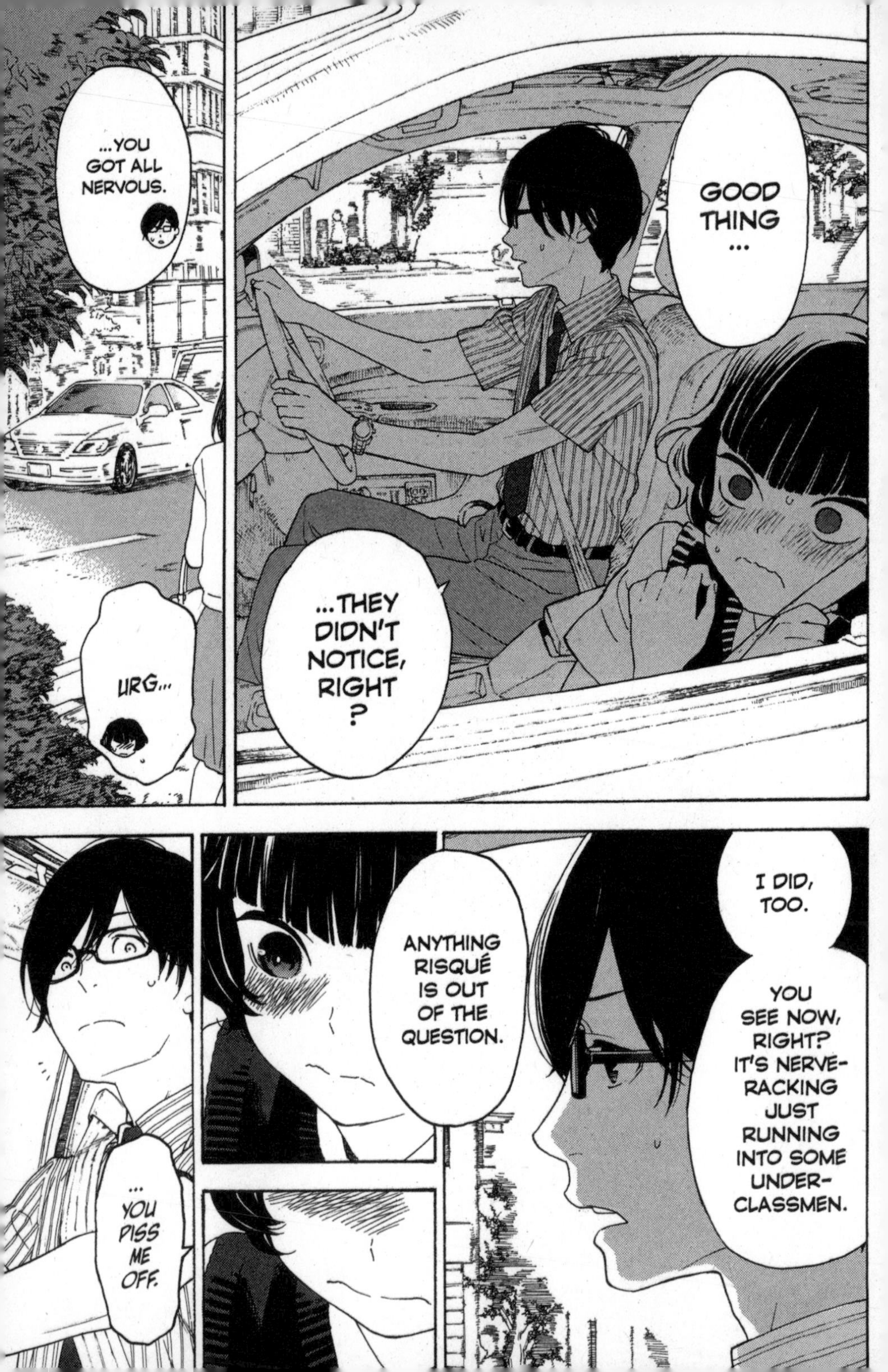
GOOD THING ...
...THEY DIDN'T NOTICE, RIGHT?
...YOU GOT ALL NERVOUS.
URG...
I DID, TOO.
YOU SEE NOW, RIGHT? IT'S NERVE-RACKING JUST RUNNING INTO SOME UNDER-CLASSMEN.
ANYTHING RISQUÉ IS OUT OF THE QUESTION.
... YOU PISS ME OFF.

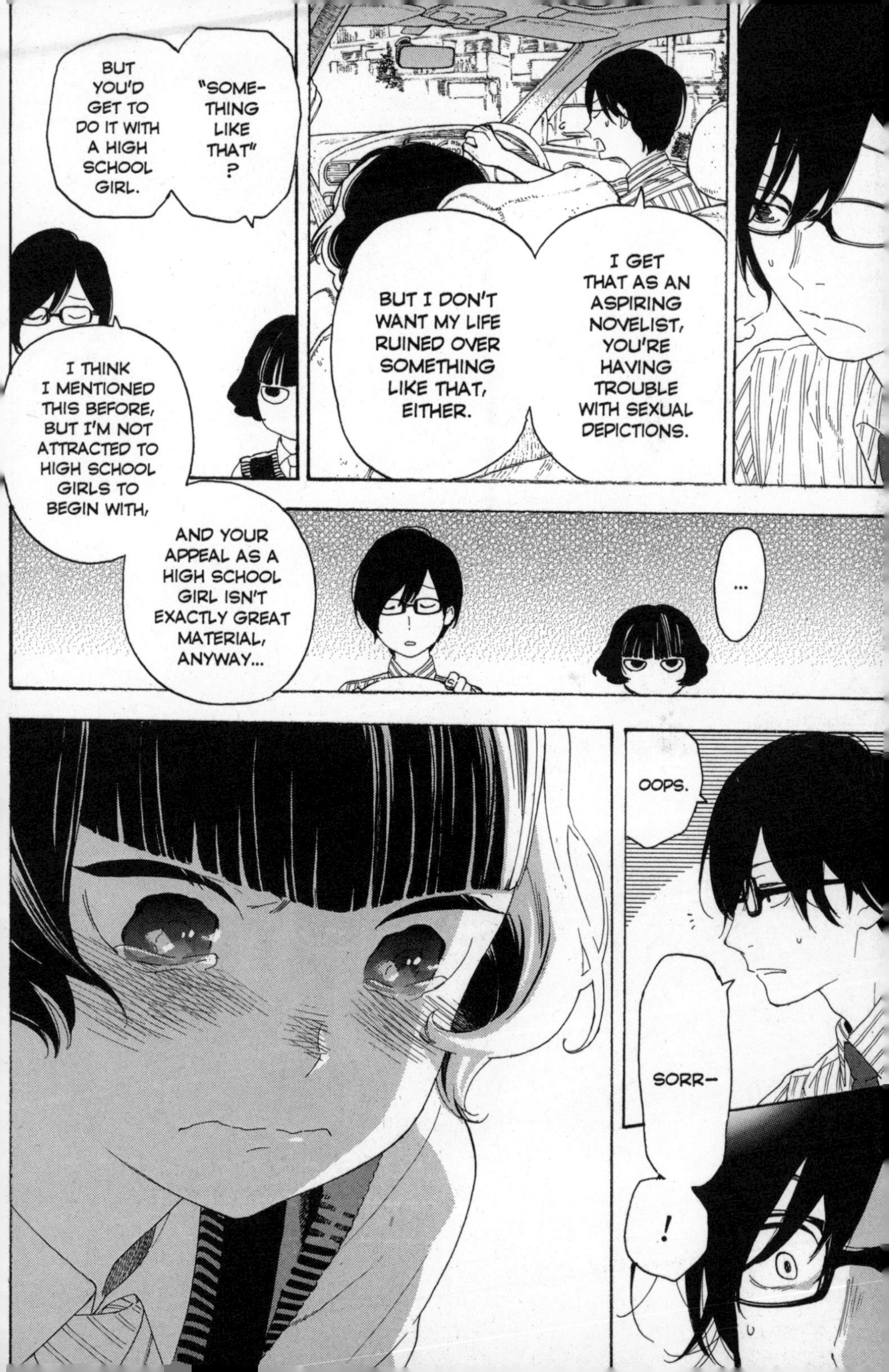
I GET THAT AS AN ASPIRING NOVELIST, YOU'RE HAVING TROUBLE WITH SEXUAL DEPICTIONS.
BUT I DON'T WANT MY LIFE RUINED OVER SOMETHING LIKE THAT, EITHER.
"SOMETHING LIKE THAT"?
BUT YOU'D GET TO DO IT WITH A HIGH SCHOOL GIRL.
I THINK I MENTIONED THIS BEFORE, BUT I'M NOT ATTRACTED TO HIGH SCHOOL GIRLS TO BEGIN WITH,
AND YOUR APPEAL AS A HIGH SCHOOL GIRL ISN'T EXACTLY GREAT MATERIAL, ANYWAY...
...
OOPS.
SORR-
!

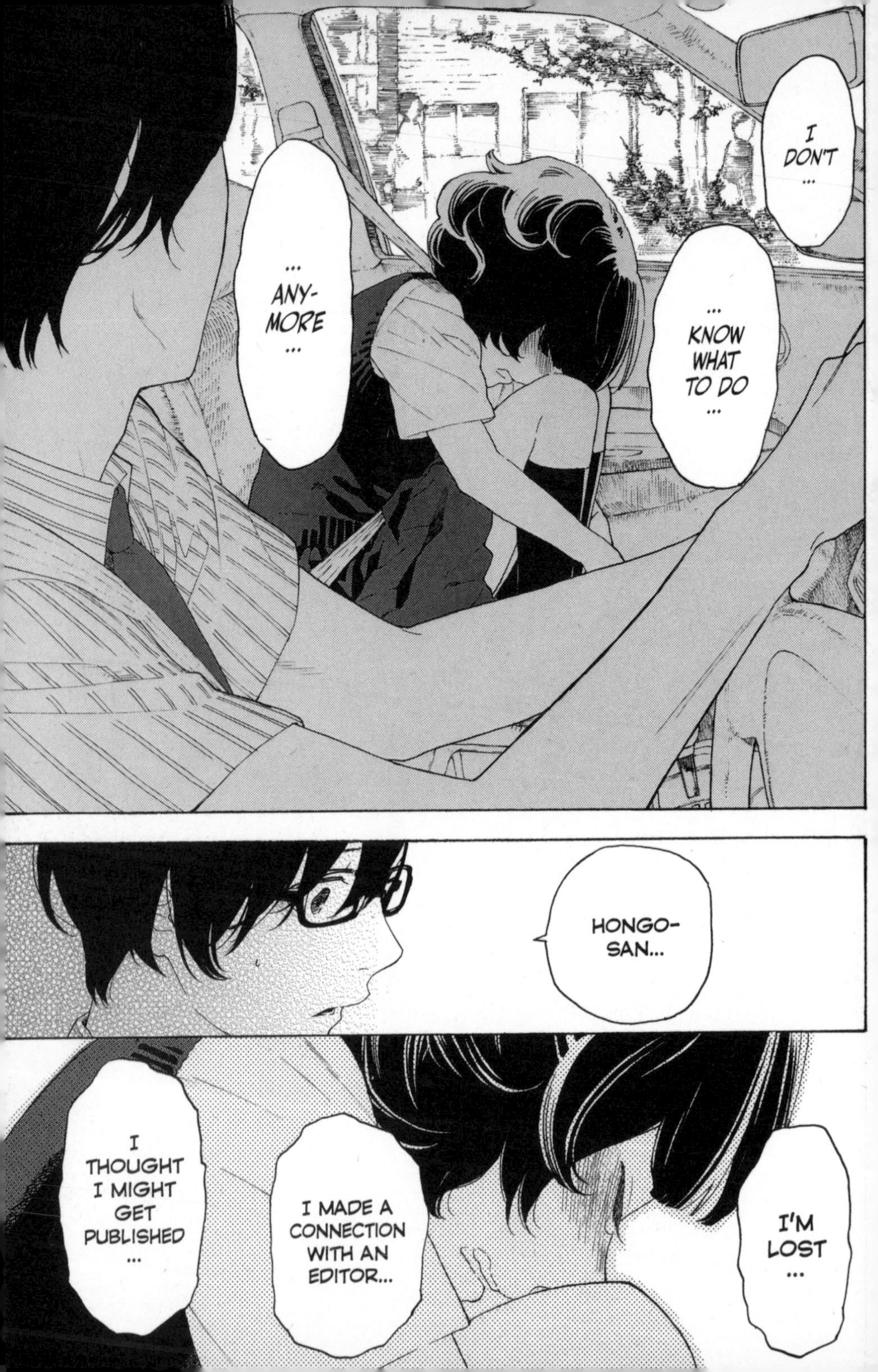
I DON'T ...
... KNOW WHAT TO DO ...
... ANY-MORE ...
HONGO-SAN...
I'M LOST ...
I MADE A CONNECTION WITH AN EDITOR...
I THOUGHT I MIGHT GET PUBLISHED ...

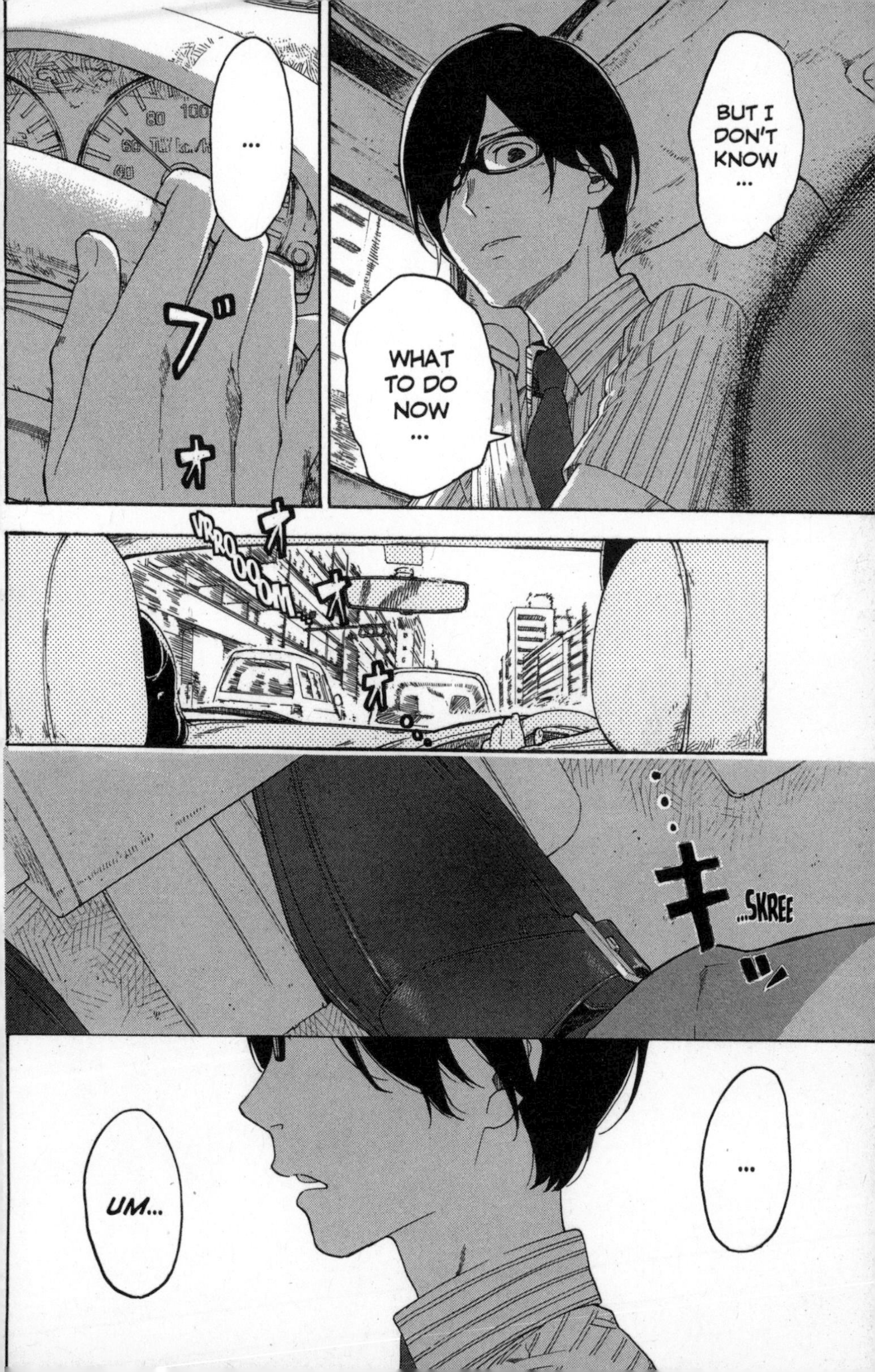
BUT I DON'T KNOW ...
WHAT TO DO NOW ...
...
ブ
オ
オ
VRROOOOM...
オ
オ
キッ
...SKREE
...
UM...

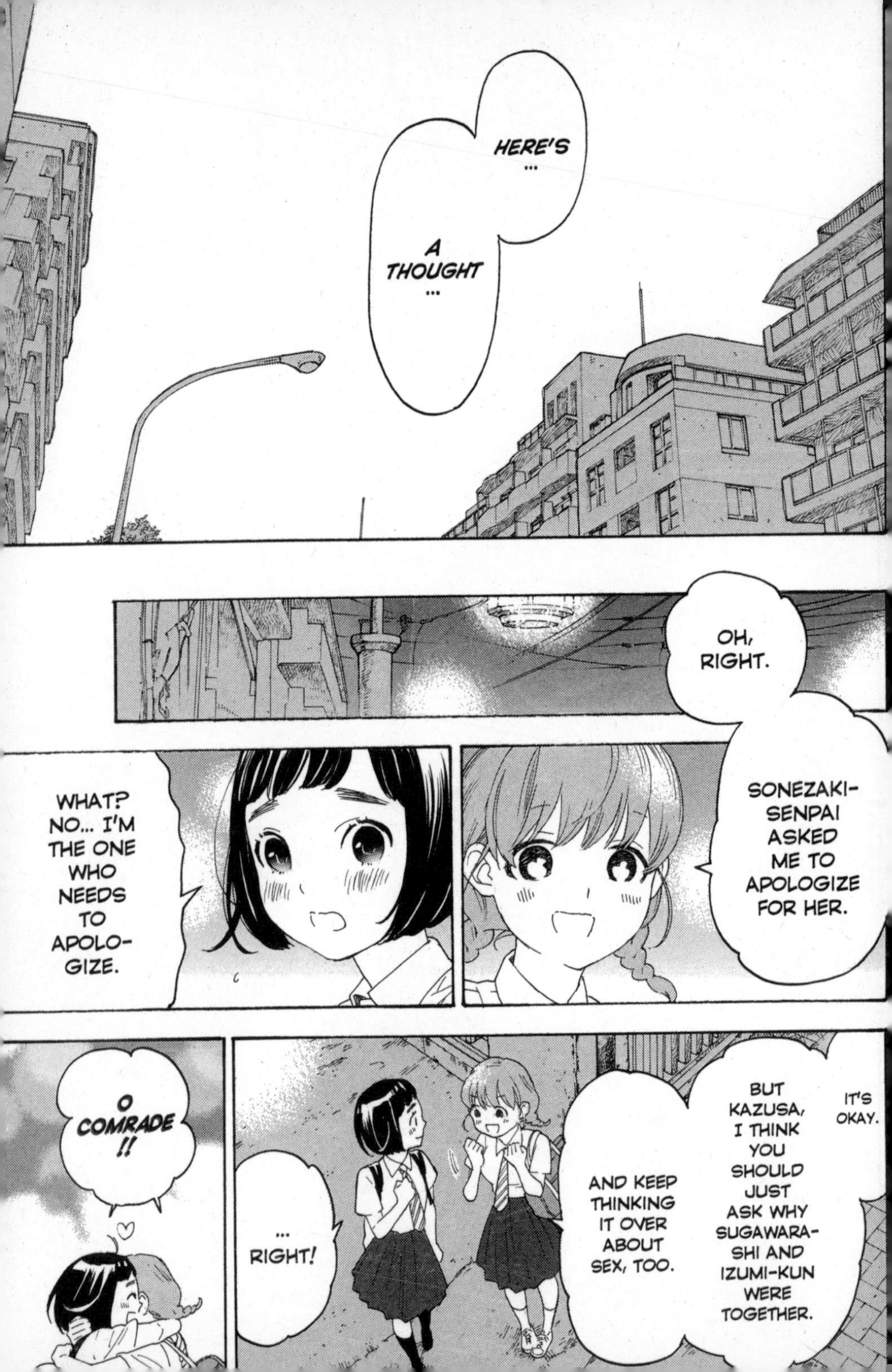
HERE'S...
A THOUGHT...
OH, RIGHT.
SONEZAKI-SENPAI ASKED ME TO APOLOGIZE FOR HER.
WHAT? NO... I'M THE ONE WHO NEEDS TO APOLOGIZE.
IT'S OKAY.
BUT KAZUSA, I THINK YOU SHOULD JUST ASK WHY SUGAWARA-SHI AND IZUMI-KUN WERE TOGETHER.
AND KEEP THINKING IT OVER ABOUT SEX, TOO.
...RIGHT!
O COMRADE!!

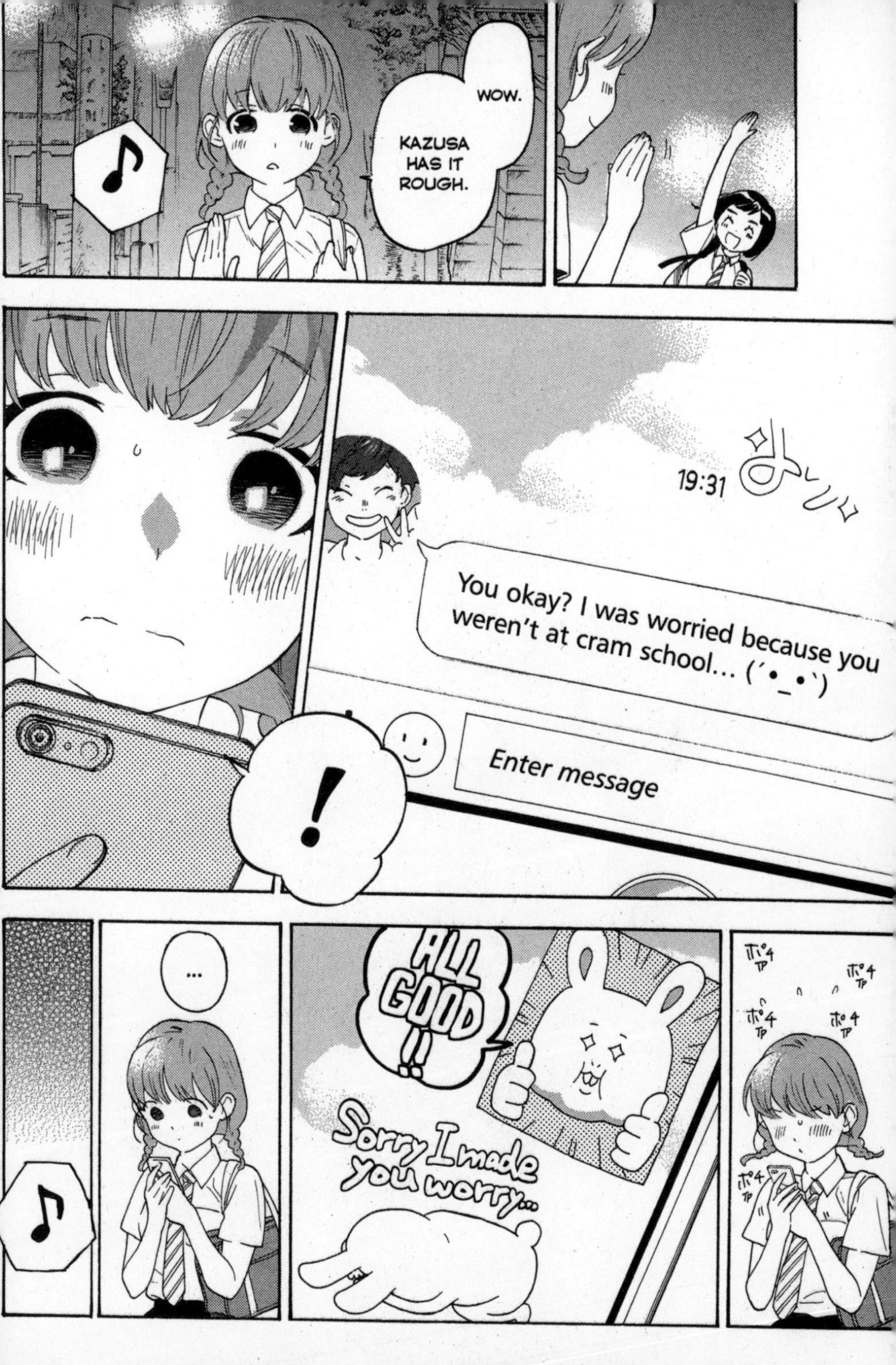
WOW.
KAZUSA HAS IT ROUGH.
♪
19:31
You okay? I was worried because you weren't at cram school... (´•_•`)
Enter message
!
ALL GOOD!!
Sorry I made you worry...
...
♪

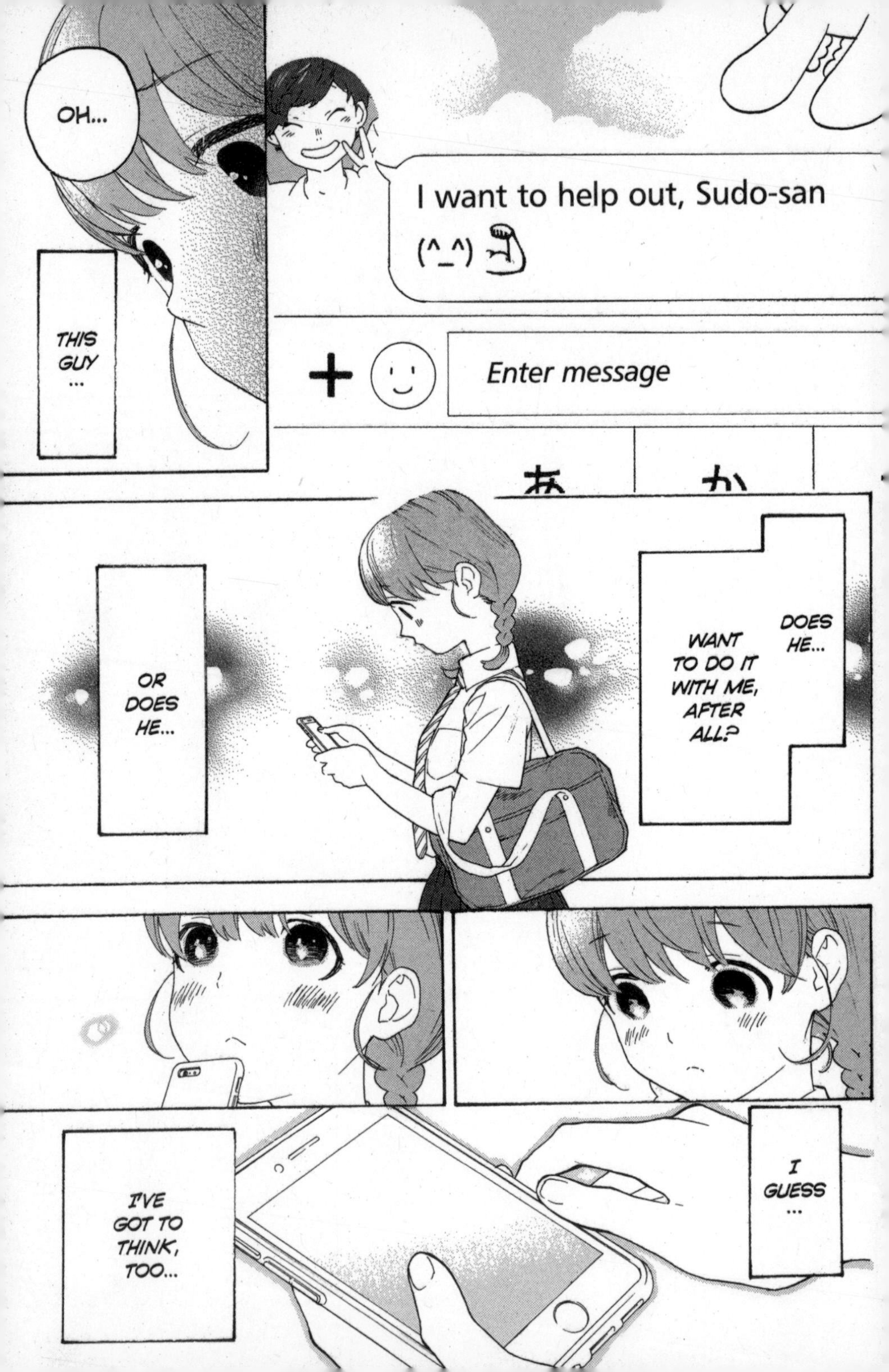
I want to help out, Sudo-san (^_^)
Enter message
あ
か
OH...
THIS GUY ...
DOES HE... WANT TO DO IT WITH ME, AFTER ALL?
OR DOES HE...
I GUESS ...
I'VE GOT TO THINK, TOO...

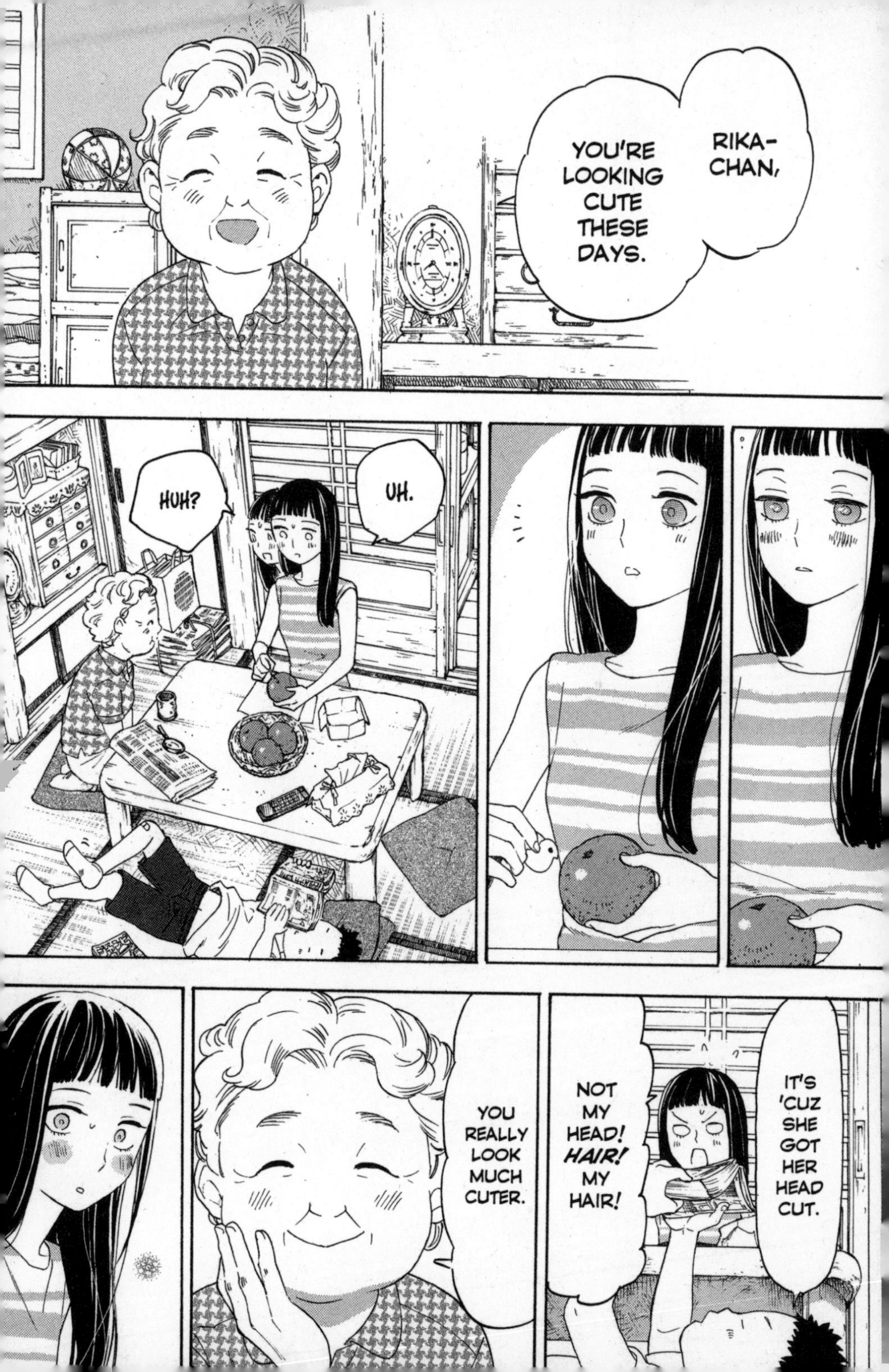
RIKA-CHAN,
YOU'RE LOOKING CUTE THESE DAYS.
UH.
HUH?
IT'S 'CUZ SHE GOT HER HEAD CUT.
NOT MY HEAD! *HAIR!* MY HAIR!
YOU REALLY LOOK MUCH CUTER.

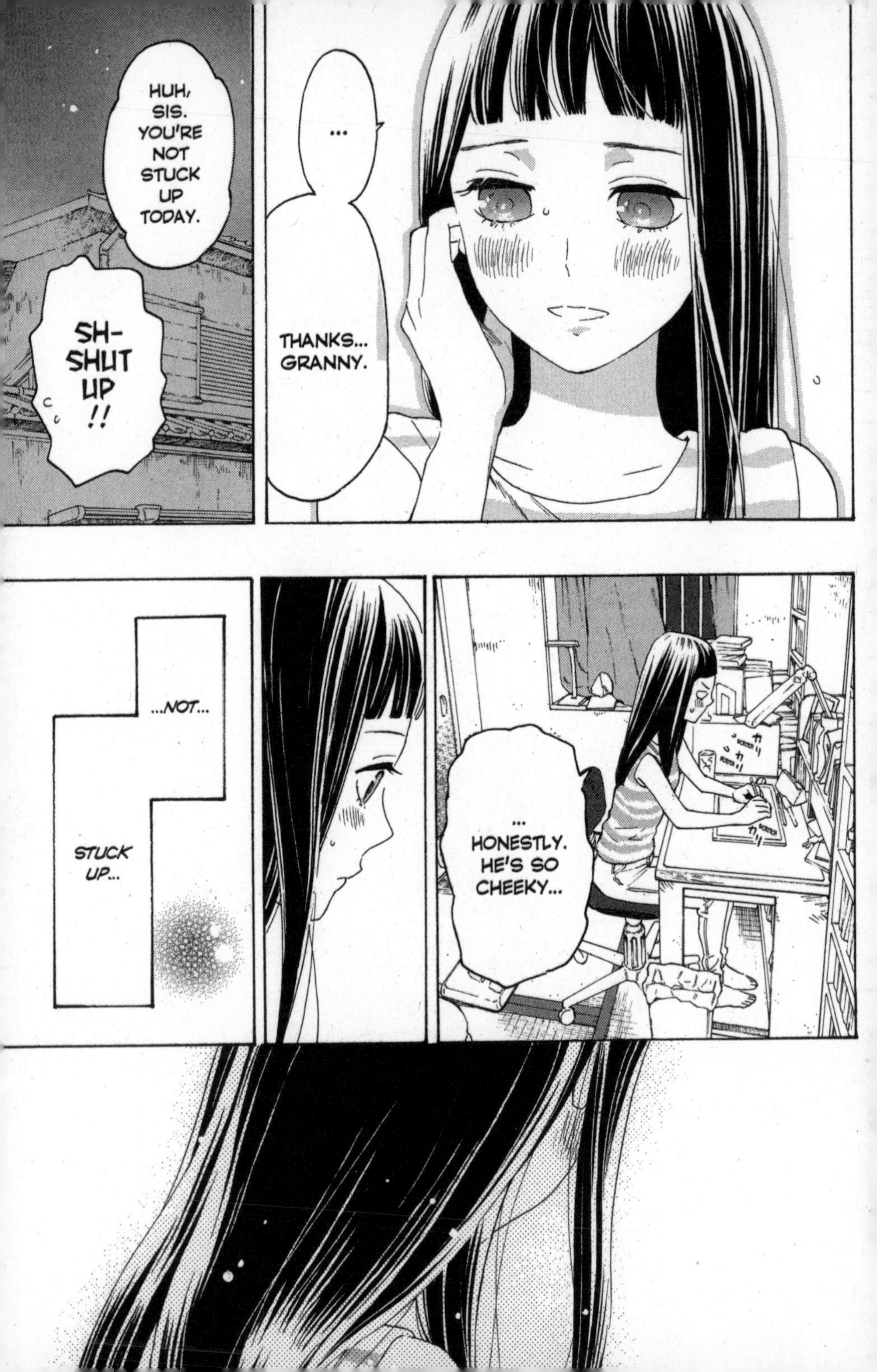
...
THANKS... GRANNY.
HUH, SIS. YOU'RE NOT STUCK UP TODAY.
SH-SHUT UP!!
... HONESTLY. HE'S SO CHEEKY...
...NOT...
STUCK UP...

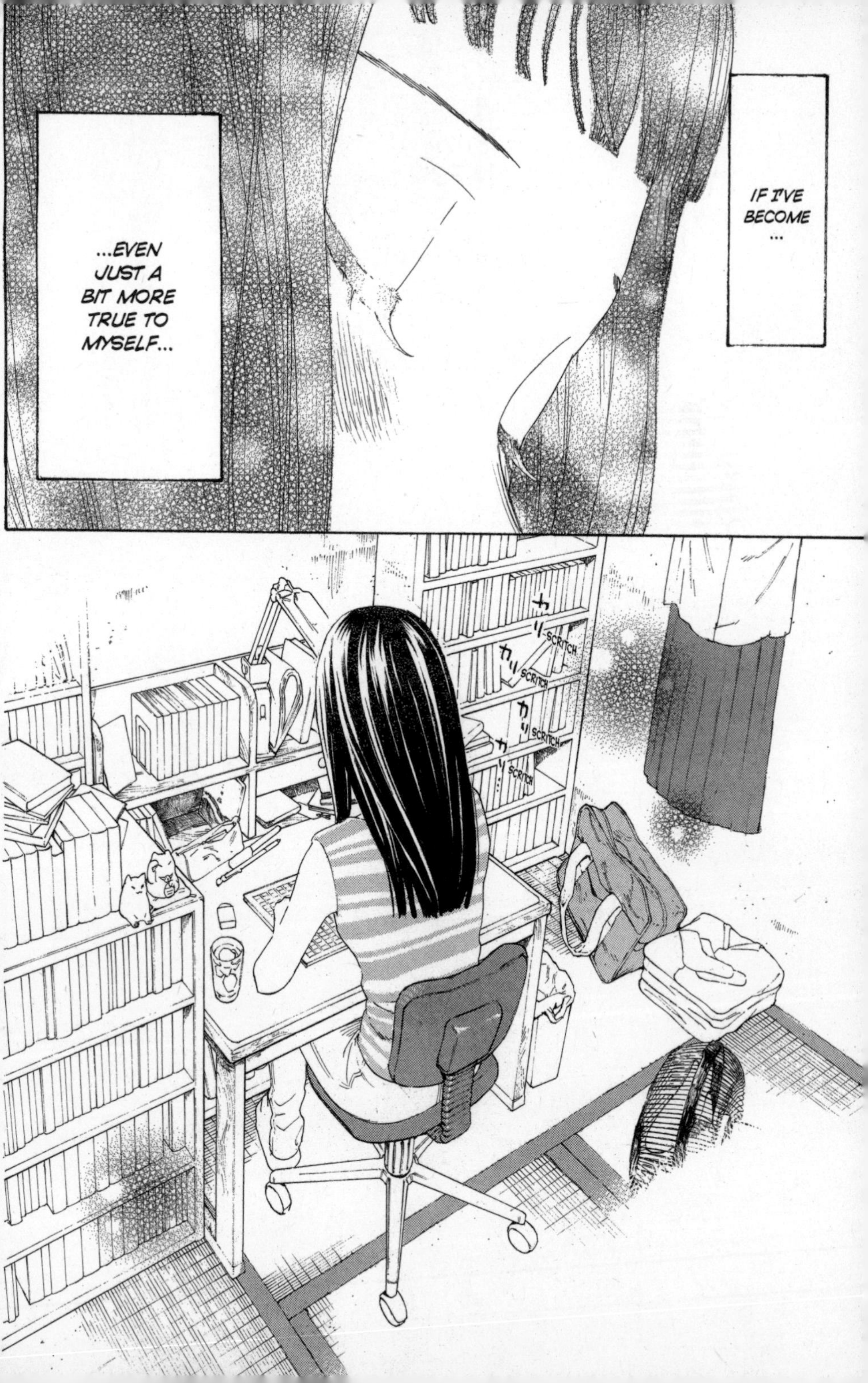
IF I'VE BECOME ...
...EVEN JUST A BIT MORE TRUE TO MYSELF...
SCRITCH
SCRITCH
SCRITCH
SCRITCH

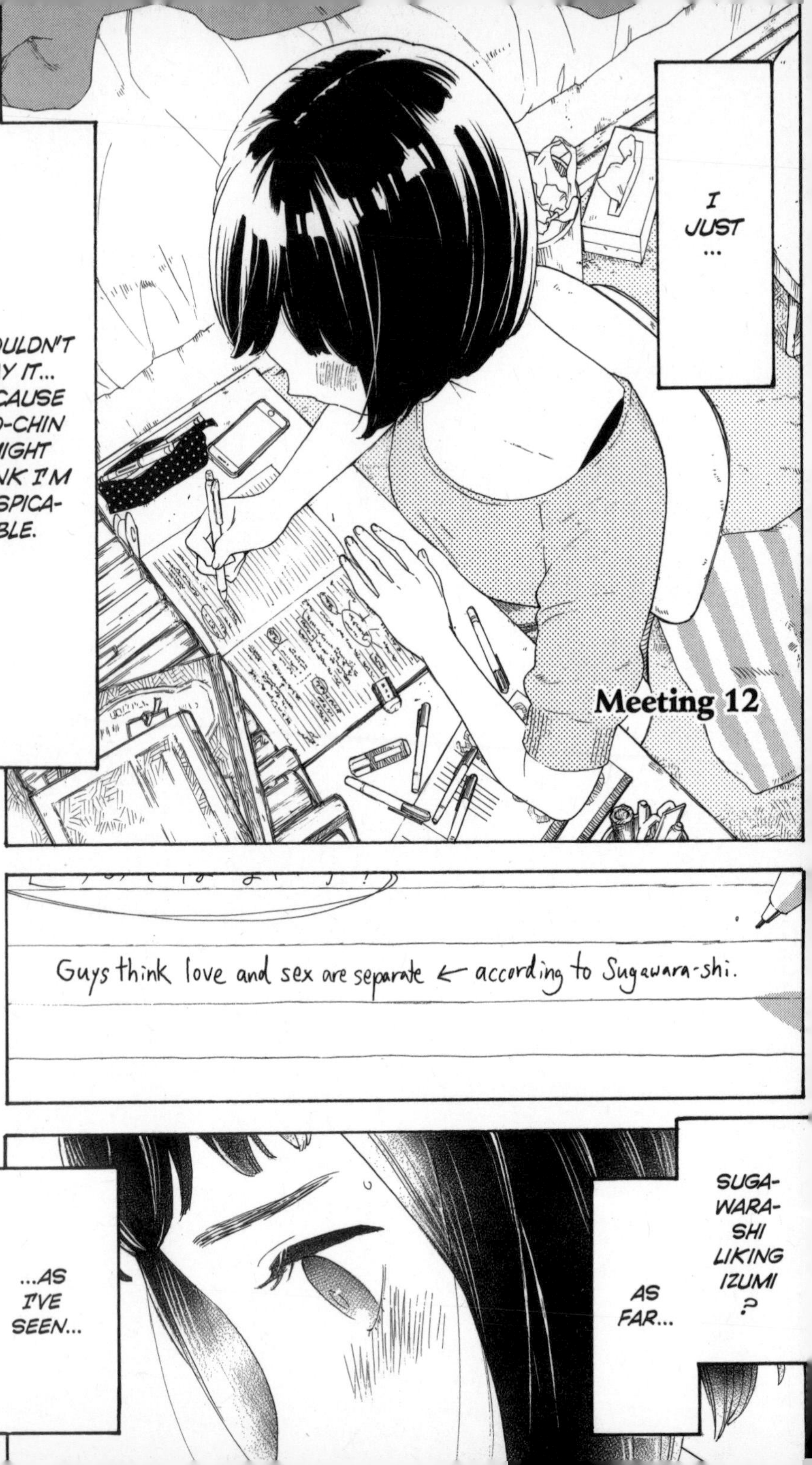
I JUST...
...COULDN'T SAY IT... BECAUSE MO-CHIN MIGHT THINK I'M DESPICABLE.
Meeting 12
Guys think love and sex are separate ← according to Sugawara-shi.
SUGAWARA-SHI LIKING IZUMI?
AS FAR...
...AS I'VE SEEN...

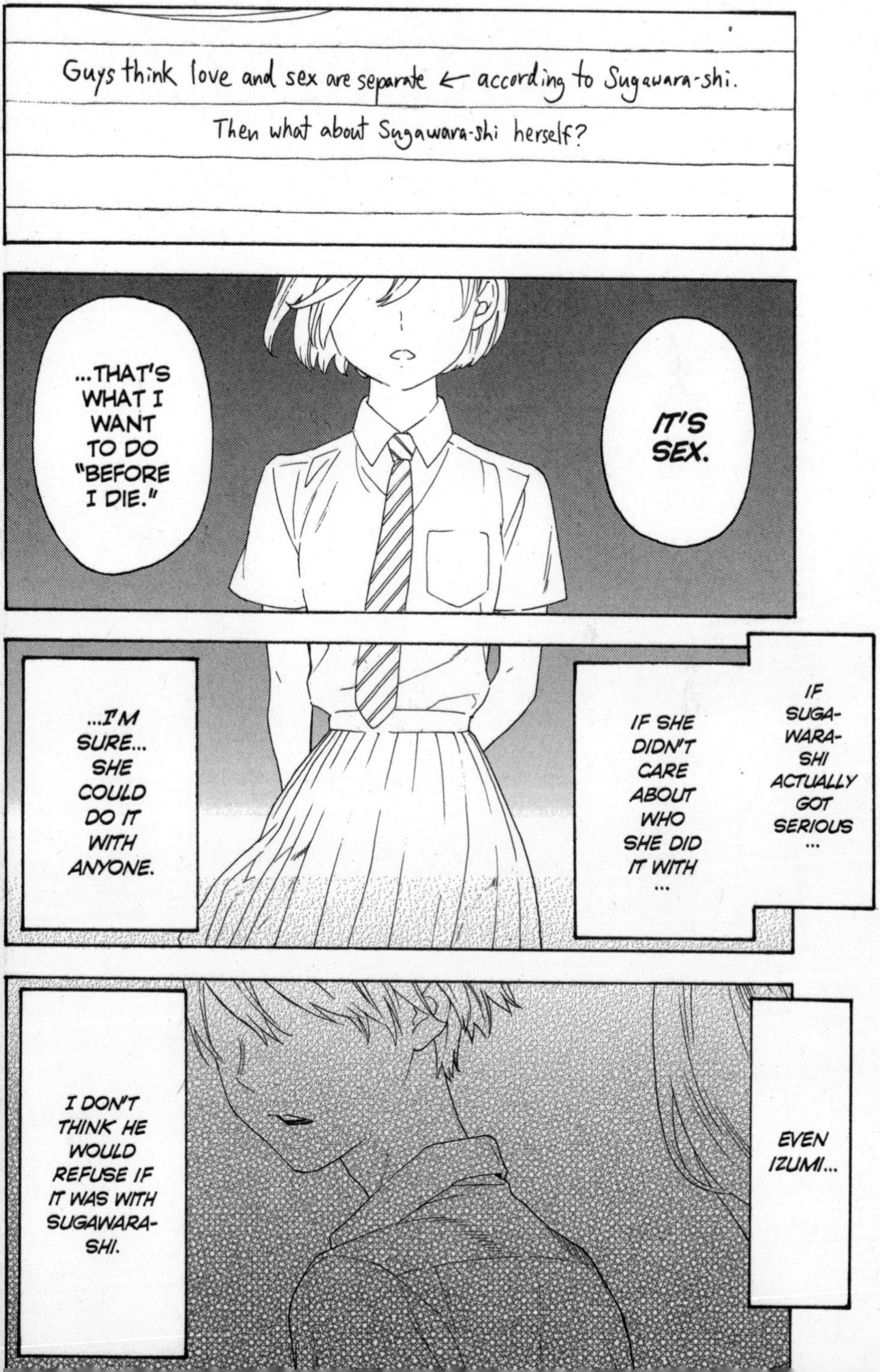
Guys think love and sex are separate ← according to Sugawara-shi.
Then what about Sugawara-shi herself?
IT'S SEX.
...THAT'S WHAT I WANT TO DO "BEFORE I DIE."
IF SUGA-WARA-SHI ACTUALLY GOT SERIOUS...
IF SHE DIDN'T CARE ABOUT WHO SHE DID IT WITH...
...I'M SURE... SHE COULD DO IT WITH ANYONE.
EVEN IZUMI...
I DON'T THINK HE WOULD REFUSE IF IT WAS WITH SUGAWARA-SHI.

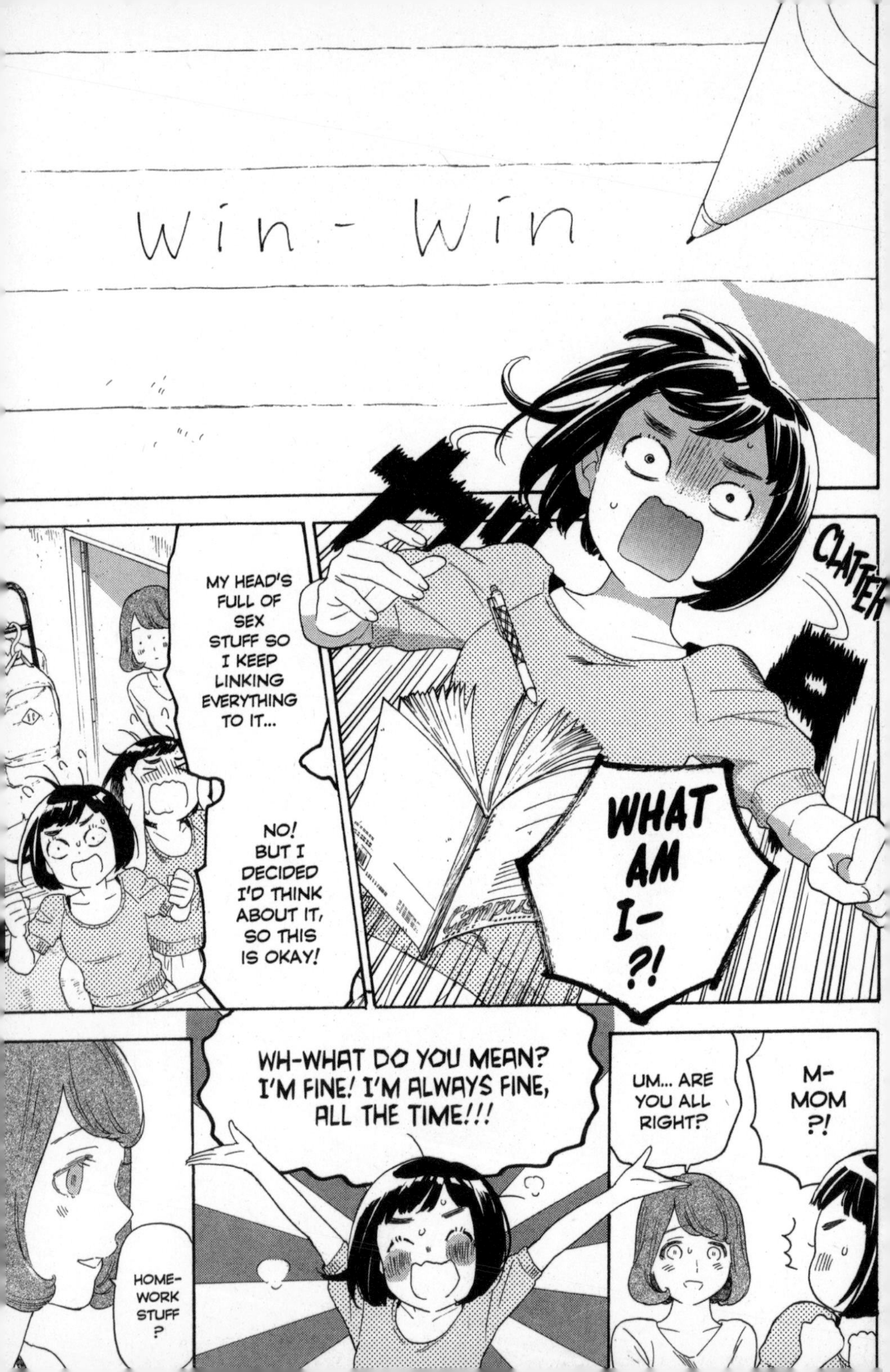
win-win
CLATTER
WHAT AM I-?!
MY HEAD'S FULL OF SEX STUFF SO I KEEP LINKING EVERYTHING TO IT...
NO! BUT I DECIDED I'D THINK ABOUT IT, SO THIS IS OKAY!
M-MOM?!
UM... ARE YOU ALL RIGHT?
WH-WHAT DO YOU MEAN? I'M FINE! I'M ALWAYS FINE, ALL THE TIME!!!
HOME-WORK STUFF?

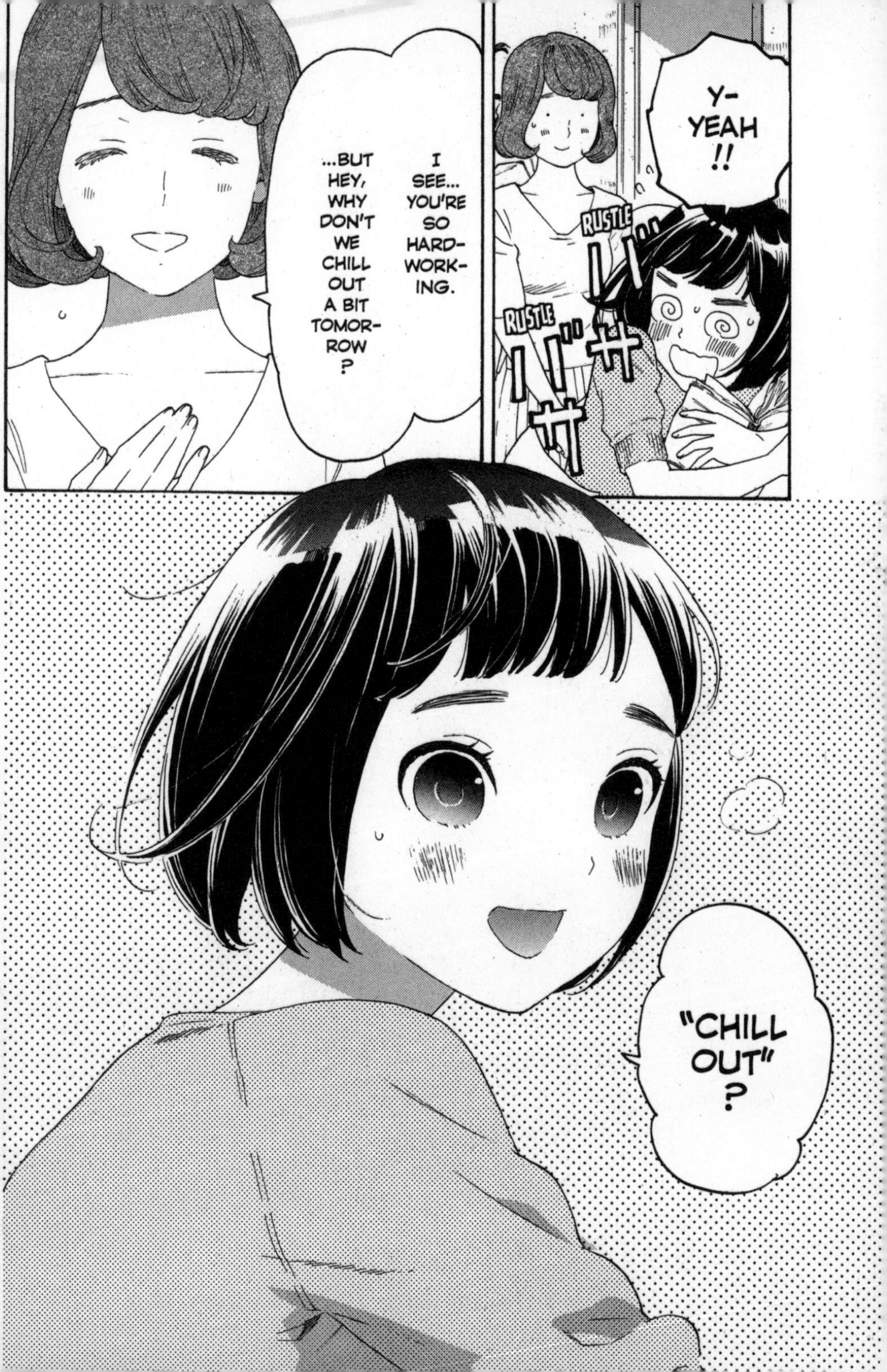
Y-YEAH!!
RUSTLE
RUSTLE
I SEE... YOU'RE SO HARD-WORKING.
...BUT HEY, WHY DON'T WE CHILL OUT A BIT TOMORROW?
"CHILL OUT"?

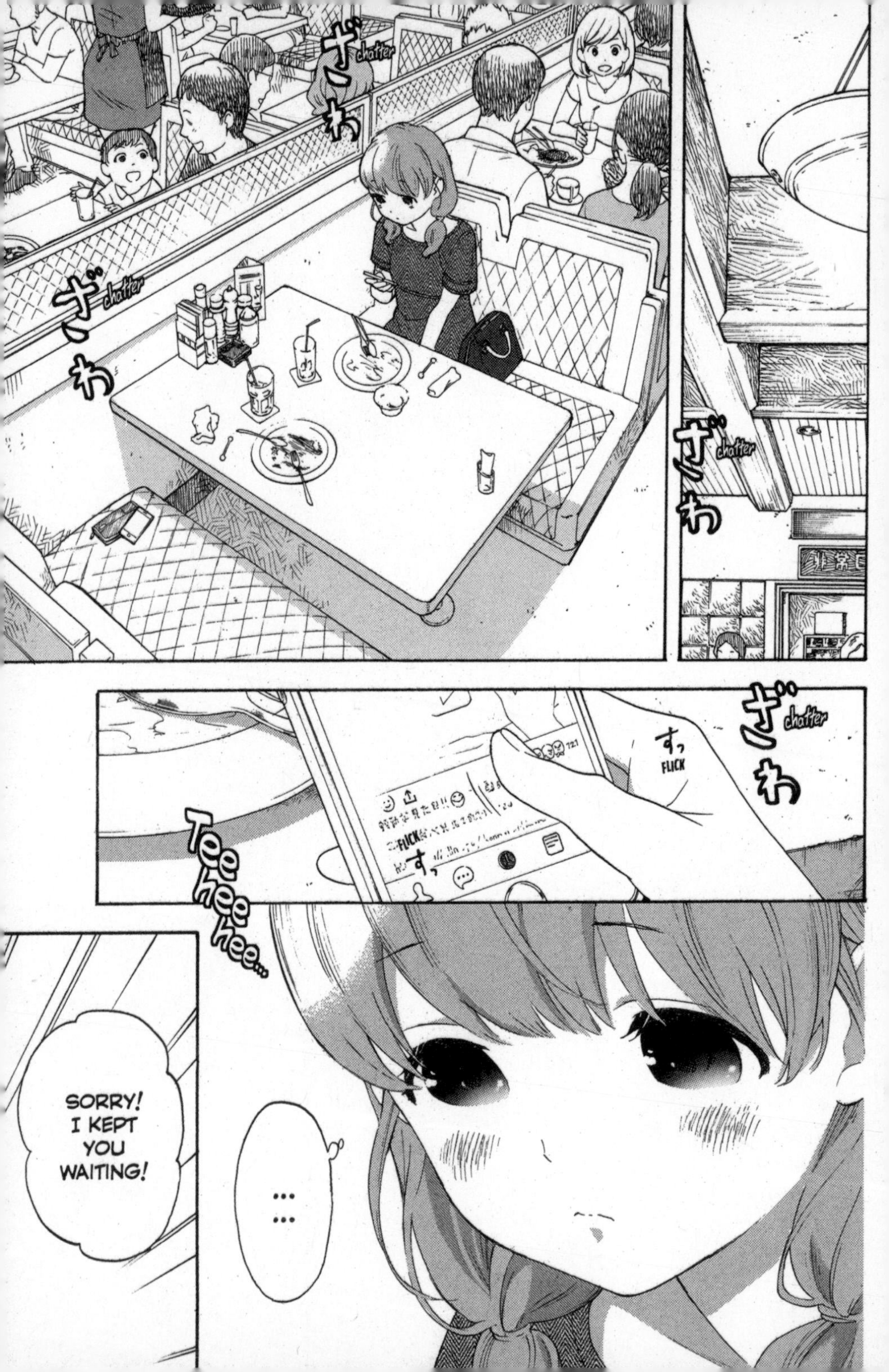
ざわ chatter
ざわ chatter
ざわ chatter
ざわ chatter
すっ FLICK
Tee hee hee...
......
SORRY! I KEPT YOU WAITING!

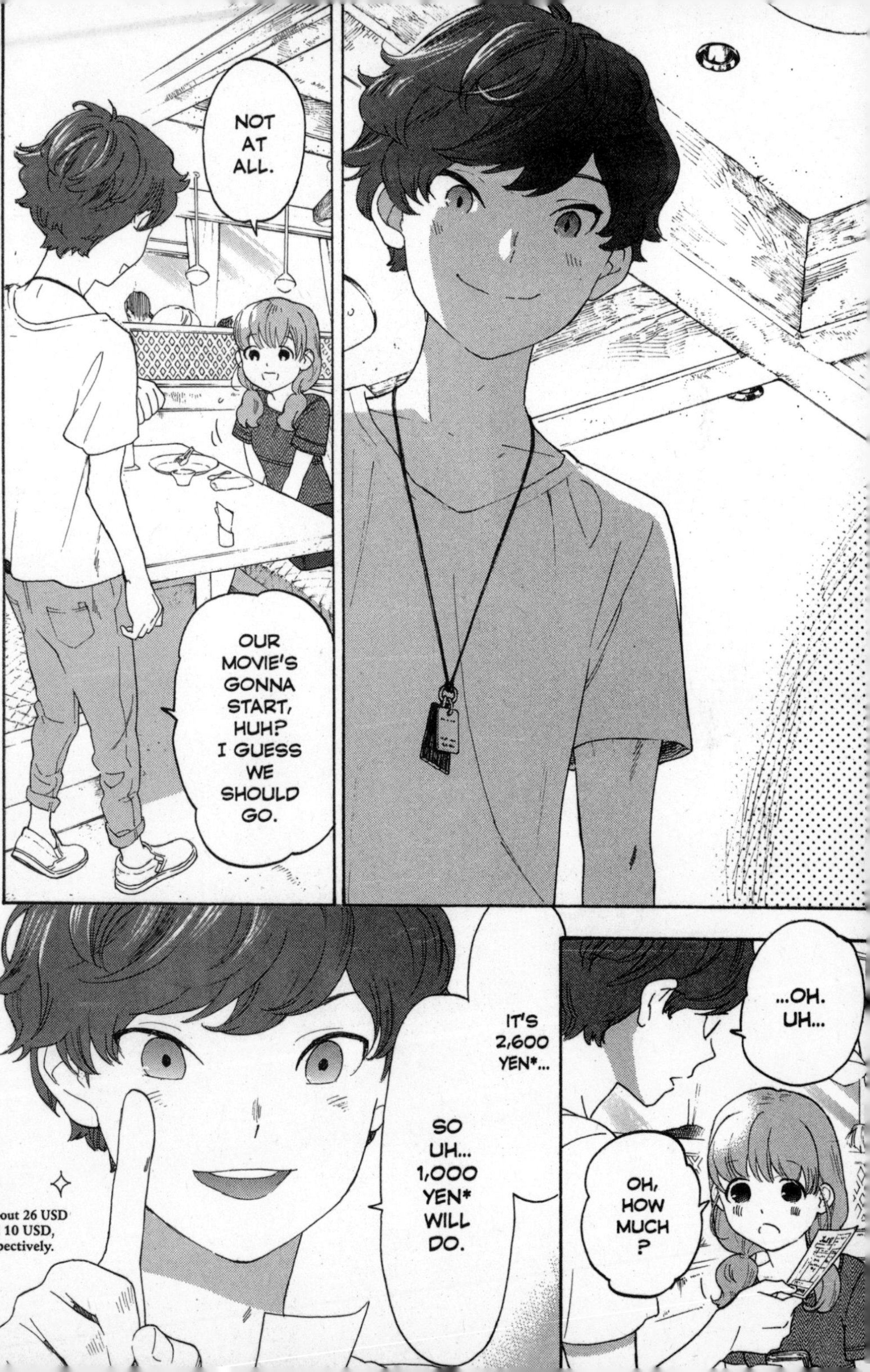
NOT AT ALL.
OUR MOVIE'S GONNA START, HUH? I GUESS WE SHOULD GO.
...OH. UH...
OH, HOW MUCH?
IT'S 2,600 YEN*...
SO UH... 1,000 YEN* WILL DO.

About 26 USD
nd 10 USD,
espectively.

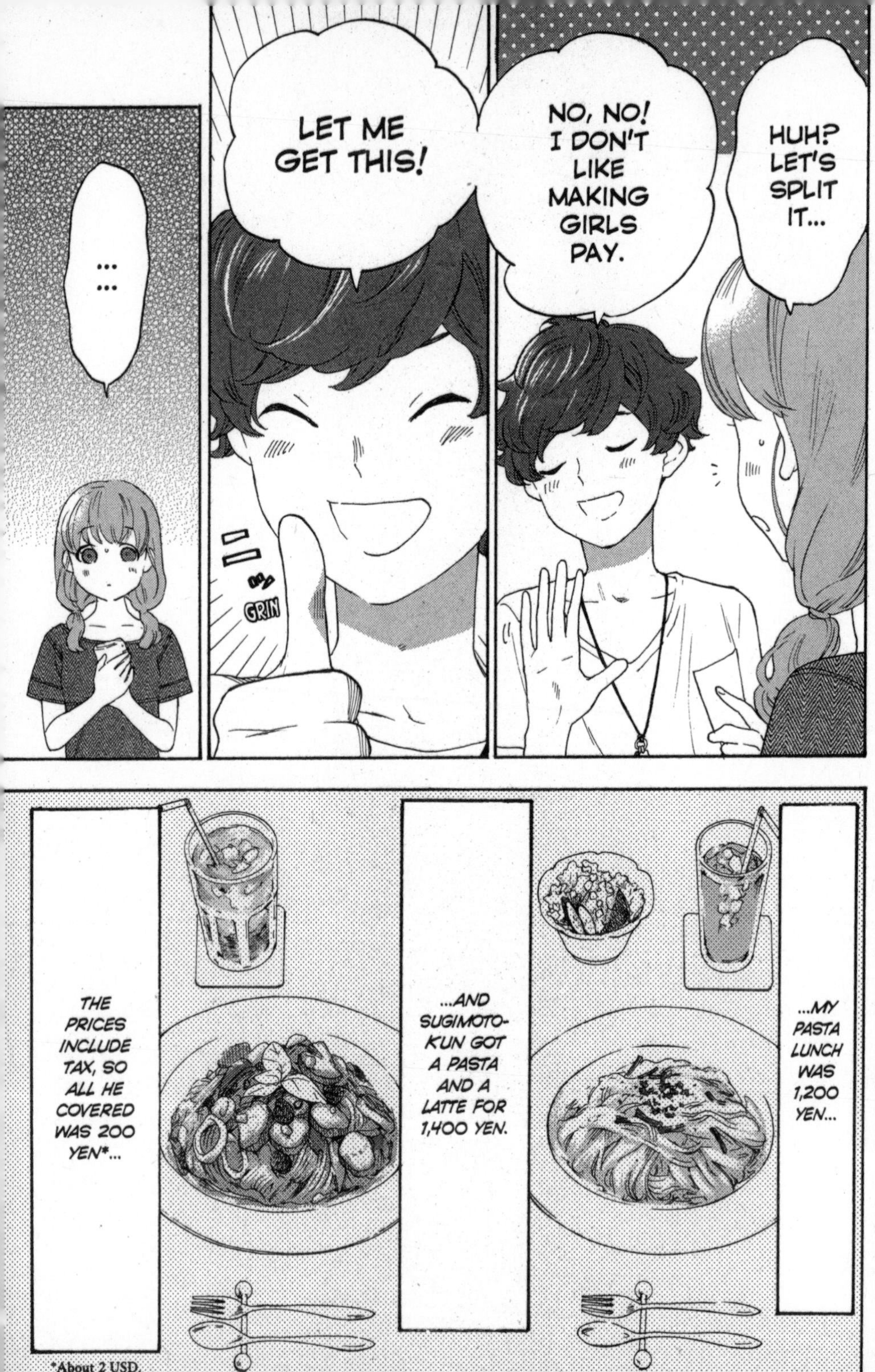
HUH? LET'S SPLIT IT...
NO, NO! I DON'T LIKE MAKING GIRLS PAY.
LET ME GET THIS!
GRIN
... ...
...MY PASTA LUNCH WAS 1,200 YEN...
...AND SUGIMOTO-KUN GOT A PASTA AND A LATTE FOR 1,400 YEN.
THE PRICES INCLUDE TAX, SO ALL HE COVERED WAS 200 YEN*...

*About 2 USD.

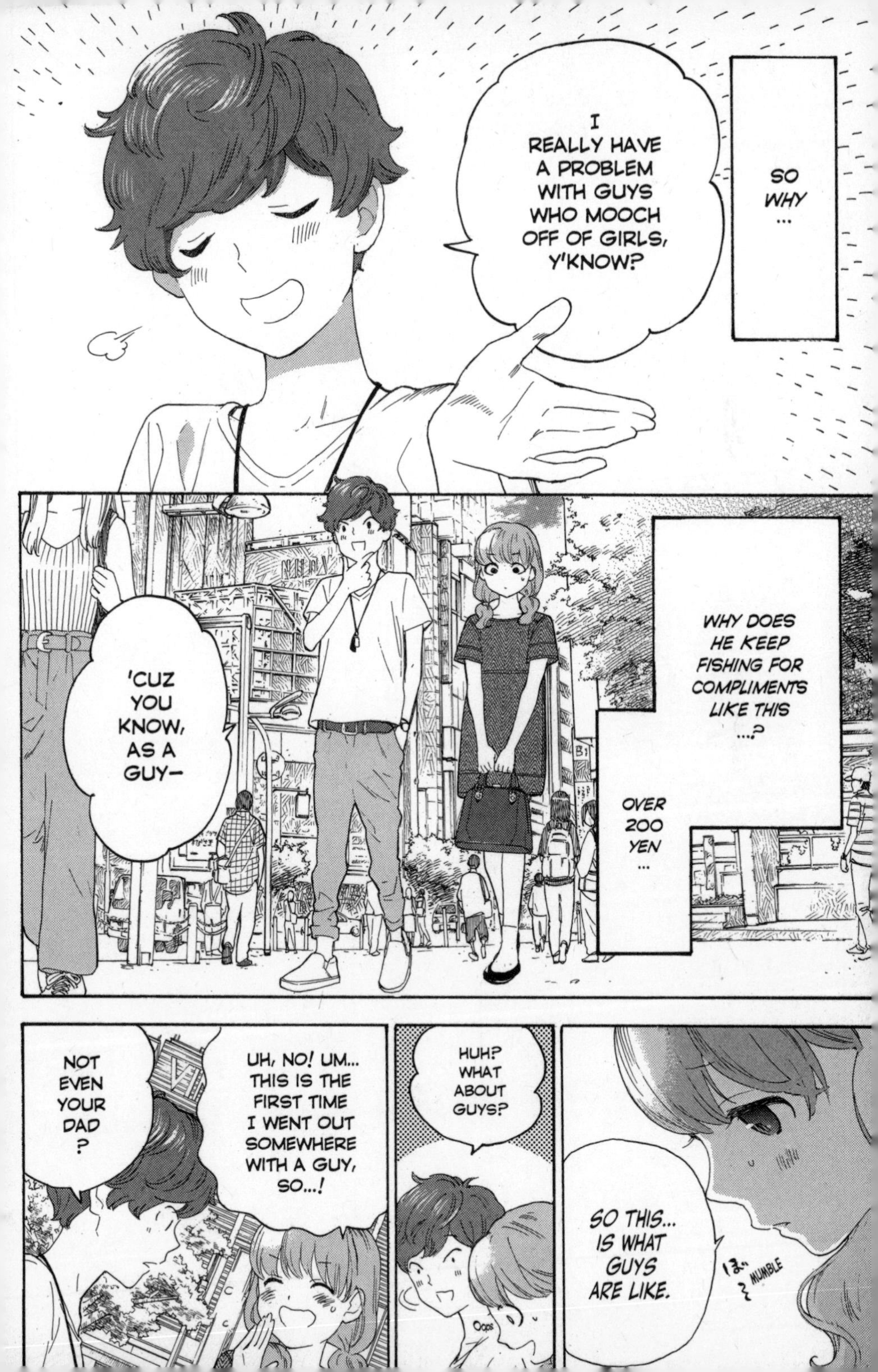
SO WHY ...
I REALLY HAVE A PROBLEM WITH GUYS WHO MOOCH OFF OF GIRLS, Y'KNOW?
WHY DOES HE KEEP FISHING FOR COMPLIMENTS LIKE THIS ...?
OVER 200 YEN ...
'CUZ YOU KNOW, AS A GUY—
SO THIS... IS WHAT GUYS ARE LIKE.
MUMBLE
HUH? WHAT ABOUT GUYS?
OOPS
UH, NO! UM... THIS IS THE FIRST TIME I WENT OUT SOMEWHERE WITH A GUY, SO...!
NOT EVEN YOUR DAD ?

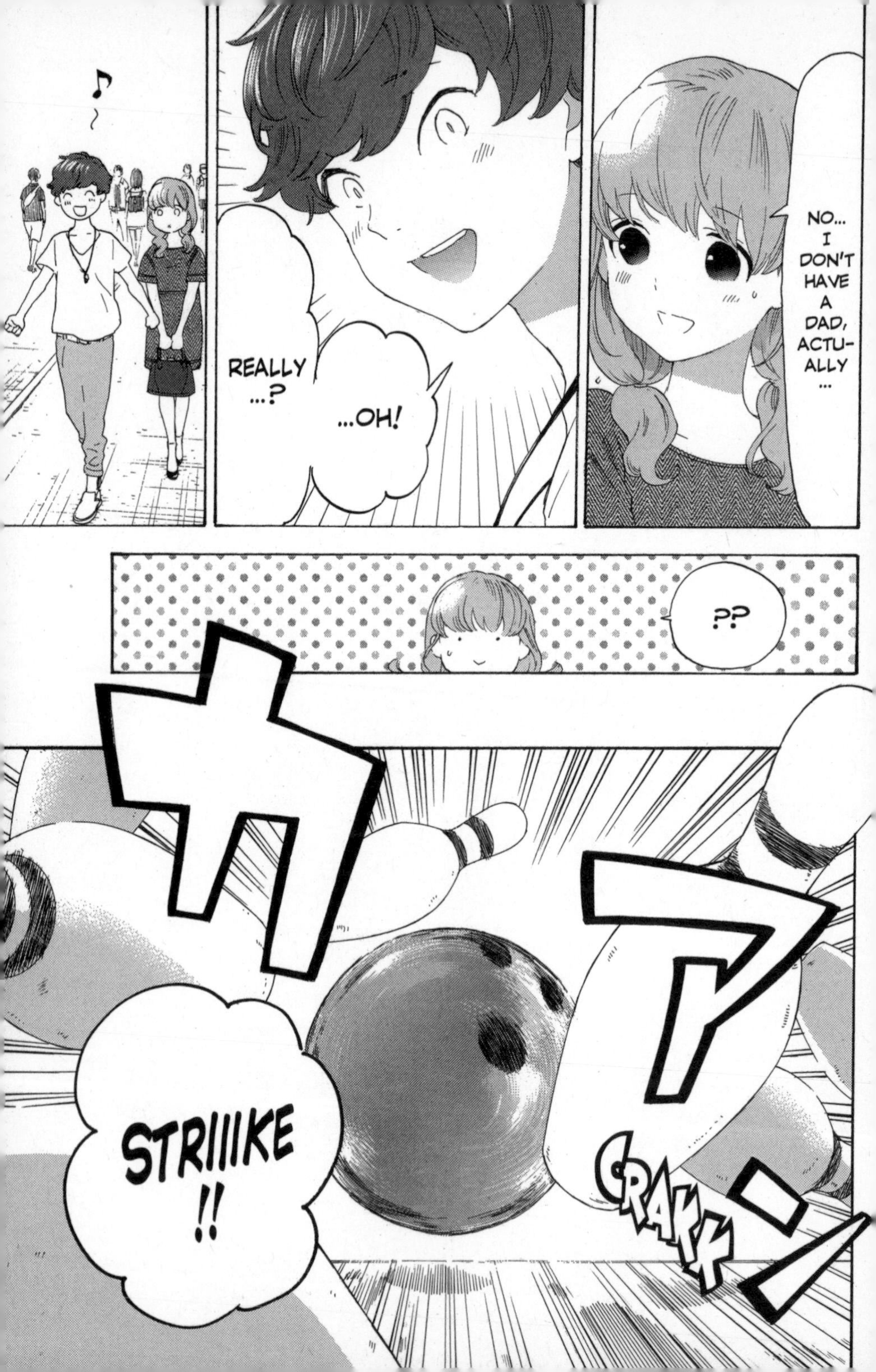

NO... I DON'T HAVE A DAD, ACTUALLY...
...OH!
REALLY ...?
♪
??
CRAKK
STRIIIKE !!

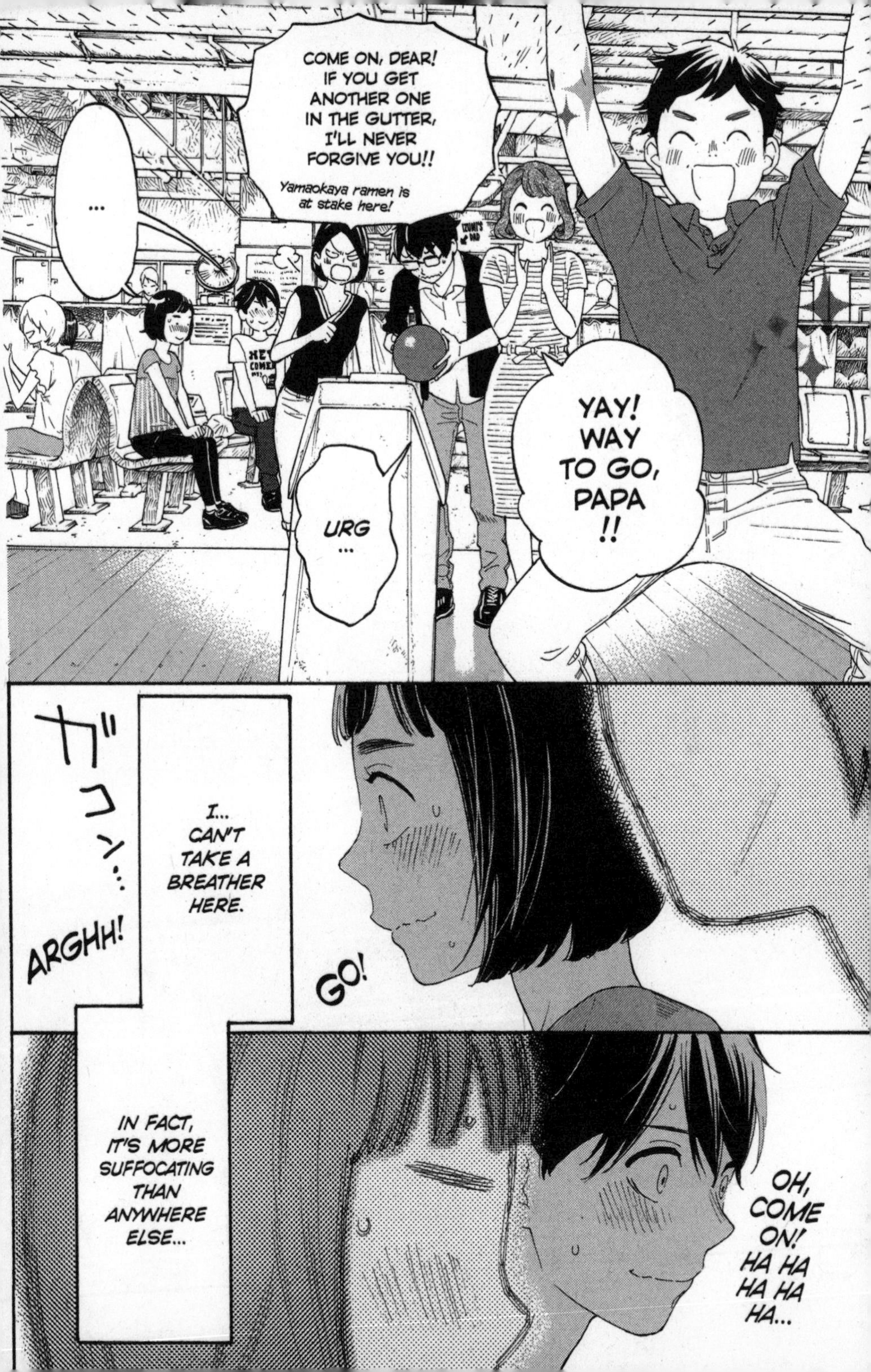
COME ON, DEAR! IF YOU GET ANOTHER ONE IN THE GUTTER, I'LL NEVER FORGIVE YOU!!
Yamaokaya ramen is at stake here!
IZUMI'S DAD
YAY! WAY TO GO, PAPA!!
URG...
...
GO!
I... CAN'T TAKE A BREATHER HERE.
ガコン…
ARGHH!
OH, COME ON! HA HA HA HA HA...
IN FACT, IT'S MORE SUFFOCATING THAN ANYWHERE ELSE...

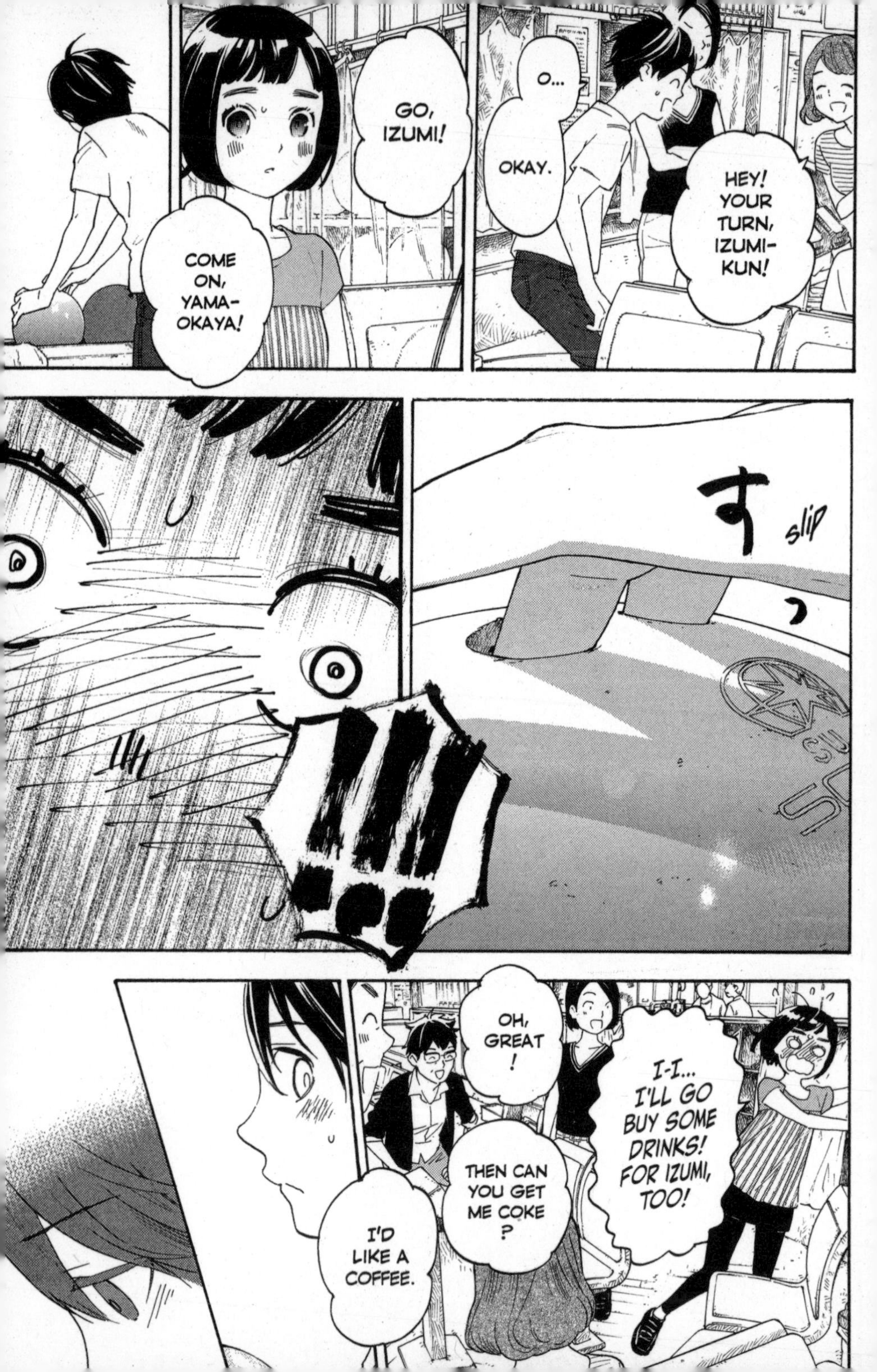
HEY! YOUR TURN, IZUMI-KUN!
O...
OKAY.
GO, IZUMI!
COME ON, YAMA-OKAYA!
す
slip
!!!
I-I... I'LL GO BUY SOME DRINKS! FOR IZUMI, TOO!
OH, GREAT!
THEN CAN YOU GET ME COKE?
I'D LIKE A COFFEE.

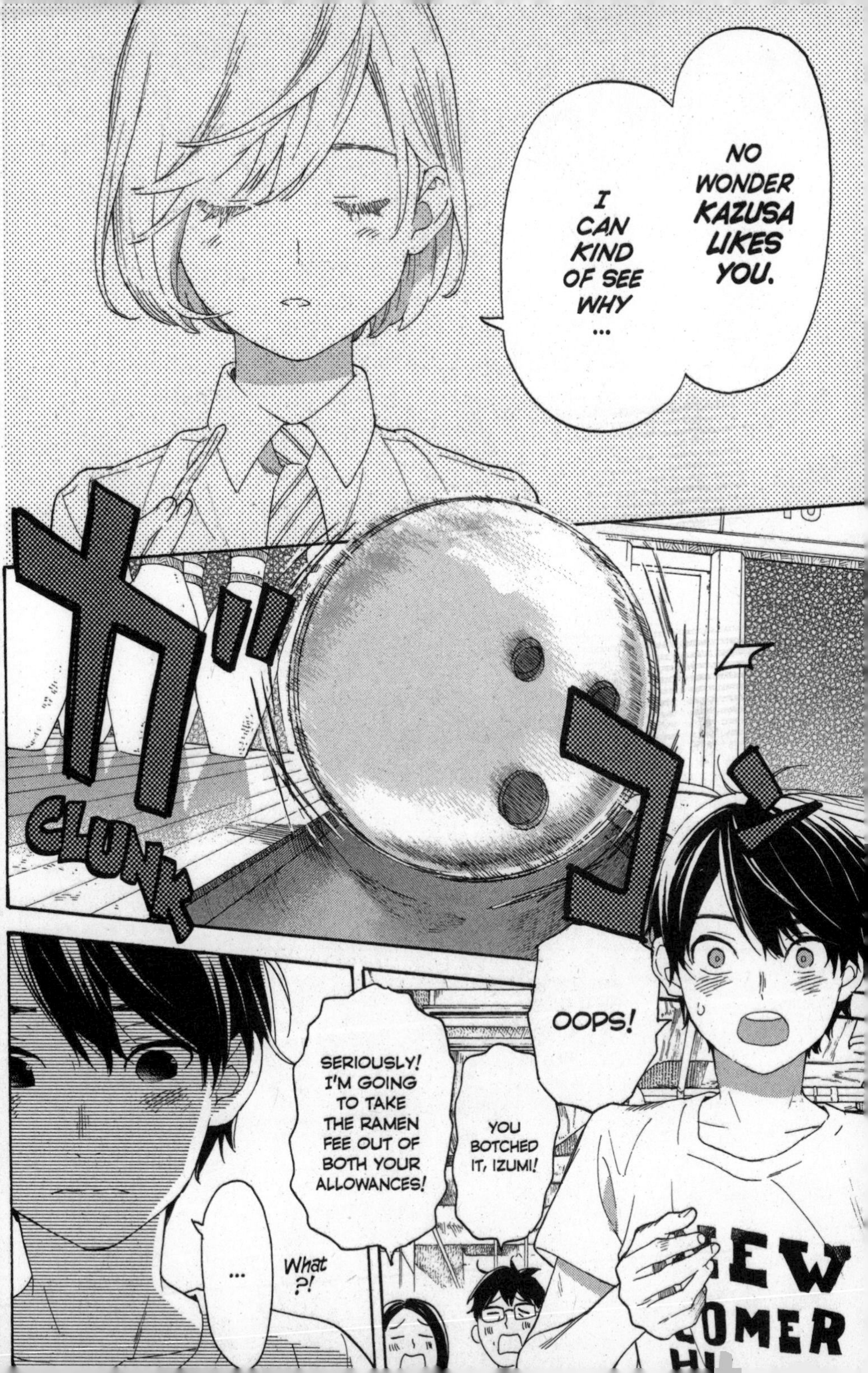
NO WONDER KAZUSA LIKES YOU.
I CAN KIND OF SEE WHY ...
ガゴ
CLUNK
OOPS!
YOU BOTCHED IT, IZUMI!
SERIOUSLY! I'M GOING TO TAKE THE RAMEN FEE OUT OF BOTH YOUR ALLOWANCES!
What?!
...

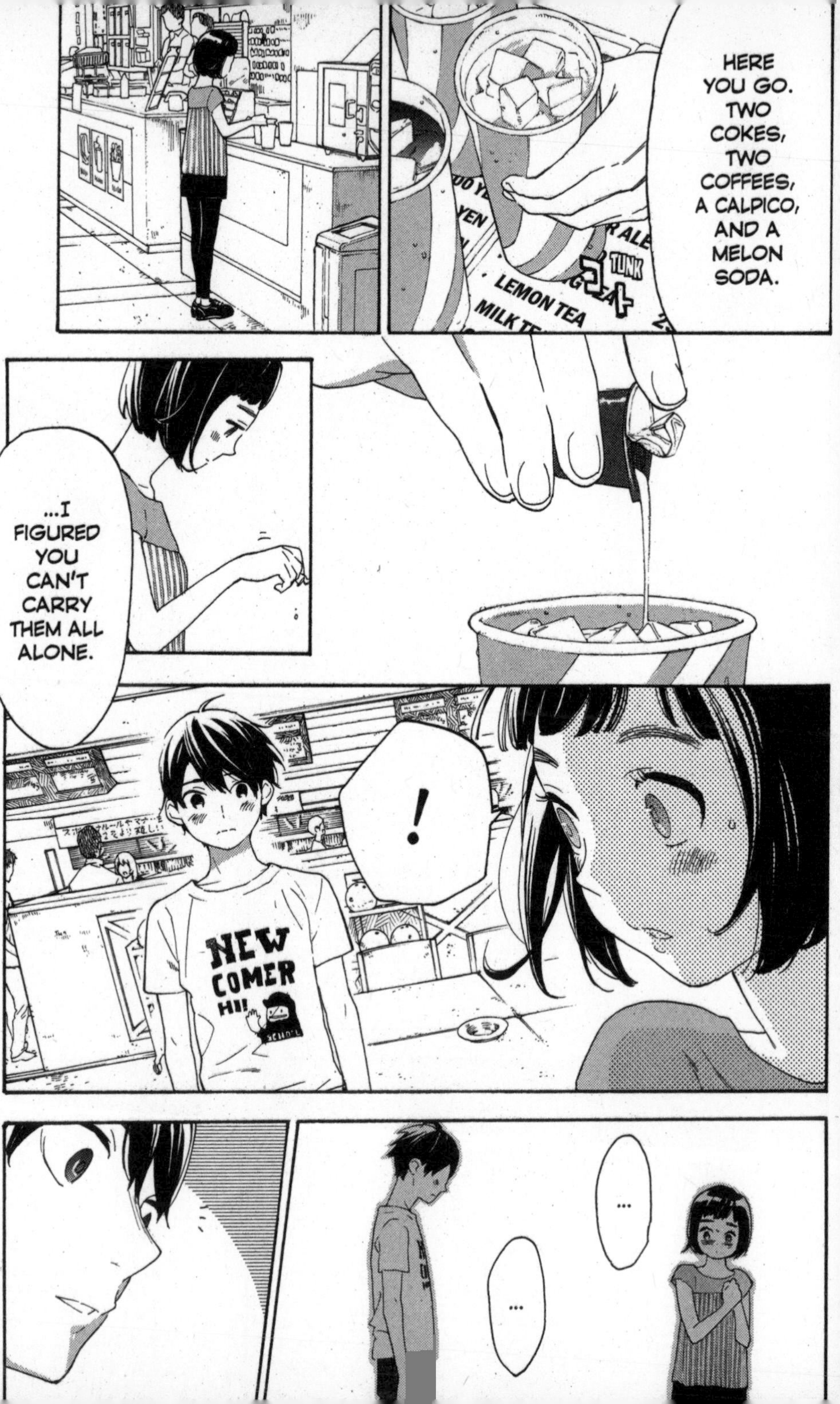
HERE YOU GO. TWO COKES, TWO COFFEES, A CALPICO, AND A MELON SODA.
TUNK
LEMON TEA
...I FIGURED YOU CAN'T CARRY THEM ALL ALONE.
!
NEW COMER HI!
...
...

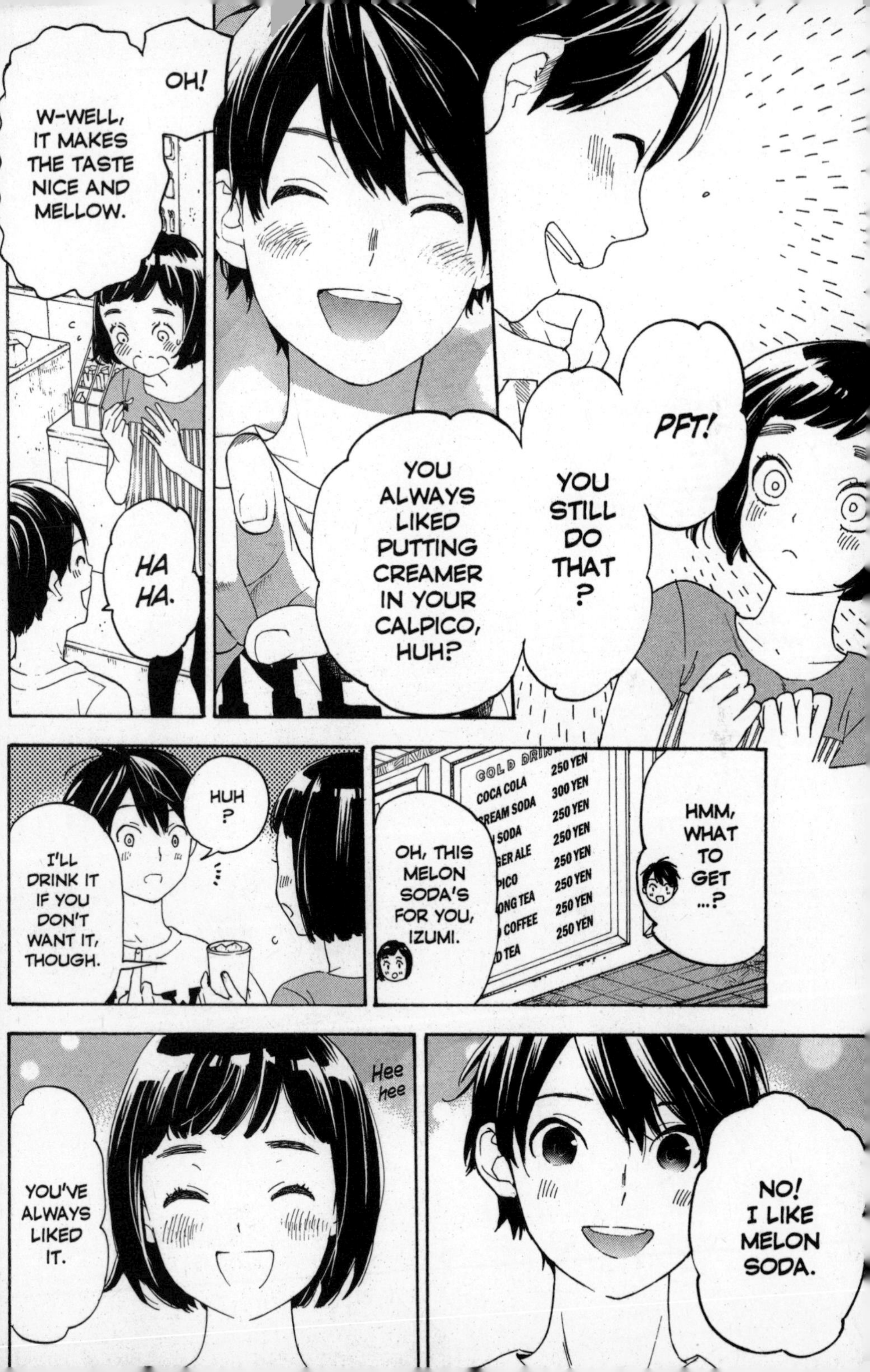
PFT!
YOU STILL DO THAT?
YOU ALWAYS LIKED PUTTING CREAMER IN YOUR CALPICO, HUH?
OH!
W-WELL, IT MAKES THE TASTE NICE AND MELLOW.
HA HA.
HMM, WHAT TO GET ...?
COCA COLA
OH, THIS MELON SODA'S FOR YOU, IZUMI.
HUH?
I'LL DRINK IT IF YOU DON'T WANT IT, THOUGH.
NO! I LIKE MELON SODA.
Hee hee
YOU'VE ALWAYS LIKED IT.

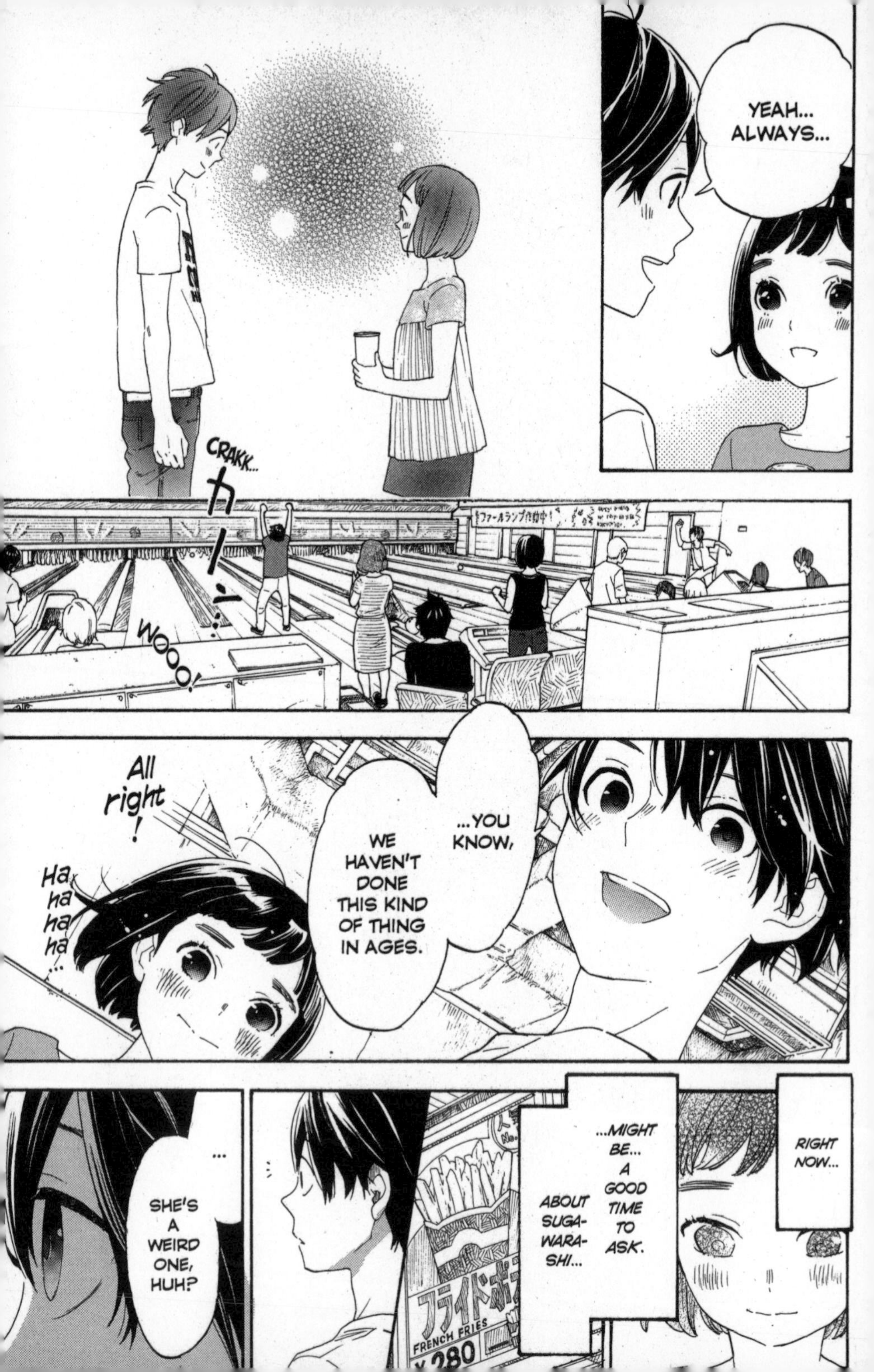
YEAH... ALWAYS...
CRAKK...
WOOO!
...YOU KNOW,
WE HAVEN'T DONE THIS KIND OF THING IN AGES.
All right!
Ha ha ha ha...
RIGHT NOW...
...MIGHT BE... A GOOD TIME TO ASK.
ABOUT SUGA-WARA-SHI...
FRENCH FRIES
¥280
...
SHE'S A WEIRD ONE, HUH?

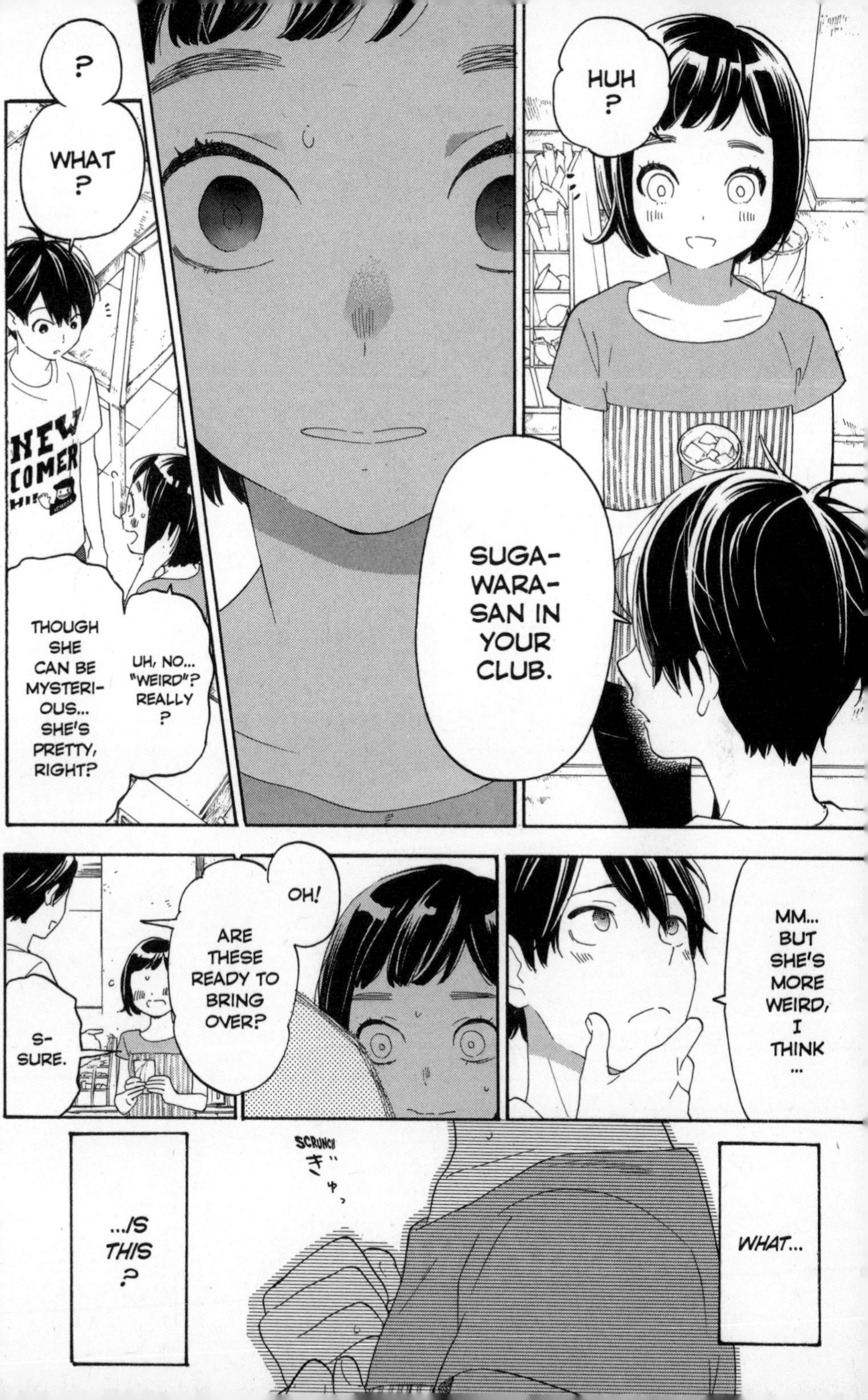
HUH ?
SUGA-WARA-SAN IN YOUR CLUB.
? WHAT ?
UH, NO... "WEIRD"? REALLY ?
THOUGH SHE CAN BE MYSTERI-OUS... SHE'S PRETTY, RIGHT?
MM... BUT SHE'S MORE WEIRD, I THINK ...
OH! ARE THESE READY TO BRING OVER?
S-SURE.
WHAT...
SCRUNCH
ぎゅっ
...IS THIS ?

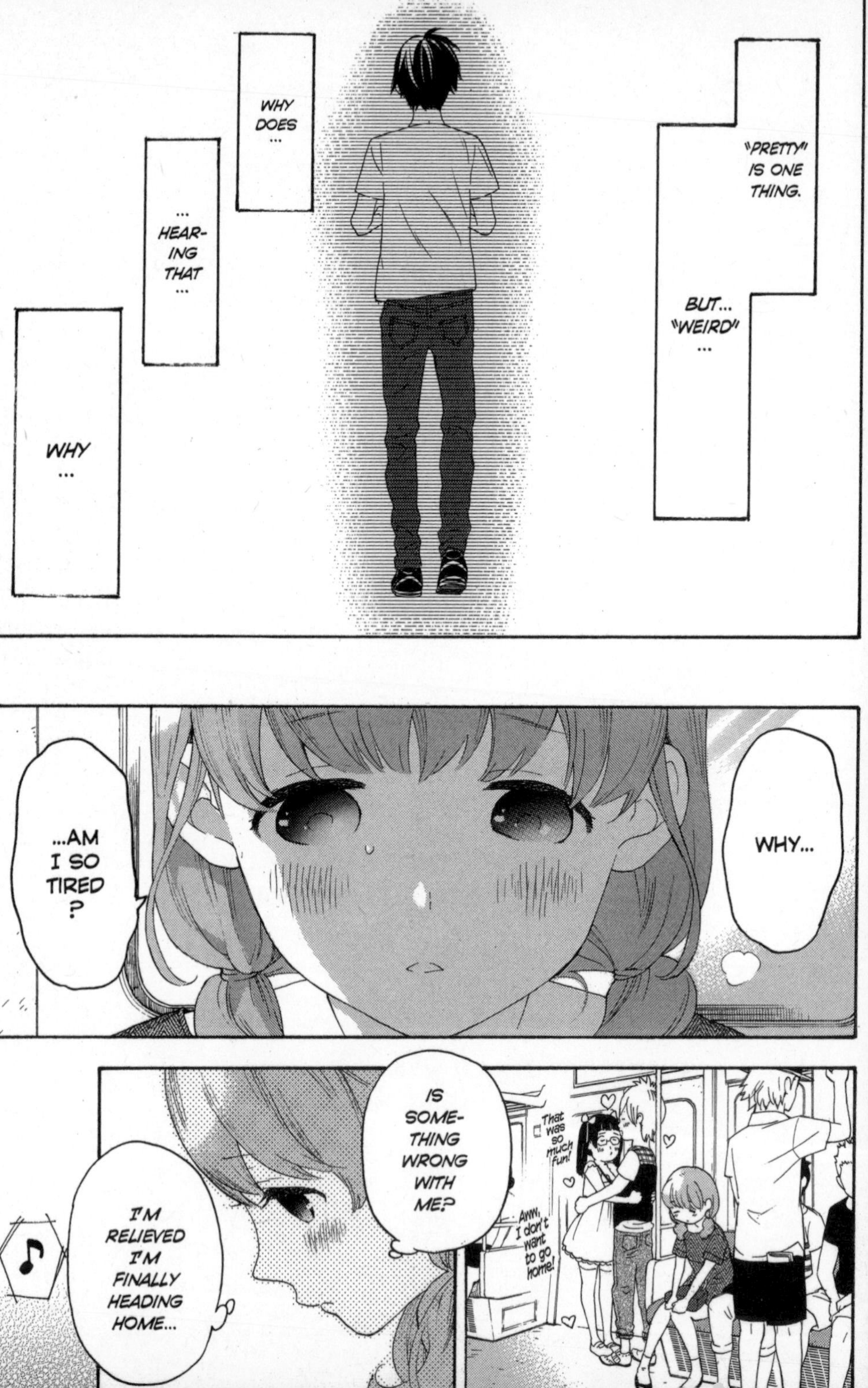
"PRETTY" IS ONE THING.
BUT... "WEIRD"...
WHY DOES...
...HEARING THAT...
WHY...
WHY...
...AM I SO TIRED?
That was so much fun!
Aww, I don't want to go home!
IS SOMETHING WRONG WITH ME?
I'M RELIEVED I'M FINALLY HEADING HOME...

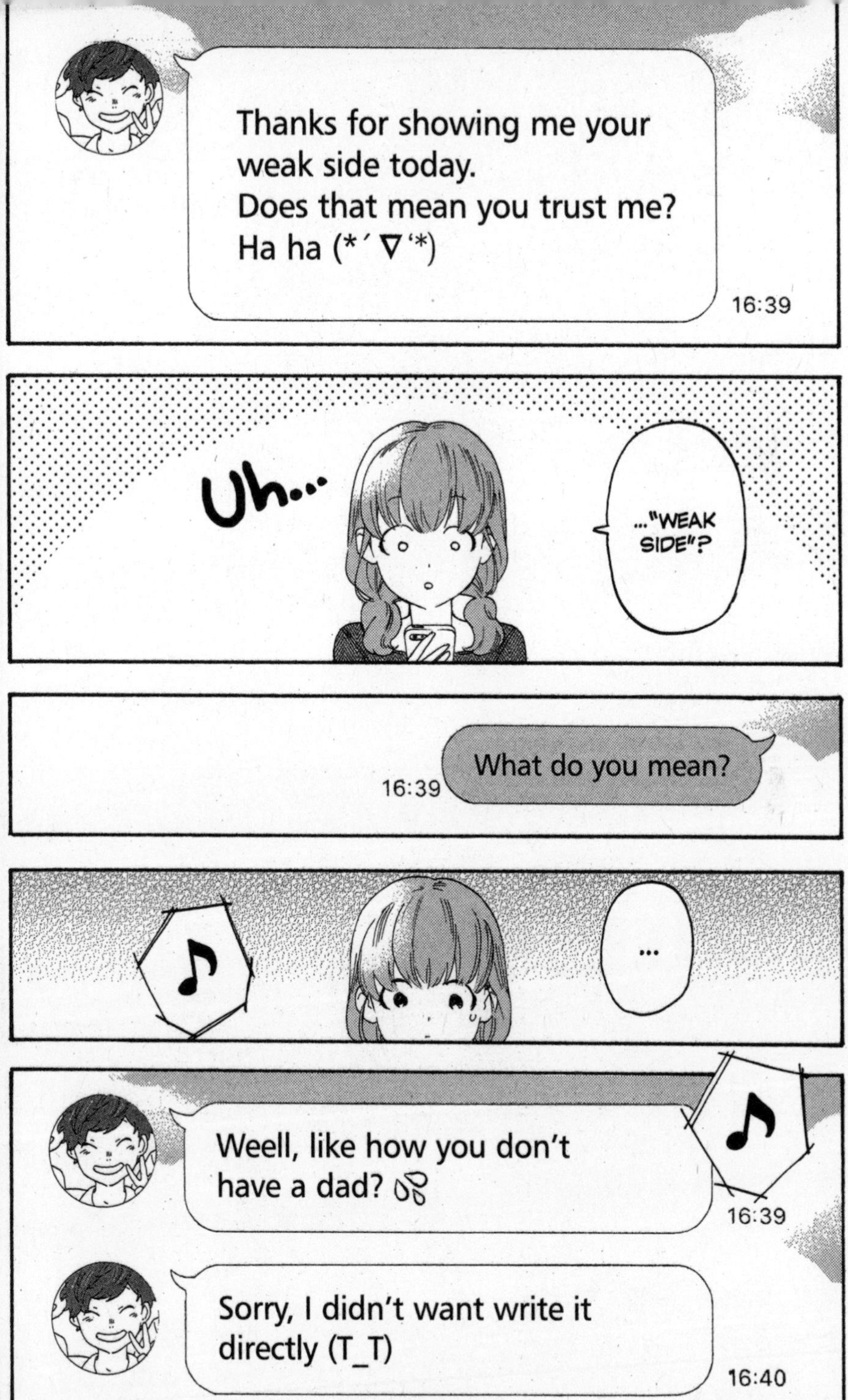
Thanks for showing me your weak side today.
Does that mean you trust me?
Ha ha (*´∇‘*)
16:39
..."WEAK SIDE"?
Uh...
What do you mean?
16:39
...
Weell, like how you don't have a dad?
16:39
Sorry, I didn't want write it directly (T_T)
16:40

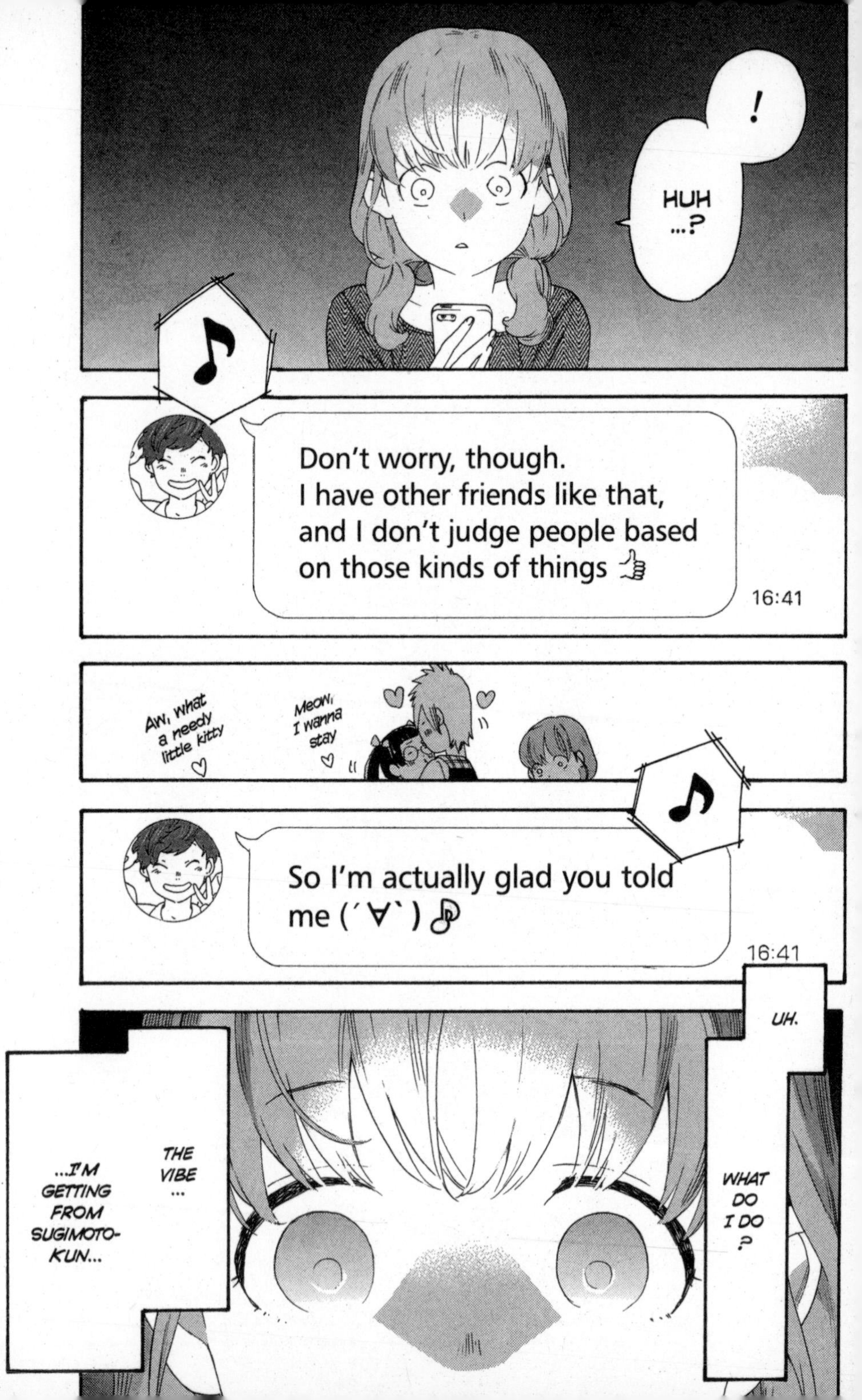
!
HUH ...?
Don't worry, though. I have other friends like that, and I don't judge people based on those kinds of things
16:41
Meow, I wanna stay
Aw, what a needy little kitty
So I'm actually glad you told me (´∀`)
16:41
UH.
WHAT DO I DO?
THE VIBE...
...I'M GETTING FROM SUGIMOTO-KUN...

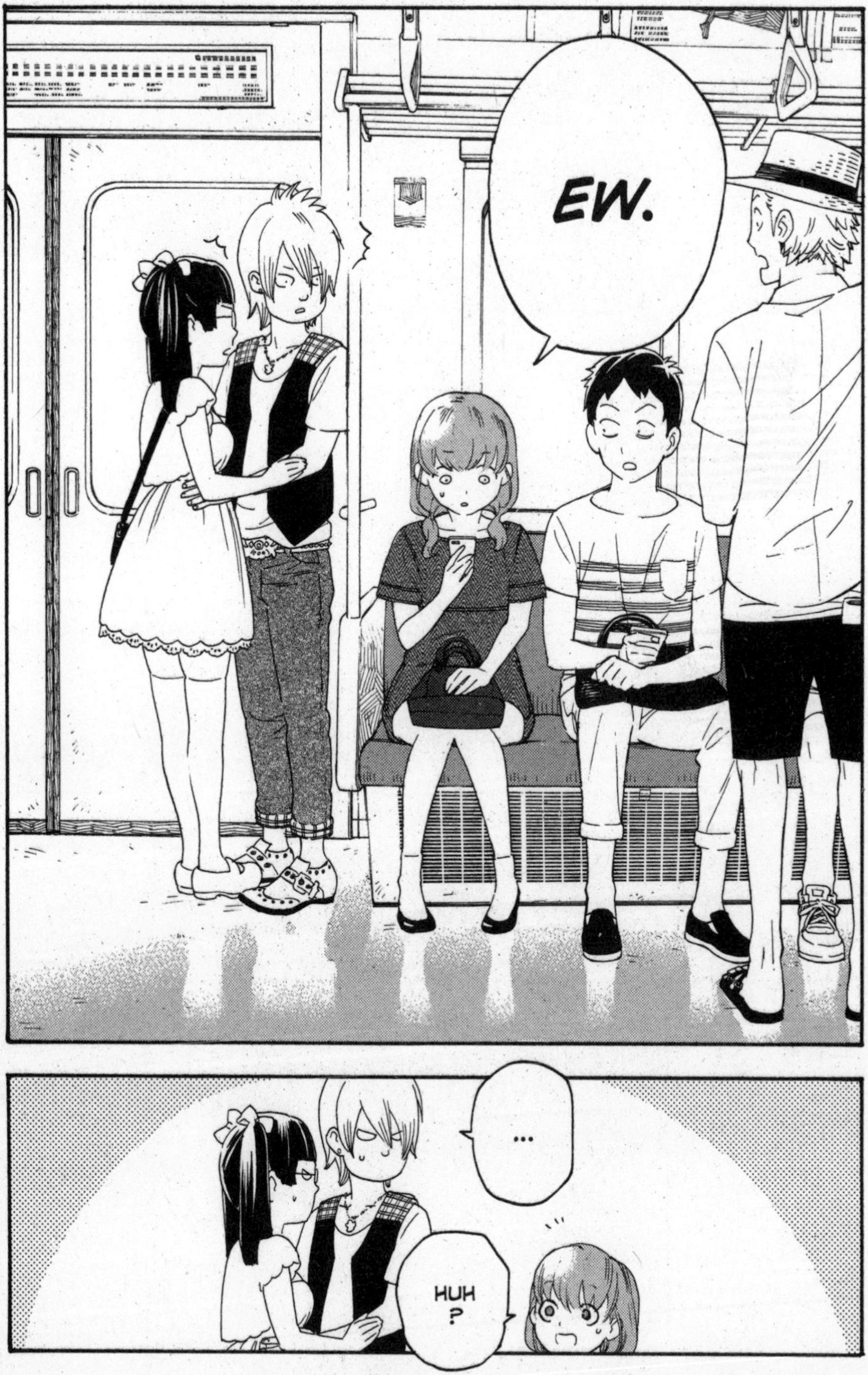
EW.
...
HUH?

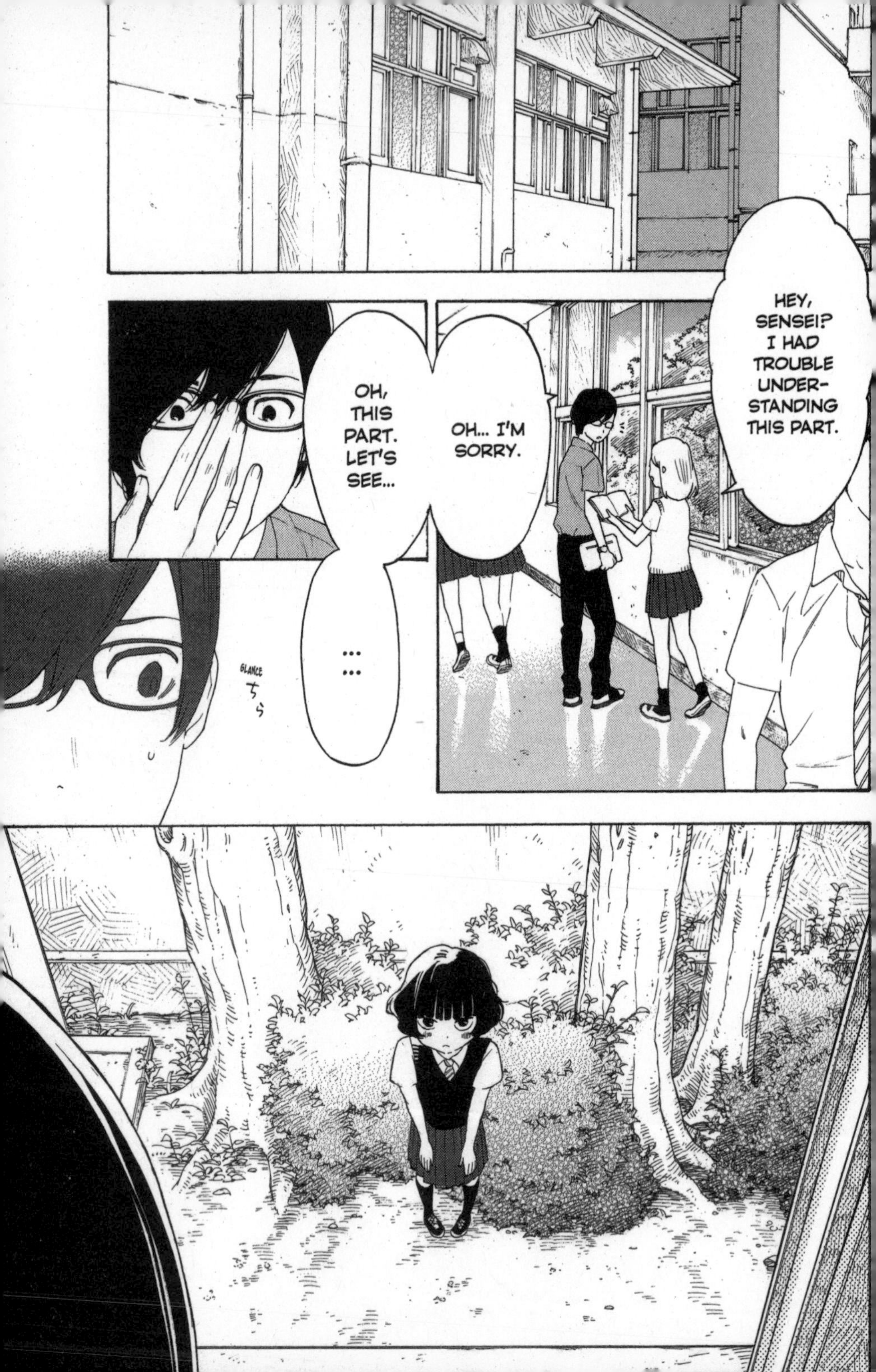
HEY, SENSEI? I HAD TROUBLE UNDER-STANDING THIS PART.
OH... I'M SORRY.
OH, THIS PART. LET'S SEE...
GLANCE ちら
...
...

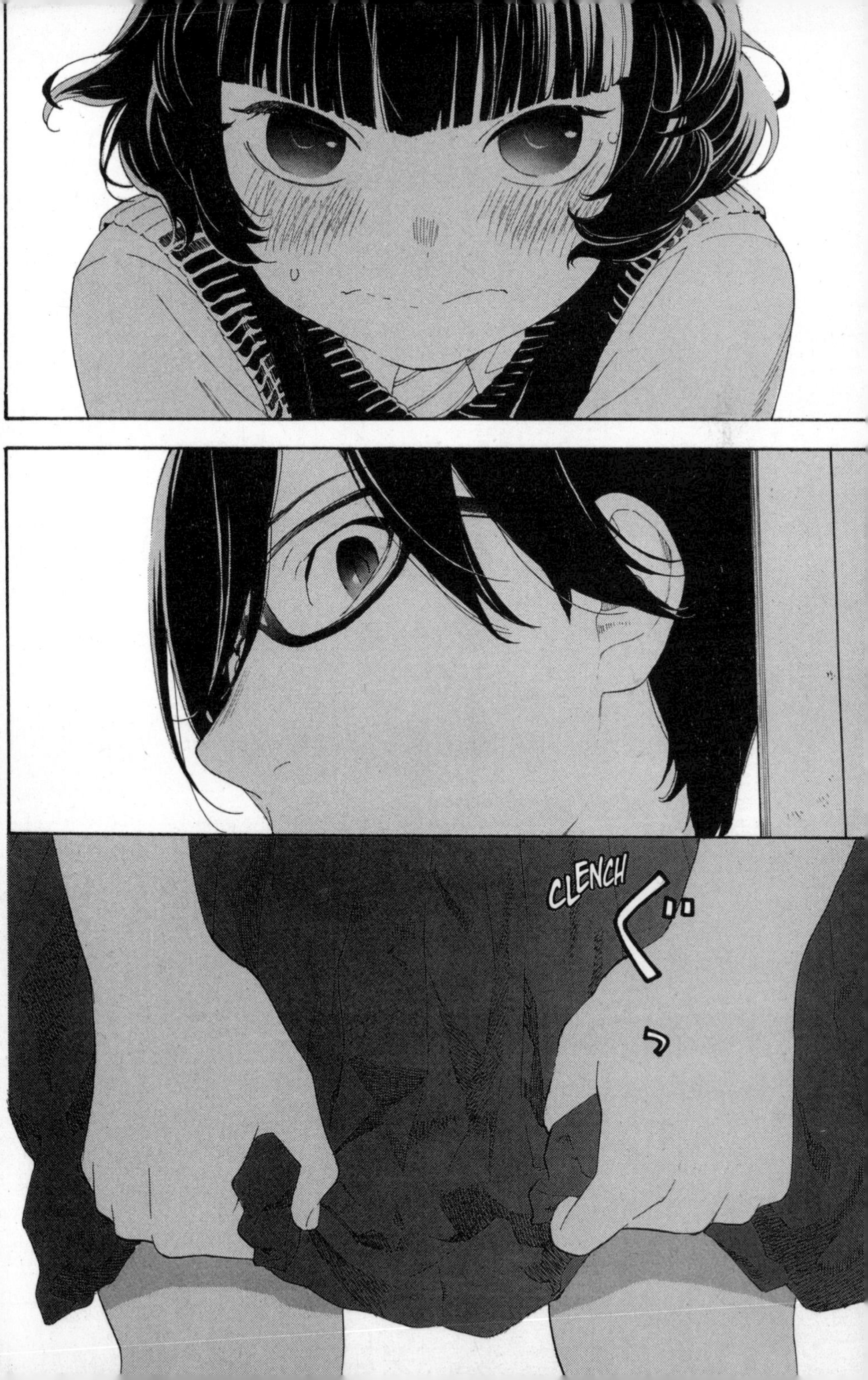
CLENCH
ぐっ

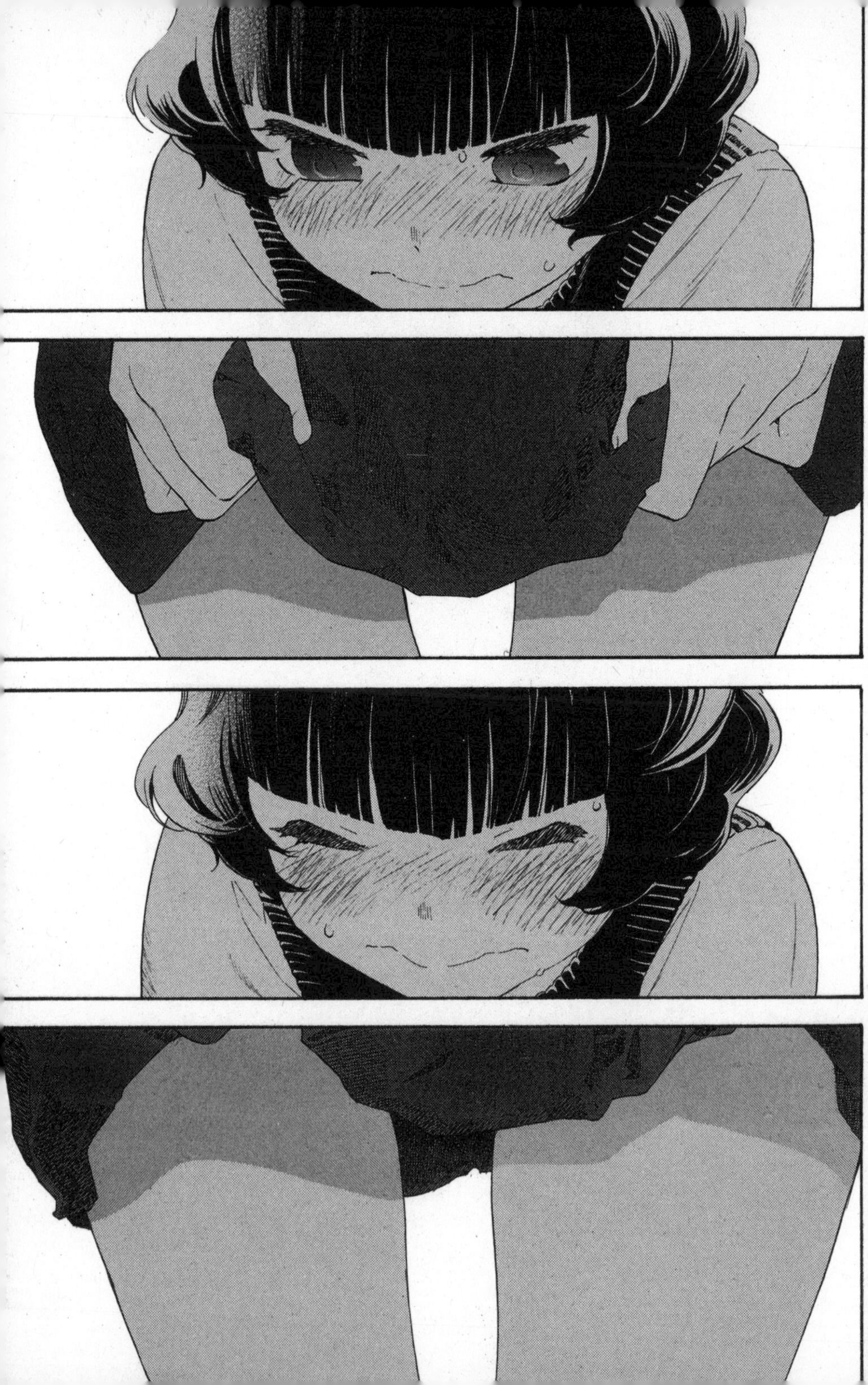

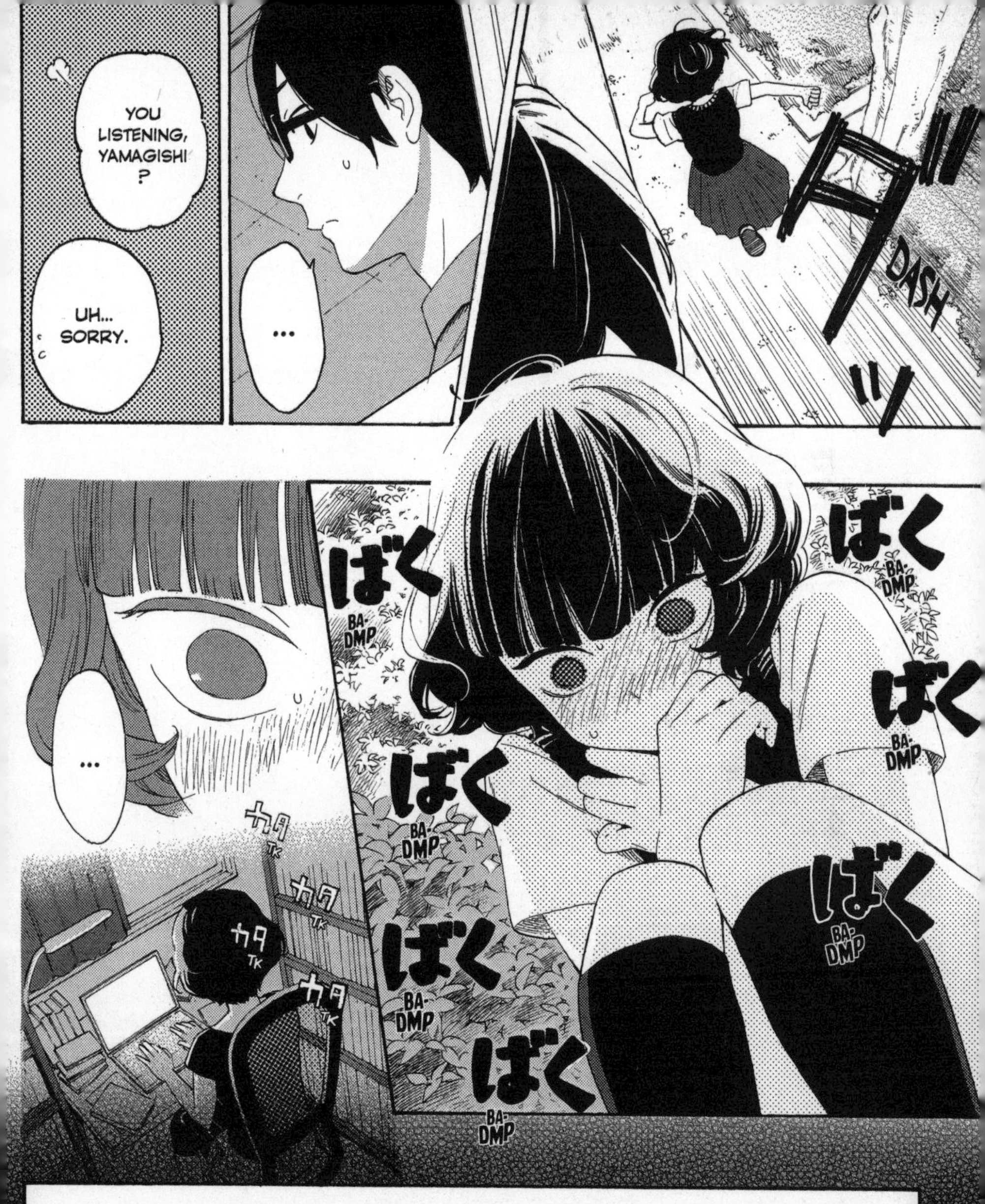
DASH
...
YOU LISTENING, YAMAGISHI?
UH... SORRY.
ばく BA-DMP
ばく BA-DMP
ばく BA-DMP
ばく BA-DMP
ばく BA-DMP
ばく BA-DMP
ばく BA-DMP
...
カタ TK
カタ TK
カタ TK
カタ TK

Hitoto> I thought over it, but I don't get it. What do you mean it's okay as long as the eroticism's conceptual and not direct?

Milo> If it isn't direct, at least I won't get arrested.

Hitoto> But what kind of things?

Milo> For example.
During break, you show me your underwear without anyone noticing.
...How does that sound?

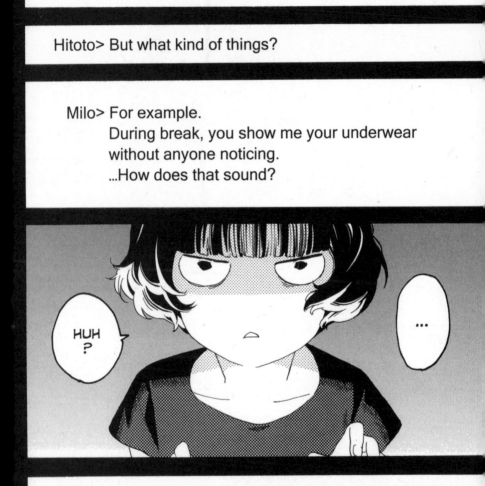

Hitoto> You're going to get excited over seeing underwear?
What are you, in elementary school?

Milo> No, I'm sure it will be really quite thrilling.
Let's just try it and see.

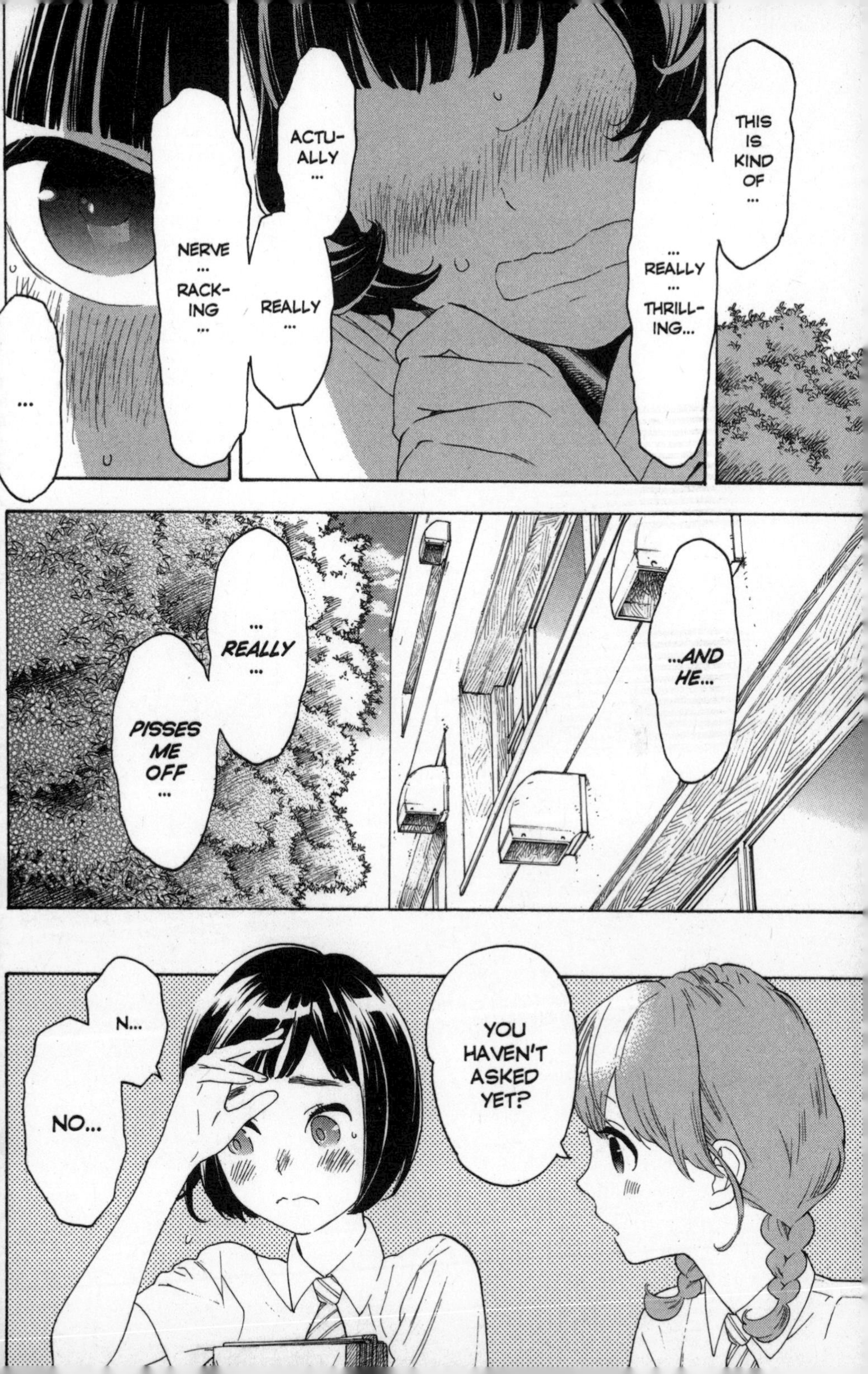
THIS IS KIND OF ...
... REALLY ... THRILL-ING...
ACTU-ALLY ...
REALLY ...
NERVE ... RACK-ING ...
...
...AND HE...
... REALLY ...
PISSES ME OFF ...
YOU HAVEN'T ASKED YET?
N...
NO...

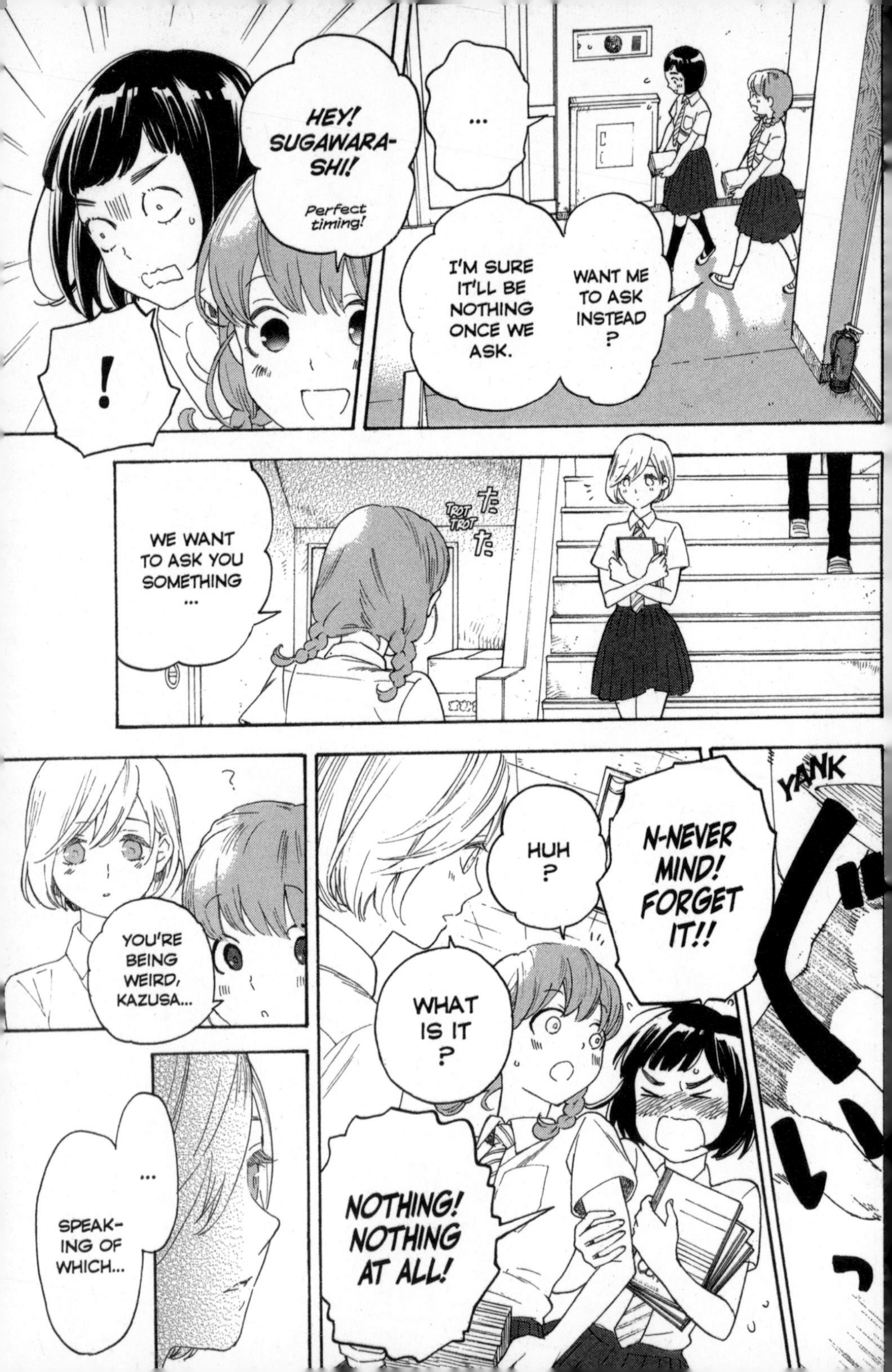
...
WANT ME TO ASK INSTEAD?
I'M SURE IT'LL BE NOTHING ONCE WE ASK.
HEY! SUGAWARA-SHI!
Perfect timing!
!
TROT TROT
WE WANT TO ASK YOU SOMETHING ...
YANK
N-NEVER MIND! FORGET IT!!
HUH?
WHAT IS IT?
NOTHING! NOTHING AT ALL!
?
YOU'RE BEING WEIRD, KAZUSA...
...
SPEAK-ING OF WHICH...

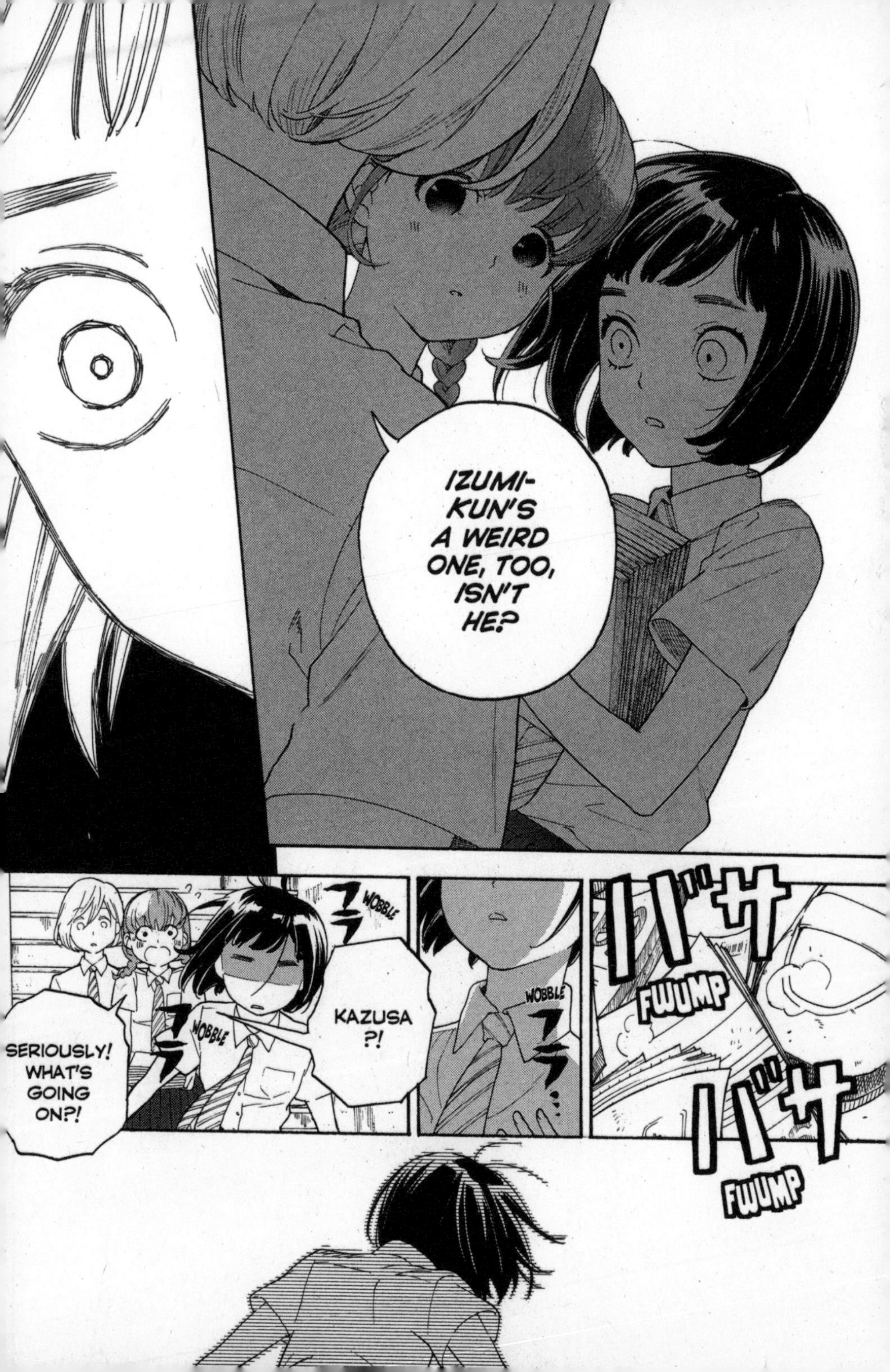
IZUMI-KUN'S A WEIRD ONE, TOO, ISN'T HE?
FWUMP
FWUMP
WOBBLE
WOBBLE
WOBBLE
KAZUSA ?!
SERIOUSLY! WHAT'S GOING ON?!

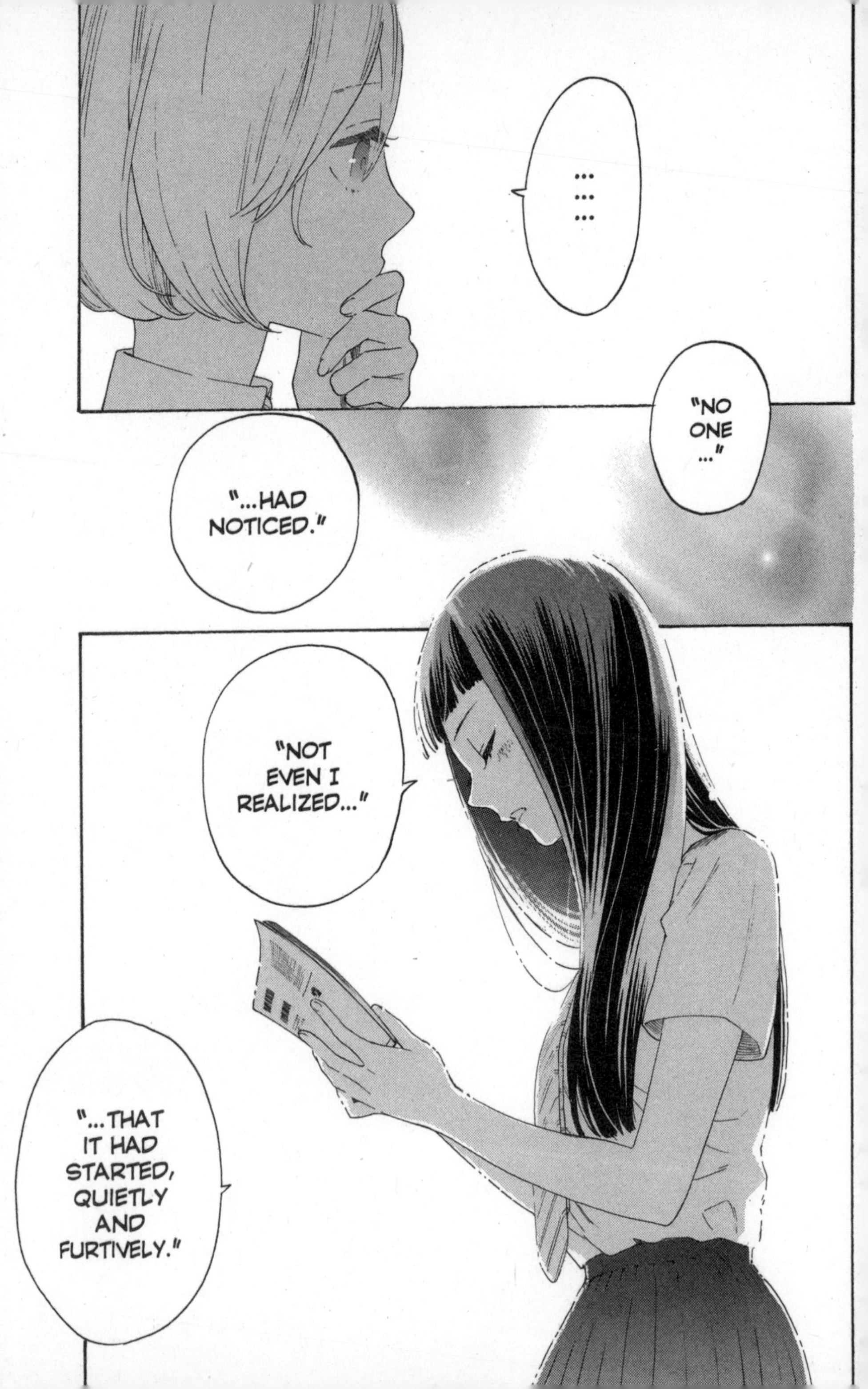
......
"NO ONE ..."
"...HAD NOTICED."
"NOT EVEN I REALIZED..."
"...THAT IT HAD STARTED, QUIETLY AND FURTIVELY."

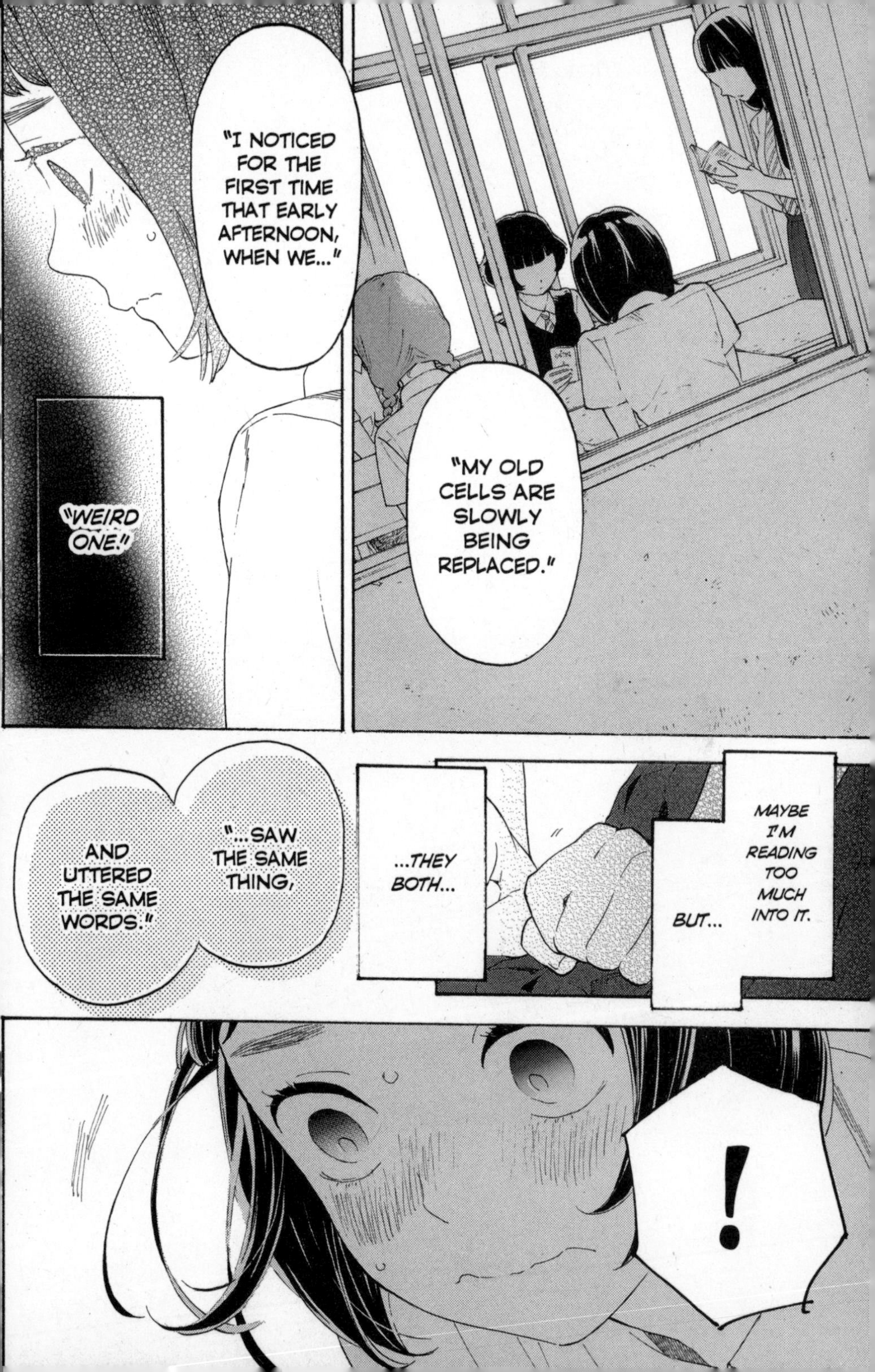
"MY OLD CELLS ARE SLOWLY BEING REPLACED."
"I NOTICED FOR THE FIRST TIME THAT EARLY AFTERNOON, WHEN WE..."
"WEIRD ONE."
MAYBE I'M READING TOO MUCH INTO IT.
BUT...
...THEY BOTH...
"...SAW THE SAME THING,
AND UTTERED THE SAME WORDS."
!

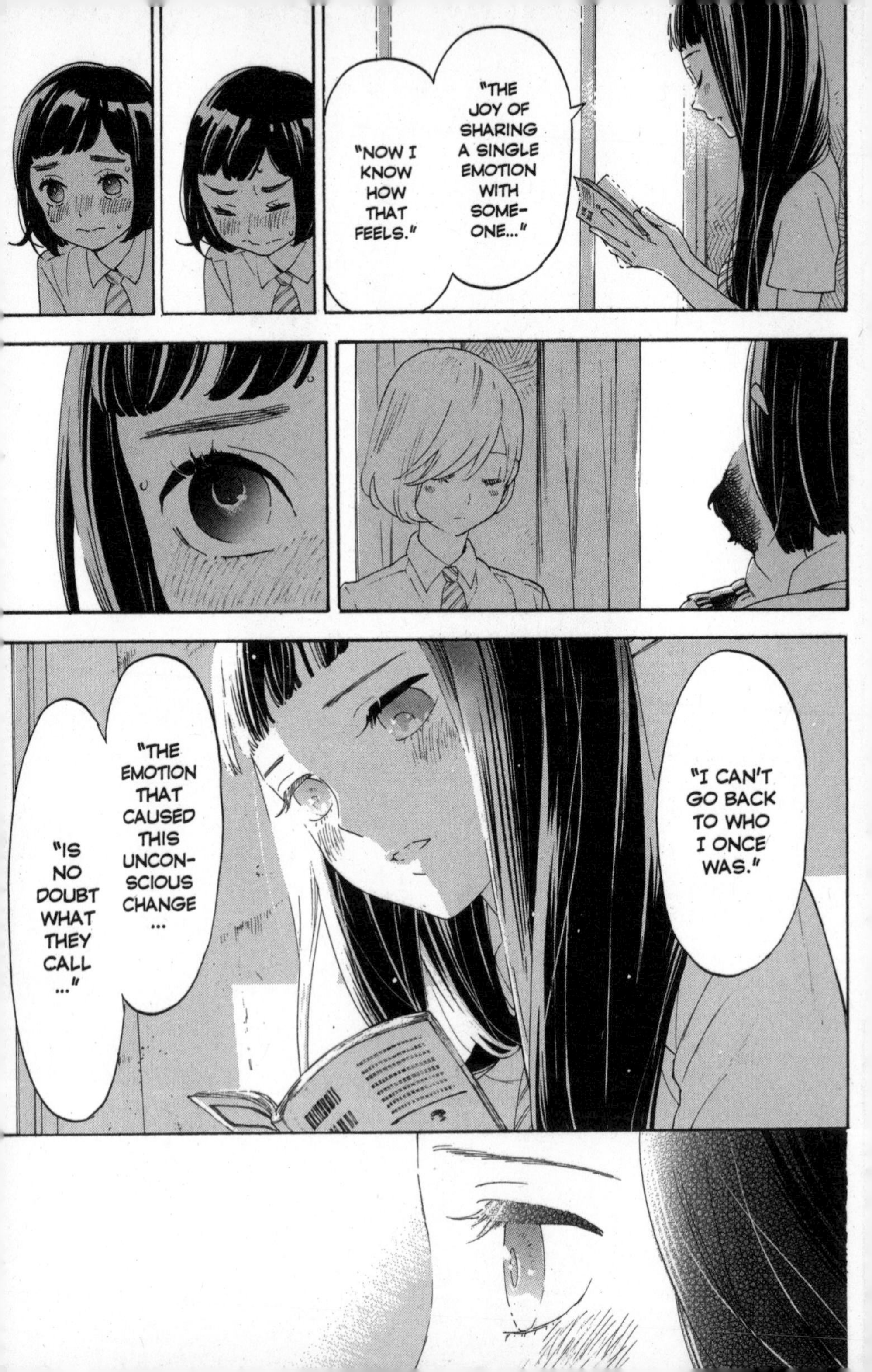
"THE JOY OF SHARING A SINGLE EMOTION WITH SOME-ONE..."
"NOW I KNOW HOW THAT FEELS."
"I CAN'T GO BACK TO WHO I ONCE WAS."
"THE EMOTION THAT CAUSED THIS UNCONSCIOUS CHANGE ...
"IS NO DOUBT WHAT THEY CALL ..."

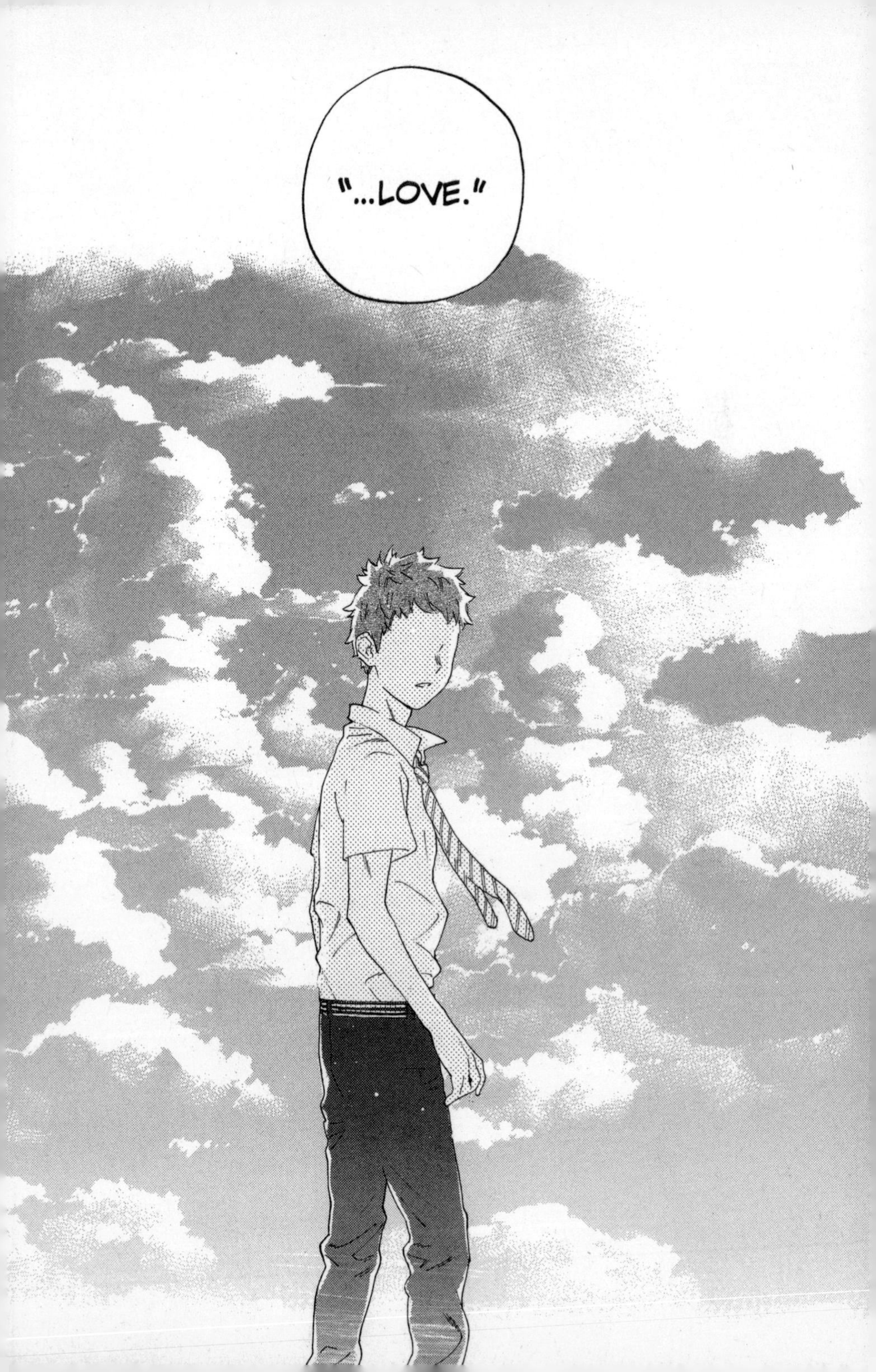
"...LOVE."

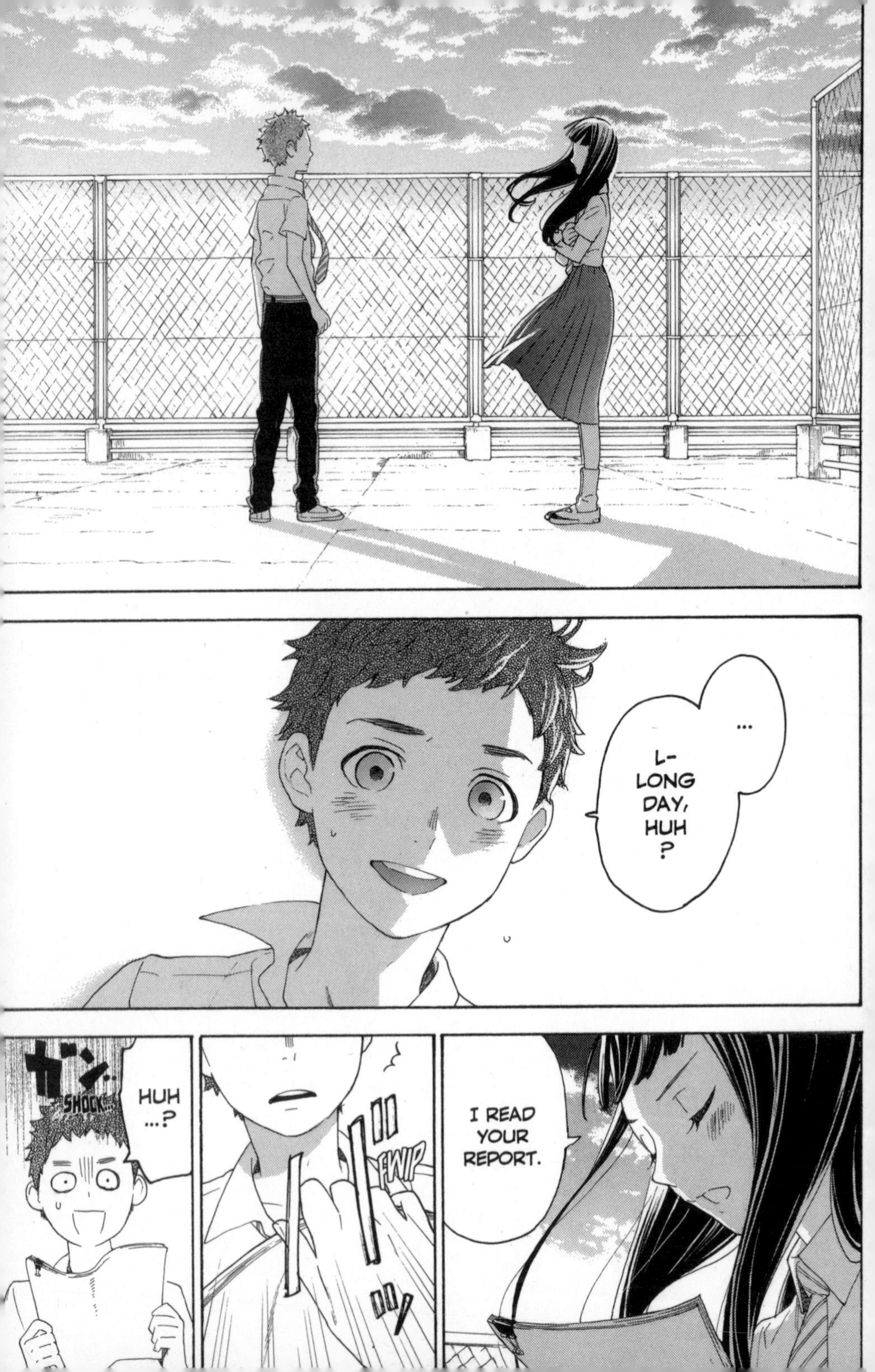
...
L-LONG DAY, HUH?
I READ YOUR REPORT.
FWIP
HUH ...?
SHOCK...

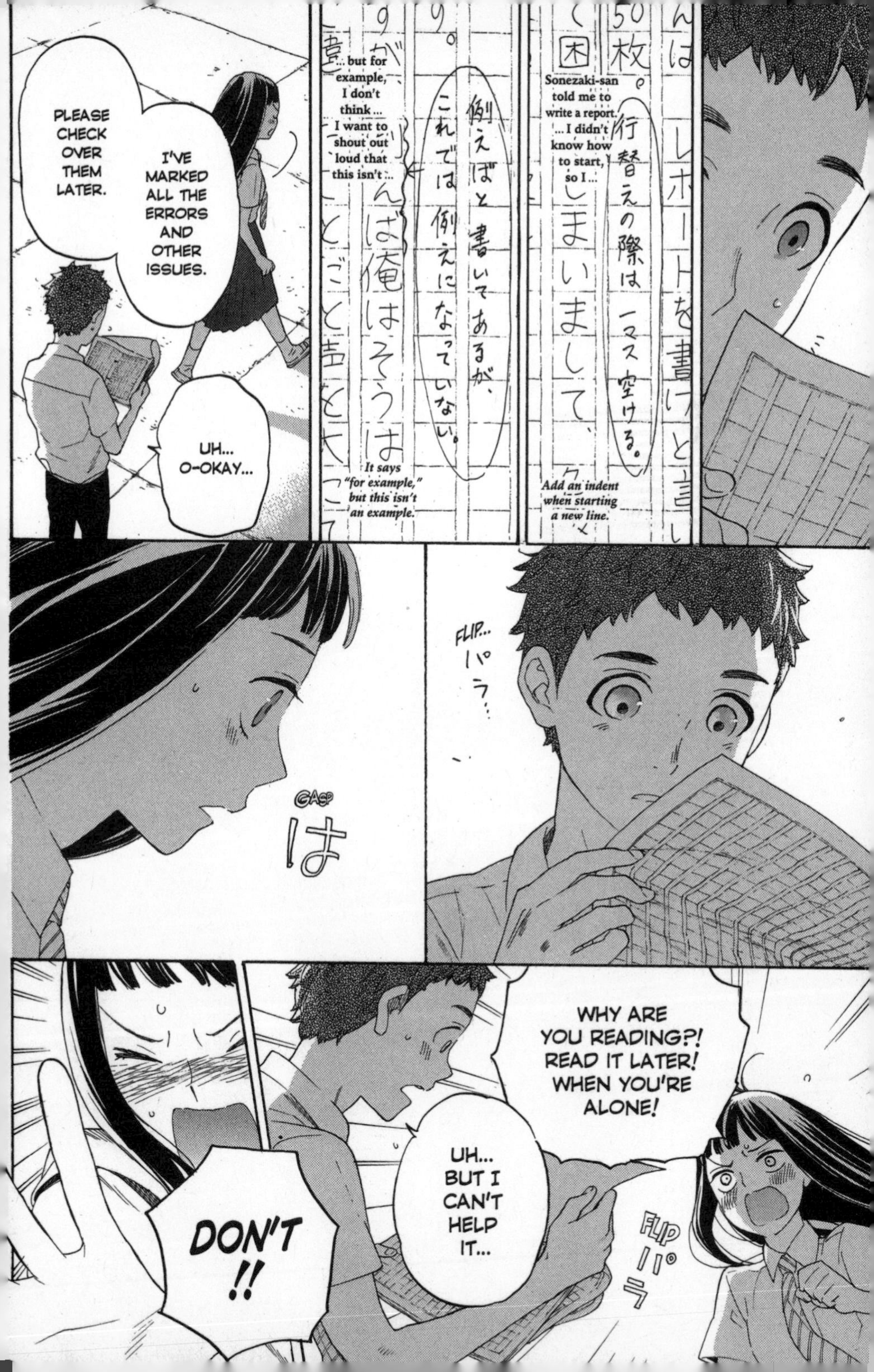
Sonezaki-san told me to write a report. ... I didn't know how to start, so I ...
行替えの際は一マス空ける。
Add an indent when starting a new line.
... but for example, I don't think ... I want to shout out loud that this isn't ...
例えばと書いてあるが、これでは例えになっていない。
It says "for example," but this isn't an example.
I'VE MARKED ALL THE ERRORS AND OTHER ISSUES.
PLEASE CHECK OVER THEM LATER.
UH... O-OKAY...
FLIP... パラ...
GASP は
WHY ARE YOU READING?! READ IT LATER! WHEN YOU'RE ALONE!
FLIP パラ
UH... BUT I CAN'T HELP IT...
DON'T!!

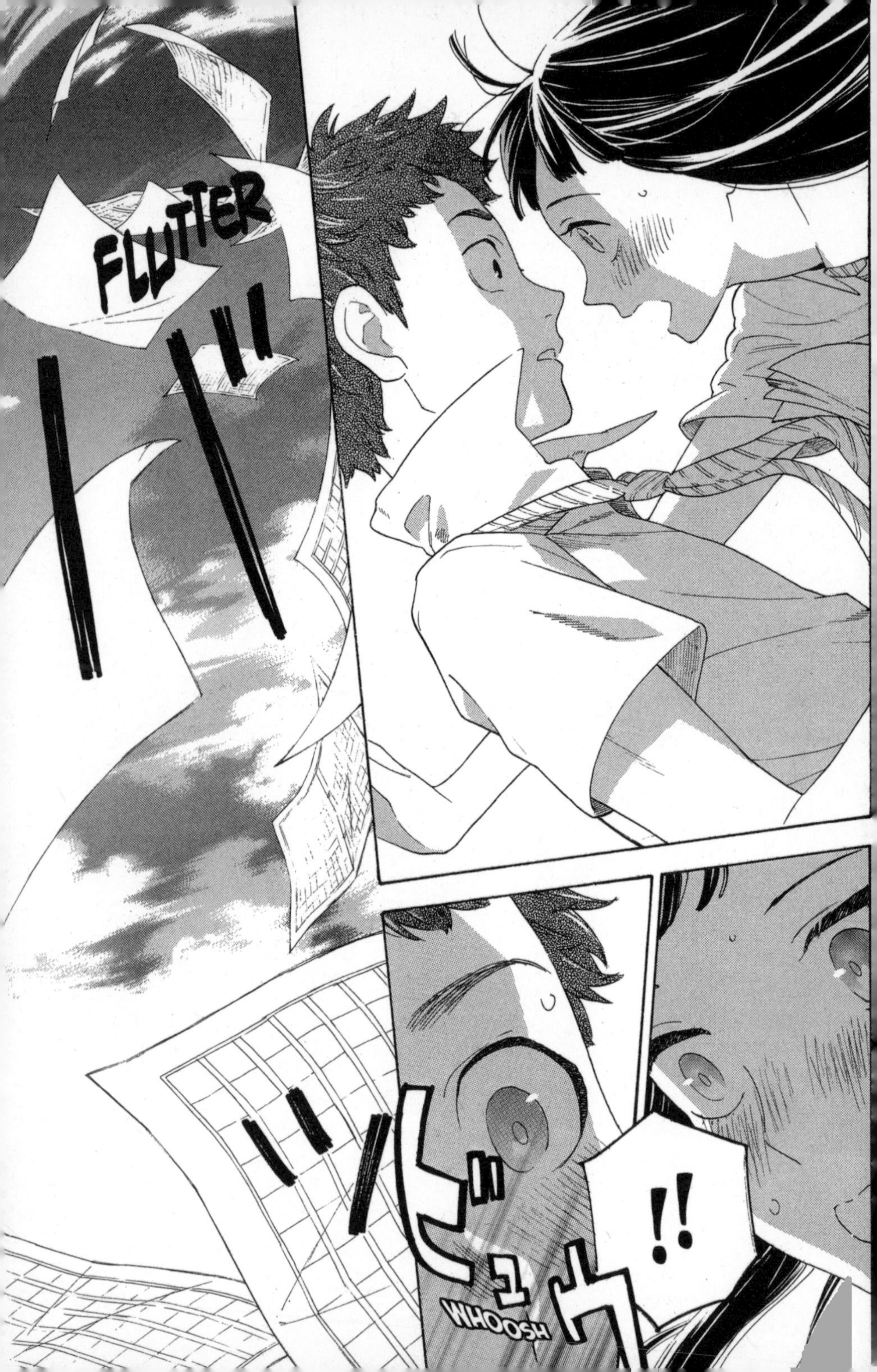
!!
WHOOSH
FLUTTER

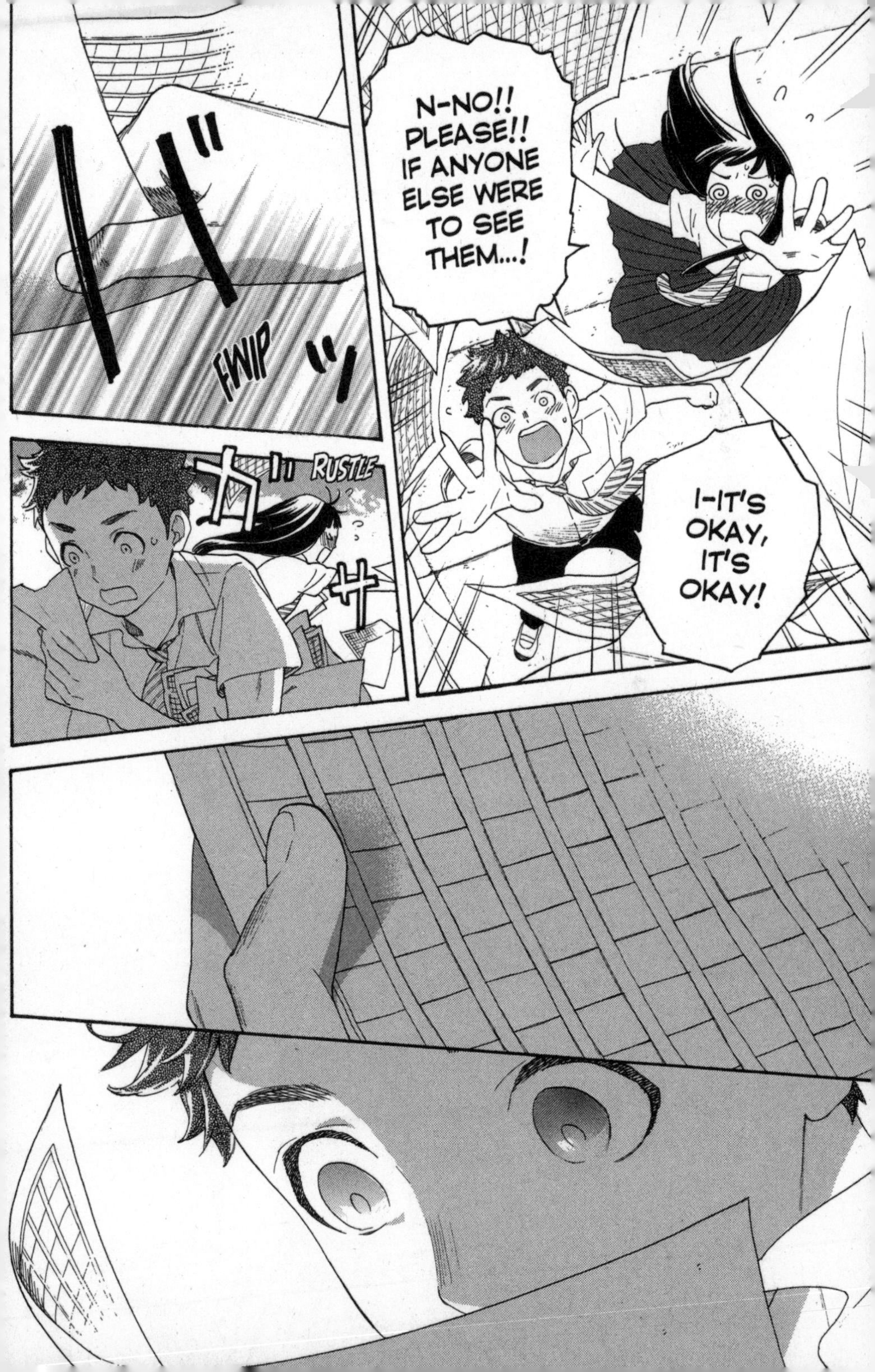
N-NO!! PLEASE!! IF ANYONE ELSE WERE TO SEE THEM...!
I-IT'S OKAY, IT'S OKAY!
FWIP
RUSTLE

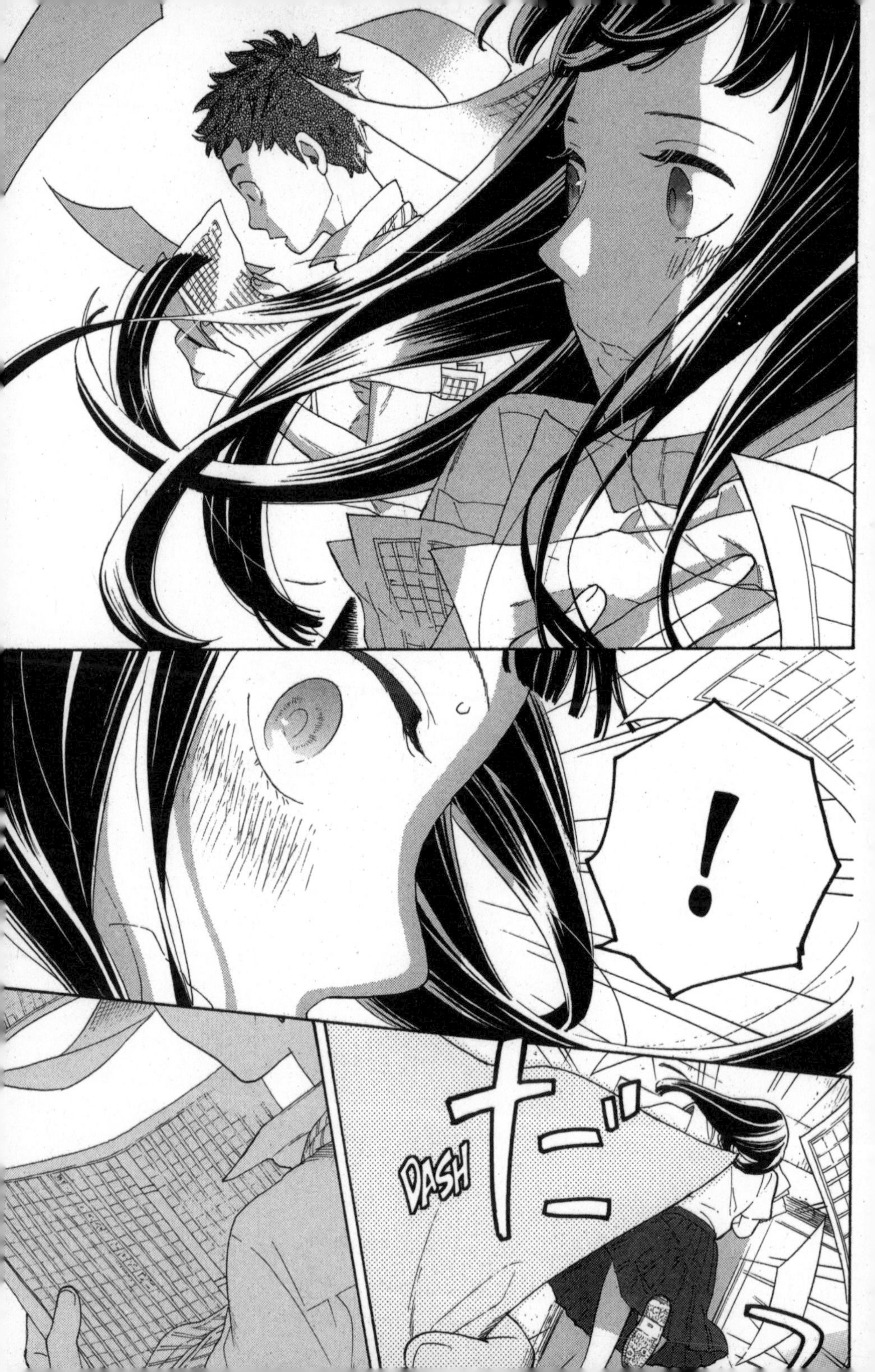
!
DASH

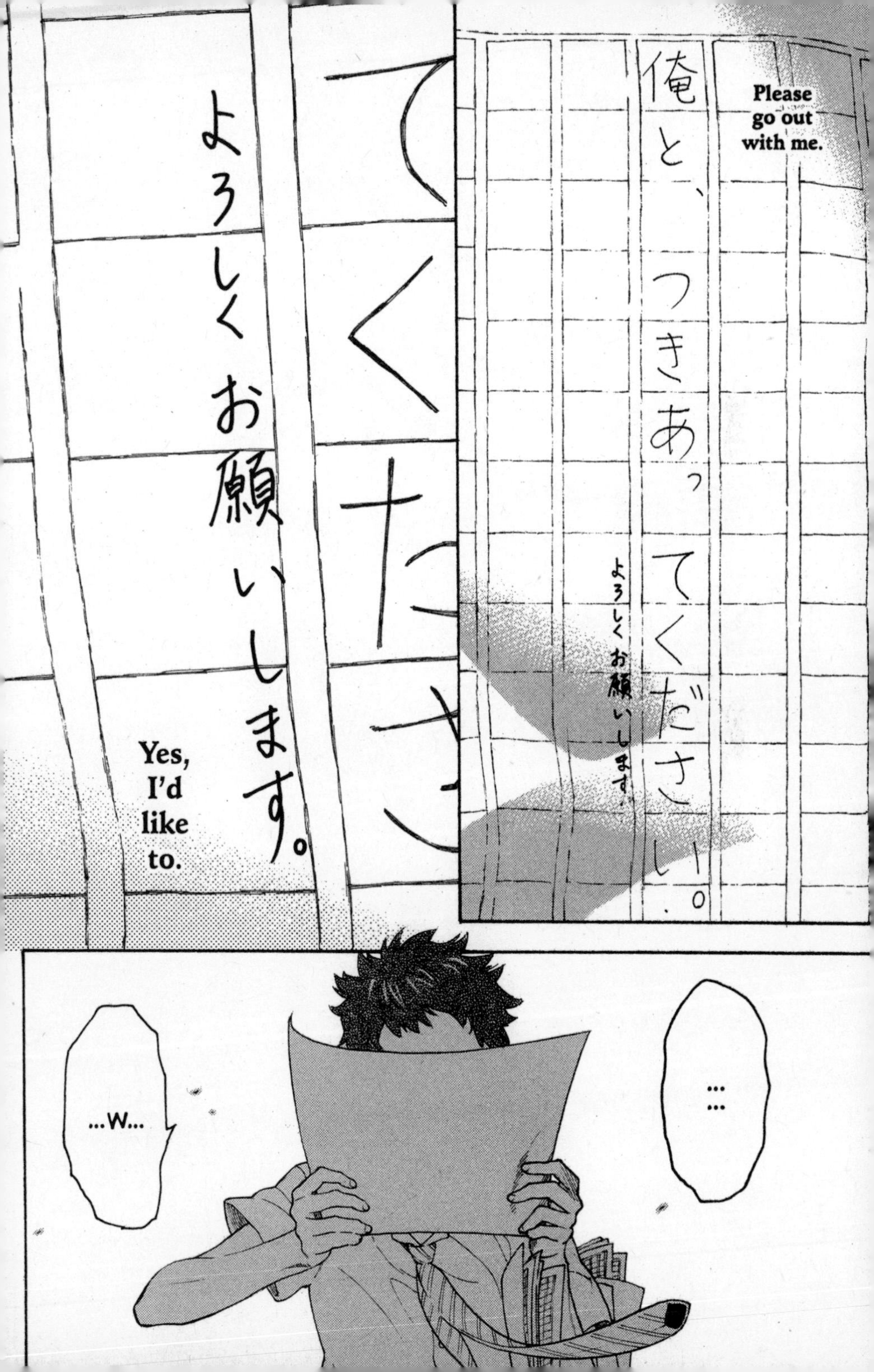
俺と、つきあってください。
よろしくお願いします。
Please go out with me.
よろしくお願いします。
Yes, I'd like to.
......
...W...

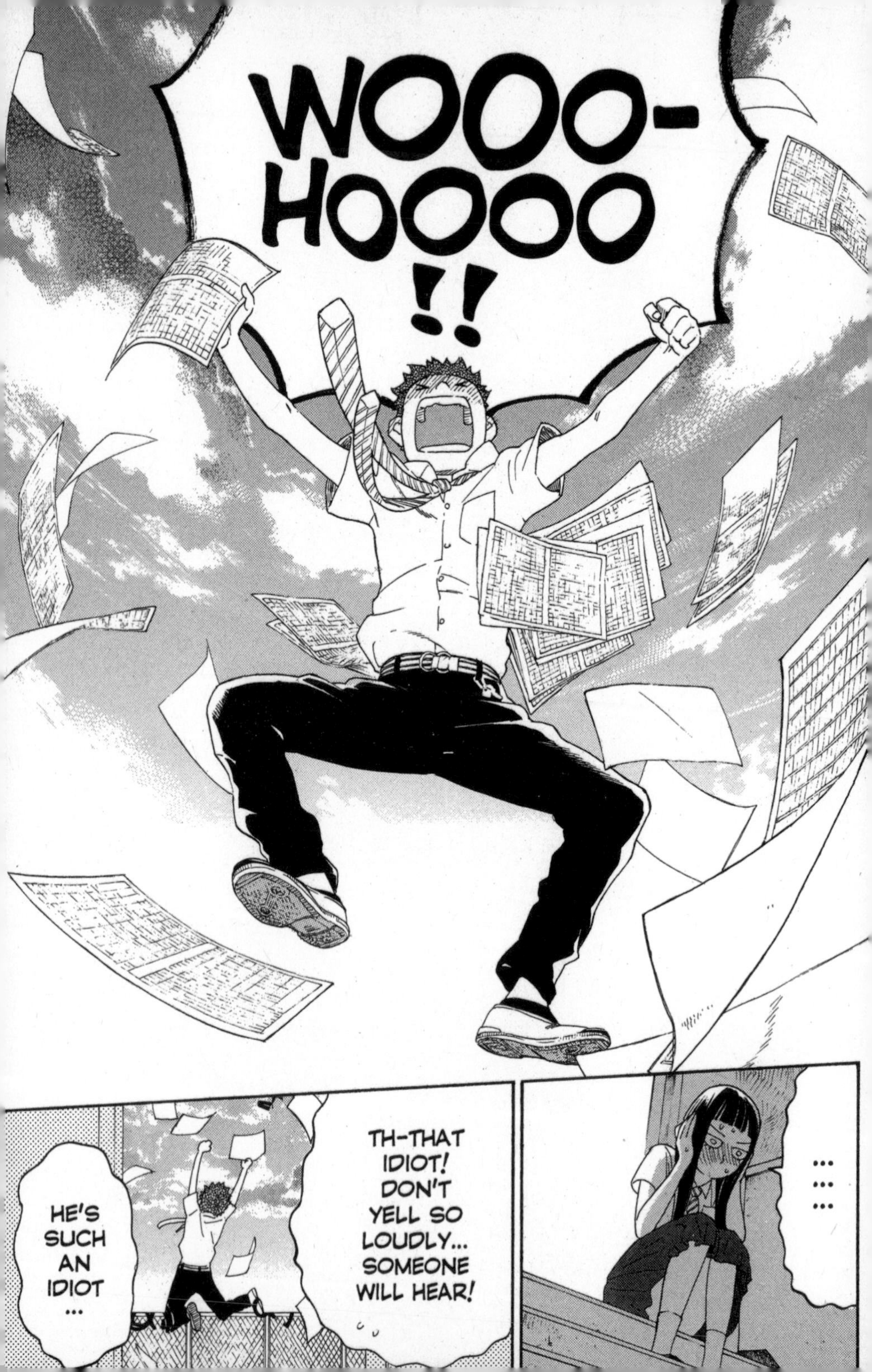
WOOO-HOOOO!!
...
...
...
TH-THAT IDIOT! DON'T YELL SO LOUDLY... SOMEONE WILL HEAR!
HE'S SUCH AN IDIOT...

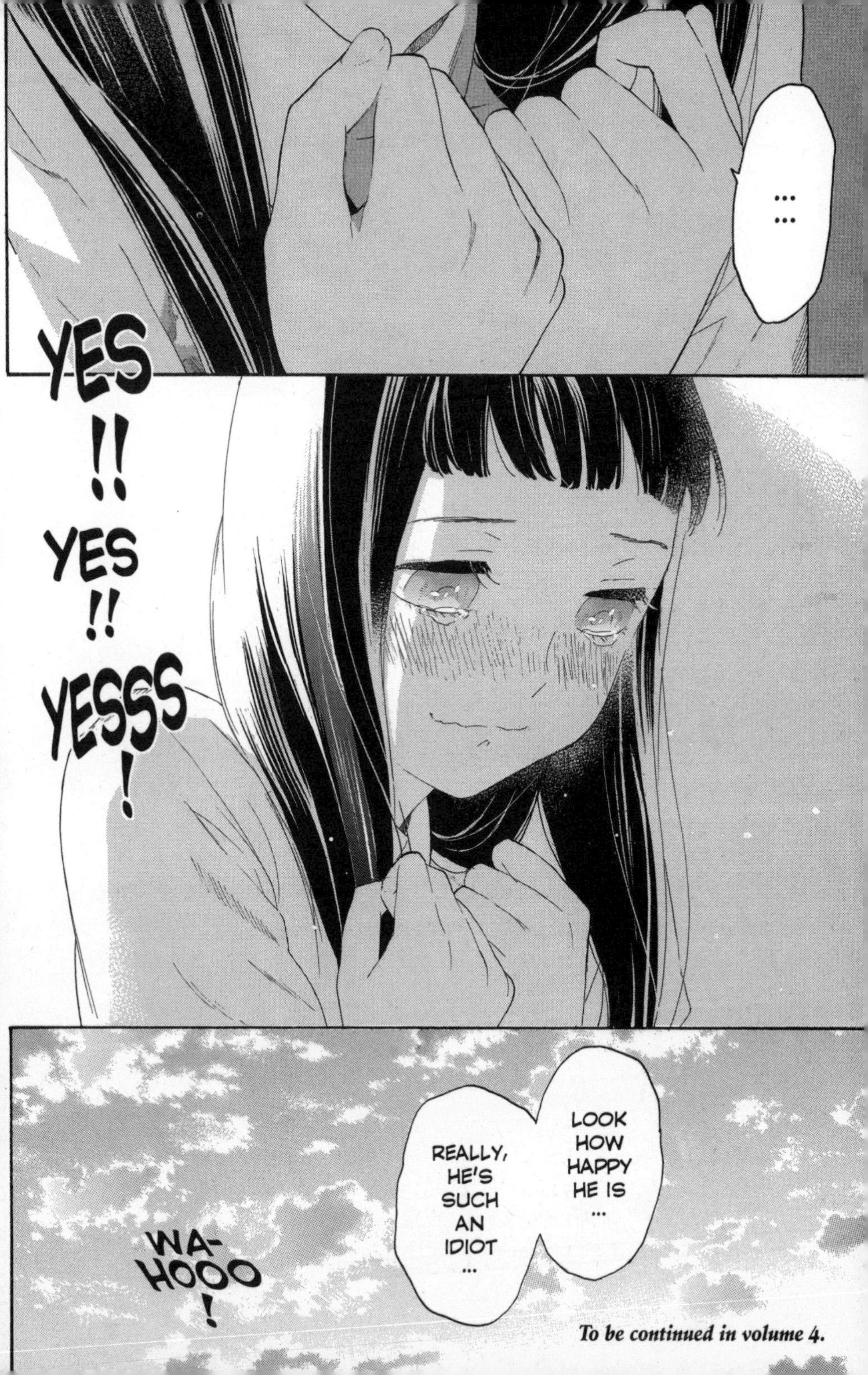
......
YES!! YES!! YESSS!
LOOK HOW HAPPY HE IS...
REALLY, HE'S SUCH AN IDIOT...
WA-HOOO!

To be continued in volume 4.

O Maidens in Your Savage Season

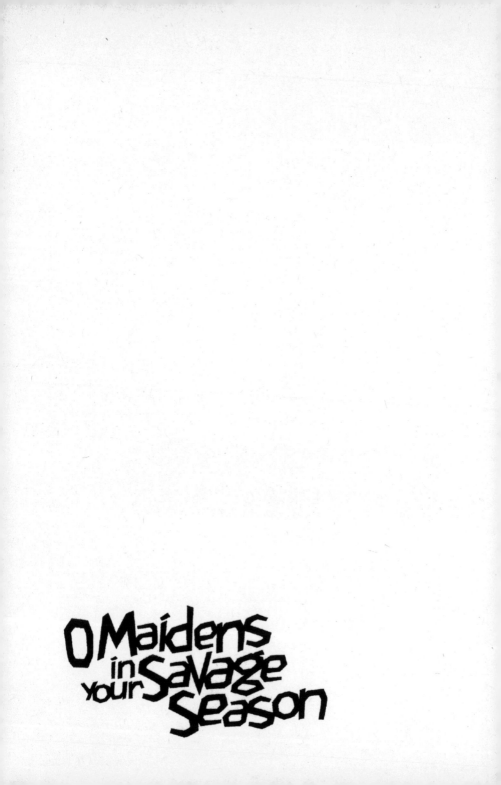

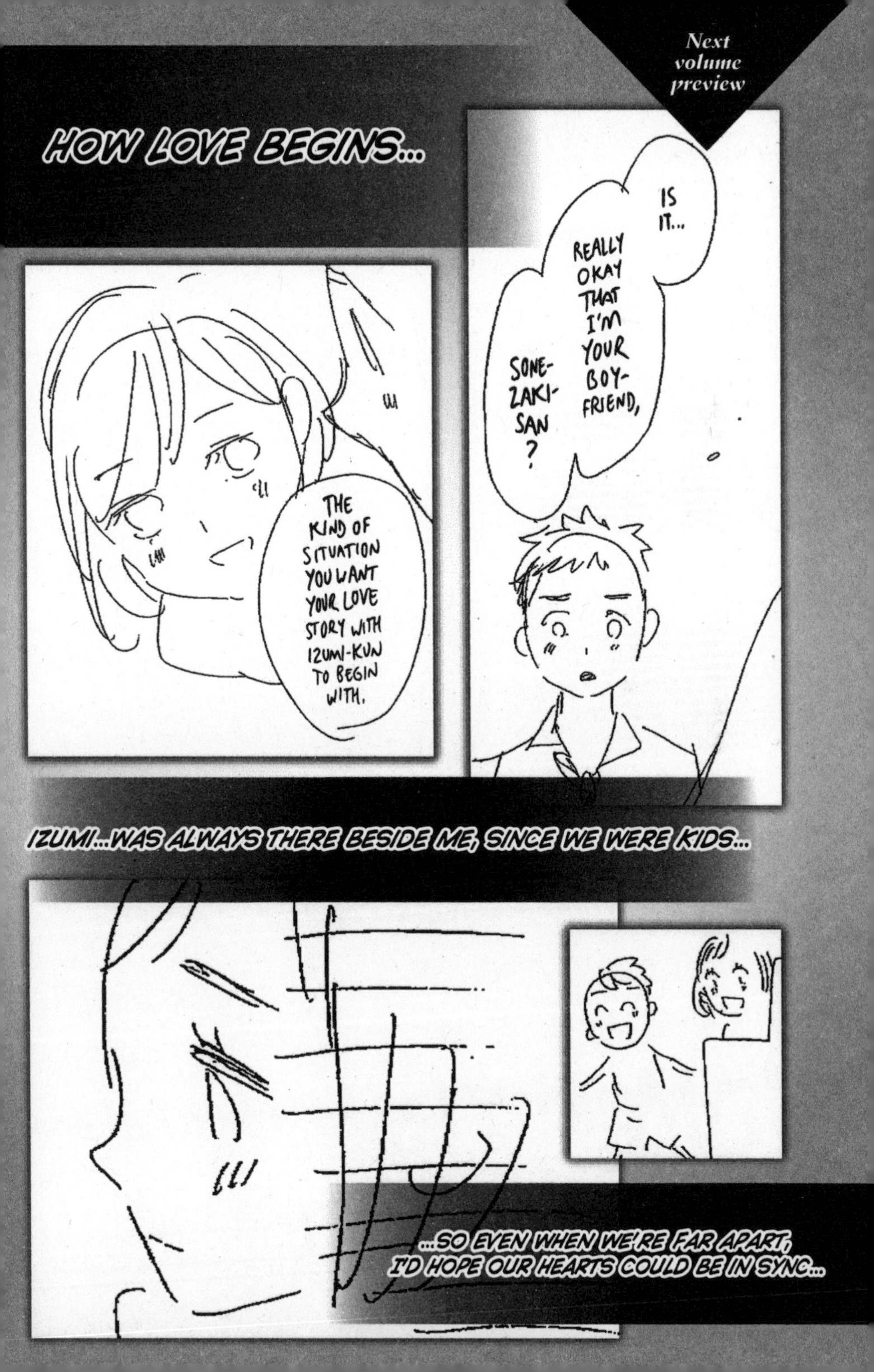
Next volume preview
HOW LOVE BEGINS...
IS IT... REALLY OKAY THAT I'M YOUR BOYFRIEND, SONEZAKI-SAN?
THE KIND OF SITUATION YOU WANT YOUR LOVE STORY WITH IZUMI-KUN TO BEGIN WITH.
IZUMI...WAS ALWAYS THERE BESIDE ME, SINCE WE WERE KIDS...
...SO EVEN WHEN WE'RE FAR APART, I'D HOPE OUR HEARTS COULD BE IN SYNC...

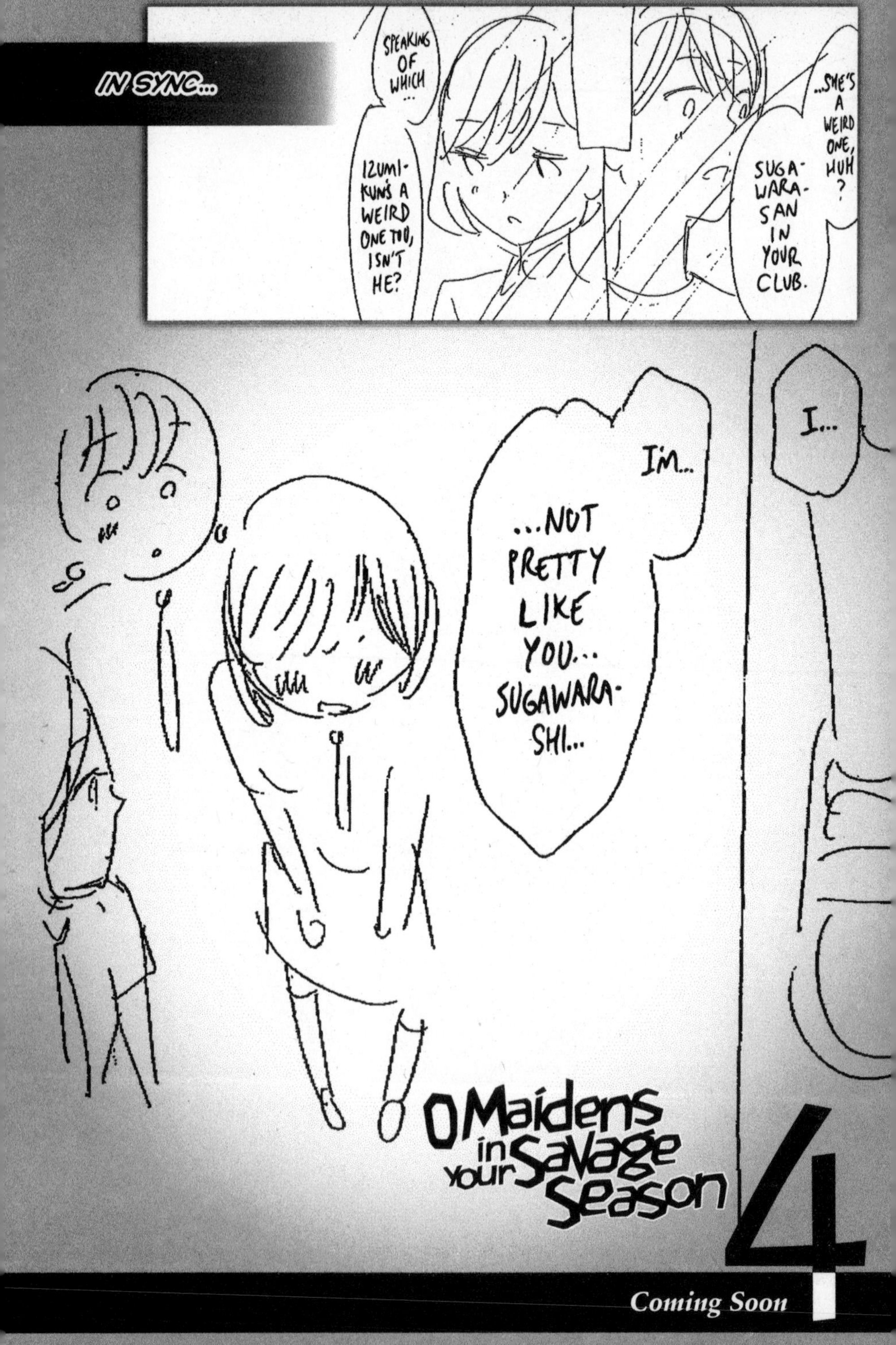
IN SYNC...
...SHE'S A WEIRD ONE, HUH?
SUGAWARA-SAN IN YOUR CLUB.
SPEAKING OF WHICH...
IZUMI-KUN'S A WEIRD ONE TOO, ISN'T HE?
I...
I'M...
...NOT PRETTY LIKE YOU... SUGAWARA-SHI...
O Maidens in your Savage Season
4
Coming Soon

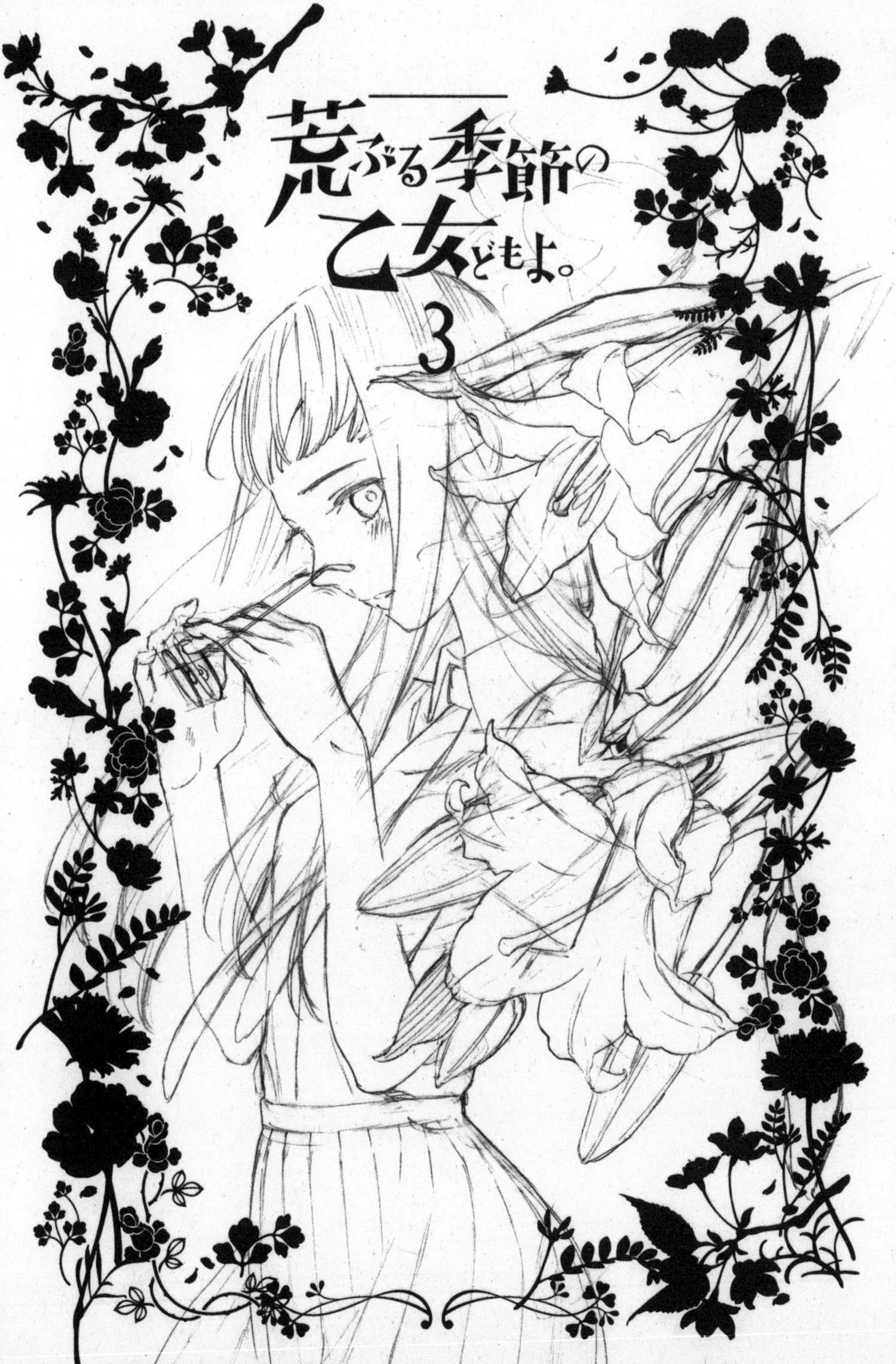
荒ぶる季節の乙女どもよ。
3

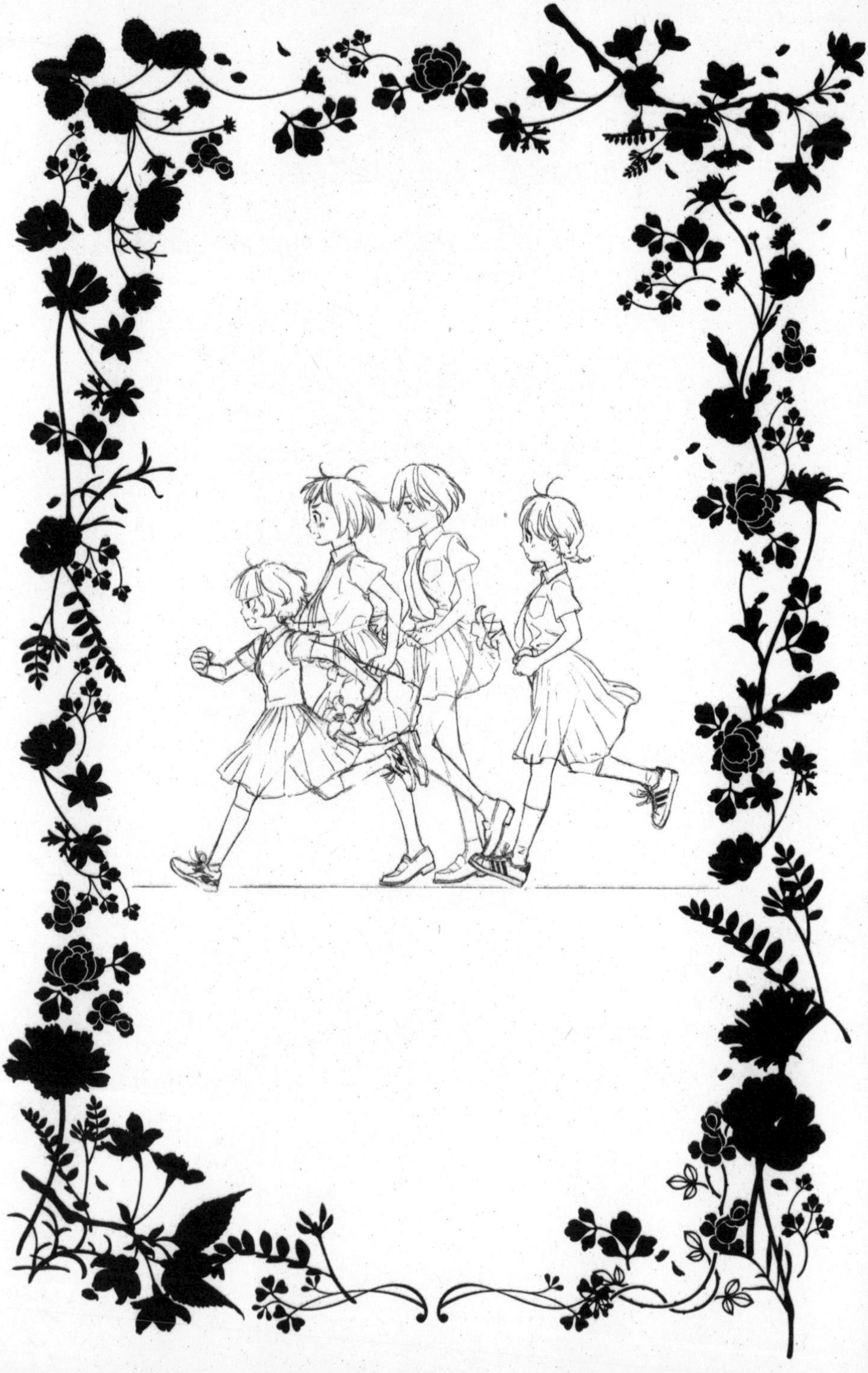

Why does my heart pound over boys?

Their skin is rough and hard, they smell unlike anything I know,

and I have no idea what they're thinking. And yet...

Does instinct make me yearn for genes that I don't have?

Then why does it have to be a human at all?

Oh... But I suppose boys...

...*are* kind of like aliens, in a way.

O Maidens in Your Savage Season

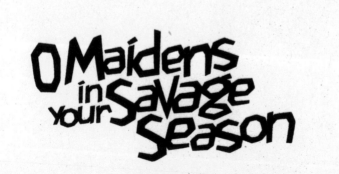

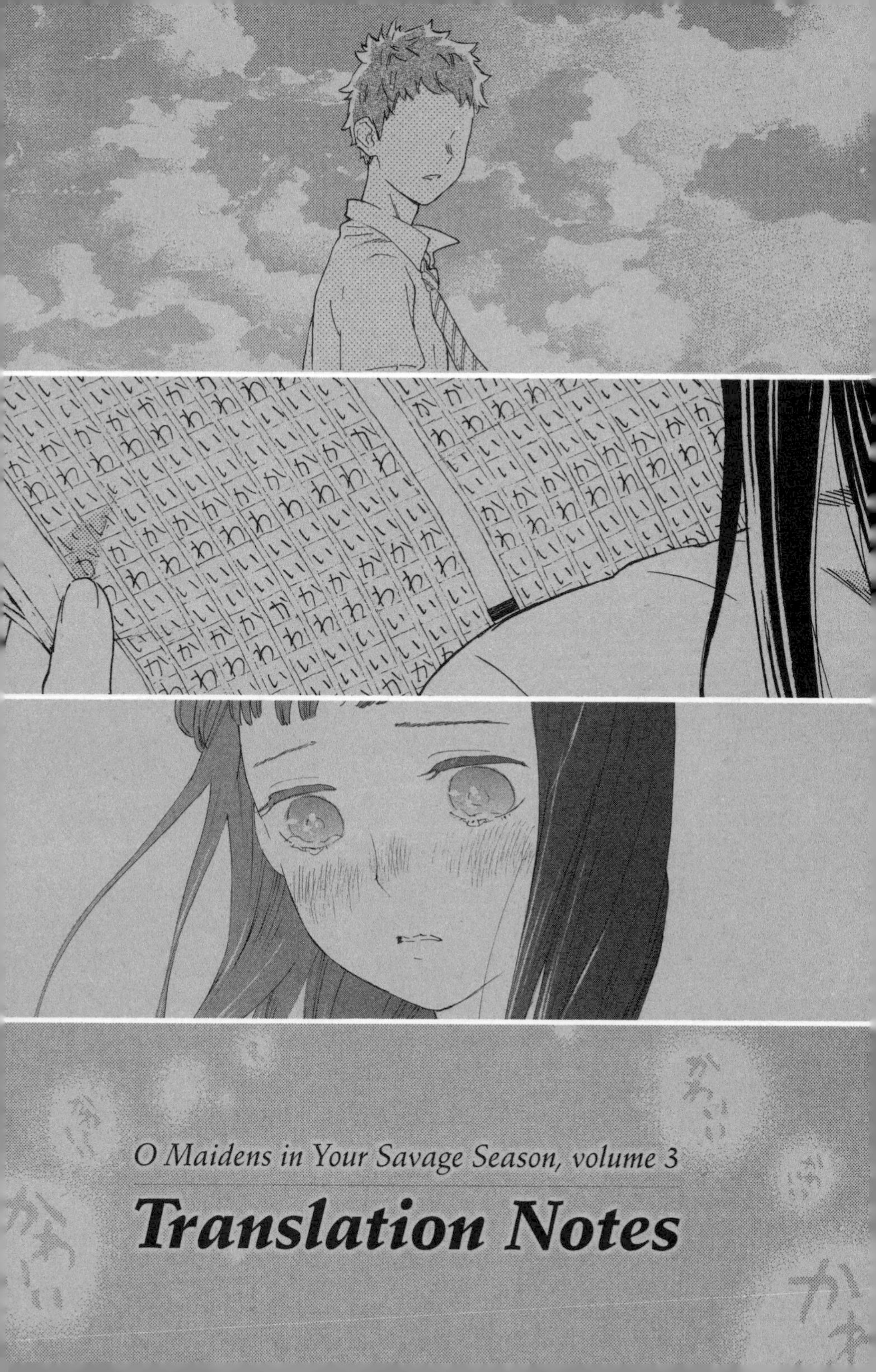

O Maidens in Your Savage Season, volume 3

Translation Notes

page 12

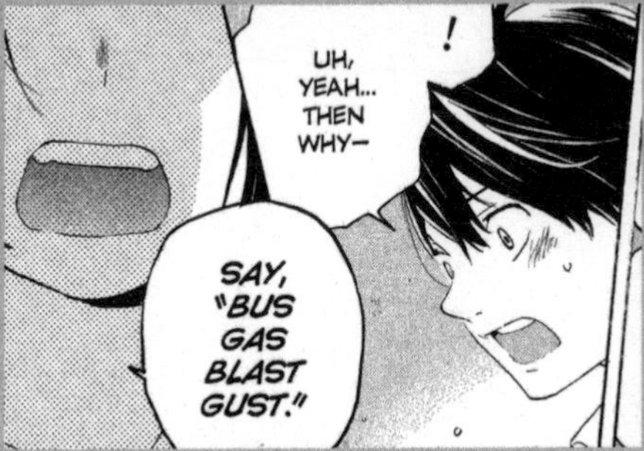
!
UH, YEAH... THEN WHY—
SAY, "BUS GAS BLAST GUST."

Bus gas blast gust

"*Bus gas bakuhatsu*," which means "bus gas explosion," is a classic Japanese tongue twister.

page 19

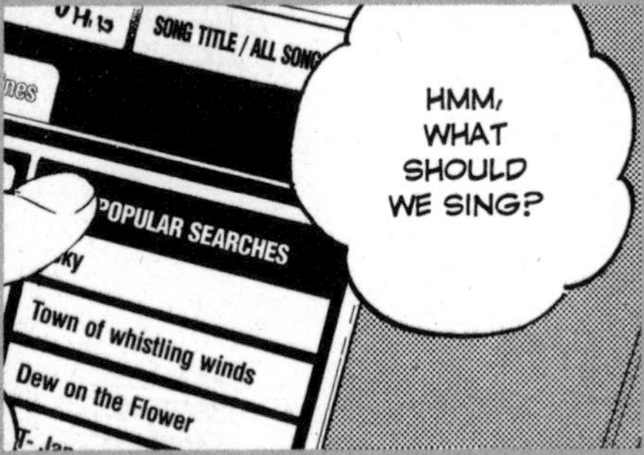
HMM, WHAT SHOULD WE SING?
SONG TITLE / ALL SONG
POPULAR SEARCHES
Town of whistling winds
Dew on the Flower

Karaoke touchscreen

The karaoke remote control is usually a tablet-like device on which one can find songs using a variety of search options.

page 27

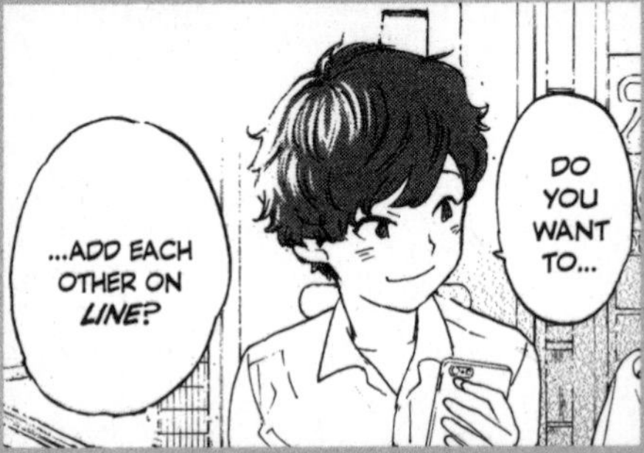
DO YOU WANT TO...
...ADD EACH OTHER ON *LINE*?

LINE

LINE is the most popular free messaging app in Japan—basically the Japanese equivalent of Whatsapp.

page 30

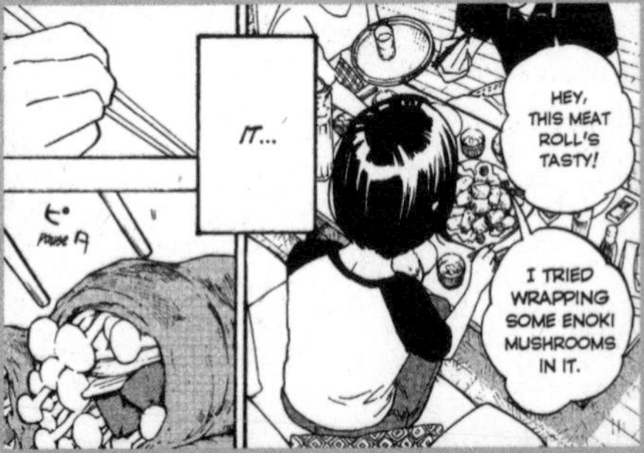
HEY, THIS MEAT ROLL'S TASTY!
IT...
I TRIED WRAPPING SOME ENOKI MUSHROOMS IN IT.

Enoki mushrooms

These are long, thin mushrooms that are used regularly in Japanese cuisine.

page 63

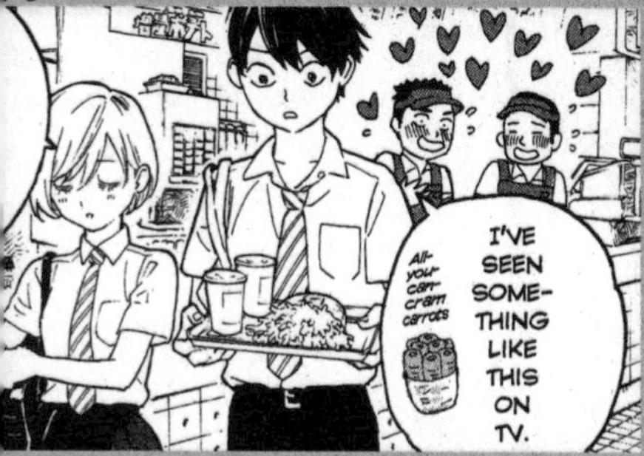
I'VE SEEN SOMETHING LIKE THIS ON TV.
All-you-can-cram carrots

All-you-can-cram carrots

Some grocery stores in Japan have special sales where you can take however many vegetables you can cram into a plastic bag for a fixed price.

page 110

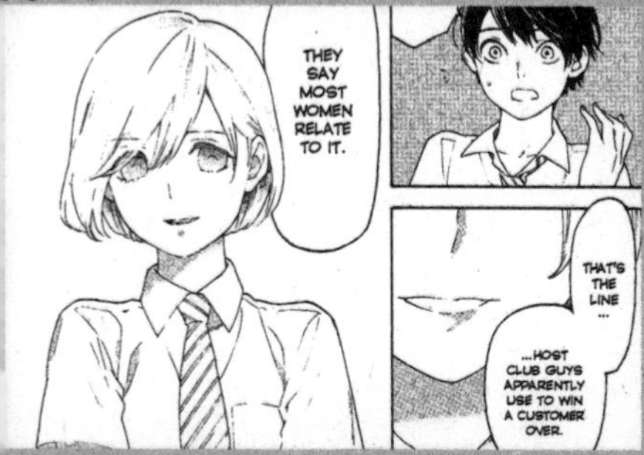
THAT'S THE LINE ...
...HOST CLUB GUYS APPARENTLY USE TO WIN A CUSTOMER OVER.
THEY SAY MOST WOMEN RELATE TO IT.

Host clubs

Host clubs are establishments where young men entertain mostly female customers with drinks and smooth talking.

page 113

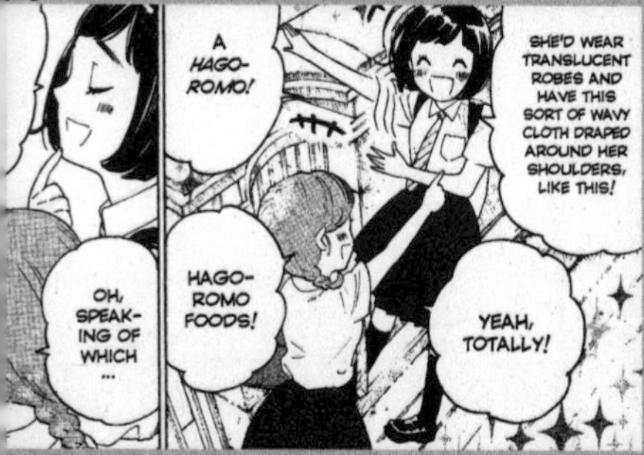
SHE'D WEAR TRANSLUCENT ROBES AND HAVE THIS SORT OF WAVY CLOTH DRAPED AROUND HER SHOULDERS, LIKE THIS!
A HAGO-ROMO!
YEAH, TOTALLY!
HAGO-ROMO FOODS!
OH, SPEAKING OF WHICH ...

Hagoromo

In Chinese and Japanese Buddhism, celestial beings have these long, flowing cloths draped around them to give them the ability to fly. Hagoromo Foods is a major canned food producer.

page 136

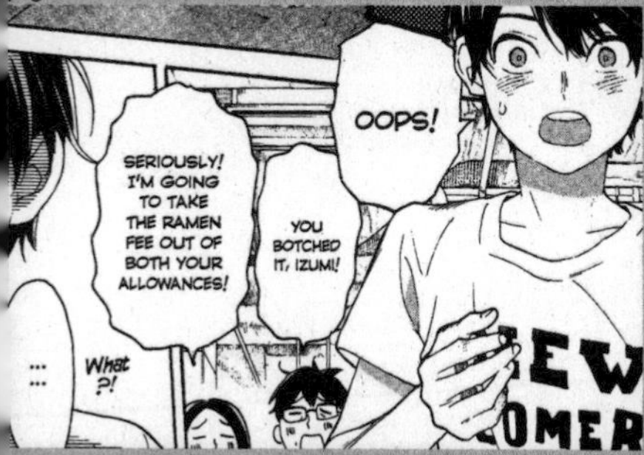
OOPS!
YOU BOTCHED IT, IZUMI!
SERIOUSLY! I'M GOING TO TAKE THE RAMEN FEE OUT OF BOTH YOUR ALLOWANCES!
What ?!
...

Allowance

In some Japanese families, the wife manages the family finances and allocates money to the husband as an allowance to use on miscellaneous purchases.

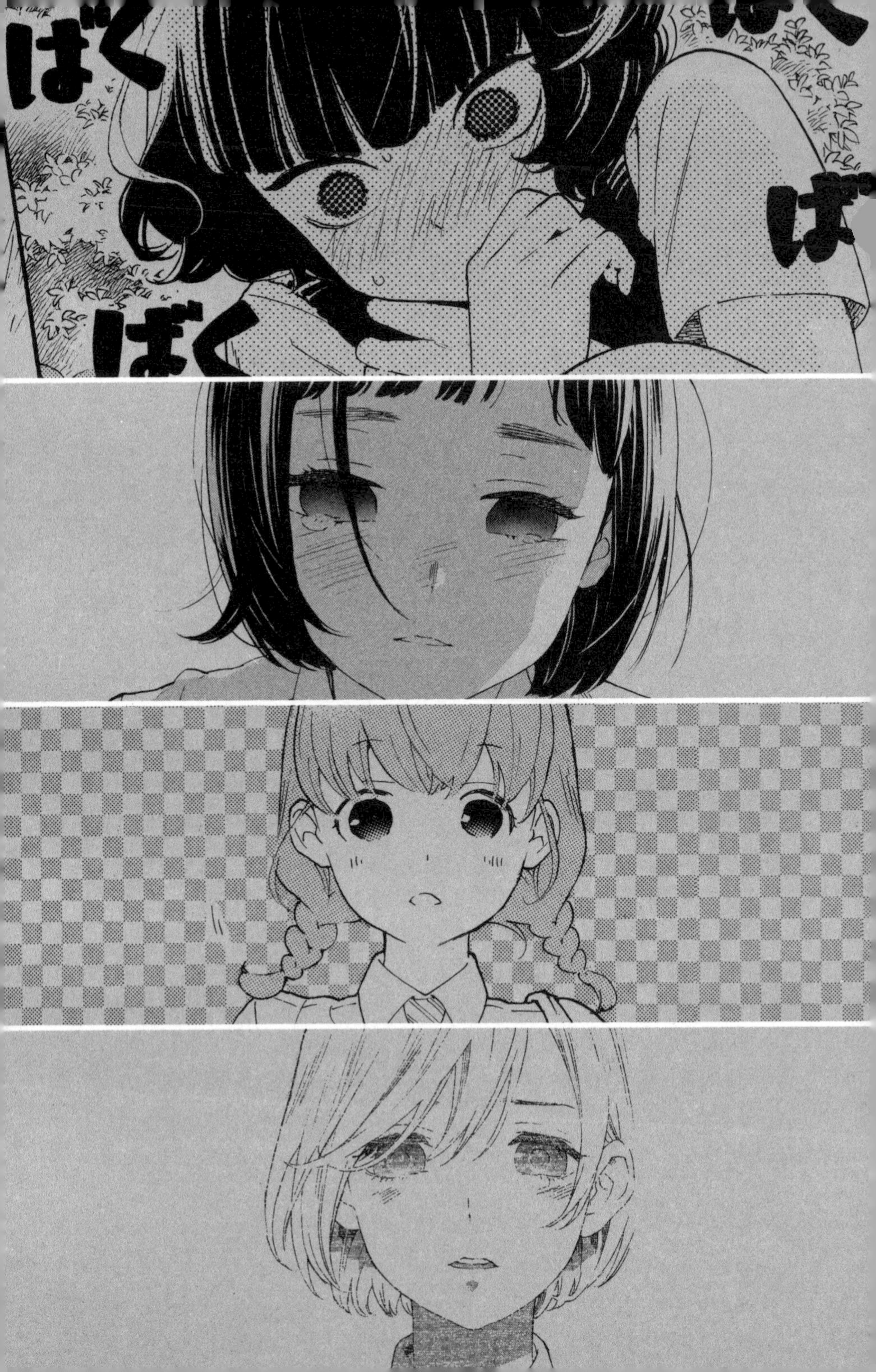

ば
ばく
ばく

O Maidens in Your Savage Season volume 3 is a work of fiction.
Names, characters, places, and incidents are the products of
the author's imagination or are used fictitiously.
Any resemblance to actual events, locales, or
persons, living or dead, is entirely coincidental.

A Kodansha Comics Trade Paperback Original

Published in the United States by Kodansha Comics, an imprint of
Kodansha USA Publishing, LLC, New York.

Publication rights for this English edition arranged through
Kodansha Ltd, Tokyo.

First published in Japan in 2017 by Kodansha Ltd, Tokyo,
as *Araburu Kisetsu no Otomedomoyo* volume 3.

ISBN 978-1-63236-820-1

Printed in the United States of America.

www.kodanshacomics.com

9 8 7 6 5 4 3 2 1
Translation: Sawa Matsueda Savage
Lettering: Evan Hayden
Editing: Haruko Hashimoto
Kodansha Comics edition cover design by Phil Balsman